DOROTHY DAY

The World Will Be Saved by Beauty

— • ◆ • —

An INTIMATE PORTRAIT
of MY GRANDMOTHER

KATE HENNESSY

SCRIBNER
New York   London   Toronto   Sydney   New Delhi

Scribner
An Imprint of Simon & Schuster, Inc.
1230 Avenue of the Americas
New York, NY 10020

First Scribner hardcover edition January 2017

SCRIBNER and design are registered trademarks of The Gale Group, Inc., used under license by Simon & Schuster, Inc., the publisher of this work.

For information about special discounts for bulk purchases, please contact Simon & Schuster Special Sales at 1-866-506-1949 or business@simonandschuster.com.

The Simon & Schuster Speakers Bureau can bring authors to your live event. For more information or to book an event, contact the Simon & Schuster Speakers Bureau at 1-866-248-3049 or visit our website at www.simonspeakers.com.

Interior design by Jill Putorti

Manufactured in the United States of America

10 9 8 7 6 5 4 3 2 1

Library of Congress Cataloging-in-Publication Data is available.

ISBN 978-1-5011-3396-1
ISBN 978-1-5011-3398-5 (ebook)

In memoriam
Tamar Teresa Batterham Hennessy

CONTENTS

PREFACE

In the last years of her life, my grandmother often woke up hearing in her mind the words from her beloved Dostoyevsky: "The world will be saved by beauty." Of all the words she wrote, of all the quotes she loved to repeat, of all the advice and comfort she gave to countless people, in all five of her books and fifty years of her column, and in a lifetime of diary- and letter-writing, this is what has come to give me the most hope. For if, after years of struggle, weariness, and a sense of deep and abiding failure, she believed in salvation through beauty, then how can we not listen?

I discovered this aspect of my grandmother while reading her diaries. They were published two weeks after my mother's death, but it took almost a year before I could bring myself to open the book. Then, once opened, I couldn't put it down. It was as if I, dying of thirst, were given a long, cold drink from the purest of wells. And as I read, I felt a growing need to add another layer to this tale, not only to portray the grandmother I knew and her daughter—her only child, Tamar—but also to somehow bring my grandmother and mother together in ways they hadn't been able to achieve while they lived.

On the morning after I finished reading I lingered in that half-asleep state where both dreams and reality take on a different quality altogether. That in-between state where you sometimes hear a voice you are certain is from someone in the room calling your name, and you wake up saying, "Yes, what is it?" but no one is there. My dream was brief, as dreams of this kind are—no beginning or end, just a flash containing all I needed to know. And in that moment I felt, sure and true, the knowledge of both Tamar's and Dorothy's lives with all their experiences and memories, and I was overcome by this knowing. I felt the weight and the miracle of their lives, and I wondered if I were strong enough—wise enough—to tell this story. But haven't I been working on it all my life, living in their wake and stumbling along trying to make my own way?

And isn't this my history also? One of the elements of what makes a person extraordinary, I have come to believe, is when their inner and outer lives are in accord. When what they do in the world is what their innermost being leads them to do. This is why the history of the Catholic Worker is the history of my mother, the history of the relationship between my mother and grandmother, and the history of my family.

The winter following my grandmother's death was bone-shivering, teeth-achingly cold, the temperature hovering between twenty and thirty degrees below zero night after night. At the time, my mother lived with her small black dog in a hand-built cabin on the edge of the woods. She was alone and grieving, and yet she turned to me—she was fifty-four and I was twenty—and in an effort to help us both through this dark time, she and I began a discussion about her mother. These talks were not often easy to follow; their paths could be just as elusive as Tamar was herself. She was unfocused and uncollected. She jumped from thought to thought, while I tried to follow her hints and allusions or the sentences she couldn't bring herself to finish, telling me her story in the grab-bag way she had—an image, a thought, a sparkle and flash of laughter, a retort of anger, regret, or loss.

We continued our conversations on the first anniversary of Dorothy's death while staying at the Catholic Worker's beach cottage on Staten Island, New York. And then in a house in the small Vermont town of Springfield, where my mother moved from her cabin, the neighborhood rough but full of poor, working-class families, just as Tamar liked it. Again and again we returned to this discussion until the last weeks of her life twenty-seven years later.

Many writers—scholars, historians, and theologians—have chosen to tell the story of Dorothy Day and the Catholic Worker, the movement she began in the 1930s grounded in performing the works of mercy, and that still exists today, decades after her death. But it seems to me that those who knew her best are often the ones most fearful of trying to write about her in all her complexity, richness, and contradictions. Tamar greeted each new book or film about her mother with fatalism, yet she couldn't stay away, and she couldn't keep from being disappointed.

Then, when such a person as Dorothy Day is your grandmother, an examination of her life isn't an intellectual, academic, or religious exercise. For me, it is nothing less than a quest to find out who I am through her and through Tamar. It is a quest to save my own life, though I don't yet know what this means. (Seamus Heaney once said that in his poetry he wrote about those moments he sensed held greater meaning within, even though he might not ever find out what the meaning was.) And I see this quest as not only for me or for my family but for anyone who senses that greater meaning and desires to explore it. There was a group of children who grew up at the Worker in the sixties and seventies who called Dorothy "Granny," as my siblings and I do, though they were not related to her, and this is as it should be. We all need to live our lives as if we are Dorothy's children and grandchildren, being comforted and discomforted by her as she invites us to be so much more than how we ordinarily see ourselves and, perhaps more important, how we see each other.

Dorothy said there was never a time when she wasn't writing a book or thinking of writing a book; whereas Tamar wasn't a writer and had difficulty expressing herself in any medium. "Dorothy was a talker, and my husband was too," she said. "That was enough." But there did come a time when she felt the desire to write. When her father, Forster Batterham, died four years after Dorothy, Tamar discovered in his apartment letters Dorothy had written to him in the 1920s and early thirties. In them Tamar finally could read of the love and longing her mother felt for this silent man, so much like his daughter. In them Tamar could once again see her mother, the Dorothy Day she so loved and who seems in danger of being lost to the world—a woman of great joy and passion, humor, and love of beauty. Tamar grieved the loss of this vibrant woman to the annals of hagiography and the desire to see her as a saint, and at times to Dorothy's own nature, especially during her "severe and pious" stage, as Tamar called it. In these letters Tamar found what she had longed for—love between her mother and father, Dorothy the saint and Forster the scientist, the two halves of her heart. And after reading these letters, she wanted to show the world this part of the story, her story.

I can see the two of them in my mind's eye, mother and daughter facing each other, loving each other, challenging each other.

"This is the story of my life," says one.

"No, this is the story," says the other.

Many of Dorothy's favorite quotes had to do with love: "Love is the measure by which we shall be judged" and "Where there is no love, put love—and you will find love." Those two are from St. John of the Cross. Then there is Dostoyevsky: "Love in action is a harsh and dreadful thing compared to love in dreams." But it is one of Dorothy's own quotes that I love the best: "God understands us when we try to love." Tamar liked to say, "All the world needs is loving kindness." Her love was of a more practical nature, the words of a mother of nine and a steward of the land, whereas Dorothy's love had an element of mystery, a quality she needed for the life she led. Dorothy also said we all feel alone and we always will. She said that we struggle against both freedom and responsibility, and with these too we always will. Tamar said we all must live our own disasters. Agony and foolishness she called these lives we lead. For me, these quotes of theirs reveal something of the love they gave and received, the lessons they learned, and the heroism it required, each in her own way. I don't think they ever said these words to each other, for if they had, maybe then they would have been able to understand the nature of their struggle with each other, and maybe their intense love for one another would have been leavened by this understanding.

But Tamar was unable to write her story, as Dorothy was unable to write her last book, in which, it seems, she wanted to make sense of this relationship between mother and daughter. And so here I am, left holding the pen, still grieving the loss of my mother, still grieving for the two of them, and led by the only thing that matters, the only thing worth writing about—love.

Part One

THE
MYSTERY
OF GRACE

CHAPTER ONE

There is no time with God, my granny said, and so I set out to find Tamar and her parents when they were still together, and where do I find them but on the beach. The beach where Tamar was conceived in a cottage not twenty feet from the water, where she learned to walk in the sand, to say the rosary while following the edge of the lapping waves as the tide ebbed and flowed, and to pray to the dead spider crab hanging on the wall beside her bed. It is Staten Island, 1927, and Tamar is one and a half years old. I want to know what happened to bring these two people—Forster and Dorothy—together and what drove them apart. I want to know why Tamar would always feel this father loss, missing him even when she was too young to know what that meant. The three of them are in a rowboat, and Dorothy and Forster are silent. The happiness they had felt with each other and with the birth of Tamar is giving way to something that seems insurmountable, that seems tied to Dorothy's constant thirst for a mystery she has yet to name. How did they get there? How far back do I need to go? To those days long before Tamar's birth?

Let me begin again . . .

My granny said there is no time with God, and so I set out to find her when she was a young woman of twenty, the age I was when she died. The year is 1918, and it's a bitter January morning in the predawn hours. While deep snowdrifts cover the streets of New York City, Dorothy's fresh, new life is giving birth to struggle, pain, and questioning. Although she doesn't yet know it, it is a time when she will turn from one path and head along another, unsure of what she is doing and where she is going. Until now, her youth and energy, her exploration and freedom have propelled her along a life of great excitement. At this moment, the hour both late and early, she is sitting in a rough, gaily decorated Greenwich Village tearoom called Romany Marie's, and she is holding a dying man in her arms.

But wait—I must go back even further in this peeling away of the layers of the past.

Ah yes, there she is—tall and thin, more bones than flesh, with a strong, clear jaw and large oddly slanting blue eyes, thin and straight brown hair with auburn highlights, and hands and feet that are long, narrow, and graceful. It is the summer of 1916, and she is eighteen and roaming the horse-manure-spattered cobblestone streets not so far from where the Catholic Worker is now, with a nervous stride as if there were never enough time, and full of an unquenchable curiosity about people and their work, families, and traditions. Burdened by heat and loneliness, she is looking for work as a journalist, scared, full of hesitation, but determined to make her own way, following her father's footsteps. Her two older brothers, Donald and Sam, had Pop's blessing to become journalists (even though he had kicked them out of the house as soon as they had jobs), but she did not.

Dorothy and her father were two peas in a pod in some ways and each as bullheaded as the other. It wasn't that John Day was against the idea of his daughter being a writer. He had started her on that path when she was a child and had helped publish her first piece for the children's page of the *Chicago Tribune*, followed by book reviews for the *Inter Ocean*, the Chicago newspaper where he worked. Their parting of ways may have begun when Dorothy, at the age of sixteen, won a three-hundred-dollar scholarship for the University of Illinois sponsored by the Hearst papers by placing fifteenth in twenty winners of a contest in Latin and Greek. John Day wasn't interested in higher education. He hadn't finished high school, and neither did his two older sons. In his view, journalists didn't need an education. They needed to start work as soon as they were able, preferably at fifteen.

But Dorothy, regardless of her love for Cicero and Virgil, turned out to be an indifferent student and careless with money. When her scholar-

ship, which should have been sufficient to see her through her degree, ran out, she got a job cooking for a family at twenty cents an hour, then gave that up and almost starved to death. After two years, penniless and bored with her studies, Dorothy left with her family for New York City, where her parents had first met, married, and had the four oldest of the five Day children.

Enamored by the socialism she had picked up reading Jack London and Upton Sinclair and while walking through the Polish and Italian working-class neighborhoods of Chicago pushing her baby brother in a carriage, Dorothy found work with the *New York Call*, a paper of socialists, Industrial Workers of the World (IWW) members, trade unionists, and anarchists. When she got the job, faced with her father's belief that it was a woman's role to stay home and be beautiful, as Tamar described it, she left her family's place in Brooklyn and, with not much more than her phonograph, moved into a room on Cherry Street in Manhattan. The flat was between the Brooklyn and Manhattan Bridges and upriver from the *Call*'s office on Pearl Street, near the South Street Seaport. While walking under the Brooklyn Bridge on her way to and from work, she began to know the men on the streets who, as the winter months approached, warmed themselves by fires lit in barrels.

For five dollars a month Dorothy had a tiny hall bedroom in a five-story tenement with a window onto the air shaft and a toilet off the stairwell for the use of two families. As with all the tenements in the Lower East Side, there was no electricity or central heating. To keep warm, people burned coal in the fireplaces, if they could afford it, driftwood if they couldn't, or turned on their gas ovens. The doors, halls, and stairs were made of wood, and fires were as common as bedbugs. There was also no hot water, and Dorothy used the public baths along with the Jewish women. The halls were dark and foul-smelling, but the room was clean, and the family she rented the room from provided her with a thick down comforter. They were Orthodox Jews, and when she came home after midnight from the paper, she would often find a plate of food by her bed with a note from one of the children—the parents spoke only Yiddish—explaining that they couldn't serve milk or butter if there was meat.

Dorothy would come to claim that it was the experience of living in rooms rented out by working-class families and the long walks through the Lower East Side that would begin her affinity with the hard up and struggling. This was how her enduring curiosity about people, about their lives and their work, began. Could she ever be part of that hard life? Could she even do it? she wondered.

The Days had never been well-off, although they often lived as if they were. When Dorothy was born, Pop was working as a clerk. When he left Brooklyn for San Francisco in search of newspaper work, Dorothy's mother, Grace, took in boarders in their Bath Beach house until she and the four children could join him. After losing everything in the 1906 earthquake, including the furniture they had shipped from New York around Cape Horn, they moved to Chicago following another one of Pop's newspaper jobs. When that newspaper failed, Pop wrote a novel sitting at his typewriter day after day in the living room while the children were forbidden to make any noise, until he was able to find work with the *Inter Ocean*. When they returned to New York in 1916, he worked as the racing editor for the *Morning Telegraph*.

The family lived week to week, though Pop sometimes had winnings from the racetrack. He was a gambling man, my great-grandfather, a Southerner from a family of Tennessee farmers, though his father was a beloved and respected doctor, described by one of Dorothy's cousins as kind, considerate, careless about his bills, and generous to all, poor or wealthy, black or white. Grace was from a family of whalers from upstate New York, a Northerner and a bitter pill for Pop's mother, who took a dislike to Dorothy because she looked like Grace, the Yankee, and preferred Della, Dorothy's sister, because her looks took after Pop. Grace came from poverty herself and had worked in a shirt factory from the age of twelve to fourteen to support her mother and three sisters after her father, Napoleon Bonaparte Satterlee, died of tuberculosis. He had been a chair maker and veteran of the Civil War—during which he was wounded in the throat and thereafter couldn't speak above a whisper—and a survivor of Libby Prison, the second deadliest prison of the Confederacy.

Grace would come to bear five children to a man whose earnings came and went on the racetrack, who didn't know how to share his wife with his children, and who never showed them any physical affection, though he ensured they all grew up well-read. He and Dorothy were much alike, strong-minded and stubborn—my way or the highway, as Tamar described it—and they fought. When Pop saw that Dorothy was determined to make her living as a journalist, he sent word to his cronies in the newspaper business to discourage her. Lore has it that he booted her out of the house when she found work at the *Call*, but then, he had booted his sons out too.

John Day liked his horses, he liked his drink, he liked his women, and he looked good at all times. He was tall, imposing, and well dressed. The Days always were beautifully dressed no matter how broke they were, and Grace, often despairing during the day, would dress up to have dinner with her children. "Get clothed and in my right mind," she'd say. Like her mother, Dorothy dressed like a well-bred young woman even as she moved from one cold Lower East Side room to another, writing articles for a pittance, and she would maintain that sense of style long after she started the Catholic Worker, still longing for lovely clothes. "Every woman needs one good dress," she often said, looking pointedly at Tamar.

Within a few months of working at the *Call*, Dorothy's salary of five dollars a week was raised to ten. She wrote a flurry of articles over a period of five months, working from noon to midnight covering child labor, strikes, fires, starvation and evictions in the slums, food riots, and antiwar meetings. She interviewed Margaret Sanger one day and Mrs. Astor's butler another. She and a young man, a radical writer by the name of Itzok Granich, who would come to love her, interviewed Leon Trotsky, one of the architects of the Russian revolution. She was in Madison Square Garden in March 1917 when it filled with workers celebrating the fall of the Russian czar and two days later when it held a pro-war rally. At night she attended socialist, anarchist, and IWW balls at Webster Hall on East Eleventh Street, while by day she picketed garment factories and restaurants, her first experiences of facing public indignation and hostility while being bored with the endless walking back and forth. And she also started to smoke cigarettes.

In the winter of 1916 and 1917, the *Call* moved from Pearl Street to St. Mark's Place, and Dorothy's walks were lengthened. She began to wander the streets and hike the Palisades in New Jersey with Itzok, and she became his girl. They sat and talked into the early-morning hours on the piers over the East River, where every now and then Itzok, or Irwin as he was now signing his work, would break into Yiddish folk songs or Hebrew hymns.

Irwin was a good-looking man with thick, black, and unruly hair he couldn't be bothered to cut so he was always pushing it away. Like Dorothy, he was generous with money. He loved to explain Marx and what needed to be done to change the world, and rarely spoke about himself or his own writings. He came from an Orthodox Jewish family, theater-loving Romanian immigrants who lived on Chrystie Street in the Lower East Side. At the age of twelve Irwin got a job working in a gas mantle factory in the Bowery. At thirteen he began working for a delivery company and fell in love with horses. He said if he hadn't become a journalist, he would have become a teamster. He had attended New York University and Harvard, but, like Dorothy, didn't finish. University wasn't nearly as exciting as the education that could be found on the streets.

Immigrants were arriving with an appetite for learning and attending night school, theater, and lectures by poets, professors, and philosophers who often spoke from soapboxes—Herbert Spencer on the corner of Delancey Street or Marx in the lecture halls. Atheism, anarchism, socialism, vegetarianism, women's rights, free love, free speech, free thought—it was all in the air. The socialists were mainly immigrants and old trade unionists who sat drinking tea in East Side cafés, often speaking Yiddish. The IWWs were American, though the heyday of the great strikes was over by 1917, and the leaders were all in jail. The anarchists were a small group—Dorothy didn't pay much attention to them—and the liberals were those who worked on the *Masses*, a collectively owned monthly begun in 1912 full of art, cartoons, and political commentary. In the Village, poetry, plays, and art—the Lyrical Left, as some called it—flourished along with the radical thinkers, and Irwin was involved with all of these groups. He had joined the IWW and experimented with anarchist communes. By 1914 the *Masses* was publishing his articles, and in 1916 he had become a member of the Socialist Party. The Provincetown Playhouse, which was housed in the stable of an old town house on Macdougal Street that the journalist John Reed had found, in its first New York City season performed his play *Ivan's Homecoming*, under what they called the "war bill," and it was through this that he introduced Dorothy to the Village.

Before the influx of the bohemians, Greenwich Village had been a neighborhood of Italian, Irish, and German immigrants, with a small segment of African Americans who helped construct the bridges, the subways, and the first of the skyscrapers. Then around 1910 a different sort of immigrant started to arrive, first from Europe and then from within the States. Some were fleeing failed marriages or family lives, drawn by something brave and new that might just might be their salvation. They were also drawn by an awareness that the world was changing, and the heartbeat of this change was to be found surrounding Washington Square Park. The north side of the park was lined with old sedate houses and tall trees in small gardens, while on the south side these bohemians gathered on narrow and crooked streets, in run-down redbrick tenement houses so miserable, people preferred to congregate in the parks, bars, and tearooms.

After rehearsals and shows, the Provincetown Players met next door at Polly Holladay's restaurant, the first of the Village bohemian restaurants, where for fifty cents you could get a leg of lamb or roast beef and gravy, though one look at the cockroach-infested kitchen could kill your appetite. Through the Provincetown Players, Irwin introduced Dorothy to two people who would come to influence her in unexpected ways. The first was Peggy Baird Johns, a small, delicate woman seven years her senior with peculiar yellow eyes who spoke with a Long Island accent and was rumored to be the first woman in the Village to bob her hair. Peggy, it seems, knew the entire Village literary and radical crowd, including Jack London, John Reed, Emma Goldman, and Man Ray, and was married to the poet Orrick Johns, one of the first of the free-verse poets. An artist, she studied at the Art Students League under Robert Henri. She painted landscapes and portraits, and wrote poetry and had a few assignments for the *Call*. She believed, for a time, in free love.

Neither Dorothy nor Peggy had any real reason to be around the Provincetown Playhouse. Peggy seemed content to paint, and Dorothy occasionally read parts for absent actors during rehearsals and once auditioned for a part but was so miserable she never did it again. She was succeeding in earning her living as a journalist, however meager her wages were, but her writing dissatisfied her. She did not take to the *Call*'s editorial pressure to distort the truth and make things look worse than they were in order to, as she saw it, promote socialism. Dorothy disagreed with Irwin in how she saw the world. His Lower East Side and hers were not alike, though Dorothy allowed that he knew it better, having grown up on Chrystie Street. Irwin emphasized the misery and degradation of the slums, while Dorothy, though she saw the misery, also saw the dignity and courage of ordinary people in extraordinary circumstances. In spite of these differences, she and Irwin became engaged, and he brought her home to meet his stern and beautiful Orthodox Jewish mother, who looked at Dorothy sorrowfully, as all three of her sons were dating gentile girls at the time. She didn't speak but she offered food. After Dorothy left, she broke the dish Dorothy had eaten from.

Dorothy quit the *Call* right before the Selective Service Act was passed in May 1917. All the young men argued about what to do while Dorothy worked briefly for the Collegiate Anti-Militarism League at Columbia University before bumping into Floyd Dell, the managing editor of the *Masses*, and becoming his assistant. She loved her work at the *Masses*. The publication took itself less seriously than the *Call*, and it published ideas Dorothy had never seen—depictions of Christ as a longshoreman or as a fisherman sympathetic to unions. "What a glowing word it was to us then," she wrote of her time at the paper almost thirty years later. "To speak to the Masses. To write to the Masses, to be a part of the Masses." Her own first contribution was a poem followed by a handful of book reviews. Generally, though, her duties were to answer the mail and send rejection slips to some of the best poets of the day with one word written on it, "Sorry." Floyd Dell also taught her how to dummy up the paper for the printers, a skill she would come to need when she began her own paper. Then the editor, Max Eastman, left to go on a fund-raising tour, while Floyd took a month's vacation to write a novel, and so it was left to Dorothy to make up what turned out to be the last issue before the *Masses* was shut down by the government for its anticonscription stance.

Though the first US forces were being sent to France, the summer of 1917 was a happy one for Dorothy. After a winter of living in unheated rooms, she had moved to a fifth-floor walk-up above the Provincetown Playhouse, rented for the summer from the novelist and critic Edna Kenton. There every night fevered young men gathered to talk the hours away as the threat of the draft hung over them. There seemed to be nothing they could do, so she and Irwin would head out to Staten Island for picnics on the beach and to gather shells and stones. At night they roamed the streets, and Dorothy would invite back to the apartment homeless people she met in the park.

"It's your religious instinct," Irwin said to her, the first of her friends to recognize this aspect of Dorothy, even though he would become a lifelong member of the Communist Party.

By November, Dorothy was back to her stream of cold rented rooms. With the suppression of the *Masses* and the arrest of the editors for conspiring to obstruct war conscription, Dorothy was unemployed and at loose ends when Peggy showed up with an offer she couldn't refuse.

Peggy may have been easy to dismiss as an uncommitted and free-spirited woman, but she was brave. Caught in one of the many riots at Union Square in 1915, she had protected a deaf and mute boy about to be battered by the police by throwing her tiny arms around the boy and berating the officers until they backed off. Then in August 1917 she had gone down to Washington, DC, to work as a journalist for the National Woman's Party magazine, the *Suffragist*. After watching women being arrested, she joined the picket line, got arrested, and was given a fifty-dollar fine or thirty days in jail. The suffragists needed more women on the picket line, so Peggy returned to New York to drum up support.

When she walked into the Hotel Brevoort on Ninth Street, another favorite bohemian haunt, the first person she saw was Dorothy. "Come down to Washington, DC, with me," she said.

"Why not?" Dorothy replied. She had no job, all her friends were being arrested for either refusing conscription or evading the draft or were being sent off to fight. The two of them left on the night train with eighteen other women.

On November 10, two days after Dorothy's twentieth birthday, she and forty-eight other women were arrested on the picket line. What had begun as a respectable picket had gotten rough. A group of sailors dragged the barricades away and attacked the women. Dorothy fought back and was attacked so furiously that the women, before they were arrested and hustled into the paddy wagons, huddled about her saying, "Are you hurt, Miss Day? Are you hurt?"

Up until that day, the women who were arrested had been jailed overnight, released, and told to go home, at which point they changed their clothes and returned to the line. But this time the oldest woman, who was seventy-three years old, received a six-day sentence, while one of the leaders, Lucy Burns, a schoolteacher from Brooklyn, received six months, and Peggy and Dorothy each received thirty days. They were sent to Occoquan, a notorious work farm in Virginia, and while traveling there by train, Dorothy, feeling oppressed by the bleak countryside, wondered why she had gotten involved. That night when they arrived at Occoquan, November 15, the Night of Terror, as it came to be known, was the worst and most brutal incident of the treatment of the suffragists. About forty guards, some dressed in street clothes and all armed with clubs, dragged, kicked, trampled, and choked the women. Some were knocked unconscious or threatened with rape. Three guards attacked Dorothy so violently the story made the newspapers. They throttled her, held her arms above her head, and smashed her several times against an iron bench, almost beating her senseless. Witnesses were afraid the guards had broken her back.

Dorothy was not a timid person. One night while working on the *Call*, she had forgotten her house key, and unwilling to wake the family, she visited police stations trying to find a women's lockup where she could spend the night. Failing that, she took a taxi to find friends and ended up being attacked by the taxi driver in a Jewish cemetery in Yonkers. She fought back, biting him until he bled, and then she demanded he drive her to the train station, which he did while cursing her until she got him to shut up by lecturing him all the way there. But the Night of Terror crushed Dorothy. Fortunately, she was put in the same cell as Lucy Burns, who, though handcuffed to the bars for three hours (a sight that would haunt Dorothy for years), recognized the fragility of the young woman and kept her calm by talking the night through about the sea and traveling and Joseph Conrad, while they shared a single cot with no blankets. The following day Lucy was put in solitary confinement, and Dorothy was left alone during the subsequent seven-day hunger strike, which she and eleven other women participated in. She wept throughout the week while reading the Psalms.

The hunger strike had begun as a demand for political prisoner status, which, according to several accounts, Peggy had first suggested. Peggy, well versed in the radical world, which most of the suffragists were not, pointed out that they were political activists arrested on trumped-up charges for obstructing traffic and were treated more harshly than other prisoners, including being fed food crawling with worms. When news of the Night of Terror and of the hunger strike got out, the women were transferred to a DC jail where Dorothy spent her time reading *Fortitude*, a dense Victorian novel that suited her mood, while Peggy sketched portraits of fellow prisoners, until President Wilson pardoned all the women at the end of November.

The warden of Occoquan, who ran his camp with bloodhounds and whipping posts, had been encouraged by the Wilson administration to terrorize the suffragists in an attempt to stop the movement, but it had the opposite effect, and money and support poured in. Eight of the women who were most brutally treated, including Dorothy, sued the superintendent of prisons for eight hundred thousand dollars in damages. They withdrew the suit in 1920 when the wardens of both the DC jail and Occoquan were fired, and when women finally succeeded in getting the vote, a law that Dorothy, in her disinterest in politics and belief that change was more effectively brought about in other ways, would never take advantage of.

On Dorothy's return from Washington, DC, Irwin introduced her to another friend who would open a door for her that no other at that time could. One of the most dark, intense, driven, and talented writers of the times, Eugene O'Neill, or Gene, as Dorothy called him, understood her dawn visits to St. Joseph's Catholic Church on Sixth Avenue after nights at the Hell Hole tavern or balls at Webster Hall. The future Pulitzer Prize winner was twenty-nine, divorced with a son, and just beginning to be recognized as a playwright of talent.

That winter, that bitter, snowbound winter, when because of the war there was a coal shortage, and they had heatless Mondays (Dorothy sometimes burned clothespins to keep warm) followed by meatless Tuesdays, was a time that would remain with them all. Decades later, Gene recalled those days and nights as the happiest period of his life.

Just as Dorothy had walked the streets with Irwin the previous winter, she walked the streets with Gene, down West Street and up the East Side waterfront. They stopped in saloons to warm up, and Dorothy drank port in the back room, as women weren't allowed in the bars. He took her to Jimmy-the-Priest's, a dangerous dive at the South Street Seaport, near the fish market, and a stranger told her, "You're too young to be hanging around here." But she felt safe with Gene. After the saloons closed, they continued to walk or rode in trucks along the waterfront, or on the Second Avenue El, and sometimes he would fall asleep on her shoulder. They would often end up at Romany Marie's tearoom on Washington Place. Romany Marie was an immigrant from Romanian Moldavia, an ex-anarchist who knew Emma Goldman from the early days. She was dark and good-looking with a lovely low voice and laugh, and she provided meals to those who needed them. Some said she kept Gene alive by feeding him during his drunks. Gene was fond of Romany Marie's, with its fireplace, batik prints, and patrons' paintings on the walls. It was lit by candles in glass wine bottles on the wooden tables as there was no electricity. "Last of the really great bohemian cafés," said Buckminster Fuller, another one of Romany Marie's many poverty-stricken visionaries who she kept fed.

People couldn't sit around the Hell Hole without drinking a few; they drank to keep going. Some would later like to talk about how hard drinking Dorothy was in those years, but Sue Jenkins Brown, writer and close friend to many of the writers of the era, told Louis Sheaffer, who would win the Pulitzer Prize in 1973 for his biography of O'Neill, that Dorothy was not as wild as people liked to portray her. Unlike many of the others, she had a job with a regular paycheck working on the *Liberator*, the successor of the *Masses*, and she supplemented it with freelance work.

Dorothy was the only one who could keep up with Gene. (She was the youngest—Irwin was three years older, Peggy seven, and Gene nine.) She matched Gene hour for hour riding the buses and walking the streets, and talking, always talking. She loved to listen and to talk; she was tireless. "No one ever wanted to go to bed, no one ever wanted to be alone," she wrote.

When Dorothy headed to work early one morning after not having gone to bed, Gene put her in an open-air horse-drawn carriage, and then an hour later, she got a phone call at the newspaper from him saying, "Come back, I am lonely." But he never seemed to want to kiss her even though he said offhandedly, "Don't you want to lose your virginity?" One night she did sleep with him, but they did not make love. No, she told him, you don't really want that. Gene liked the way things were—relaxed, companionable, uncomplicated—but he also didn't want to be left alone, even for a minute. He liked her, Dorothy thought, for her vitality and her companionship and because she was in love with his writing.

It was Gene who taught Dorothy to take people seriously and never to laugh at them, to listen to their stories and turn what could have been tawdry into something with dignity, maybe even with romance. It was one of the fine things about Gene, Dorothy said. He gave her his plays to read, and she felt flattered. He wanted her to read Strindberg and Baudelaire. Face the tragedy of life, he said to her. He burned toilet paper and used the ashes to darken her eyebrows and eyelashes, saying that anything can be used for theater makeup.

Their friendship broke Irwin's heart. Gene tried to gently kid him, and one night when the three of them were the only ones in the Hell Hole, a fierce blizzard outside, Irwin poured all his feelings out and told them how jealous and brokenhearted he was. Gene said, let's go for a walk, and the three of them walked through the streets, pushing through the snowdrifts, while Irwin sang songs in Yiddish, and Gene sang sea shanties. Dorothy was Irwin's girl, but she wasn't serious about their engagement, and Irwin knew it.

The Hell Hole was the back room of the Golden Swan tavern on the corner of Sixth Avenue and Fourth Street. It was a dark, dirty, and dank place—the sawdust covering the floor smelled of urine, and two pigs lived in the cellar—but, Peggy said, it had more ideas and ideals than any bar at the Waldorf. It had a small wooden window you'd shriek into or pound on until it opened and a ghostly hand passed out a bowl of soup. There was always a man whom no one ever saw enter or leave, thin and short with a limp, sitting alone in the back with a derby hat on the chair next to him. When he got drunk he stood up and for hours played his cane as if it were a violin. The bartender Lefty Louie was short and dark with one bad eye that shot out to the left and who walked with a crablike limp. The owner of the Golden Swan, a blind man named Tom Wallace, lived upstairs and would bang on the floor with his cane calling for Lefty, and Lefty would slowly climb the stairs yelling, "Coming, coming!"

The pickpockets, pimps, and Hudson Dusters, a West Side gang who bought Gene drinks and listened when he recited poetry, stayed in the bar in the front, while the Provincetown Players and their crowd stayed in the back room. They were always coming and going—no one could sit still for long. Helen Westley, the actress, coming straight from the theater with her stage makeup still on, or Charles Demuth, the painter, with his clubfoot and diabetes, all aflame with revolution and art, writing and politics. Many were either writing plays or acting in them. No one owned much more than the clothes on their backs, a box of paint, or a typewriter. They were barely able to pay eight dollars a month for cheap furnished rooms, and all hoped for a commission, a publication, a role—something that would bring in a bit of money.

Gene was the genius of the crowd, Peggy said. She knew him well, as she had been one of his lovers in 1915 when he took her to meet his mother at the Prince George Hotel, where they had tea. Gene took care of Peggy when she was ill and brought her food and medicine several times a day. "Divorce Orrick and marry me," he said to her, but Peggy left with Orrick to live at the Johnses' family farm in St. Louis, where they were happy for a time. A year later their marriage fell apart, and Peggy returned to New York to find that Gene had fallen in love with Louise Bryant. They remained friends—people always did with Peggy—and when she was broke years later, Gene gave her a hundred dollars, half of what he had in his bank account. But it was how Gene would later come to divorce his second wife, Agnes, that Peggy found unforgivable.

That winter of 1916 Gene finished writing his play *The Moon of the Caribbees*, which he gave to Dorothy to read. She believed it was as good as *Candide*. A year later, the Provincetown Players opened *The Moon of the Caribbees*, and performing in it was a young man, Forster Batterham, the man Dorothy would come to love more than any other. But before she fell in love with Forster, she had other battles to fight.

At the Hell Hole, Gene recited with somber eyes, bitter mouth, and a monotonous grating voice, Francis Thompson's poem "The Hound of Heaven," his elbows resting on the table, chin cupped in hand, and looking at no one—*My heart is a broken fount*. He recited it to her only, Dorothy thought. No one else was listening.

Then Dorothy would sing to Gene "Frankie and Johnny" in a way few would forget, this self-possessed girl of twenty, cool-mannered, tweed-wearing, drinking rye whiskey straight with no discernible effect and smoking like a chimney at a time when women weren't allowed to smoke in public. And who brought into the Hell Hole rough-looking men she had encountered at the steps of St. Joseph's Church in need of a warm room and a stiff drink.

They were joined by Max Bodenheim, the poet from Chicago, who, with a red beard and pale face, recited his poems with a stutter, his corncob pipe anchored in a gap where he was missing a front tooth. "I know not ugliness. It is a mood which has forsaken me" was a line of his that Dorothy would remember all her life. Max was another who would come to her in need years later, but then he was young, serious, and hardworking, and everyone chided him for not drinking.

One evening, Gene, Max, and Dorothy sat around a table working on a nonsense poem, each adding a line on a napkin that Dorothy kept until it was destroyed years later in a fire. On other nights, Gene, Dorothy, and Harold de Polo, a pulp fiction writer who would soon come to be a fishing buddy of Forster's, often got in a singing mood. De Polo sang "The Spaniard That Blighted My Life," Gene sang the sea shanty "Blow the Man Down," and Dorothy sang "In the Heart of the City That Has No Heart."

Gene watched Dorothy as she sang in her true yet odd voice, and he listened to her during those rare moments he was not talking himself. If something pleased him, Peggy said, his whole face lit up, his eyes shone, and his melancholy slipped away, and you felt you had been given a warm and intimate gift. He listened until Agnes Boulton's beauty in the candlelight took his admiring eyes away from Dorothy.

Was Dorothy in love with Gene? Louis Sheaffer asked Sue Jenkins Brown, but Sue didn't reply. No one could say if this was so. Dorothy never spoke a word of it, and she said she wasn't years later when there was no reason to hide it. Agnes Boulton, who would become the second of Gene's three wives, believed she was. There was some undeniable connection between them—Dorothy stopping in at St. Joseph's (Agnes, as a Catholic, claimed she accompanied Dorothy to her very first Mass), while Gene quoted Baudelaire and the "downward path to salvation," his hand trembling as he reached for his drink. But there was no pulse there, no physical attraction for Dorothy. He would devour his friends and lovers because he was devoured by his talent, his all-consuming urge to write. Dour and melancholy Gene, as Dorothy described him, with his great sense of futility about life that led him to reject anything that might save him, couldn't really love anyone.

"Marry me and come to Provincetown," he had asked Dorothy, but then, he had also asked Peggy and others. Peggy said he wanted someone to take care of him, but everyone knew he was in love with Louise Bryant.

Dorothy said, "He wanted a girl for a companion, but I was a virgin, and then Gene went with Agnes."

Agnes Boulton was a successful writer who, in the years before she married Gene, published more than forty-five short stories. She was smart and beautiful and worked hard. She went to bed early and wasn't able to keep up at night with the others. She was quiet but strong-willed, and she wanted Gene.

"Agnes loved the man," Dorothy said. "I loved the writer."

Agnes's feelings for Dorothy were a mixture of liking and jealousy, fear and annoyance. Dorothy would stride into Agnes's apartment early in the morning, not having been to bed all night, and get up Agnes's nose by telling her what to do even though Agnes was five years older. Agnes didn't trust Dorothy. Dorothy had met Gene first, and Agnes was unsure of their friendship, but she was also unsure of Gene, so she said nothing when Dorothy would fall asleep on the bed fully dressed while Gene sat on the couch talking until Agnes would lie down beside Dorothy and go to sleep. Gene, Dorothy told her, always had to have someone to listen while he talked, and he never stopped talking.

"Gene should have married you," one of her old friends said to Dorothy almost fifty years later. "If he had, he would be alive today." But would Dorothy have married Gene? He failed her the night that Louis Holladay, brother of the owner of Polly's restaurant, died.

Louis Holladay was tall, blond, slow of speech, and, like all the others, loved Baudelaire. He was an old friend of Gene's and had introduced Gene to the Village crowd when both were eighteen. Louis had just returned to the city after being away for a year getting clean from his drug addiction. On the night of January 22, 1918, Louis, Gene, and Dorothy left the Hell Hole to eat at an Italian restaurant on Prince Street. At the restaurant, Dorothy saw Louis exchange money for a small bottle with one of the waiters. They then went to Romany Marie's and sat near the fireplace drinking coffee with Charles Demuth and the writer Robert A. Parker. Louis put some white powder from the bottle on the back of his hand near his thumb and sniffed it. Somebody asked him what it was.

"Heroin," he replied.

"You fool," Gene said, and got up and left.

Louis soon slumped over onto Dorothy's shoulder, and someone cried out, "He's dead!" The room cleared out until only Louis, Dorothy, and Romany Marie remained. Dorothy, who had just met Louis that night, gazed steadfastly at this beautiful young man as he died in her arms.

"Where's Gene?" Dorothy asked Romany Marie.

"You're not leaving too?" she said.

"I'll be back," Dorothy replied, and left for Agnes's apartment at the Hotel Brevoort, where she found Gene in bed.

"Here you are," she said. She looked at him intently for a moment. "Louis is dead."

Gene rolled over and turned his back to her. "It's not my mess," he replied.

Dorothy returned to Romany Marie's with Agnes to find Polly and Max Bodenheim there.

"He died in my arms," Dorothy said to Agnes, and turned away, weeping silently.

Some say it was Dorothy who took the bottle of heroin from Louis's pocket before the police arrived, and when the cop wasn't looking she slipped the bottle into Max's pocket. Agnes claimed Louis had deliberately taken an overdose over a failed love affair. Polly told the coroner that her brother had a history of heart trouble, and his death was put down as chronic endocarditis.

Polly, even though she had just lost her brother, took pity on Dorothy and accompanied her to the Greenwich Village Inn, where Dorothy had a bath and went to sleep.

Dorothy didn't remember Gene getting drunk that day, as Agnes recalled. She claimed Louis's death sobered him up while Agnes said he sat in the Hell Hole drinking himself senseless with Old Taylor whiskey. He stayed with his brother until he could pull himself together, and then showed up at Agnes's door, and they left for Provincetown together. That April they got married, even though Gene was still writing love letters to Louise Bryant. Dorothy wouldn't see him again for a year.

Dorothy never wrote about this other than to say that "a succession of incidents and the tragic aspect of life in general began to overwhelm me and I could no longer endure the life I was leading." She would come to write an unpublished four-page essay after Gene's death in 1953. Though it irked her that some believed her glory lay in that time when she was Eugene O'Neill's companion, it was Gene's faith that was on her mind as she wrote. People said Gene had no interest in religion. Dorothy felt differently. He wasn't interested in politics—he was interested in man's relationship with God, and Gene's relation with his God was a war in itself. Gene, Dorothy said, rebelled against man's fate.

CHAPTER TWO

After the death of Louis Holladay, Romany Marie closed down her tearoom, while John Reed told Dorothy she should leave town. He gave her the train fare to Washington, DC, to work on the *Suffragist* magazine, but after a month, she returned to New York. That April, the same month as Gene and Agnes's wedding, she began training as a nurse at Kings County Hospital in Brooklyn.

Dorothy said she turned to nursing because she was sick of playing at writing, but her nursing skills had begun when her mother had the last of her five children. Grace was in her forties when John was born eleven years after Della, Dorothy's only sister and fourth of the Day children. Grace did not recover easily from the birth and neither could she nurse the baby, so Dorothy took care of him, though he was so difficult to feed he almost starved to death.

Dorothy's work as a nurse that spring of 1918 almost ended before it had begun. In mid-April the editors of the *Masses* were put on trial for conspiring to obstruct war recruitment and conscription, and Dorothy was called as a witness for the prosecution. She was lucky not to have been arrested, as she had been responsible for choosing some of the cartoons and articles that were used in the trial, but her name had not been on the masthead. She wasn't helpful to the prosecution and claimed she couldn't remember much. "I am taken by surprise by this testimony," the prosecutor said. The trial ended in a hung jury—ten had voted for conviction—as did the second trial, for which Dorothy was not called, although now eight voted for acquittal, and as the war was ending by that time, the matter was dropped.

During the trial, Dorothy lost her position at the hospital, but she got it back because most of the doctors and nurses had left for Europe in the war effort and the first wave of the Spanish flu had just begun. She couldn't have chosen a more benighted time to become a nurse, but she was always one to be doing something, doing what needed to be done. While her two older brothers were serving in the war—Donald at an air and coastal patrol station at Montauk Point, New York, and Sam as a radio operator on a mine sweeper in the English Channel—Dorothy was coming onto the ward in a city hospital, the last stop for the dying poor, to lay out as many as eight bodies a day. People healthy in the morning could be dead by night. The autumn of 1918 brought on a second wave of the flu, and the fatality rate was so high and death so quick that if the rate continued, people feared the US population would be wiped out in a matter of weeks. The flu weakened its victims' bodies but they retained their clearness of mind, and it left people with no idea of whether they or their friends or family would survive. While she was caring for the ill and dying, Armistice Day, three days after Dorothy's twenty-first birthday, passed by without her being aware of it.

As the worst of the flu abated by the end of November, she started to write again, half an hour in the morning and a half hour late at night. She became restless and went into the city on her half day off, and it was there, back with the old crowd, that she met a man whom she would come to love beyond reason and hope—a newspaperman named Lionel Moise. In June 1917, at the age of twenty-nine and while living in Missouri working as a reporter for the *Kansas City Star*, Lionel had registered in the Officers' Reserve Corp as a second lieutenant, and when Dorothy met him he was in uniform. In her autobiographical novel *The Eleventh Virgin*, Dorothy wrote that the fictional character based on Lionel was working at the hospital as an orderly to pay off his medical bill after being drugged and robbed by Mexican sailors. He had arrived in New York after working his passage on a freighter from Caracas, Venezuela, where he had been a cameraman for a film company. This may or may not have been true of Lionel, but it has become accepted history. Peggy's second husband, Malcolm Cowley, the literary critic, spoke of Lionel only as a reporter working at the time for the *New York American*.

Lionel was a man who loved to laugh and who threw himself into life. He was a romantic, Dorothy said, and he reminded her of Pop the way he typed with two fingers while smoking cigarettes. Wrung dry by the Spanish flu pandemic, in which she found herself surrounded by the dying young, men and women of her own age, she had encountered a man who seemed to possess the passion and bravery that Gene did not. Lionel, beloved of women and idolized by young reporters, cracked her heart wide open, and Dorothy was no longer the unengaged and self-possessed woman she had been.

Big and blond with blue eyes, Lionel was a handsome—no, by all accounts he was a beautiful—Jewish man who looked and acted like the fighting Irish and who loved to sing and write poetry. The history that has come down of Lionel begins with the *Kansas City Star*, which in 1917 was one of the half dozen best American newspapers. Great ego and undisciplined talent were his colleagues' favorite assessment of Lionel, and they often remembered him more for his personality than his writing. Lionel was famous at the *Kansas City Star*, but he wouldn't become the most famous of its writers. That would be an eighteen-year-old cub reporter named Ernest Hemingway. Lionel had by then already worked for at least nine newspapers, crisscrossing the country as he would do for most of his life. When he tramped and beat his way from New York to Missouri and out to the West Coast, it made the papers of one of the towns he passed through. He hit every hobo jungle and worked the harvest fields searching for material for his stories and poems. In 1910 he had written a poem describing the life of the track worker, rock splitter, and migrant laborer—work he had personally experienced. He could sniff out a tramp with a fantastic but true story within ten minutes of speaking to him in a hobo dialect no other reporter could understand. He was one of the last of his kind—opinionated, hard drinking, hard fighting, and loyal to no one but himself, and a boomer, a footloose reporter, moving from one city to another, one newspaper to the next, always able to get a job because of his talent. By 1917 Lionel had already become a legend in city newsrooms across the country, and no one underestimated his intellect. His stories, entertaining and erudite, men said, stood out when the rest faded away. He had a thirst for knowledge and a quick grasp of topics many reporters couldn't comprehend. The literary critic Malcolm Cowley called Lionel a brilliant reporter, though half-baked by reading Nietzsche, with enough talent, if not the discipline, to make him a famous writer.

Lionel held strong opinions about writing, which he was happy to share. He believed pure objective writing was the only true form of storytelling, by which he meant one should use dialogue, action, and a minimum of description. His favorites were Twain, Conrad, Kipling, and Dreiser. "No stream of consciousness nonsense; no playing dumb observer one paragraph and God Almighty the next. . . . In short, no tricks."

He also spoke of " the regrettable indication of a great nation's literary taste when it chooses a national anthem beginning with the words, 'Oh, say.'"

Lionel advised Dorothy to write with "simple, declarative sentences, personal articles, and to write like a woman."

"And that," she said toward the end of her life, "is what I've been doing all these years."

In December Dorothy quit her work at the hospital and moved into Lionel's studio, a large room on Fourteenth Street, where she would find that Lionel was not an easy man to love.

"I had been going with Gene O'Neill," she said. "Lionel was jealous, and he punched Gene. Gene was a gentle man, and he said, 'Why did you do that?'"

Gene forgave Lionel, and they soon became good friends. Gene offered him a part in one of his plays, and by February, Lionel was a Provincetown Player performing in two productions. Earlier in December, Forster had performed in *The Moon of the Caribbees*, the play Gene had just finished when he and Dorothy were wandering the streets together the previous winter. By the time Lionel arrived, Forster was no longer acting—some say after he walked off the set to avoid a confrontation, but this could also have been when he came down with the Spanish flu. The Provincetown Playhouse had difficulty putting on their performances as their members fell ill.

Another to succumb to the flu was Malcolm Cowley, Peggy's new love and soon-to-be second husband. Lionel carried him to the hospital in his arms. "Just like a Pietà," Malcolm said. Malcolm would later become one of the best literary critics of the era, but in 1919 he was just another young poet nearly fainting on the sidewalk from starvation. Malcolm's poetry, Peggy said, was gentle and sweet, but she wouldn't come to remember it as she did the poetry of her first husband, Orrick Johns.

"You must meet Dorothy," Peggy had said to Malcolm, and went on and on about the line of Dorothy's jaw, which Malcolm would come to agree was extraordinary.

Greenwich Village was still cheap, and you could rent a furnished hall bedroom for two or three dollars a week or a top-floor flat in a derelict house for thirty dollars a month. Fifty cents was enough to buy breakfast for two, and fifty-five cents would buy you a cheap bottle of sherry. Friday nights there were still the dances in Webster Hall, and on Saturdays everybody gathered at Luke O'Connor's saloon, the Working Girls' Home, as the Hell Hole had closed. But many of the newcomers to the Village weren't interested in being starving artists and instead opened antique shops, nightclubs, and real estate offices, while the old-timers, who were now reaching the age of thirty, talked about the good old days of 1916. The era of the old *Masses* had come to an end, and the war had changed everyone. In October 1917, after the Bolsheviks took power in Russia, the suppression of antiwar dissent escalated into the Palmer Red Raids, with wholesale arrests and sentences of between five and fifteen years for simply stating an opinion, written or spoken. In this atmosphere of fear some of the Village crowd joined the army, some joined intelligence and spied on their former friends, some went to prison, and others fled to Mexico, including Irwin Granich, who had changed his name to Mike Gold after a Jewish Civil War veteran who had fought to help free the slaves.

By the time the men started to return from the war, the neighborhood was changing. The Seventh Avenue subway had opened, and the old firetraps that had been a steady source of cheap studios for poor artists were torn down to make way for new apartments. Soon both bohemians and radicals, including Malcolm and Peggy, began an exodus to

Paris or the South of France, where, of course, many of them planned to write their one good novel.

And Dorothy? How was she doing? While walking down the street, she and Malcolm came to an Episcopal church on Hudson Street, St. Luke in the Fields.

"Come in with me," she said to Malcolm.

After sitting in the pew for a while, Dorothy knelt and prayed with tears streaming down her face.

"Don't tell anyone," she said to him as they continued on their way.

He was a compelling man, that Lionel Moise. He taught Dorothy how to write as a journalist; together they read *The Possessed*, by Dostoyevsky, an author they both loved; and he introduced her to Pascal's *Pensées*. But he fought bitterly against being tied by love for any woman and was cruel to those who did love him. And he walked out on, abandoned, fled from Dorothy on the day of her greatest need.

"It never occurred to me," she would come to say in her eighties, "to keep the baby."

It was a bitter summer of 1919 for Dorothy, pregnant and witnessing the marriage of two of her closest friends, Peggy and Forster's sister Lily Batterham. She told no one of her pregnancy until Peggy cried out in a letter, "What's wrong with you? Are you dead or something?" Peggy, who was unable to have children, tried and failed to talk Dorothy out of the abortion. She dismissed Dorothy's belief that she couldn't bring a child into the world as a single mother. If everyone waited until the circumstances were perfect, Peggy said to her, no one would get born.

Dorothy couldn't bring herself to tell Lionel. While he worked, she walked the streets and peered in the windows of families in their homes. "Why couldn't I too have home, husband and babies?" she wondered. She did no writing but spent her time sewing and reading Anatole France. The Provincetown Players knew of her difficulties, but they could do nothing but stand by helplessly. All that summer she kept her pregnancy hidden from Lionel, and in September, when he announced he was leaving for Chicago, where he had a job offer, she finally told him.

"I'm sorry for you," he said, "but I'm still going to Chicago."

Lionel had always been a waterfront brawler kind of guy, and maybe he tired of the sad faces of those who considered themselves true bohe-mians mourning the lost days of 1916. Maybe Chicago, where the radical life and the IWW were now showing their strength, called to him. But Lionel had always been a wanderer and would be for the rest of his life.

Dorothy followed him to Chicago, living within three miles of him that autumn and winter, but there are few clues about this time. Maybe this was when Lionel told her, perhaps not unkindly, to marry a wealthy man who could support her and give her children. And this was, as far as I have been able to discern, where she had her abortion. She didn't speak of the abortion to Grace. Don't get caught, Grace had said to her, she who had sat with her three sisters in the kitchen discussing methods of at-home abortions, while Dorothy, a young girl, overheard from the bedroom.

The doctor who performed the abortion was Ben Reitman, a Mid-westerner born in poverty who ran away from home to ride the rails. He got himself into medical school and became known as the "hobo doctor" for his free care of hobos, prostitutes, and radicals. He opened the Hobo College in Chicago and later became known as the "clap doc-tor" for his pioneering work on sexually transmitted diseases. Like most people who knew Ben Reitman, Dorothy was repelled by him. He was a tall, heavy man who wore a black cowboy hat and silk tie, walked with a cane, and would have been handsome but for the filthy hair, hands, and fingernails. He was arrogant, unbearable, and a pathological woman-izer even throughout his relationship with his great love of ten years, Emma Goldman.

The abortion left Dorothy so ill and traumatized that for decades she couldn't bring herself to admire or like Emma Goldman, even though they would, oddly enough, come to share some things in common. Like Dorothy, Emma would never sway from her beliefs, she was unin-terested in the usual discussions of feminism, and she believed in the power of love.

Sometime in early 1920, Dorothy, heartbroken and suffering com-plications from the abortion, returned to Greenwich Village. There it seems she tried to commit suicide twice, once by overdosing on lauda-num and another with the gas oven, but in each instance she was saved by her friends. Dorothy believed it was Sue Jenkins Brown who saved her from the attempt by gas, though Sue claimed it was Spanish Willie, seller of bootleg liquor during Prohibition, who had smelled the gas while walking up the stairs past Dorothy's apartment.

That spring Dorothy took Lionel's advice when a much older man named Berkeley Tobey said to her on the train to Groton, Connecticut, "Let's get married." It was her fourth marriage proposal. The first had been while sitting on a tombstone in Illinois when she was seventeen, from a young man who planned to become a chicken farmer and who thought Dorothy would make a good farmer's wife. Then there was her engagement to Irwin, followed by another proposal while she was in Washington, DC, with the suffragists from a man who would go on to become a Wall Street lawyer and send money to the Catholic Worker.

Berkeley Tobey was one of the few in the Village with any money. He came from a wealthy Boston family—his grandfather had made his money manufacturing steamships for the US government during the Civil War. Berkeley dabbled as a writer and an actor, became business manager of the *Masses*, and gave the paper two thousand dollars he had inherited. He also had been a journalist for the *New Republic*, and he would become one of the founders of the Literary Guild. A man with money, plenty of ideas, and no need to work, Malcolm said. Dorothy was his third wife, and there would be six in total that his children knew of, though he never admitted how many times he had married. Rumor had it that he would give each of his new wives the family silver, which would then be "stolen" to find its way back to him after the end of the marriage. According to Malcolm, he would also insist on getting married in Connecticut and not consummate the marriage there, making it invalid under state law.

Dorothy and Berkeley got married in Connecticut in 1920. She was twenty-two, he was thirty-nine, and the best man was the editor of the *Daily Worker*. They lived in Berkeley's apartment on Washington Square, from where Dorothy would phone Lionel, who was now in Canada, until they joined the exodus to Europe in June of that year. They traveled in London, where she visited Dickens's home, drank tea, and ate watercress sandwiches, followed by Paris, Naples, and the island of

Capri, where they stayed for six months. Dorothy worked on her novel *The Eleventh Virgin* and in the hot afternoons fell asleep on a yacht or took a boat into Naples for the outdoor opera. There she was, married to a man she didn't love, writing about the man she did.

They returned April 1921 to live at the New Yorker Hotel, and Dorothy woke early one morning—she was always an early riser—while Berkeley was still asleep and placed all the jewelry he had given her, including her wedding ring, on the kitchen counter. She then went home to her mother feeling a sense of shame she would never fully overcome. "I married Berkeley on the rebound," Dorothy said. "I married him for his money." The marriage was dissolved, and she rarely spoke of Berkeley again.

Having finished her novel in which she declares she will get her man back, Dorothy, perhaps tired of the literary world she had immersed herself in since her marriage and ready to return to the kind of radical life she led in those happy times with Mike Gold and the *Masses*, headed for Chicago to find Lionel and get him back. And there she took up with him again, on and off, hot and cold. They argued over authors, and Lionel threw Dorothy's copy of James Joyce's *Portrait of the Artist as a Young Man* out the window of the Elevated onto North Avenue, offended by Joyce's stream-of-consciousness writing.

H. L. Mencken, the writer and literary critic, called Chicago in 1920 the literary capital of the world, and there too radicals and bohemians congregated in the tearooms. Chicago's Greenwich Village was North Side bohemia, as some called it, with its cafés like the Green Mask, along with Jake Loeb's house, which was full of everyone who was anybody, including Sergei Prokofiev, who Dorothy met. Dorothy already knew many of the artists and writers who had also come from New York, such as Max Bodenheim. Anarchists, Wobblies (of the IWW), and socialists mingled with gangsters, circus performers, actors, and grifters at the Dill Pickle, a renovated barn around the corner from Bughouse Square where anyone who felt he or she had something to say could get up on a soapbox. Dorothy attended Sunday workers' meetings in Lincoln Park, where she had walked as a fifteen-year-old with her infant brother John and sister, Della.

Jobs were easy to find, and Dorothy roamed from job to job as artist's model, Montgomery Ward department-store clerk, public library clerk, restaurant cashier, and night-shift clerk at a print shop. She worked briefly as secretary to Robert Minor, the cartoonist who gave up the highest paid political cartoonist position in the country to turn editor of the *Liberator*, the successor to the *Masses*, now based in Chicago, and the paper of the newly formed Communist Party. It was at this job that Dorothy would sneak into the nearby cathedral at lunchtime. She was often sick and depressed, and she still gazed at others' lives, peering in through the windows of houses she walked past at night. People seemed so normal—family, church, and girls "keeping themselves" for their fiancés. She didn't understand her own restlessness and recklessness that kept her from this. She felt driven—by what, she didn't yet know. Haunted. Greenwich Village, the Lower East Side, the cafés of Paris, the North Side of Chicago—wherever she was, Dorothy cornered people at parties to talk about God. Lionel at the time was city editor of the *Chicago Post*, and his assistant, Sam Putnam, later to become a communist, lent Dorothy J. K. Huysmans's *The Return*, *The Oblate*, and *The Cathedral*, in which Huysmans wrote of his return to the Catholic Church. Dorothy would never forget how Sam Putnam had recognized something in her.

Chicago in the early 1920s was an exciting if violent and dangerous place for radicals, and the Chicago IWWs were the toughest, strongest, and most active in the union movement. Lionel was a member, organizing and agitating and lucky to survive in a time when union organizers were being tortured, maimed, and killed, inside and outside the law. The brutality was worse than the Palmer Raids during the war. In 1922, while working with the American Unity League, an interfaith group led by Catholic priests, Lionel helped track down and reveal names of local Ku Klux Klan members. At that time, the KKK was at the peak of its power nationwide, and in their first year in Chicago in 1921 it claimed fifty-five thousand members. By 1925 it was down to ten thousand, in large part because the American Unity League's weekly publication, *Tolerance*, had published the names, addresses, and occupations of thousands of KKK members.

What a set of contradictions Lionel turned out to be: a brawling womanizer who supported his widowed mother for decades; who had a keen sense of justice; who wrote poetry and loved to tell stories and sing and knew every Wobbly and hobo song, every barroom ballad; and who was quick-witted and talented and yet unable to tame himself and focus on his writing. But a man who, Malcolm Cowley felt—through passing advice on to all those raw, young writers who idolized him, from Kenneth Rexroth to Dorothy Day—had made his mark on American writing.

Dorothy continued to fling herself about, taking on jobs wherever whim and fancy took her, still in love with Lionel, even though he had other women and she also sometimes dated other men, until the summer of 1922. Then she found herself caring for a woman, Marie Cramer, who had tried to either commit suicide over love for Lionel or give herself an abortion by taking twenty-five tablets of bichloride of mercury. Sold at the local drugstores, bichloride of mercury was used in the treatment of tonsillitis and syphilis, but desperate women also used it to induce abortions, leaving almost all of them to die tortured, prolonged deaths during which their bodies would begin decomposing even while they remained alive and alert.

How this must have torn at Dorothy to be reminded of her own abortion and suicide attempts, and it was through trying to help Marie that Dorothy found herself arrested for the second time, while they were both staying the night in one of the IWW's rooming houses. At the time, radical headquarters all over Chicago were being raided by the police, and, in an unlikely coincidence, that night just as Dorothy and Marie had gone to bed, the police raided the place. Well used to the raids, the men fled out the windows and down the fire escapes, while the women were arrested as inmates of a disorderly house—that is, prostitutes. It was a good thing, Dorothy would later say, that she didn't know, as she stood there in the glaring light of the streetlamp, she was being arrested for prostitution. The experience would turn out to be very different from her arrest in 1917. There were no headlines, no recognition of being a political prisoner, no Lucy Burns or Peggy to help her through, and no presidential pardon. After the arrest, she became full of irrational fear—afraid of being accused by any policeman she walked by and afraid of being pushed in front of the El. But it also opened something up in her that helped her to share in the suffering of the other jailed women, many of whom were going through drug withdrawals, that the first arrest had not. But then, she too had grown and suffered.

After Dorothy was released three days later, Lionel got her a job with the City News Bureau covering family court, and Della came over from New York to stay with her until the end of 1923, when Dorothy left Chicago and Lionel forever. She first went to New York and then on to New Orleans, while Lionel left for Minnesota with another woman—in a fit of pique, Dorothy claimed to one friend, and "to get away from me," she said to another. But what had happened was that Lionel, in a jealous rage, had held a gun to Dorothy's head, and after more than four years in love with the man, Dorothy walked away.

"I was scared," she told Stanley years later. "I was glad to get away from him, but I was deeply in love with him."

Even in the face of such abuse, Dorothy would never publicly put any blame on Lionel. She took responsibility for all she did and didn't do. So much of Lionel is inexplicable, and no one seems able to forgive him or to understand him, whether it is because no one can understand why Dorothy loved him so much and for so long, or because of what she was willing to do to stay with him. Or because this reminds us all that she was not always the clear-eyed visionary that we now see her as. Lionel was a man on the run—from women, from jobs, from life. He was tormented, it is clear, and because my grandmother loved him, and because more than fifty years later she still prayed for him, as she did for Gene O'Neill and those others she remembered with pain and love, and because Lionel was the father of her unborn child, Tamar's only ghost of a sibling, I find myself much more open to forgiveness. He is, after all, a member of the family.

I can feel my grandmother over my shoulder as I write. How she hated it when people wrote about her, especially of those early years. What do you know of me? I hear her asking me. How many people have looked at her life, including herself, searching for the earliest signs and elusive elements of religious impulse, searching for that exact moment of conversion? I can see no separation, no tears in the fabric in any aspect of her life. It is all of one piece. It's true, there is so much I don't know. I would like to know more about Lionel, and I have only the barest of clues. Sometimes the best clues are those moments of silence from my grandmother, those things she did not write or speak about. "Least said, soonest mended," she liked to say, as did her mother.

As painful as it is for me to read, I am glad my grandmother wrote *The Eleventh Virgin*. I read Tamar's copy, a discard from a Massachusetts public library with one corner chewed through by one of Tamar's budgerigars, who left no page untouched. For in this book, through its sad and disturbing qualities, I am able to reach out to my grandmother, knowing what it means to love a man against all reason and intelligence, loving without blindness but in full knowledge of your madness. And if there is only one thing I know in this quest to understand and tell the tale of Dorothy and Tamar, it is that I have to work from the heart, that mad, uncontrollable heart, which, regardless of this madness, is our one true connection with God.

Dorothy regretted writing *The Eleventh Virgin*, and she claimed that to speak of her licentious past would give young people permission to lead their own licentious lives and take that "downward path to salvation" (as if any young person needs permission). Her memories were painful to her, and she keenly felt misery at having her life raked over and commented on. But the book reveals the power and love and beauty of a young woman who in the small dark hours, with Gene's voice in her ear, harsh and bitter, battling against God and reciting "The Hound of Heaven," sought out the mysterious and silent places of the heart to listen to the voice of God. And I know that in the rawness of love gone awry, particularly in that awful summer and fall of 1919 and the lonely years of loving Lionel that followed, God is to be found, so much more intimate and profound, loving and immense, than at many other wiser or more pious times.

CHAPTER THREE

Like Grace, Dorothy was always seeking water. It gave her comfort and strength, and she could never do without the beach and sea for long. In the spring of 1924, she bought her first home for twelve hundred dollars, a cottage on a beach of Staten Island. With this move began the chain of events that led her to that moment so many of us chew on like a bone as we wonder what it means to us personally. Wonder if we too have what it takes to hear our call.

The cottage was on a lot twenty by eighty feet on Raritan Bay. It had enough land for a flower and vegetable garden, though the soil was heavy with clay, and there was a hedge of irises, forsythia, wild cherry, and apple, and a honey locust outside the porch. In front of the cottage, steps led down a steep bank of sumac, wild grape, and goldenrod and out to the beach. The cottage had a barrel woodstove in which she burned driftwood and a row of windows, some looking out to the meadows and hickory trees. Her writing table stood at a window overlooking the bay to the lighthouses and deep purple shadow of the New Jersey Shore. There she lived with the smell of seaweed and the sound of waves crashing high with the wind or softly lapping on calm days, and there she fell in love again.

It was the sale of the movie rights to *The Eleventh Virgin*, that book she so regretted writing, that made it possible for Dorothy to buy her first home. And that home provided her with ground beneath her feet, which in turn enabled her to fall in love with a man who loved the sea with the eye of a biologist and who helped her to see the beauty around her more intimately than any man had ever been able to do before. Then this man, however unknowingly and unwittingly, helped her to solidify what she felt and believed, to become strong enough to live the life that she would come to lead. Home, love, motherhood, and commitment—although she didn't yet know what she was committing herself to—all conceived at a seaside cottage with no electricity and twenty feet of beachfront. It is from there that she would be able to see further, where she could begin to hear the call and prepare herself for it.

After her years of wandering from New York to Europe to Chicago and on to New Orleans, Dorothy returned to New York City when her book was published. Maybe she felt she could return at that time because she had finally proved herself to be a serious writer, a novelist, that dream to which everyone from her father to Mike Gold succumbed. The book reviews for *The Eleventh Virgin* were mixed, with a few favorable ones in the Boston, Detroit, and Los Angeles papers and a dismissive one in the *New York Times*, though both Gene O'Neill and Floyd Dell helped as best they could by getting the book to reviewers. But it was the sale of the film option, of which she received twenty-five hundred dollars, that got her a home of her own in New York.

"Don't fritter the money away on your friends. Buy a house," Peggy advised, knowing how little Dorothy cared for money, how she could for weeks leave a payment for an article sitting on an editor's desk when she had so little.

Dorothy listened to Peggy, and the two of them went house hunting on Staten Island, which was still rural, with clean, empty beaches surrounded by meadows. They found the cottage on the west end of Huguenot, and Peggy helped to fix it up. That first summer there, Peggy showed Dorothy a different side to the jailed political activist or the Village girl who liked to party and drink. Peggy wandered along the beach collecting shells and harvesting clams, and she had such a love and enthusiasm for what she found, it led Dorothy also to feel this. With the good food and fresh air, Dorothy regained her health, for while living in Chicago she had gotten down to 108 pounds, which was emaciated at her height of five feet ten inches.

"Dorothy wasn't thin then," Peggy said. "She was skinny, just plain skinny. Nothing but skin and bones. A lot of bones! Beautiful teeth, though."

Dorothy put on some weight and grew strong and tanned from swimming in the sea. She immersed herself in the works of Balzac while her book continued to sell, and by summer the first printing had run out and a second printing was meant to be in the works. Her brother Sam came across a copy in a bookstore window. The owner of the shop told him it was selling well, and he had to order more.

Once Dorothy moved to Staten Island, her friends began to follow her, beginning with Peggy and Malcolm, who bought a cottage less than two miles away. Then Mike Gold and his brother and wife bought a place nearby, and Mrs. Granich, she who had looked sorrowfully at Dorothy when her son was engaged to her, visited bringing her own kosher dishes.

Dorothy filled her cottage with everyone she loved, including her siblings Della and John. Her closest neighbor was Smitty, who lived on the beach in a six-by-eight-foot shack he had built from driftwood that was just big enough for a bed, chair, and woodstove. To get by, Smitty painted the neighbors' boats or rented his own in exchange for kerosene, and he bartered clams, flounder, and lobsters for groceries and haircuts.

Peggy and Malcolm had heat and hot water in their cottage, so Dorothy often went over for a bath, bicycling up the lane in the dark, or she went to join the parties. Prohibition was in full force, and everyone, including Dorothy, made their own wine using whatever they could lay their hands on—dandelions, raisins, rice, rhubarb, or parsnips—and Peggy would always have far too much to drink.

It was then that Dorothy became reacquainted with Malcolm's close friend since grade school Kenneth Burke, who would go on to become a renowned literary critic, linguist, and philosopher, and his wife, Lily, who had become good friends with Dorothy in 1919. With Lily came her younger brother William Forster Batterham, and while Dorothy and Peggy went swimming off Dorothy's beach, Malcolm and Forster went fishing. Dorothy had already known Forster from when she first met Kenneth and Lily, but she had been so involved with Lionel she hadn't taken much notice of him then.

Thirty years old, with gray eyes and blond hair, Forster was tall and thin like Dorothy. He always dressed in jacket, vest, and tie even in the heat of summer, and was profoundly color-blind, which he passed on to one grandson, and had a heart murmur he passed on to most of his grandchildren. He was different from Lionel and the other men Dorothy had dated, like the Englishman Charles Ashleigh, a conventional poet and yet one of the founders of the US Communist Party and who had been arrested for being a Wobbly and deported. Or John Brooks Wheelwright, college friend of Malcolm's and a Boston Brahmin turned Trotskyite whose poetry was more experimental than Ashleigh's. They were men of ideals who grabbed after life. Forster had his ideals, but he turned inward. He did no writing other than the occasional book review and research for his pulp-fiction-writing fishing buddy Harold de Polo, who had sung while drinking in the Hell Hole with Gene O'Neill, Agnes Boulton, and Dorothy in the winter of 1917. Harold was convinced that Forster, if he wished, could earn his living as a pulp writer. "Why not?" Harold asked. "You're good enough." But Forster declined.

It is difficult to know what Forster believed, for the only writings that explore this are Dorothy's. He never called himself an anarchist. It was she, in her desire to make some sense of him, who said he was more of an anarchist than anything else in his philosophy, but Forster never joined any philosophy or any group. He was a radical who did not accept the way things were, and he also dabbled in the literary and artistic worlds. But what made Forster different from both crowds was that he wasn't a talker, he refused to tell anyone what they should do, and the world he felt most at home in was the natural world. He had studied biology at the University of Virginia before he went on to become a biology instructor, while also studying law, until World War I interfered. Peggy sparked Dorothy's love for the beach, but Forster helped her see it. He was also a gardener, and he would rush home on weekends from his machine-shop job in the city to check the vegetables with a flashlight. Influenced by Forster, the soil around the cottage, Dorothy would say years later, became holy to her.

They would row a small boat out in Raritan Bay to fish for flounder and eel, or lie in the bulkhead in the dark, surrounding themselves with nothing but the rhythmic sound of waves lapping against the boat. Or they rowed along the shore examining the flotsam and jetsam, while gannets and gulls flew against the hazy horizon where oyster boats and four-masted schooners seem to float in the sky.

"Atmospheric conditions leading to mirage," said Forster, the scientist, drawn to what can be explained.

"How the senses can deceive us," replied Dorothy, the mystic, drawn to what can't.

They explored the pools at low tide, observing killies, snails, and hermit crabs, and collected mussels or clams for dinner. They lined the walls of the cottage with their specimens—horseshoe and spider crabs, the shell of a large sea turtle, a mounted fish head, starfish, sea horses, pipefish, and filefish.

Like Dorothy's father, Forster was a Southerner. He came from Asheville, North Carolina. His father, Harry Batterham, was from Norfolk, England, and came from a family of farmers and soldiers. When Harry's father lost everything in an agricultural crisis, the Batterhams immigrated to America, where they had no family and knew no one. Harry claimed he arrived in Asheville with only a dime, which he'd bring out to show his children. He would sit in his morris chair, bushy mustache down around the corners of his mouth, a droop in his left eyelid, feet on the footrest, reading the newspaper. "Dry up and blow away!" he'd say to shush his children.

People took to Eleanor, Forster's mother—even Forster's hard-boiled buddy Harold de Polo. A vigorous old Englishwoman, Dorothy called her, who swam and played croquet into her eighties and who liked to listen to Churchill on the radio.

Both Harry and Eleanor remained loyal to England and never became US citizens. They thought of themselves as a British family, and the children spoke in a mixture of Southern and English accents. Eleanor read the London *Times* and cooked only English meals of roast beef and boiled potatoes, Yorkshire pudding, and Lancashire sponge cake.

Harry was an excellent gardener, and he loved to plant trees, just like his granddaughter Tamar would come to do. Forster was also a gardener, though because of his color-blindness he could not see the red blossoms. He was curious about the natural world and would borrow his father's mare and ride into the mountains to collect specimens. It was during one of these excursions that he drank water contaminated with typhoid, but unlike his grandfather and aunt, who both died of the disease, he survived.

The Batterham children were lively and smart. They played tennis and croquet and loved to hike into the mountains, gathering their friends to join them, including Fred Wolfe and his younger brother, Tommy. Tommy would go on to become, according to William Faulkner, the greatest writer of his generation, and his autobiographical novel of Asheville, *Look Homeward, Angel*, would include an English family based on the Batterhams. Harry had become friends with Fred and Tommy's father, a stonecutter who set up a socialists club, but Harry refused to join because Mr. Wolfe drank too much. Both Harry's and Eleanor's fathers had been teetotalers and brought with them to America teetotaler literature with illustrations of neglected children waiting at pub doors.

Forster and Fred, the more outgoing one of the Wolfe family, were classmates and close friends, and they left Asheville together to attend Georgia Tech. There Forster, a lover of opera like his mother, became an extra at DeGive's Opera House and heard Geraldine Farrar and Enrico Caruso sing. The following year, he entered the University of Virginia to study biology. Like all of the young men of that time, Forster's scientific and academic career was interrupted by the war draft in the summer of 1917. He sought an exemption due to a heart condition but was refused. What followed is unclear. Forster may have suffered a breakdown and was hounded in Asheville for still being at home after all the other young men had left to fight. On March 19, 1918, a day Harry claimed never to have forgotten, Forster left for New York City, where he disappeared, leaving the family frantic. His sister Rose found him in what she called a substandard army hospital on the Hudson River, near death and having lost eighty pounds from the Spanish flu. He was never sent overseas to fight.

Unlike Malcolm, who returned to his interrupted studies at Harvard at the end of the war, Forster didn't return to the University of Virginia. It took him years to recuperate from his illness, and when he and Dorothy fell in love, he was still obsessed with the war.

To Malcolm and others, including his own family, Forster lacked ambition. Malcolm blamed it on having too many sisters (Kenneth Burke would say after a sojourn in Asheville that the Batterhams were a family of undercurrents) and an obsession with fishing, though he had to admit that Forster was an excellent fisherman. Forster didn't argue. To his way of thinking, it wasn't a lack of ambition but the refusal to *be* ambitious. He created a simple life for himself, as simple as he could make it, living from day to day, gardening, fishing, digging bait at low tide under a full moon, studying the stars, and sometimes sleeping on the beach for nights on end or staying out in his boat until the small hours. He endured life in New York City because that was where his friends and family were. He became good friends with Kenneth Burke, and the friendship survived Kenneth's divorce from Lily and subsequent marriage to Lily and Forster's younger sister Elizabeth.

Bright, energetic, and with an insatiable curiosity, Forster dragged Dorothy away from her books to go for long walks along the beach, no matter how bad the weather, and to examine mussel larvae along the way. Nature became a healer for Dorothy at this time, for even though Lionel and those years of misery were past, she was still reeling from them, and Forster was the agent of this healing. He taught her how to look at the world closely, to know what she was seeing, and her writing for years afterward retained details she learned from Forster, though not having the mind or the eye of a scientist, she often got things wrong, which drove Tamar, who liked to be precise with the facts, to distraction.

Dorothy and Forster shared a love for opera, and in the winter at the old Metropolitan Opera House they stood in the balcony high above the stage. They ate breakfast together—buttered toast and tea—and read the *New York Times*, from which Forster could not keep himself away, though he would read articles aloud indignantly. *Indignant* was a word people often used to depict Forster. Malcolm described him as "indignant with the tragedy of existence." Dorothy said he read the news with such indignation and passion for people's suffering that she couldn't help but listen, though at that time she was often in her own world, content as a cow.

It was a lovely June day in 1925 that Dorothy knew for certain she was pregnant. She felt happy, secure, and settled while at the Tottenville circus in a tent with Malcolm, Peggy, and Forster, drinking dandelion wine and eating pickled eels, homemade bread, and butter, and for dessert popcorn and root beer. She had been longing to have a child, saying to a pregnant Caroline Gordon, the novelist, when she came to visit, "Oh, I hope I am pregnant." And again, when Caroline left, "Oh, I hope I'm pregnant." The baby had been conceived at the beach cottage in late spring. Forster fed Dorothy clams and fish fresh from the sea in July, pickled eels and squash and tomatoes from the garden in September, and salted whitefish in the winter.

"I had found what I was looking for," she said, though this would not be the only time she would come to say this in the journey ahead. As for Forster's desires, it is Dorothy who tells us he was not interested in the responsibility of raising a child, but he was a loving and loyal man, and he would not tell Dorothy she couldn't have a child, believing so firmly as he did in individual freedom.

In September, her pregnancy beginning to show, Dorothy headed down to Florida to spend time with Della and Grace. Della soon noticed Dorothy's expanding waistline and was delighted, while Grace was too delicate to inquire. Dorothy wrote Forster intense love letters that were funny, risqué, loving, simple, and joyous. Her morning sickness over, she felt marvelously healthy and got a pineapple bob haircut. She described in detail her changing body along with her plans to plant strawberries the following spring. She wanted to buy a farm, live off the land, and have ten children, and she told Forster not to snort derisively over this.

In early October she headed back north and asked Forster to have a supper of pickled eels, squash, and tomatoes waiting for her when she arrived. She also had a dream that he didn't meet her at the train, and she went "weeping and heavily laden to Huguenot by myself only to find you lackadaisically out fishing, saying it was too much trouble to come into town. I awoke in a fine rage."

The winter before her child was born was harsh. She, Forster, and Della moved into an apartment with no running water above a tavern on West Street overlooking the Hudson River docks. They immersed themselves in the literary bohemianism of their friends, Dorothy on that pendulum between the radicals and the literati. The poet Hart Crane showed up for breakfast and recited poetry to Dorothy, while she was reading at the time *The Imitation of Christ*. On an early-spring day, she and Della took a taxi crosstown to Bellevue Hospital, where on March 4, one day earlier than she had calculated, she gave birth to a daughter, Tamar Teresa. One of the Staten Island neighborhood children was named Tamar, and Dorothy liked the name, though she knew little about it other than that it was Hebrew for palm tree. She chose Teresa for St. Teresa of Avila, whose autobiography Dorothy had been reading.

Six weeks later, spring in full bloom, Dorothy returned to the cottage and nursed Tamar in a rocking chair in front of the window overlooking the beach. On July 3, four months after her birth, Tamar was baptized a Catholic at Our Lady Help of Christians. Forster caught lobsters for the celebration but left in the middle of it, silent and angry.

Tension between Dorothy and Forster had already existed long before Tamar's baptism. Dorothy had always felt unfavorably compared to Forster's sisters. Three of them had their master's degrees; they wrote novels and were scholars, mathematicians, and travelers. The Batterhams were a long-lived, well-educated family of thinkers, writers, artists, and musicians, and they had children and grandchildren who also became well-educated thinkers, writers, artists, and musicians, one of whom, Lily's grandson, was the folk singer and world-hunger activist Harry Chapin.

There were also tensions and resentments over money. Like his father, Forster was frugal, while Dorothy, like her father, spent money as it came. Forster also hated the rounds of parties, which to Dorothy made him seem afraid of the world. The things that Dorothy didn't understand in Forster—the inarticulateness, the extreme sensitivity, and the close attention paid to world events even as he had no desire to take action—she later didn't understand in Tamar.

It is hard to know which was most insurmountable—Forster's refusal to marry or his refusal to accept her burgeoning religious feelings. When Forster and Dorothy fell in love, she was already known by her friends for her religious leanings. In New Orleans, she was stopping by the cathedral to attend benediction each night, so often that one of her communist friends gave her a rosary. "Dorothy will never be a good communist," Fred Ellis, a cartoonist for the *Daily Worker*, said. "She's much too religious." Reading William James's *The Varieties of Religious Experience* led Dorothy to read the writings of St. Teresa of Avila. At no point did she hide this from Forster. Before Tamar's birth, she was stopping in churches, sometimes during Mass, and she was praying and studying the Catholic catechism. Their arguments became bitter but brief.

As the writer, Dorothy was the one who got to tell the tale of their relationship. In her book *The Long Loneliness*, she writes a scene in which Forster comes to bed smelling of the cold and of the sea. There is something that haunts in that image—the loss of that simple pleasure and the knowledge that it was on her mind twenty years later. "The very love of nature and the study of her secrets," Dorothy wrote, "which was bringing me to faith, cut Forster off from religion." She also wrote, "He was an anarchist and an atheist, and he did not intend to be a liar and a hypocrite."

This was all I knew about Forster for years, that he was an anarchist and an atheist. It was the phrase many repeated when speaking of him, and, I heard in their voices, that because of this, he walked out on her. Because Forster was a silent man, he did not answer these criticisms or the false accusation that it was he who walked out on her. Even in the face of biographers getting his name wrong, of journalists claiming he was dead long before the fact, or of criticisms by those who had never met him, Forster always kept his own counsel.

"I'm a disappearer," he said. He couldn't bear tension or difficult scenes and would sleep on the beach or head out on his boat, immersing himself in the natural world rather than argue. But whereas Forster wanted to retreat to places of solitude, Dorothy wanted to throw herself into the fray. She believed that not only could she change the world but it was her obligation to do so. What did Forster feel called to do? I look to my mother for an answer. She could be all indignation also, and she couldn't keep herself from reading the news every day, but she also knew that there are ways in which you can make a difference. They just weren't Dorothy's ways. Dorothy believed Forster loved nature and children because they were not men. This was also much like Tamar, but perhaps Dorothy had it wrong, and it wasn't simply because nature and children weren't men but because of what they could teach men that Forster loved them. Forster also questioned the sincerity of Dorothy's religious feelings, but he never attacked her or the decisions she made and actions she took in the way that many others—Catholic and non-Catholic alike—would attack her in the years to come.

Forster didn't believe in tying yourself up in knots over what you thought you should do or should be, and maybe this is what led Malcolm Cowley to declare that Forster didn't let anything interfere with his whims. Forster believed in living up to one's ideals, even if he wasn't willing to speak of his own at the weekend dinner parties, and the worst thing for him was to be a hypocrite. And perhaps because hypocrisy was on his mind, it was also on Dorothy's. Dorothy feared hypocrisy because she had seen it. It had been in the bohemians who fled at the dying of one of their own. It had been in the radicals who spoke passionately about justice but weren't so kind to each other. And it was a question she asked herself repeatedly throughout her life—was she living up to her ideals or was she being a hypocrite?

Dorothy came to believe years later, when she and Forster had become good friends again, that their separation came about because she felt gratitude toward God and desired to say thank you, while Forster did not. The paradox is that life with Forster, with the stability it brought through exploration of what love for a man meant, of motherhood, of opening her to the beauty of the beach and sea, led to a spiritual hunger, to mystery, sacrament, and symbolism, things that do not often concern scientists. This then pushed Dorothy to enter the church, which in turn led to the dissolution of their life together and divided father and daughter.

In one of her letters to Forster, written in the months after her own Catholic baptism, Dorothy wrote, "I do love you more than anything in the world, but I cannot help my religious sense, which tortures me unless I do as I believe right." Forster, in spite of his stance against religion, would understand this in his own way. He too had integrity along with his stubborn pride. There is so much that was unyielding in her throughout the years—was this his influence? She must have had him in the back of her mind—he was so adamant against any hypocrisy, and she, for her part, had given him up for her beliefs.

It wasn't only religion that was insurmountable. Forster also believed marriage was a tyranny that he wanted no part of, no matter how much Dorothy desired it, and it wasn't simply a tyranny that limited his whims, as Malcolm interpreted it. Forster saw marriage and parenthood as being full of danger in how people control one another in ways they should not. That power corrupts even between husband and wife, parent and child. Forster also had no hope for humankind, and this was devastating to him and paralyzing. Dorothy wasn't paralyzed by anything. Even though Dorothy badly wanted marriage and more children, she could not have been anything other than who she was—a person who made no differentiation between her inner self and her outer self. They were the two most bullheaded people you'd ever find, each determined not to be a hypocrite, and in this determination found themselves in an insolvable conflict.

Sometimes I wonder that, though Dorothy wrote of not wanting her daughter to flounder as she had done, what she couldn't bring herself to say is that she was scared, she who was fearless in so many other ways. That she had to take one step at a time in her thirst for order, instructions, and a way of life, and it was easier to first have her daughter baptized than it was to be baptized herself. Tamar is the first Catholic in this tale (other than Gene O'Neill, Agnes Boulton, and Max Bodenheim, that is), a Catholic whose father not only did not believe in God but was certain that people's beliefs were fraught with hypocrisy and corruption, while her mother was drawn to Catholicism but still couldn't see her way. Only Dorothy would baptize a child into a religion neither parent belonged to, though Forster, as an ex-Episcopalian whose father was far more devout that Dorothy's, was familiar with the sacraments. Dorothy believed with the fervor of a new mother that she could protect her daughter from the self-inflicted wounds of a rootless and careless youth, but she didn't yet understand the workings of her own faith. She didn't know why she was pulled time and time again to what seemed to her and to her friends to be a church of crude, medieval thinking and, worst of all, obliviousness to the poor on whose sweat and toil it built its churches. All she knew then of her own strivings was connected to the rosary she had been given as a gift, the solitary visits to churches, and the voice of Gene she could still hear reciting that dark and disturbing poem. Nevertheless, she was going to give her daughter a grounding in faith that she herself did not yet have. Dorothy had yet to learn that faith isn't something you can simply hand over to someone else, even your own daughter.

Dorothy's decision to baptize Tamar would set her on a path she never could have imagined, and it would set her daughter on a different path that would take a long time for Tamar to disentangle herself from. And it would break all three of their hearts—Dorothy's, Forster's, and Tamar's. But things mattered to Dorothy in a way that imbued them with an intangible element, an element of the sacramental, and the birth of her child was a gift of a sacred manner that she was not going to squander.

The summer after Tamar was born, Dorothy had thyroid trouble and lost weight. She read her missal daily, went to Mass, and said the rosary while walking on the beach. At night she danced on the sand draped in shawls while the neighbors played guitar and sang Russian gypsy songs. One night she swam naked in the sea and gave Forster a scare when she swam out too far. Dorothy's friends were all watching this struggle, of course, first with interest but without surprise, and then with growing concern. Peggy, in whom Dorothy confided, kept quiet when asked by others about it.

Dorothy wandered through her days amid deep moments of happiness filled with beauty and deep moments of struggle filled with doubt; blind flashes of exultation and realization, and floods of joy mingled with moments of confusion. It wasn't the best Catholic minds or even the church's teachings on social justice that drew her. She knew nothing of that. It was reading the Psalms in Occoquan with a sense of returning to something she had lost. It was Gene reciting "The Hound of Heaven" with all his Catholic sensibilities, and Dorothy feeling that she too was being followed by something that desired her. It was getting up at five thirty to go to Sunday Mass with her fellow nurse at Kings County Hospital. It was the simplicity of the Catholic girls she shared a place with in Chicago that hard winter after her second arrest, who introduced her to Catholic language as she read Huysmans.

Things stumbled on between Dorothy and Forster, and the year of 1927 began the tradition of planting radishes on Tamar's birthday. That summer Dorothy wrote nothing but a few articles for the *New Masses*, the paper Mike Gold and others, who were unhappy with the *Liberator* as successor to the *Masses*, had begun in 1926. Her article on the birth of her baby would become among her best known. With Forster out on the weekends and the cottage full of visitors, Dorothy would slip off to Mass or wander the beach with Tamar, feeling keenly the silence and solitude, the pain and restlessness. She prayed daily on the way to the village to pick up the mail, and she recited the Te Deum, which she had learned from the Episcopalians, on the beach where Tamar was learning to walk. (For years, when things got too oppressive at the Worker, Dorothy and Tamar headed to the beach and said the rosary as they walked.) She collected driftwood with Smitty, which Forster chopped, and they sat around Smitty's fire at sunset while the bells of St. Joseph's rang the Angelus, and they ate buttered toast with mushrooms collected from the fields. She studied the catechism with Sister Aloysia, a retired second-grade teacher who Dorothy met by chance on the road and who had introduced her to the priest who baptized Tamar. Sister Aloysia's head would appear through the window when it was lesson time, and Forster would leave with a slam of the door. (Dorothy never quite memorized the catechism and years later had to ask people what the seven deadly sins were.)

Dorothy was groping in the dark, undergoing a long, slow fundamental shift that would continue to the end of her days. Toward the end of her life, Dorothy said she often didn't remember there was a time she wasn't Catholic, but she also said she wished she had spent more time trying to grasp what was going on at that time.

That August two Italian immigrants, Nicola Sacco and Bartolomeo Vanzetti, were executed for murder, an act that sent Forster into a virtual catatonic state. The executions knocked the wind out of both the radicals and the bohemians for daring to imagine something new during the 1920s, which had been a decade of pushing the boundaries of gender and class and exploring ideas and creativity. Eugene O'Neill changing the voice of theater, Igor Stravinsky changing the sound of classical music, Pablo Picasso changing art, and socialism and communism changing people's beliefs about what was possible economically. All were making society uncomfortable and bewildered, fearful and dangerous, and all were reduced in history's eye to flappers and Prohibition, and then finally killed off by the stock market crash and forgotten in the Depression.

Dorothy would never forget Sacco and Vanzetti's execution, that day of grief, as she called it. Della was in Boston walking a picket line between the writer John Dos Passos and her good friend the writer Katherine Anne Porter. Dorothy stayed on Staten Island caring for Tamar (an echo of what she would do years later, bathing her grandchildren during the execution of the Rosenbergs), while Forster lay with his face to the wall. The executions sent him into shock at a time when his grief at the disintegration of their relationship was already reaching breaking point. To him it was the death of all decency in the world. He could barely eat or speak, and he sat around the cottage for days in silence. (As a teenager, he had witnessed the public hanging of a man for murder in Asheville and refused to speak of it.) He buried himself in books on marine biology or stayed out in his boat night and day with the wind and the sea to return only to be with Tamar.

Dorothy's health was worsening, and she thought she was having thyroid trouble again, but the doctor put it down to nervous strain. Her priest tried his best to help. Wait, he said, and try to hold the family together. The bond between father and daughter is also sacred. Late in December, one and a half years after Tamar's baptism, Forster left after a quarrel when Dorothy and Tamar moved into the city for the winter, banality often opening the door to what lies deeper, and when he returned, as he always did, Dorothy refused to let him in. She closed the door on her bewildered and angry partner, and the next day, "a most miserable day," December 29, Dorothy left Tamar with Della and took the ferry back out to Staten Island to be baptized. It was a grim ferry ride with no peace and no conviction that baptism was the right thing to do. It was just something that had to be done. She walked around and around the ferry as it sailed, and when it landed, she disembarked and headed down to Tottenville and Our Lady Help of Christians, where she was baptized conditionally, acting as swiftly and thoroughly as she always did when she made what seemed like a rash and sudden decision. Forster lived by his principles, and she could do no less. But it was a quiet affair that gave her no joy, and afterward she quickly left.

"I have to get home to my child," she said.

One of the women assisting said, "I didn't know you were married."

"Oh, I'm not," she replied, and the shock was so visible on the woman's face that Dorothy wondered if the woman was questioning just what kind of person they were bringing into the Church.

Dorothy didn't know if she had any faith or belief or just wanted to believe. Faith, she would later say, is so much an act of will. She doubted herself. Was she praying because she was lonely and unhappy? Even twenty years later, she couldn't tease it all out. Was she happy or unhappy during this period that she called "Natural Happiness" in *The Long Loneliness*? Dorothy had done what she thought was right, but she also wrote about a hideous depression during which her newfound religion, her family, work, and the beauty of Staten Island weren't enough. Her loneliness, unhappiness, and restlessness seemed to be a spiritual hunger, and maybe it was pushing her, reminding her of what needed doing, but she didn't know. Even with this specter of depression, she writes that she seldom had such quiet, beauty, and happiness as she then had. As with so many aspects of my paradoxical grandmother, I know that both of these two contradictory statements are true.

When Dorothy was forty, she wrote, "A conversion is a lonely experience." She wrote *The Long Loneliness*, her account of her conversion, in her early fifties, at a time when Tamar was going through the loneliness of a young mother in a difficult marriage living in exile and isolation from her beloved Catholic Worker family. Dorothy saw Tamar's loneliness, but she believed she had provided her with a faith that would get Tamar through.

By her seventies, Dorothy was no longer silent on the disorderly life she led before her conversion, and spoke often and easily of "the friends and the drinking and the talk and the crushes and falling in love and the disappointments." And the joy and seeking and questioning.

"We're born to ask questions," she said. "It's a tragedy to go through life not asking." She then added, "God wants us to ask."

CHAPTER FOUR

One day in the early 1990s, Tamar thrust a stack of folders at me and said, "Read these." The folders contained dozens of letters, most typed on onionskin or cheap and yellowed pulp paper that crumbled to the touch, but some were handwritten in that unmistakable, cramped, barely decipherable, pointed hand of Dorothy's. The bulk of them, over forty letters, began in 1925 and ended seven years later, just before the inception of the Catholic Worker in 1933, with another two dozen from the sixties and seventies. "Dearest Forster," most of them began. Tamar had found them in Forster's Greenwich Village apartment after his death.

Forster wasn't a talker, and he wrote little. Nothing of what he wrote has survived except one brief letter to Dorothy. But he saved the letters he received from her, including the most painful ones after Tamar's birth when Dorothy wanted to marry him and have more children. The letters came from California, Florida, and Mexico, where she had fled to keep herself away from him. Tamar's first reaction was to put them in a safe-deposit box, where they lay untouched for three years. She then showed them to Rita Corbin, one of the three most prolific and influential artists of the Catholic Worker. "Publish them," Rita said. At first Tamar said no, she wouldn't, but then she thought, "Why not?" She wondered if this was an opportunity to repudiate, at one end, the images of Dorothy's loose-living younger days, and at the other, the saintly images of what Tamar described as those "ghastly, severe, sad faces," reflected in those moments when Dorothy would settle back, and her vibrancy would be lost. People who didn't know Dorothy spoke of this grim and dour woman, and it pained Tamar that that was the image people so often wanted.

"The joyful side of Dorothy is being missed with all this saint stuff," she said. "Dorothy always pointed out that the saints were joyful, and Saint Teresa of Avila led her nuns in dance."

Tamar wanted to write an answer to all those who, she felt, believed they knew enough to write about Dorothy, and for a time she felt a sense of purpose, though she didn't know if her mother would be pleased or outraged by the idea. Perhaps this would be her book that people kept asking her for. She was torn between feeling there were things she should not speak of and things she must speak of. She longed to be able to speak to Stanley Vishnewski about it. He had arrived at the Catholic Worker, as a seventeen-year-old, in its first year and became another beloved member of Tamar's extended Catholic Worker family. Though Stanley had been dead for years, she wondered what he would have said in his discreet, sensitive, and wise way. But she couldn't pull her thoughts together, and the years went by until, provoked by the making of a movie on Dorothy in 1995, she sent copies of the letters to Ade Bethune, the first Catholic Worker artist, whom Tamar had known since she was eight and to whom she had been an artist's apprentice as a teenager. Ade would know what to do. She had always been sensible.

Ade was delighted by the letters. "Yes!" she said. "This is the Dorothy Day I first met in 1934—bright, lively, witty, sarcastic, enthusiastic, energetic, open-hearted."

But again Tamar did nothing until, sixteen years after finding the letters, she gave them to the Catholic Worker archives at Marquette University.

When my mother handed the letters to me, I tried to read them, but I felt I was eavesdropping on an intimate conversation that was not mine to listen to. I wasn't ready to hear this young Dorothy so much in love and so much wanting marriage and more children. I read some, glanced through others, and then gave them back to Tamar without saying much. I didn't know, as I do now, that those letters contained clues to the innermost workings of my mother's heart, to the joys and wounds she felt to the marrow of her arthritic bones.

*   *   *

After Dorothy's baptism on December 29, 1927, she writes in *The Long Loneliness* of the beginnings of the Catholic Worker, dropping all mention of Forster as if her baptism put all that behind her. But she was still in love with him and he with her, and back and forth they went, on and off again for another five years. We wouldn't know any of this if it weren't for Forster saving her letters and Tamar finding them. Those years between Dorothy's conversion and the beginning of the Worker were years of wandering, a Catholic but still feeling divided within herself. She and Tamar traveled out to California and Mexico, and then shuttled between Staten Island and Florida, where Grace was living. Dorothy worked a variety of jobs as a cook, columnist, secretary, bookseller, researcher, and script reader, while always writing. But she also was raising a child and forging bonds strong enough to see them through the pressure cooker of the Catholic Worker.

The spring of 1928, Dorothy and Tamar returned to the beach from yet another dismal apartment in the city in time to plant radishes on Tamar's second birthday. In preparation, Smitty—Tamar called him "Mish"—had cleaned up the cottage, filled the wood box, and brought them flounder and clams. Dorothy collected driftwood from the beach, and they lived on oatmeal and fish from the two wooden tubs of salted whiting that she and Forster had put up the previous summer. She went out fishing for eels and flounder with Smitty, leaving Tamar with the neighbors. Dorothy planted the garden while thinking she might be pregnant again and worried about Tamar, who had whooping cough.

She wrote Forster sad, painful, lonely, and argumentative letters. Forster would not back down in the face of any threat to his independence, she said, and yet now that she was giving him up, she accused him of pursuing her. "You are so contrary," she said.

Forster had started his own business and would eventually settle in a narrow, six-story building that still stands on Broadway near city hall, from which he sold household appliances, bicycles, Lionel train sets, Erector sets, typewriters, radios, and wedding rings. He sent Dorothy money when he could but never nearly enough and not the five dollars a week she hoped for. The new business was slow, as were her efforts to get published. She sold an article to the *New Masses* for five dollars and bought a bathtub for Tamar, while yet another novel made the publisher rounds.

Forster came out on occasion for tension-filled weekends. He helped with the cottage, fixing the ceiling, the floor, and the plumbing. She begged him to leave her alone and yet she wrote him almost weekly. "I should like to hold you and kiss you and kiss you, but I can't and my arms ache for you." The following winter, the last line of her only letter was, "The baby speaks of you often . . . she gave me a sweet, fervent kiss and said, 'Forster kisses you like that.'"

Dorothy and Tamar were living that winter on West Fourteenth Street, while Dorothy worked for the Fellowship of Reconciliation at one of her rare and brief salaried jobs. She grew depressed after visiting Forster's sisters and seeing their happy homes. "I wonder how you would feel if one of your sisters had to go through the struggle that I do," she said, and told him to put up with her religiousness just as she did with his fishing obsession, but the arguments were old.

Dorothy finished writing a play that interested some directors and producers, and celebrated it by attending a *New Masses* ball. Her past life and her present life were colliding. Visiting priests sometimes gave lifts to her communist friends, while Father Zachary, after giving her absolution in the confessional, whispered, "Have you sold your play yet?"

On the Feast of the Pentecost 1929, she was confirmed, a joyful celebration, not at all like her baptism a year and a half earlier. That summer, Dorothy was having difficulty paying the mortgage and taxes on her cottage, so she rented it out while she and Tamar lived at a Marist novitiate in Prince's Bay, where Dorothy cooked for the monks during their summer holiday. The days were long and hot, the kitchen a furnace, and Dorothy wept during moments of sadness at the kitchen counter. On her breaks, she sat outside under a tree, smoking cigarettes and listening to the cicadas, which reminded her of Italy, while Tamar helped Father McKenna with the barn chores and found a nest of field mice she saved from the mower and kept in a muffin tin.

Dorothy prayed to St. Anthony that she could make a living as a writer, and in mid-August she received a call from Pathé, a Hollywood film studio that had read her play. They offered her a job in Los Angeles to write dialogue for the talkies, which were still only a few years old. The salary was $125 a week, a fantastic amount of money, and she accepted the offer. After years of writing prolifically but largely going unpublished, Dorothy's successes were a book that was a failure in the eyes of those whose opinions meant the most to her yet allowed her to put a down payment on a home and a play that was never produced but led to the best paying job she would ever have.

Dorothy and Tamar's departure for California in early September brought Dorothy and Forster together again, and he saw them off at the train station in a cloud of love and possibilities. The separation would not be for long, Dorothy thought, as she planned to be gone for the length of her three-month contract.

By Indianapolis, both she and Tamar weren't feeling well. Tamar had motion sickness, while Dorothy briefly thought she might be pregnant. "Just as well, I suppose," she wrote to Forster when she realized she wasn't, and added that it would be better to first insulate the cottage, so they could live in it year-round, before having more children.

When they arrived, they stayed at the Hotel Washington, opposite the Pathé studios, which Pathé had recently bought from Cecil B. DeMille and where they would soon be filming *All Quiet on the Western Front*. Dorothy read scripts in an office overlooking a swimming pool and a lawn with bush geraniums. There was little for her to do. Out of twenty-four writers—Dorothy was the only woman—half were doing nothing.

Dorothy and Tamar settled into a small house a mile from the studios, and Dorothy found an Englishwoman to care for Tamar. At first Dorothy was wretched and hated the place. Even the beach couldn't compare with Staten Island, and she walked the streets weeping. "I have felt nothing but a blank loneliness since I left you," she wrote Forster. She asked him why he didn't ask her to come home and marry him. "We could be so happy together." Even if they fought, it would be better than this "blank, dead feeling." "I don't want to marry anybody else. Do I have to be condemned to celibacy all my days just because of your pigheadedness?" She reminded him of their long evenings on the beach, and of eating buttered toast and drinking tea, reading books and making love. Forster wrote back at once. He often wrote twice a week, sweet letters, but none have survived.

Tamar too grieved and talked about him often, while watching other kids with their fathers. She asked, "When is my friend Forster coming back?" She called him "my Forster father" and made up songs about him.

By the end of September, Forster wanted more passionate letters, but Dorothy was slipping into despondency. "What's the use?" she asked. "Go find yourself some other affair." She alternated between berating him and writing of her desire to marry him and have more children. "You and Aldous Huxley," she said, "both have the same superior hate for the rest of the human race and wouldn't go one inch out of your way to help anyone. Evil has far more reality than good in your minds." She went over the ground of their quarrels, but still, it was such a struggle. "I've never loved anyone but you and Lionel and that early affair seems but the dimmest adolescent crush compared to the love I have for you." After writing every three days in September, Dorothy sent no letters until early November, just after the stock market crash, when she wrote to say she had stopped writing because of "the seeming hopelessness of it all."

At the studio, Dorothy was sitting around doing nothing but reading novels and writing one of her own. Her stomach was in a constant knot, and she wondered when she would be let go. Only three writers remained, including herself, which she attributed to her low pay, but by mid-December her contract was up and not renewed. This didn't surprise her, as all of her ideas and synopses had been greeted with indifference, the best comment "pretty good," leaving her with a lack of self-confidence over her writing talent. But the situation had nothing to do with her work. Pathé had been taken over by another studio, and all of the studio heads, writers, and secretaries were being laid off. Pathé offered to pay her way back to New York, but she headed to Mexico instead, a thought that had been on her mind when the euphoria of that short time of being back with Forster had worn off. She planned to stay safely away until Tamar was seven, by which time she hoped she would be over him.

Dorothy left for Mexico with Tamar, her typewriter, her phonograph, and two hundred dollars, driving a 1926 Ford she had bought for eighty-five dollars and that couldn't go over thirty miles per hour. It was in this car that Dorothy first learned how to drive, beginning a lifelong love of cars, and it was in this car that occasioned Tamar's earliest memory of her mother driving slowly down a street in Escondido late one night, looking for an address. She pulled over to the side of the road, and a speeding car smashed into them.

Tamar, seeing blood on Dorothy's face and on the steering wheel, said, "Why can't you be more careful?"

"I was a dreadful child," Tamar said. "I used to scold Dorothy all the time."

"I really am an excellent driver," Dorothy wrote to Forster concerning the accident, but she didn't mention getting injured.

They arrived in Mexico City on the same day a letter from Forster arrived. Dorothy was hoping to get a job with the English-language sections of the newspapers but instead found work as secretary to two writers—Della's friend Katherine Anne Porter, the novelist who would go on to win the Pulitzer Prize, and Mary Heaton Vorse, the writer and labor activist whom Dorothy had known in her Greenwich Village and Chicago days. Dorothy also received enough money for three months' rent from a connection she made through Della with Otto Kahn, a wealthy financier and patron of the arts who had also helped support Hart Crane, George Gershwin, and Arturo Toscanini.

Dorothy, with her usual ability to sniff out interesting people wherever she went, soon met the artist Diego Rivera, who looked at Tamar and said, "I know this little girl." While in Russia, he had read Dorothy's article on Tamar's birth published in the *New Masses*.

Not many details of their sojourn in Mexico have survived, mostly just the names of the flowers and vegetables that surrounded the cottage in the village of Xochimilco, where they lived part of the time, Dorothy continuing her practice of having a city place and a country cottage. Tamar picked up the language easily. "Now we have no more thank-yous, only *gracias*. And we have no more good-byes, only *adiós*," she said to her mother.

The Xochimilco cottage, which they rented for ten dollars a month plus two dollars and fifty cents for the boat they needed to get to it, was stone with a thatched roof and a garden of geraniums, heliotropes, roses, and cacti. The house was dark, as it had only one window and a door, and Dorothy had to write outside, her typewriter propped amid the melons and squash on the stone wall that enclosed the house.

Dorothy and Tamar lived in Mexico for six months, until June 1930, when Tamar came down with malaria, and they sailed home from Veracruz. Tamar was already a sickly child. As an infant she was in and out of the hospital, once for a week with abscessed ears, and she came out looking so gaunt and starved that Dorothy wept over her all the way home. The doctor tried to reassure Dorothy. "It's hard to kill a child," he said. News of Tamar's illness spread quickly, and Eleanor wrote Forster asking for information. "We are so grieved about it as Tamar has not a very strong constitution to battle anything like malaria." She ended the letter with what she would say in each letter to Forster until her death in 1954, "Please give my love to Dorothy and Tamar." Tamar stayed in the hospital (Forster paid the bill) for eleven days and was dosed with twenty grams of quinine daily.

That autumn, after being gone for a year, Dorothy and Tamar returned to Staten Island. The garden was overgrown with weeds, the perennials were now living at the neighbors', and the cottage was full of fishing poles and dead worms. Tamar, possibly having another attack of malaria, said her prayers to the spider crab over the door that had replaced the cross, which Dorothy later located in the attic. Dorothy felt she had returned home after a period of exile, and she was home to stay, but she was still restless, still struggling with her feelings for Forster, and still unsure of what she was doing.

Dorothy and Tamar spent the winter with Grace in Florida, where she and Pop had been living since 1924. Pop had been instrumental in opening the Hialeah Park racetrack, a venture he failed to reap the benefits of. "Done out through dirty business," Dorothy said. He then went to Cuba to work at the Havana racetrack, which was where he was that winter. He was no longer an editor, but he was still writing articles, though now at sixty-two he had rheumatism in his hands and could hardly type. He paid the bills while Dorothy wrote and kept Grace company, and he told Grace not to let Dorothy do any housework, that he had sent her down to Florida so she could write all winter. Maybe Pop wasn't so much a tyrant about her writing as he had been when she was eighteen, but then, maybe he felt guilty for leaving Grace in Florida while he was working at the Havana racetrack, another venture that would leave him broke.

Even though Pop had given her one hundred dollars for the train fare to visit Grace during the autumn of Dorothy's pregnancy, and even though he had met her early one morning at the station in Washington, DC, to spend the half-hour stop with her, things between them were still fraught with tension. "I won't have her around me," he said to others, and Dorothy and Tamar stayed with their cousins when he was at home. Pop was mostly in Havana, but even so Dorothy worried about Tamar getting in his way.

At first Dorothy couldn't believe it—three months of no worries about bills and doing nothing but be with her daughter, mother, and aunt and write articles and short stories. But the dream did not last long. Pop and Grace were not living as luxuriously as they had been the winter Dorothy was pregnant, when they had a chauffeur to drive them to the beach. This time Dorothy had to beg money from Forster for Tamar's clothing and fees for kindergarten, and Forster's business was not prospering in those years after the stock market crash. He had agreed to send five dollars a week—she got it twice in five weeks. Pop sent twenty-five dollars every two weeks, leaving the four of them to live on sixty dollars a month. And so Dorothy again worried about money. She couldn't seem to escape it. She had to spend the money from Forster for Tamar's school on medicines for Tamar and for her own frequent migraine headaches, as Grace, a Christian Scientist, wouldn't have any medication in the house.

"It's the state of your mind," she told Dorothy. "Holding the thought, you know."

Grace asked Dorothy to sell the Staten Island cottage and move to be near her, and Dorothy thought about it. Perhaps she could return to nursing. Property was more reasonable, and life in Florida was easier with its warm weather and good cheap food, and Dorothy was gaining weight.

"I think I am actually getting a figure," she told Forster.

It was during that visit that Grace began to open up to Dorothy about the true state of her marriage. She and Pop spent little time together—he was either in Havana in the winter months or in New York during the summer, while Grace remained in Florida—though they weren't separated. Grace thought about moving back to New York so she could be near her children, but she hadn't told Pop of her plans, afraid he would think she wanted to take in John, who was still only eighteen, and Pop would refuse to support her. Pop had always been jealous of his sons and Grace's attention to them. She told Dorothy that he had tried to kick Donald out of the house because she ran his bath for him. Until that winter, Dorothy hadn't known just how bad things were between them.

"He is a strange man, Pop is," Dorothy wrote to her brother John, and a tyrant because of how little money he gave Grace. "I'm terribly fond of him in spite of saying these things," she added.

Dorothy learned how to tat and play bridge that winter, but she was bored and lonely. The writing was not going well, even though she was, as always, hard at work. She endured many blows when it came to her writing. Neither Katherine Anne Porter nor Malcolm Cowley believed she had talent, and the rejections never let up. Yet she kept at it, writing articles, short stories, and novel after novel, seeking freelance work, a success here and there from *Commonweal*, a Catholic publication, and the *New Masses*, a Communist one. In Mexico, she had tried to publish articles about the political situation there, but all were rejected until she recalled Lionel's advice to write personally. It was only when she started to write about Tamar and herself that she began to get more acceptances. She received two dollars for a book review for the *New Republic*, a windfall considering they were living on sixty dollars a month, but she had no luck with the ten stories she sent out.

Dorothy heard from Forster every two weeks, and when she didn't, she would dream of him. Her letters to him were changing. They were tension free and chatty, and she slipped into the conversation a mention of Forster's new love, a twenty-two-year-old Jewish woman from Pennsylvania named Nanette. Dorothy suggested they stay in her cottage while she was in Florida, which they did on occasion. She had a dream one night of Forster, Nanette, and herself "living together most amicably down in the bungalow."

Even knowing of Nanette, Dorothy wrote to Forster, "What do you say you marry me, when I come up in the spring?" And in another letter: "My feeling about our night together was one of sadness because we couldn't be always together. I feel that Tamar and I belong to you and when I am with you in that way it leaves me with a feeling of our close presence in my heart for weeks afterward. Aren't we ever going to be together again?" They now had been apart four years if one didn't count the slipups.

Grace's plans to return to New York came to nothing, and her health was poor, so Dorothy waited for Pop to return from Havana before she and Tamar headed north in the spring, all ideas of remaining there erased by the worsening economic times and by the heat, sores, and rashes afflicting them.

It's difficult to follow Dorothy and Tamar's moves during these years. Rents were cheap and housing plentiful, and Dorothy could rent an apartment in the city for twenty-five dollars a month during the winter, and then, come spring, head to Staten Island. As an adult, Tamar had given up trying to keep the chronology of their whereabouts, and the addresses of all the apartments they lived in blurred together, but all these moves were hard on her, which Dorothy didn't realize, as she was never bothered by the many moves of her own childhood. Houses and apartments meant little to any of the Day family.

But it was Staten Island that Tamar and Dorothy both loved and always returned to. They dug for clams, harvested mussels and seaweed, and collected specimens of horseshoe and spider crabs, whelks and stones. Dorothy got a job writing the garden column for a Staten Island paper, and in a 1923 car she bought for thirty-five dollars she and Tamar visited the best parts of the island. Driving twenty miles per hour,

Dorothy's favorite speed, they visited the old estates and farmhouses, where the owners talked about their gardens and gave Tamar plants for her own garden. When Dorothy and Tamar were done for the day, they sat on the beach next to Smitty's shack while he skinned eels and washed clams for dinner, and Tamar played with her kitten.

"Doddy," Tamar said, "flowers and grass, things are so beautiful, they just hurt my feelings."

Tamar called her mother Doddy before she could say "Dorothy," and she would never come to call her "Mother," as Dorothy wished, except briefly when she was at school in Canada as a fifteen-year-old, and the mother superior insisted Tamar begin her letters with "Dear Mother."

"Why don't you call me 'Mother'?" Dorothy asked her.

"I don't know," Tamar replied. "I'm used to calling you Dorothy. I'm just used to it."

"But no one will know that I'm your mother if you call me by my name."

"But I know it," she replied serenely.

The situation hurt and confused Dorothy, but Tamar would not budge.

When I asked her about it, Tamar shrugged and thought that maybe it was the influence of growing up with that "Hudson Street crowd of bohemians." She didn't seem to think it as fascinating as others did. "Everyone called her Dorothy, and 'Mother' didn't sound right to me."

Now that Tamar was six, Dorothy looked closely for signs of piety in her, listening to her recite the Creed, the Lord's Prayer, the Hail Mary, and "the bless 'ems" all delivered in order to put off going to sleep. They went for long walks along the beach, where Tamar learned to say the rosary, while wanting to know if there were beaches in heaven with crabs and snails and shells. Whoever got to heaven first, she said, would wait for the other. Dorothy recounted a theological discussion with Tamar, who understood what it meant to believe, but Tamar was beginning to reveal questions she would think about hard and long for years to come.

"Why do we believe in Him?" Tamar asked.

"Because the Church tells us to. You know, the sisters tell you in school and the priest tells you."

"Just like you tell me about when I was a little baby and I believe you. I don't remember either."

Tamar was quiet for a moment before she added, "But good people will go to heaven anyway, won't they, Dorothy?"

"I think they will," Dorothy replied.

The summer of 1932 was a happy one. Dorothy and Tamar were living in an apartment on East Fifteenth Street, with a backyard, hot water, and heat, for Tamar's sake, and a rent of twenty-five dollars a month, which was more than Dorothy was comfortable with. She had rented out the cottage for six months, and the mortgage she had obtained from Forster's father four years earlier was finally paid. She had a job she enjoyed researching for the Paulists at the New York Public Library on Forty-Second Street, while Tamar was in a day nursery at $1.20 a week. (The previous two winters, Dorothy had put her in an understaffed Catholic charity nursery for working mothers where she suspected Tamar had been neglected.) And she was home by three to work on the perennial novel. Things were going well; it was as stable a life as Dorothy could provide.

That fall, Dorothy's brother John moved in with his new wife. While in Florida the previous winter, they had had news of John's marriage to Tessa de Aragon, a daughter of Spanish aristocrat immigrants who had a summer cottage in Huguenot. It took Grace a while to come around to the marriage, as John was only eighteen. But, she acknowledged, at least he wasn't on the racetracks, drinking, betting, and frequenting the brothels, all legacies he'd inherited from Pop, and the behavior that had led Grace to send him, three years earlier, to live with Dorothy on Staten Island.

Like all the Day men, John wanted to be a newspaperman, but unable to find a job, he and Tessa, who was expecting, moved in with Dorothy on Fifteenth Street.

"All the world loves a pregnant woman," Mike Gold said wistfully when he visited, wishing to start his own family.

Dorothy and Mike were still loyal friends, even though their beliefs and ideals took them in opposite directions. Coming from an Orthodox Jewish family, Mike never appeared to be concerned or afraid of Dorothy's religiosity. He had seen and identified it years before, in 1917, and, in any event, it was her business. Her other friends, after their initial alarm, had gotten used to it and often helped care for Tamar so Dorothy could go to Mass.

It was because of this enduring friendship with Mike that Dorothy knew of the hunger march planned for that December in Washington, DC, and organized by one of Mike's brothers. She decided to go down to cover the march for *Commonweal* and the Jesuit publication *America*. The Depression was worsening, and farmers had come from all over the country to ask for a moratorium on evictions and forced sales, and for cancellation of mortgages and seed loans. They also were angry at being told to raise fewer crops while people in the cities starved.

Things might have gone on for years with Dorothy struggling to make her living as a writer, writing novel after novel only to see them all rejected, moving back and forth between the city, the beach, and Florida, grabbing whatever job interested her at the time. After being away from the radical scene for years, Dorothy found herself standing on the sidelines observing her old friends, communists and socialists, marching with the farmers and unemployed workers. But being a bystander did not sit comfortably with her. Her radical friends were out on the front lines, and she too wanted to be involved in some way and not simply observing as a journalist while others acted.

"Where are the Catholics?" she asked.

After the march, Dorothy visited the Shrine of the Immaculate Conception on the Feast of the Immaculate Conception, December 8. This visit would become much treasured by her and a time when one of her most profound prayers was heard. No wonder she was able to survive all the years of struggle and poverty that were to come, a task that was Herculean and mad. She was, as she said, on the brink of losing her faith in the face of the Church's apparent indifference to what called to her most deeply—compassion for the downtrodden. Though it had been five years since she said those first prayers as a Catholic and felt like a hypocrite, she still didn't yet know how to proceed with this sacramental view of the world that had begun with a small being, Tamar, and led her to see her own life as sacred.

Love, motherhood, religion—how many of us on finding ourselves embraced by any one of these would have stopped, rested, and remained? But this is the mystery of those forces that led her to go one step further, and another step, and another. And in one of the most grace-filled moments of a life full of grace, Dorothy finds herself praying to the Blessed Mother. *Here I am—what would you have me do?* Isn't this that in-between time, that liminal space cherished by the Irish, that mysterious time of waiting and wandering? Isn't it about hearing the call?

CHAPTER FIVE

In coming to this part of the story, I feel I'm holding in my hands my mother's most treasured memories and her most vulnerable self. I am holding my grandmother's creation, the *Catholic Worker*, this physical manifestation of the Mystical Body of Christ, the answer to her prayers at the Shrine of the Immaculate Conception, birthed within a mere six months of her visit. What an honor, a gift, a fearful task I have been given. All that was dear to Tamar—a life of hospitality, the natural world, creativity, and family. All that came out of Dorothy's spirit, all of what passed before readying her to hear the call—the loves, the failed novels, the literary life that eluded her—to lead her to write that most wonderful tale of all, the story of the Worker. A creation story, a Dostoyevskian tale, an exploration of the soul pouring out in a river of columns, articles, diaries, and letters, examining, molding, and telling the story of the lives of people who would have been forgotten, loving portraits of the unknown or despised who mean nothing to the world's affairs. The great American novel birthed in the winter and spring of 1933 and lived and written day after day for forty-seven years.

They were glorious, exuberant years, the first years of the Catholic Worker. "That early zeal, that early romance, that early companionableness," Dorothy described it. Or as Grace said when she visited, "Dorothy bites off more than she can chew."

Two days after her visit to the shrine, Dorothy wrote Forster a letter that contained strength that hadn't been there before. She laid out her beliefs about marriage and how she would no longer have sex outside of it, both because of Catholic teachings and the mores of society. These protect the family and children, she said. Even though she and Forster had briefly gotten back together yet again earlier that spring, she would now no longer accept his rejection of what was dear to her. She had finally given up any hope of marrying him; it was over.

Within days of writing this letter to Forster, the last one in Tamar's collection until they started up again in the 1960s, the Blessed Mother, Dorothy believed, sent her a teacher, and those years of waiting and wandering came to an end. Dorothy returned home from work one evening to meet a man who insisted on speaking with her. He was in his mid-fifties, short and broad-shouldered with beautiful fingers and strong hands. His face was square and weathered, and he reminded her of a tree trunk, a man rooted in the earth. His clothes were neat but worn and looked slept in. He spoke precise and rich English in a thick French accent and used his whole body as he did so, arms flinging about and index finger stabbing the air to emphasize his points, while he quoted from memory philosophers and writers from all schools of thought. His name was Aristide Pierre Maurin, or Peter, as he now answered to.

By the time Peter showed up at the door announcing to John's wife, Tessa, that he was here "not to bring a Red Revolution, but a Green Revolution" (Tessa thought he was mad, but she sat him down and gave him a cup of coffee anyway), Dorothy had met scores of radicals and crackpots. "People with blueprints to change the social order," she said, "were a dime a dozen around Union Square." At first she didn't see much in Peter; she was tired and distracted and wanted to spend time with Tamar, John, and Tessa. She continued with her research job for the Paulists, walking to the library after dropping Tamar off at the nursery, and returning home most days to find Peter waiting for her.

Peter didn't say hello or good-bye, and every time he arrived he began talking where he had left off. He didn't hold conversations—he wanted to indoctrinate, as he put it, and provoke people into thinking, and in Dorothy he found someone who listened, though often it was with only half an ear. Day after day he arrived to talk to anyone he could collar, standing over Tamar's bed when she had measles and lecturing the doctor who was trying to care for her. He could talk a person deaf, dumb, and blind, even Dorothy, but she found herself listening in spite of herself for she was hearing things she hadn't heard before. Radicals may have been a dime a dozen around Union Square, but here was someone different. Here was a Catholic radical.

Dorothy was still hungering for something, and the Church had asked very little of her—attend Sunday Mass and confession, and make your Easter duty. Peter didn't talk personally about religion, though he seldom passed a church without stopping in, and he went to daily Mass followed often by an hour of meditation, during which he'd get lost in thought with finger pointed at the tabernacle. He gave Dorothy lessons on the social teachings of the Church, and he spoke of people's material needs—their need for work, food, clothing, and shelter. He brought books and his own writings, though Dorothy couldn't remember which of his essays he first showed her. He carried them around in his large coat pockets, sheaves of paper jammed in between the pamphlets and loose pages he had ripped from books that he would read aloud from or give away. Peter didn't begin his indoctrination of Dorothy with the social encyclicals of the popes—those would come later. He first spoke of the saints, the prophets of Israel, and the fathers of the Church. Peter introduced her to current Catholic thinkers such as Romano Guardini, G. K. Chesterton, Hilaire Belloc, and the two men who influenced Peter the most, Peter Kropotkin and Emmanuel Mounier. Kropotkin was a son of Russian aristocrats and a scientist who came to believe that Darwin's theory of evolution was profoundly misunderstood, that it was not competition but mutual aid at the heart of evolution. Mounier emphasized the value and dignity of each human being, personal responsibility and freedom, and living a life of poverty that was not destitution but one of simplicity and detachment. Peter also spoke of St. Francis of Assisi and of the modern desert father Charles de Foucauld. (Peter, Dorothy often said, came to her with Kropotkin in one pocket and St. Francis in the other.)

"Study history," Peter advised, "so to live in the present as to make the future different." He then would walk Dorothy through the entire history of an idea, sometimes taking four or five hours and leaving her head reeling. Only when he was finished would he tie it all together to deliver his point. Peter looked for inspiration from all sources, from the popes to thinkers of utopian socialism. He wasn't afraid of the word *communism*. The word, he claimed, had been stolen from the Church. At first he claimed he was a Christian communist to shock people, but when the shock turned them away he dropped the term, along with other labels, and it became difficult for people to pin Peter down. He would never say, "I am an anarchist," or "I am a pacifist," for he came to believe these labels set people against one another. He didn't believe in majority rule or in elections because lobbyists and politicians divided people. He didn't want to argue but to exchange ideas. He patiently listened to dissent, but if people dismissed his ideas as crazy, he clammed up. Peter did not like confrontation; dialogue was his method. He didn't like stirring people up, which he felt happened when reporting injustices. He was afraid of inciting class war. He wanted people to sift out the truth, not create controversy.

"People are always saying, 'they don't do this, and they don't do that,'" he said. "WE is a community; THEY is a crowd. Be what you want the other person to be."

Dorothy understood Peter in part because his was the soapbox tradition she had been exposed to from Bughouse Square in Chicago to Union Square in New York.

When a man once asked Peter, "What university did you graduate from?" he replied, "Union Square."

He had taken his cue from the Irish *seanachie*, the storyteller, and liked to speak in verse with a cadence. Dorothy's brother John came to call his verses Easy Essays, and the title stuck. He liked to shout out one-liners: "Everyone take less so that others can have more! Freedom is a duty more than a right! Workers should be scholars and scholars should be workers! Fire the bosses!" He said we need to get away from thinking solely in terms of a job or a wage. Everyone has a vocation, and we must find the work we are best suited for, what we are called to do, and then do it single-mindedly. Artists and musicians do this. They are willing to risk poverty in order to do what they must do, what they love. Not only did Peter believe in a philosophy of work that spoke of love of work rather than work ethic, he also believed that we must have a philosophy of poverty. True reform begins with oneself, he would say, and voluntary poverty and manual labor are where we begin. Proud of being a peasant, Peter worked as a day laborer on the railroads and in mills or smashing rock to build roads. He had no home and owned nothing but the clothes on his back and the books in his pockets. When Dorothy met him he was a laborer at a Catholic boys' camp in upstate New York earning five dollars a week.

Dorothy liked to refer to Peter as the leader of the Catholic Worker, but he was not a man to tell anyone what to do. He offered his vision and ideas to provoke people into thinking for themselves, but it was up to them to take it or leave it. He did not offer practical ways to achieve things, and when people asked him what they should do, he answered, "I am not a question box; I am a chatterbox." But he spoke of a philosophy of action that Dorothy could understand, and he had one ambition—to change the hearts and minds of men and give them a vision of a world where it was easier to be good.

Peter's program, which was simple, direct, and Catholic, and there-fore caught Dorothy's attention, began with roundtable discussions where people could contribute their ideas and where there would be "clarification of thought." He wanted people to be well-read and articu-late, and he believed this was within everyone's grasp no matter the level of education or state of mind. All who asked deserved to be taught the best and to be treated as equal scholars, as everyone could and should have a philosophy to live by. He included even the mentally ill who, through their illnesses, could sometimes wring out every bit of his own vitality in his effort to give them his full attention and respect.

Second in his program was the establishment of houses of hospitality with priests at their head, based on the bishops' hospices for wayfar-ers in the middle ages. Then those at the houses of hospitality would form farming communes, or "agronomic universities," as he liked to call them, where workers and scholars together would rebuild society within the shell of the old, and where people could find their vocations and no longer would need to work in factories or for corporations.

"There's no unemployment on the land," he'd say, and to lessen the need for money we needed to "grow what you eat and eat what you grow."

He called this agrarian movement he envisioned the Green Revolution, decades before the phrase came into use in the 1960s to refer to the push to feed the world through monoculture and the use of petro-chemicals and fertilizers, the antithesis of all Peter meant. He loved to play with the English language, listening to conversations on the street for clichés and odd turns of phrase, or reading signs and slogans trying to find everyday catchphrases he could use to grab people's attention. He was happy to keep repeating his Easy Essays and restating his position, as he believed that sooner or later the ideas would get across. He used any place and opportunity to teach—park bench, subway car, coffee shop, or lodging house. He became enthusiastic when people agreed with him, and he would begin to shout, his eyes shining.

People either loved Peter or they ridiculed him. His style of indoctrination did not suit everyone, and he would chant his Easy Essays mournfully in his thick French accent, which many could not understand. Because he didn't believe in small talk and spoke simply, sometimes people confused his simplicity with simplemindedness, and he could be treated badly because of his shabby appearance or laughed at because of his peculiar way of speaking. But Peter never took offense. He was accepting and nonjudgmental of everyone he met, asking about their vocation, what they read, and what they were enthusiastic about, and then he'd connect them to other people who had the same interests. He rarely spoke of himself and his past, though sometimes they seemed to emerge with moments of sadness and regret. He never answered letters and did not write personally as Dorothy did. Many people said they had never met a man more detached from personal relationships and material needs than Peter. He even gave away his books, never keeping more than what he could carry in his pockets.

Peter may have been a day laborer, he may have owned nothing, but he was, to those who listened to him, the most well-read person they had ever met. He would often head up to Columbia or Fordham to speak to professors of religion and philosophy or down to Wall Street to speak about economics and lending money at interest with John Moody, head of Moody Investment Services, or Thomas Woodlock, editor of the *Wall Street Journal*. One afternoon Dorothy overheard him speaking with a Russian theocrat, a Mexican general, and a German Benedictine priest, and she tried to write the conversation down, recalling the conversations between Kenneth Burke, Malcolm Cowley, and John Dos Passos she had witnessed in the twenties though she couldn't understand a word of them.

Dorothy would remember and repeat some of Peter's sayings all her life: We are trying to make a world where it is easier to be good. The rich make their money by the machine and then buy handmade things to have in their homes. The poor are the ambassadors of God. And he said all are called to perform the works of mercy—to feed the hungry, give drink to the thirsty, clothe the naked, harbor the harborless, ransom the captive, visit the sick, and bury the dead.

"Without him," Dorothy said in the last decade of her life, "I would never have been able to find a way of working that would have satisfied my conscience." His ambitions for Dorothy were great—he wanted her to follow in the footsteps of St. Catherine of Siena and advise the popes.

After several months of listening to Peter, Dorothy asked him, "How do we begin?"

"The way to start is to start," he replied. "Let's start with a newspaper." Or, at least, that's what she heard him say. He hadn't a newspaper in mind at all, but broadsheets and pamphlets he could hand out while talking in Union Square.

"How?" she asked. "I have twenty-four dollars, and that has to pay the rent."

Peter didn't believe in worrying about money, and no sum was too big to ask for when working for a world where it is easier to be good. Dorothy gave up her rent money, a friend gave her twenty-five dollars, the editor of a Catholic publication gave her ten, as did a priest in Newark, and one dollar came from a nun, Sister Peter Claver Fahy of the Missionary Servants of the Most Blessed Trinity, who Dorothy had not yet met but who would become a lifelong friend.

She didn't know if the paper was going to be a weekly or a monthly. It all depended on donations. It was planned, written, and edited in the kitchen of her Fifteenth Street apartment, on subway platforms, on the Elevated, and on the Staten Island Ferry. The three editors were Dorothy, Peter, and Dorothy's brother John, even though he wasn't a

Catholic, and the Paulist Press printed twenty-five hundred copies for fifty-seven dollars. On May 1, 1933, the worst year of the Depression, and during the May Day demonstrations in Union Square, Dorothy and Joe Bennett, a twenty-two-year-old man with a heart condition, sold copies of the first issue of the *Catholic Worker* for a penny a copy. The name itself caused some of the two hundred thousand trade unionists and communists gathering that day to stop and take notice.

That first issue was idealistic, enthusiastic, and afire with the zeal of two oddly paired people—a thirty-five-year-old woman and a French-man twenty years her senior, both with a unique vision of faith and action at a dark time. Peter contributed seven Easy Essays, while the title and articles were Dorothy's. The paper, she wrote, is "For those who are sitting on park benches in the warm spring sunlight. For those who are huddling in shelters trying to escape the rain. For those who are walking the streets in the all but futile search for work. For those who think that there is no hope for the future, no recognition of their plight." She wanted people to know that the Catholic Church had a social program, and that it had both their spiritual and material wel-fare in mind. This wasn't an easy message as most people didn't know about the Church's social teachings—Dorothy hadn't before meeting Peter—and they thought Dorothy was trying to fool them by claiming the Church had such a program. Many of the copies were destroyed, but enough contributions trickled in for another issue.

By the second issue there was an almost complete turnover of staff. John found a paying newspaper job, and he and Tessa moved out. Peter thought Dorothy would help him disseminate his message, but their dif-ferences were apparent from the start. He wanted to call the paper the *Catholic Radical*. The word *radical* means getting down to the roots, he said, and they must get down to the roots. Dorothy's choice, the *Catholic Worker*, came too close to class warfare, which he abhorred. When the first issue came out (in which his name was spelled wrong), he walked out, saying, "Everybody's paper is nobody's paper." While he saw the paper as a way to print his Easy Essays, he also wanted to talk about how things should be and could be, whereas Dorothy, the journalist, wanted to report things as they were to arouse the conscience. (This was one of

Peter's favorite responses to a situation that seemed unbearably unjust—"It makes to arouse the conscience.") But Dorothy had begun and could not be stopped, and so the paper became hers alone. Peter took no further part in it except to submit a handful of Easy Essays for each issue.

"Man proposes and woman disposes," he said, which could be read in two ways. It stuck in Dorothy's mind for years to come, so much so that she wrote of it in the last line of *The Long Loneliness*, and again in her seventies, when she wrote of Peter's disappointments with their lack of success for his ideas such as the farming communes that she, as the practical one, had had to initiate.

"I considered that I was putting some flesh on the dead bones of his thinking. It is one thing to dream of Utopias, it is another thing to try to work them out," she wrote.

What Peter brought to Dorothy changed her life, but she was the first to admit she sometimes didn't understand him or his program of action. Peter did not relate to others on a personal level, and he and Dorothy had little in common. He did not share her love of music, and he felt no connection with Dostoyevsky. For her part, she wasn't beyond hearing what she wanted to hear. Six years after the beginning of the Catholic Worker, she claimed that Peter had come to her back in 1933 urging her to start a Catholic labor paper, which was unlikely given his disinterest in the labor movement.

Dorothy, after years of listening to radicals, was tired of the call for revolution. It was always the revolution, she said, and Peter agreed. He had studied the French Revolution and did not like its violence. He didn't wish to perpetuate the proletariat, and he belonged to no union. Strikes don't strike me, he'd say, while Dorothy was writing of the hundreds of strikes going on around the country. Peter had no interest in what he saw as short-term solutions, and he had seen the price people paid for the Industrial Revolution. He was interested in the long view, while Dorothy still had her loyalties toward the labor movement and would for a long time. When Peter spoke of workers, he saw what he had come from in France—farmers and craftsmen living on the land. When Dorothy spoke of workers, she saw what was in New York City—factory workers living in slums.

Even though Peter had withdrawn his name from the paper's mast-head, and John and Tessa had moved on, Dorothy wasn't left alone. Young people began to find their way to her door, and among the very first were Dorothy Weston, a recent college graduate, and Eileen Corri-dan, a newspaperwoman. Peter then brought in three young men from off the street. One became the bookkeeper, the other the circulation manager, and the third married Dorothy Weston, beginning the tradi-tion of Catholic Worker marriages.

The growth of the paper was phenomenal. From its first run of twenty-five hundred, it reached twenty thousand four months later. Dorothy rented an old barbershop in the Fifteenth Street building and turned it into the Worker's office. She typed in the hot summer evenings to the sound of children playing and mothers calling out from the apart-ment above, and communist speakers shouting under the light of lamp-posts to people sitting on their stoops seeking a breath of cool air and listening because there was nothing else to do. Visitors and subscrip-tions flooded in. Priests ordered hundreds of copies for their working-class parishes, and the mailman stopped to chat about his working conditions, as did a worker for the electric company who said that their union members didn't dare talk about their working conditions.

Dorothy reported on the strikes covering the country and affecting tens of thousands, from steel workers to silk workers to cotton pick-ers whose bosses, in response to the strike, took the strikers' children out of school to pick the cotton. The mood was ugly. Men, women, and children were beaten, teargassed, clubbed, shot, and killed. A judge in California, speaking of strikers, said from the bench, "In some places they take men like these out and hang them. Don't be too sure they won't do it yet, right here." A steel worker handing out union literature was arrested and sent to an insane asylum.

Dorothy also wrote of lynchings and of the lives of sharecroppers. She wanted a paper not only for blacks and whites but written by both, to impress on her readers that the paper was for all workers. On the back page she published one of Tamar's sketches in which she had drawn a picture of black convicts in Florida though she had not made them black. She didn't see the color, only the stripes, Dorothy wrote, and that's how children see before prejudice is instilled in them. By the sixth issue, Dorothy was tackling Hitler's persecution of the Jews and anti-Semitism not only in Germany but also in the United States.

When asked why she wrote of such misery and bleak events, Dorothy said that we need to try to help, and this begins by recognizing people's situations. If we don't, then there are only the communists who are trying to change things. Most Catholics spoke of communists with horror, and yet the communists, she said, "are apt to stand more chance in the eyes of God than those indifferent Catholics who stand by and do nothing."

While Dorothy published the paper, Peter started a workers' school and held lectures and roundtable discussions chaired by a philosophy professor from Fordham University. Peter invited the talkers and thinkers of the day, priests and laymen, writers and professors, who gave lectures to an audience sitting on boxes in the backyard among the privet hedge and petunias. These talks were held every evening for one wildly enthusiastic year before it wore thin and no one could keep up the pace Peter had set, and they settled on Friday nights only. Jacques Maritain, the French philosopher, gave his first talk in English at the Worker, but his accent was worse than Peter's, and no one could understand him. A theologian priest gave a talk on the Trinity, at the end of which an Irishman said, "I haven't heard one mention of the Blessed Mother. I don't believe any of you are Catholic."

Everyone was out talking in those days—soapbox orators in Union Square and Columbus Circle and people arguing at large street meetings all over the city. They had nothing but time since so many were unemployed. At the Worker, discussions could start in the morning and continue into the afternoon and evening. Dorothy could leave for the printer, meet friends for dinner, and return to find people still talking, while Peter rocked back and forth in his seat waiting for the speaker to get done so he could make a point. If there were no visitors, Peter went out into the streets, heading over to Union Square or giving loud lectures to his companions on the subway, hoping to indoctrinate everyone close enough to hear and open-minded enough to listen.

Fifteenth Street drew many of the crowd that Tamar grew up with and loved for the rest of her days. In the fall of 1933, a shy nineteen-year-old artist, Ade Bethune, a Belgian immigrant from an aristocratic family, showed up having heard about the two Dorothys—Day and Weston—who were publishing a paper and offering hospitality to the homeless. On the subway home, Ade looked at the paper and asked herself, "Where's the artwork?" and before she knew what she had gotten herself into, she was making illustrations. "This is what I want," Dorothy said without introduction or preamble to Ade, who was in something of a panic on meeting her. "St. Catherine of Siena and John Bosco. Pictures of working saints."

Ade's art began to appear in the ninth issue of the paper in 1934, and a year later she designed a new masthead. Ade was so taken by Dorothy that for a brief moment of madness she wanted to smoke cigarettes like Dorothy did. Even though she was a timid and introverted art student, Ade took her courage in hand and sold the paper on the streets.

Big Dan Orr, an ex-policeman and unemployed truck driver from New Jersey, six feet tall and over two hundred pounds with bad feet and full of Irish wit and happiness, had been sleeping on the docks when he stopped in at the Worker. When Dorothy asked what he needed, he said, "To soak my feet." They brought him a tub with hot soapy water and a copy of the paper. He returned the next day and began selling the paper and handing out clothing.

He would come into the office and shout, "Is everybody happy?" And they all would groan and shout in reply, "No!"

Big Dan knew how to handle a horse and cart, so they rented a horse from a neighbor, a German Nazi sympathizer, as they eventually found out, to pick up the paper from the printer and deliver the bundles. Big Dan drove along Fifth Avenue with the horse and cart shouting, "Read the *Catholic Worker*!" He called the horse Catholic Action and used one of Dorothy's blankets to cover him. That first summer they borrowed the horse and cart to help evicted families move, many of them Jewish, the irony of which delighted Dorothy, given the horse's owner.

Stanley Vishnewski arrived at the Worker in 1934, a tall blue-eyed boy about to turn eighteen. He was the son of poor Lithuanian immigrants who lived near the foot of the Williamsburg Bridge in Brooklyn. Stanley had just finished printers' trade school but hadn't been able to find work when he picked up a copy of the *Catholic Worker* from the local library. He showed up at the office to help and soon was walking across the Williamsburg Bridge to Fifteenth Street every day.

"Dorothy had the most wonderful quality of treating someone who was eighteen almost like an equal," he said. "She took me in. She talked to me as though what I had to say really mattered."

The youngest member of the Worker, Stanley was set to work the "street apostolate." He sold papers walking from Union Square down to Wall Street, and he liked to talk with strikers about God, surprising the police, who thought all strikers were godless communists. It wasn't easy selling the paper. At some of the rallies, copies were ripped out of his hands and flung into his face, and he was sometimes yelled at and spit on.

The Worker drew Stanley in because of his dissatisfaction with what the local churches were offering, called the "Five Bs"—bridge, beer, bazaars, bowling, and bingo. (For the young women, it was fashion shows and parties.) At the Catholic Worker you could get discussions on the personalism of Mounier, the philosophy of the English distributists, or the social encyclicals of the popes. And at the Worker you didn't merely write about the news; you took part in it. By the time Stanley turned twenty-one he had witnessed seven riots. The first broke out when seamen were picketing on Eighth Avenue and Fortieth Street, and police on horseback and swinging clubs rammed into the picket line. Stanley ran for two blocks while Dorothy hid behind a car. Forty people ended up in the hospital, and Dorothy told Stanley he wasn't to go on any more picket lines until he turned twenty-one. But he didn't listen, and it was Stanley who, when he and Dorothy were at a demonstration during the National Biscuit Company strike, flung himself between Dorothy and a mounted policeman about to crush her against a wall, saving her, she believed, from grave harm.

Ade, Big Dan, and Stanley each arrived at the Catholic Worker with differing needs and each found a role within it. Though Ade would never come to live at the Catholic Worker, as would often happen to young people who showed up, Dorothy put her on the road to her life's work by paying her tuition to attend a course on liturgical art. Big Dan would leave several years later when he found work as a chauffeur and taxi driver, and he would cheer as he passed by Workers selling the paper on the street, or, if he had no fares, give them lifts. Stanley moved into the Worker permanently in 1936 and, barring two or three years when he went off to find adventure, stayed until his death in 1979.

On the first anniversary of the paper, May Day 1934, when hundreds of thousands of demonstrators gathered around the country, more than a dozen students helped distribute the paper in Madison Square and Columbus Circle, and people of all nationalities approached them asking for copies. They were now printing one hundred thousand copies per issue, and Dorothy was thrilled. "Let's head for a circulation of two hundred thousand," she cried. Stories began to trickle in of how far and wide the paper could be found, including a copy discovered in a Nova Scotia coal mine four and a half miles underground.

At the Catholic Worker's headquarters, there was little to indicate just how successful the paper was. Dorothy's desk was a damaged antique rolltop with a missing leg held up by a copy of the *Catholic Encyclopedia*, and next to that was the circulation desk, which was a metal table with two filing cabinets where the paper was folded, stuffed into hand-addressed envelopes, and stamped before being delivered to the post office. Beyond the office, in a room with no windows, they stored back issues of the paper, packing crates of clothes to hand out, and belongings of those who were homeless and out looking for work. Peter slept there, and he tacked up on the wall quotations he had copied in his beautiful script. He liked to quote Eric Gill, the English artist: "Every man is an artist and artisan."

In Dorothy's apartment, she had a small kitchen with a table that sat eight, and Stanley set the table every night with one extra plate for whoever came in, but soon that wasn't nearly enough. While Peter exhorted the bishops to open houses of hospitality, as called for by canon law, and exhorted individuals to practice the works of mercy, people showed up in need of food, and so the Worker began to serve meals. The vision was a kind of Wobblies-style flophouse with a pot of soup on the stove at all times, but the pots were small and the fire slow, so they went to the pushcart market and bought a ten-quart pot for seventy-nine cents, the first of many large soup pots. They began to receive food donations, including thirty dozen fresh eggs from Indiana, delivered by train. "Fresh eggs!" Dorothy wrote. "Soft-boiled for breakfast, with the morning paper and a symphony on the radio, preferably the first Brahms!"

Dorothy began to hear from people telling their stories of being homeless, and as she wrote about it, the homeless began appearing at the door. By the end of 1934 the Catholic Worker opened its first house—a six-room apartment big enough for ten women. Throughout the city, well-dressed women were begging, and the lines for food and refuge at the municipal shelters were full of girls and women who looked comfortably well-off and yet were homeless and destitute. Dorothy was herself mistaken several times for a woman in need, even though her heels were not run-down and her clothes were neat.

Peter brought in men he met on the street—Mr. Minas, an Armenian anarchist, who walked about the city with sheaves of poetry in his pocket that only he could read, and Mr. Breen, an out-of-work journalist with a gentlemanly air who became a scourge at the Worker. He was a dignified old man, the oldest in their household, with a beautiful beard and a cane. On occasion he wrote poetry and reviews for *Commonweal*. He looked like a poet, but he had a terrible temper and was virulently racist. Dorothy often had to write letters of apology to those he had insulted in his efforts to help with the growing correspondence. His family was gone, he said, and with the Depression he had fallen on hard times. Before meeting Peter, he had slept in what was called the world's longest bedroom, a municipal shelter on a dock at South Ferry that put up more than two thousand people a night. Mr. Breen would listen only to Dorothy. To Ade, he said, "My only home in all the world is with her."

There was also one of Peter's bosom friends, a man known only as the Professor who had been a pianist, a promoter of the language of Esperanto, and a linguist but lost his job to drink. He stole five dollars from Dorothy to go on a bender. "The only thing is to be oblivious, as Peter is, and go right on and on," she said.

People came by accompanying those too troubled to make their own way to the Worker—a young woman in danger of committing suicide, a young man out of prison, a sick mother with a baby to whom they read Peter's Easy Essays in an effort to get the baby to sleep, and a fellow who tried to whip up hatred against the Jews. "I shall read Conrad and forget my troubles," Dorothy said on one of her more difficult days.

People kept arriving and stayed, drawn by need or by Dorothy's powerful interest in them, and soon the Catholic Worker was renting three apartments funded by donations from readers of the paper. "It's amazing how quickly one can gather a family," she said.

And Miss Day's daughter? How did Tamar fare during those early years of her mother's movement? She learned her arithmetic by playing with the money in the cash box and loved every bit of what was happening—well, most of it. At the age of seven she was asked—and would continue to be asked throughout her life—for a sacrifice that possibly would have damaged a less wise and sensible child. But Tamar loved to sit with the adults in the office, the room full of radical excitement, and listen to them talk, especially Dorothy and Peter.

"I didn't understand them, of course. I just listened," she said. "They all smoked like chimneys back then, so I'm not so sure this was good for a young child. But they all were such wonderful fools. So full of hope. Those early years were magnificent. So much enthusiasm, and everyone found what they really wanted to do. People came in off the streets and blossomed at the Worker." Then she added, a bit sadly, "It was the world that taught me that people weren't always so kind and hospitable. Growing up at the Worker, I thought everyone was good and kind."

It was a hard time of transition for Tamar. After having the exclusive attention of her mother for years, the family exploded from just the two of them to dozens and then to hundreds. For first and second grades Tamar attended a parochial school on Fourteenth Street while living at the Fifteenth Street apartment, but it was hard for a little girl who already had battled a life-threatening illness and whose health continued to be fragile. When her doctor said to Dorothy, "This is no life for a child," meaning the atmosphere of the Worker, Dorothy found her a small, newly formed school in a convent on Staten Island. The Academy of St. Dorothy was a yellow-brick mansion full of antiques on the former estate of a wine family and with grounds of sculpted gardens, fountains, and grape arbors facing the bay. With Forster paying tuition, in the fall of 1934, Tamar, through Dorothy's ignorance, was placed in second grade when she should have gone into third. She boarded at St. Patrick's, four miles away in a decrepit building—the dormitories were old classrooms—near a jail, and the girls would shout up to the prisoners, who would shout back down.

Though Tamar was no longer living at home, during the weekends Dorothy continued to read to her, cook her little treats, and take her on spontaneous trips to the beach, but Tamar knew from an early age that she would always be sharing her mother with countless others. And as Miss Day's daughter, she dreaded people's expectation that she would be like her mother. They would ask, "Are you going to be a writer? Are you going to be a speaker? Are you going to take over the Catholic Worker when you grew up?"

In the spring of 1935 Dorothy rented a Victorian house with half an acre in Huguenot on Staten Island overlooking the bay. They called it the garden commune, as it couldn't, at that size, rightly be called a farming commune. Dorothy's own cottage had burned down under unknown circumstances possibly that same year. Tamar thought it might have been one of Dorothy's friends who accidentally set it on fire, but Dorothy was silent on the topic. It must have been a huge blow to lose what had been so dear to her. Her books, early writings, journals, articles, the play, novels, letters, and the nonsense poem she, Gene O'Neill, and Max Bodenheim had written on a napkin had all gone up in flames.

That summer Tamar and Dorothy often went for a swim before supper, when the water was calm and the tide high, and when the tide was low, they dug for clams. After dinner they went for walks with Stanley, or Stanley would cut the grass while Tamar picked bouquets of buttercups, daisies, clover, and honeysuckle. On the morning when the first of the cicadas sang, Tamar woke Dorothy to tell her, and they lay in bed listening. And then Dorothy would have to wrench herself away to make the long trek back into the city with its endless tasks of court cases, evictions, hospital visits, letters to answer, articles to write, and people to feed.

Tamar returned to St. Dorothy's in the fall, and when Dorothy visited, they went to the beach before eight o'clock Mass and then breakfasted at a little Chinese shop. They walked along the back roads through the fallen leaves, and through the woods, fields, and hills. They collected sassafras and seed pods from eucalyptus trees and tried to find the crickets in the rock gardens, while Tamar talked about her days at the school and how she went with Mother Chiarini to the bakery and watched the baker fling a huge wad of dough over his shoulder.

Tamar came home from St. Dorothy's to be often met not by her mother, who was spending more time giving talks around the country and visiting migrant camps, but by two young men, Gerry Griffin and Joe Zarrella. Gerry, Joe, and Tamar formed a group called the Hot Chocolate and Walking Club, and they explored the city, visited the Cloisters and the museums, and on the way home stopped at the Automat for hot chocolate.

Dorothy had begun her public speaking almost with the inception of the Worker. While attending an event at a Catholic high school, she was invited to speak for the first time. She was so petrified that she sat in the chapel before the talk reciting the Memorare over and over again. But soon invitations from all over the country began to come in and so began the element of Dorothy's work that would become crucial to keeping the Worker going but would send her away from Tamar for months on end. Speaking publicly remained agony for Dorothy throughout her life. She would start out nervous and tense, but she spoke simply and vividly, peppering her message of social change with stories and descriptions of what it was the Catholic Worker was doing in the slums of Manhattan. And people responded—some to the message and some to her.

She was beautiful, some said.

"No," said Grace, who had been a beautiful woman in her youth. "My daughter isn't beautiful—she has presence."

As Dorothy became better known, rumors about her began to fly.

"Is it true that you have ecstasies and visions?" a woman asked her.

"Visions of unpaid bills," Dorothy replied. This was her official reply, but back then her language could be salty.

Jack English, another early Catholic Worker, who first heard Dorothy speak when she visited his college in 1934, claimed to recall seeing her at her typewriter at the East Fifteenth Street apartment, a beret covering her short hair and a cigarette in her mouth, when two nuns visited.

One of them said, "Miss Day, we want to ask you a question."

She took the cigarette out, and said, "Yes, of course."

"Is it really true that you live on only the Blessed Sacrament?"

Dorothy looked at them and said, "Hell no!"

Rumors spread that she had stigmata she managed to conceal or, when someone confused her with another writer at that time named Dorothy Day, that she was living the good life in the Upper West Side.

During these years, Dorothy tried to make sense of her faith and conversion to herself and to others. She felt she had to explain to her friends what had happened. Mike Gold had stopped visiting because he believed that now that Dorothy was a Catholic, she was aligning with the fascists in the Spanish Civil War. But what may have been hardest for her to bear was his faint praise of the *Catholic Worker* as "an earnest little paper" and Dorothy as an "honest" person. It didn't help that in 1936 the paper published an article critical of Russia's totalitarianism, and Mike Gold would not hear of any criticism of the Soviet Union.

In response to questions her brother John asked about her religion, Dorothy wrote an essay that would expand into her first book since beginning the Catholic Worker, *From Union Square to Rome*. Perhaps John was a good device, as he and Tessa were communists. Perhaps these questions were what she sensed not only from John and Tessa but from Peggy, Malcolm, Forster, and Mike Gold. Or perhaps they were questions she was asking of herself.

It isn't true that religion is a deliberate turning away from life, she wrote. Though maybe it seemed morbid in that it led you to struggle with dark questions of doubt and with the shadow of death. But there is greater struggle in turning away from God, of succumbing to a life of just getting by, just doing enough. And she couldn't do without the sacraments and the guidance of St. Teresa, who understood the weariness of the soul, of St. Francis de Sales, who said be gentle with ourselves, of

Jean-Pierre de Caussade, who advised abandonment to divine provi-dence, and of Father Considine, who spoke of a God so kind and loving that he would give us everything.

Dorothy now attended Mass most days of the week. She sat in the little Italian church on Twelfth Street early in the morning before Mass and looked out on the herbs and tomatoes growing on the fire escapes and roofs. During Mass, the Italian girls sang the Kyrie Eleison, and the priest moved about intently and silent in his heavy robes. Through-out the day, young and old came in from the hot streets, and on the hottest days, the parish priest opened up the fire hydrant in front of the church so the children could cool down. The church was the com-munity, she felt, and Mass became a time to stop and take note of the sunlight and of her fellow humans, to take a breath and feel God touch-ing the heart and the mind. In such moments of peace and stillness, all her fears and questions would fall away, the path would rise up to meet her, and the calling would feel so clear it was as if it had all been taken out of her hands.

CHAPTER SIX

Then came Mott Street, glorious, miserable Mott Street, with its opera-singing Italian neighbors and Mussolini statues in the shopwindows. The Catholic Workers were delighted to move to Mott Street after spending a year and a half on Fifteenth Street, where they kept four different flats for twenty people, followed by a year of living in a derelict building on Charles Street on the outskirts of Greenwich Village. The Charles Street house had seemed a good idea at the time. It had enough room for everyone, including the cat named Social Justice, the goldfish, and a terrarium Tamar called the farming commune, and they could watch the tugboats on the Hudson River. But the building was filthy and had no heat, gas, or electricity; it was as if they were squatters in an abandoned building.

In April 1936 with the help of striking longshoremen, they moved into 115 Mott Street, a seventy-six-year-old tenement that wasn't much better—five stories of twenty rat-ridden rooms in a rear building with garbage filling the halls and courtyard, and permeated with the smell of urine from the alley behind the building, a stench so powerful Tamar never forgot it. But with fresh paint, linoleum, and curtains, the place began to improve. "We cannot promise always to be so orderly," Dorothy wrote.

Mott Street runs through the heart of Little Italy. At the north end of the street, mothers sat with their baby carriages against the warm, sunny graveyard walls of St. Patrick's Old Cathedral. Farther south the buildings were taller and the street narrower, turning it into a canyon with little sunlight except in the middle of the day. There you entered

the poor working-class slum of Little Italy and the most thickly popu-
lated section of New York, crowded with tenements, factories, baker-
ies, livery stables, laundries, and fish markets. The Bowery was two
blocks away and lined with flophouses, pawnshops, secondhand-
clothing shops, cheap movie houses, penny arcades, taverns, and a
thieves' market where nearly everything—from razors to pants—could
be found. Those who couldn't afford the twenty or thirty cents a night
for a room lay on sidewalks or slept in doorways or against house
fronts.

Men slept in tightly stacked bunks in rat-infested and overcrowded
tenements, one of which caught fire, and many of the men died. There
were drugs, alcohol, and the occasional gunshot, when women would
rush from their homes afraid for their men, and almost every building
had a boy in jail. The neighbors were large Italian families who grew
basil, tomatoes, and fig trees on their fire escapes, and Chinese, who
were steadily moving north of Canal Street and lived in their storefronts.
All summer long, men, women, and children lived their lives out on
the street, sitting on stoops, benches, or boxes. The noise never stopped
from dawn to midnight—the calls of the hucksters and pushcart peddlers, music and dancing on the cobblestone street, and everyone stayed
up late to escape the hot and airless tenements. Babies slept in carriages
and toddlers played on the sidewalk while the older kids played in the
playground, filling the air with the sounds of shouts and laughter. The
women knitted and chatted while the old men played cards, and everyone kept an eye on the young children, who would say to the nearest
adult, "Cross me," when they wanted to get to the playground on the
other side of the street.

"People cared for each other and looked out for each other," Tamar
said. "When my Susie was three years old, we were visiting Mott Street,
and she wandered out into the traffic. A quick-witted fifteen-year-old
boy grabbed her. That was a neighborhood!"

It was also a neighborhood of festivals and street fairs. In the fall,
Mott Street reeked of wine as the backyards, including the Worker's,
were filled with huge barrels, and from early morning until late at
night grapes came in by the truckload, and they made wine for the

whole neighborhood. During the Feast of the Assumption, a band of fifty musicians sat on the planks set up for Peter's roundtable discussions in the backyard, practicing for two hours and ended up drinking and fighting. People strung colored lights and set up food stalls selling fruit and nuts, or charcoal stoves to cook sweet corn, sausages, and liver. All week there were processions, food, music, and dance, and on Saturday night women and children in white carrying lighted candles and bouquets of flowers escorted the statue of the Blessed Virgin along the streets, blessing everyone as they passed. In September they celebrated the Feast of San Gennaro. Colored lights and flags were strung across Mulberry Street, and processions passed from Columbus Park to Grand Street and from Baxter over to Mott. A twenty-piece band performed in a bandstand while other bands paraded through the streets. The statue of San Gennaro was removed from the Church of the Most Precious Blood and placed in a shrine on the street for the rest of the week. There was a dance in the playground with Japanese lanterns, and swing music played on a phonograph with loud speakers. Couples danced up and down the street, while little girls whirled with their dresses flying. Chinese neighbors passed by listening to the music; old peddlers, stooped and gnarled, shuffled along; and young couples sauntered arm in arm. On New Year's when the clock struck twelve everyone flung open their windows and hurled out milk bottles, electric lightbulbs, bags of ashes, and garbage, calling out wildly as glass crashed against the sidewalks, and no one dared be on the street, not even the police.

The neighbors at first were distrustful of the Worker, believing they were missionaries. "Why did you move down here?" they wanted to know. "We are all Catholics." When they read articles in the paper opposing fascism they asked, "Why don't you like us?" With Mussolini statues in their windows and Mussolini photos in their homes, they sang and shouted their allegiance to him, and the women donated their wedding rings to help fund his Ethiopian war. But soon they began to not only feel free to talk about the Mussolini regime with the Workers but also to donate their cast-off furniture and come to Friday-night meetings.

The front building on Mott Street was filled with Italian families who left their doors open and filled the hall with smells of their cooking and sounds of their singing. As these apartments became vacant, the Worker took them over, always outgrowing its space. It also took over the two storefronts. In one, they fed people in the morning, provided space to read in the afternoon, and held meetings on Friday nights. The other storefront became the office for distribution of the paper.

In the rear building through the courtyard where one of the men repaired shoes (another fellow ran a sewing machine to repair clothes) there was a print shop for stationery, leaflets, and bookplates, a photography darkroom, and the offices, painted bright blue with blue curtains, where Dorothy, Joe Zarrella, and Gerry Griffin, who were in charge of managing the place, had their desks, file cabinets, and typewriters. The next floor was the heart of the house and the busiest—the kitchen and the dining room, run by Shorty. The third floor had bedrooms for the men, and the fourth and fifth floors were for the women; Tamar lived on the fifth floor when not at school.

Each floor had one toilet but no bath; they had to heat water on the gas stove and take bucket baths behind screens. The coal they burned in the fireplaces was delivered by cart in bushel baskets. The women collected wooden grape crates from winemakers, and the courtyard rang with the sound of hatchets. During the worst days of winter, they nailed the windows shut and stuffed the cracks with rags, and even then the wind blew in and the fires had to be watched day and night.

The building was so bleak it could unnerve visitors, and in an effort to brighten it up, a local priest gave them a statue of St. Joseph, which they placed in one of the storefront windows, and Ade Bethune's family gave them a statue of the Blessed Mother that had been blessed by a pope and then brought from Rome to Spain and on to South America. They hung an oil painting of St. Anthony, a large tapestry of Christ made by Tessa de Aragon's mother, and another one of Our Lady and the Child that Ade Bethune designed and made.

"Ade, along with Peter Maurin," Dorothy wrote, "ranks in the minds of the Catholic Workers as the genius of this concern."

As Dorothy had asked Ade to do for the paper, she asked her to decorate the walls depicting the saints as working, including the Blessed Virgin Mary attending chickens. One woman took exception to Ade's depiction of St. John the Baptist, which portrayed him half-naked with wild hair and beard, and called it a disgrace to the Catholic Church. Some unsympathetic wit responded, "Lady, if you had been in the desert for forty years, how would you look?"

Ade also designed a mural on the dining room wall of St. Benedict in his garden, Martín de Porres feeding a sick man, and St. Francis sweeping. Even the Holy Family was at work—the Blessed Mother sewing, Jesus measuring wood, and St. Joseph sawing. As often was the way at the Worker, five years later an overzealous student from Fordham University scrubbed the wall clean of Ade's mural.

Twenty people moved into Mott Street, and within the first year it grew to more than sixty. Germans, Lithuanians, English, French, Canadians, Irish, Italians, Japanese, and Americans from all over the States, young and old, arrived, all with stories to tell. It was also the year of the seamen's strike, and the seamen hung around singing and playing Stanley's ukulele, with the Italian girls from the neighborhood joining in. One of the seamen, John Filigar, or Farmer John, as we called him, arrived in need of food and a bed. One of the first things he did was clean the chimney by lowering a gunnysack full of bricks on a long rope and swinging it back and forth. He ended up staying for the rest of his life to help plant and harvest at all the Worker farms. "Scratch a seaman and you'll find a farmer," the men would say to John, quoting an old saying.

The Italian neighbors gave no complaints about the breadline, which formed every morning and grew for a block and a half, impeding traffic and blocking doorways where the men huddled on rainy days. The neighbors sent their leftover bowls of spaghetti, ravioli, greens, and pickled eels. The baker down the street, a Seventh-day Adventist, gave them sacks of day-old bread. He offered to teach them how to build an oven and make their own bread.

"I've nothing against the Catholics," he said. "We should all love one another."

Macy's department store donated vegetables and the neighboring

Chinese restaurants their leftovers. A police sergeant brought confiscated loaves of pumpernickel and real butter, and a pushcart peddler
brought in a hundred-pound bag of string beans.

The Workers' daily schedule revolved around the bread-and-soup
line. Beginning at five o'clock in the morning, as the sun rose at the
foot of Hester Street, they would peel onions, carrots, and potatoes for
the soup. Up to a thousand men showed up each morning for coffee
and bread, served from the tiny kitchen behind one of the storefronts.
They were men from the road in search of work, striking seamen from
the waterfronts who had been all over the world, longshoremen, team-
sters, gandy dancers, sandhogs, restaurant workers, sailors, coal heav-
ers, dock workers, and bricklayers. There was also the spillover from the
Bowery, two blocks away, of ragged, dirty, and unemployable men who
had led hard and dangerous lives, men from prison, some for murder.
They were Irish, Italians, Poles, Hungarians, and Slavs, and all peaceably standing in line.

"We never meant to have a breadline," Dorothy said. The Worker's
program wasn't meant to be a soup kitchen, but what was she going to
do? Talk about social justice and yet turn away people in need, saying,
"Go thou, be filled"?

By 1937 the house was serving one hundred fifty loaves of bread and
seventy-five gallons of coffee a day along with twenty pounds of sugar
and twenty cans of evaporated milk. They rented a storefront on Tenth
Avenue, around the corner from the seamen's strike headquarters, which
Dorothy rarely visited as the place was too dangerous. It was thronged
with seamen from eight in the morning until midnight. They kept three
five-gallon pots of soup on the boil and each day served one hundred
twenty-five loaves of bread, fifty pounds of peanut butter, apple butter,
and cottage cheese, plus uncounted pounds of coffee, sugar, and milk.
For two months the men lived on stew, worn-out by the long strike but
ready to stick it out through the winter.

The grocery bill mounted, with a thousand striking seamen to feed
in addition to those on the breadline and the two hundred men and
women who came for lunch. People ate in shifts of twenty-four at a
time, and everyone took turns, in teams of three, serving the line. They

served homemade bread and the best coffee they could afford, but often things were desperate. In one year the line doubled, yet they continued even as weeks went by with nothing in the bank. They worked with the stress of unpaid bills piling up and often no food for the next day, or the soup bordered on inedible, concoctions of turnips, parsnips, and lamb fat. "It is an insult to St. Joseph, our provider, to serve such meals," Dorothy wrote.

They tried to keep the dining room cheerful with the sound of the radio and the smell of freshly made coffee, but Dorothy's heart ached as she passed the line. There were now so many men she no longer could converse with each of them. "Every morning I break my fast with the men on the breadline. Some of them speak to me, many do not. But they know me, and I know them."

The line almost reached Canal Street, and the men had to stand shuddering in the cold or dripping in the rain, many without coats or sweaters. They built fires in the gutters using trash and wood collected from the street, and as the line moved each man got a chance to warm himself. Every morning beginning at five thirty, Dorothy could hear them coughing and talking beneath her window, the reflection of the fires on her walls and brilliant against the dark street, the sky just beginning to be lit by the sunrise.

"It was a miracle," Tamar said. "The line was for two, three hours every morning. The neighbors were so accepting. This wouldn't happen today, but back then everybody in the neighborhood was poor."

In addition to the breadline, the house was filled with young people, with Joe and Gerry running the house, Big Dan Orr making himself seen and very much heard on the streets selling papers, and everyone working until late at night, long after the street noise had died down, as they tried to keep up with the correspondence that poured in. There was much to be done, and none of it was getting done right. They felt they were neglecting each other, as someone was always sick or in trouble. There were sporadic attempts to bring order to the chaos in the house, and for a time Dorothy tried to enforce a few house rules—no drinking and bed at a reasonable hour. They said grace before meals and joined in spiritual readings in the evening, and Dorothy would have liked to see people attend daily Mass. But the rules never stuck, and she hated it when others tried to institute their own, for she was repelled by the often humiliating rules or confessions of faith that other houses for the homeless required, and she was determined not to inflict that on those who came to the Worker.

The office swarmed with visitors who arrived at any time of night or day, and they all fell into doing what they loved best—talking. People came from around the country and from Catholic Worker houses in Milwaukee, Detroit, and Boston. In less than two years, houses larger than the New York house were springing up, with no prompting from Dorothy, in Pittsburgh and Chicago, and others had opened in England and Australia, all loosely associated with the New York Worker but independently run. Word spread like wildfire among priests, and they came from California, Texas, and Wisconsin, from France and Chile, or on their way home from China. But it was the nuns, Tamar claimed, who were the first to understand and respond to what Dorothy was trying to do, and the invitations for Dorothy to speak at their schools and convents poured in. These speaking engagements began to bring in more money, so the Workers didn't have to wonder quite as often how they were going to keep up the line, and they were able to buy better-quality food and coffee. "The best coffee served," the men on the line said.

During these years, Peter Maurin flourished. He had a room near the house library for a time, which he delighted in and was apt to give all the books away, but usually he took whatever bed was available. Like Dorothy, Peter loved his coffee, and he loved the Automats, where for a nickel he could on a cold winter's night have a cup of coffee and sit until four in the morning talking. Peter stayed up late and slept late to get up just in time for the noonday Mass at St. Andrew's Church near city hall. He then went to what were known as the horse markets, cheap restaurants in the Bowery, where the menus were written with soap on the windows. There, while sitting at long tables with baskets of black bread, Peter ate boiled dinners with big knucklebones, lumps of fat, enormous potatoes with black spots, and cabbage soup, food for only the very poor and hungry. Then he was back to the office to indoctrinate whomever he could find, and if there was no one, he went to the universities or he would head up to Union Square or Columbus Circle, where the young volunteers gamely tried to be his foil.

"To give and not to take!" Peter boomed out.

"That's what makes man human!" they shouted back.

This idea, though, failed to get off the ground.

Sometimes he'd come in to pound the bedroom doors of the young men at two o'clock in the morning, shouting out, "I have a point to make!"

Peter liked to throw out his catchphrases, his plays on words, which often made Dorothy wince. He sometimes quoted Father Coughlin, the radio priest, making Dorothy uncomfortable, as they were taking a stand against the very things Father Coughlin stood for, but then she allowed that sometimes she quoted Marx, Lenin, or, later, Mao to shock people into examining old thinking in new ways. "It makes for clarification of thought," Peter would say happily.

For the roundtable discussions, the Mott Street office and dining room were often so crowded that they carried benches into the backyard and sat under the diapers hanging from the clothesline to listen to Peter, his voice echoing out from the courtyard into the canyons of the tenement houses. The neighbors leaned out of their windows to listen as he shouted out, "We're not an organization—we're an organism!"

And in the midst of it all, there was Dorothy, chain-smoking and sarcastic, with graying hair, fabulous hats, and an elegant manner, much of the time fleeing what she had created, and then coming home to cheer everyone up with her generous laugh and sense of humor and joyfulness that made them all, especially Tamar, love her dearly and long for her returns.

"When Dorothy gets back," they'd say of some problem or another, "she'll sort this out."

Sometimes what needed sorting out was so overwhelming that Dorothy would immediately turn around and head off to somewhere else.

Dorothy realized she needed additional help in caring for Tamar, so she enlisted Steve and Mary Johnson, a couple who had arrived at the Worker in need of help. This was often the way Dorothy worked, leading people to see her either as a genius in helping them find a vocation or a niche at the Worker or as a dictator telling them what to do. The Johnsons were older than Dorothy and often not very respectful of her, though they got on well—they were great friends and loving enemies, as one of the Workers described it. Mary had lost her job at the National Biscuit Company factory during a bitter strike in which the workers were demanding a pay raise from nine dollars to fourteen dollars a week. Steve was from Ireland and haunted by the Irish Civil War, in which he had been involved. He had been a political speaker and was highly educated, spoke and wrote in several languages, played the piano, and personally knew Eamon de Valera, considered by the Irish to be their first president before independence, who would go on to become prime minister for three terms and then finish his career once again as president. But Steve was now an invalid, a shattered man who couldn't work.

"He lost his voice," Dorothy said of his inability to speak in not much more than a whisper, "and therefore lost his livelihood."

"Oh, he still talked," Tamar said. "He liked the sound of his own voice."

Steve was a skilled writer and wrote for the paper, but he was a sore trial to Dorothy because he liked to comb through each issue searching for heresy.

The Johnsons fed Tamar good meals and provided her with a lovely bedroom in their sunny apartment in the front section of the Mott Street building. They were a haven of comfort and sanity not only for Tamar but for Workers in need of a break or for visiting bishops and abbots who seemed uncomfortable in the chaos and grime of the Worker. Mary and Steve were so good at providing a home for Tamar that once when Dorothy came back from a speaking tour she said to Tamar, "You're being pampered," and made her eat with the men on the soup line, which was difficult for a child who never forgot some of the wrecked souls she knew.

"I have pictures as though it happened yesterday," Tamar said. "Dorothy is dragging me down into the back room. They used to serve the soup line on plank tables in two tiny rooms. Any time I could get out of it, I would. I was the kind of child who would gag. We were sitting at the table with all these people, poor decrepit people trying to eat, to gobble it down, and there was one tremendously handsome man. A Maori seaman—beautiful, beautiful man. Dorothy immediately started up a conversation with him. Normally people would resent him. 'What's he doing here? He doesn't look like he needs anything.' But right away she got him talking about himself, his family, and his background, because she had such warmth. There was not a shred of any judgment in her. He was a wonderful story to her. He had come ashore, drank, got robbed, and missed his boat."

This was another part of Dorothy's genius: her tremendous interest in people, no matter who they were, young or old, sane or insane, and this is so often how people remember her.

"One of the images I'll always have of Dorothy," Deane Mowrer, a Worker who arrived in the 1950s and remained until her death in the 1980s, once said to Jack English, "is of her sitting with her knitting and listening to somebody pouring out some terrible story."

"I can remember her sitting doing the same thing on Mott Street," Jack replied, "except then she always had a cigarette in her mouth."

Then, as usually happened in the wake of one of her severe moments, Dorothy's generous spirit would break through, and off she and Tamar would go to the movies or to spend the day at the beach.

"We must spend more time at the beach," Dorothy wrote Tamar while on one of her speaking trips.

Dorothy also made sure that Tamar visited Forster regularly, meeting at Lily's apartment on West Tenth Street, the apartment where Tamar and I would visit him almost fifty years later. At Christmas and family gatherings they met with Forster and his family, and Tamar played with her cousins. Forster and Tamar were so shy they didn't seem to have much to say to each other, and this shyness would last their lifetime even though they were happy to be together. They had a lot in common, including their love of biology, and for her birthdays Forster gave her books on the natural sciences, a microscope, a chemistry set, and growing kits.

"I had so much," Tamar said, "even in the height of the Depression.

A toy train, dolls, and a dollhouse with electricity. Sometimes I wonder if everyone doted on me because they felt sorry for me not only at how often Dorothy left to go on speaking tours, but at how distracted she could be. She would let me stay up late while she was talking, and I'd be forgotten while playing in the bath. Once this caused me to get a bladder infection, and I had to spend two weeks at St. Vincent's Hospital. When Della was dying, her mind had slipped and was permanently in the past, and she kept saying, 'Oh, that poor child, poor child.' Meaning me."

Most of Tamar's things—the gifts, the collections of seashells, the microscope, all her treasured belongings—regularly disappeared, either stolen or thrown out by someone in a cleaning frenzy. Tamar stored things under her bed, and then when she came home from school, they would all be gone. Even Peter once walked off with a small suitcase of her doll's clothing, thinking it was his. At one point when Dorothy and Tamar lived in an apartment on Bayard Street—the Worker was always outgrowing its space, and Dorothy would rent cheap places—Dorothy went down to visit Grace in Florida, and when she came home she decided to close the apartment and throw everything out.

Kate Smith, a twenty-four-year-old woman who had come to East Fifteenth Street in 1934, ill with what she said was an inoperable and incurable brain tumor, although she ended up rallying and staying, often shared a room with Tamar and Dorothy. Kate, the first to be jealous of Tamar, stole her clothes and toys and destroyed her specimens. She called Dorothy "Mother" or "Mummy" and wrote her letters signed "your stepdaughter" and "kisses for you only and my love." But Tamar held no grudges. Kate had no family. Her two brothers had disappeared, and she had nowhere to go but the Worker. Tamar grieved the loss of her possessions but never blamed Kate and would defend her when she was attacked by others, just as she stood up for the impossible Mr. Breen. Years later, Tamar would laugh delightedly when she spoke of Kate Smith.

Tamar also had begun to experience painful episodes caused by people's expectations of her as Dorothy Day's daughter, and she was developing differently than Dorothy had hoped. In addition to having been slow to talk and to read, Tamar was deeply shy and, as her aunt Della observed, sorely lacking in social skills. She was an odd child who rarely looked people in the eye and kept her face turned away, leading some to believe she was rude. She would never become articulate like her mother, never be able to write the letters Dorothy longed to receive from her, never be able to have those long talks between mother and daughter. These were handicaps that bedeviled Tamar all her life, and she could not, hard as she tried, find a way to change.

The nuns at St. Dorothy's gave Tamar (or Teresa, as they called her) much of what she needed—acceptance for who she was and a stable environment to grow up in. Unfortunately, Dorothy often couldn't leave things as they were, particularly when she had periodic attacks of guilt for not spending enough time with her daughter. In the early winter of 1938, when Tamar was twelve, Dorothy pulled her out of St. Dorothy's and took her down to Florida to visit Grace, who had had a heart attack. Dorothy also was not well at that time. She had chest pains and was listless and exhausted, so she rested for a month, and in the late afternoons they walked along the beach and down to the lighthouse, to watch the sunset and listen to the waves lap quietly at low tide. It would be a long while before mother and daughter would again spend so much time together.

Dorothy became determined to stay closer to home, and she entered Tamar into Transfiguration School on Mott Street, so they could live together. Dorothy felt at home wherever she was, and as a child her parents had moved her from school to school, so it never occurred to her that all these changes might be misery for Tamar. In trying to explain to her readers why she had put Tamar in a boarding school to then bring her back to Mott Street, she said, "The only reason I sent her away was because with all my speaking trips I could not take proper care of her. But now I am to be at home for a year. I am grieved always at this talk of not raising one's children in these surroundings."

As the sun rose they would go to early-morning Mass before Tamar headed down the street to school. After school they'd meet for a quick lunch, and then walk to the library, where Dorothy tried to help with Tamar's homework. Tamar was instructed to use the words *analysis*

and *allotment* in sentences. "The only sentences I could think of," Dorothy wrote, "were provocative. 'An analysis of Fascism shows that it is
anti-Catholic,' was one. 'Has Mussolini given allotments to the widows
of the men who were killed in Ethiopia?' But I am afraid those sentences
would not sound like Tamar."

When the dark streets and tenements became unbearable, and they
longed to see sunshine over water and feel salt air on their faces, they
walked along the East River or down to the Battery to look out over the
bay. They went to the fish market to see live eels and blue-black mussels
with seaweed still clinging to them and to the fruit-and-nut stalls selling figs, almonds, and peaches, or they bought hot roasted sweet potatoes and roasted chickpeas from peddlers. Children ran in between the
stands, while the storekeepers sat in the sun next to the beggars, and
the smell of spaghetti, ravioli, olive oil, and roasts wafted from the little
restaurants. They sometimes stopped at a little cheese store around the
corner on Hester Street where the owner smoked the cheese underneath
barrels on the curbstone, or they visited the bakery down a steep flight
of steps to a whitewashed cellar, and on the street the smell of freshly
baked loaves mingled with the smell of pizza and focaccia. The baker
worked all night mixing, kneading, and baking in a long coal-fueled
oven, sliding the loaves in with a long paddle and a twist of the wrist. In
the morning he delivered the bread by horse and wagon. Dorothy would
sometimes buy a fresh loaf or hot rolls and bring them home, where the
aroma of the hot bread and freshly ground coffee filled the dining room,
and things didn't seem quite so hard.

But Dorothy couldn't do as she had planned and stay close to home
at Mott Street for a year. The financial needs of the house never let up,
and she had to, yet again, head out on speaking tours, and Tamar, yet
again, changed schools.

"Oak Knoll was very different from what I was used to," Tamar told
me years later. "The kids at St. Dorothy's were mostly the children of widows or widowers, single working parents. Oak Knoll was full of daughters of Hollywood moguls. It was run by the Sisters of the Holy Child
[Jesus] who had offered me a full scholarship. It was a nightmare. One
of the nuns took it upon herself to change me. She would catch me not

eating properly and called me a sneak with my moral values. She'd sit behind me in Mass and shake me to keep me from fainting, whispering through gritted teeth, 'Don't you dare.' I was always fainting. And she tried to force me to stand up straight, even though I had been born with a spinal curvature."

Realizing that Tamar was in danger of having a nervous breakdown, the other nuns put her in the infirmary, where she spent her days reading Ruth Fielding novels—the kind of trash her mother would not let her read—until Dorothy returned from a speaking tour.

"I don't know what they told her, but she took me out of there immediately," Tamar said. Dorothy claimed it was the sisters who had requested she come and take Tamar out of the school. As a result, Tamar returned to the safety and unconditional love at St. Dorothy's, where she received a stream of postcards and letters from Dorothy from around the country, including a description of the auto-manufacturing city of Flint, Michigan.

"What I really want," said Tamar, who already had a habit of taking in stray animals, "is a hedgehog. They are little and not at all prickly if you train them, and they are very bad for cockroaches. But they like to curl up in garbage cans so you are liable to throw them out if you are not careful." So Dorothy put an appeal in the paper asking if anyone had a hedgehog to donate to the Worker.

When the Mott Street house would become too dreary, when damp weather brought out the smell of moldy mattresses and the walls were wet to the touch, when the rats and bills seemed overwhelming, or, even worse, when one of the tightly packed neighboring tenement houses caught fire, and men, crowded into bunks, died, then it was time to head out to Easton. They named it Maryfarm, but most people just said "Easton." I grew up hearing that word often from Tamar. "At Easton," she'd say, and begin to tell us a story of her childhood. The farm in Easton, Pennsylvania, was the first property the Catholic Worker owned. They had bought it the same month they had moved to Mott Street, in April 1936.

"What do you think of the Worker?" a visitor asked Tamar when she was ten.

"I like the farming idea," she replied. "But there is too much talk about the rest."

Tamar had gravitated toward Peter's call to return to the land long before she understood it, and it was at Easton that she spent one of the two happiest times of her life, and where she blossomed in that ever-widening family of Catholic Worker aunties and uncles. So much love and hope was poured into that farm, though it was Peter's ideal and not so much Dorothy's. He saw it as a place where there would be a daily schedule of Mass, five hours of work, three hours of discussion, lectures or lessons in handicrafts, and three hours of rest or study. During this time, Dorothy said Peter was sent to her because she believed in his farming commune.

I can hear Tamar snort over this. "That aspect of Peter's program," she said, "Dorothy didn't get at all."

The work so far had been grueling, stressful, and without much hope. The breadline, that never-ending line of misery, need, and hope-lessness, that "drain on resources" (according to those who preferred focusing on the newspaper) could wear people down, and because of this, for the first years of its eleven-year existence as a Catholic Worker farm, Easton was beloved of Workers, guests, mad hermits, fractious families, and even readers of the paper who never saw it but sent them roses and vegetable seeds. Everyone, it seemed, wanted to go back to the land—seamen, ex-prisoners, soldiers, and young married couples. But Easton would come to break everyone's hearts, including Dorothy's and Tamar's.

After a year of looking for a place, a small group of Workers, includ-ing Dorothy, found themselves in a borrowed car driven by Big Dan Orr, seventy miles outside of New York City, heading up a rocky road with hairpin turns to the top of a hill, where they saw a rolling landscape with a house and barn nestled in a small valley amid large fields and woods. Even though they could smell soot from the nearby towns and the hillside seemed barren with the bare trees of early spring, they all cried out, "This is it!"

The view was glorious and looked out over New Jersey and Pennsylvania, the Pocono Mountains, and the Delaware Water Gap. In one
direction you could see the rolling farms across the river in New Jersey; in the other were the factory chimneys of Easton, two miles away,
and several miles to the west was the town of Bethlehem, which was
"devoted to gunpowder and munitions and tagged with such a lovely
name it irks me." This was written in an unsigned farm column, which
meant it had been written by Dorothy. (Much of what was unsigned in
the paper was hers, as was observed by her brother Donald, who commented that either she was writing the entire paper or everyone at the
Worker was starting to sound like her.)

They bought the farm for $1,250 from a Polish family whose chil-
dren had married and left. It had a large barn, eight acres of woods, and
twenty acres of cleared land, hilly but recently cultivated. There were
peach, apple, and cherry trees, strawberries, raspberries, blackberries,
elderberries, currents, half an acre of asparagus, rhubarb, and plenty
of sumac. The seven-bedroom house was in bad repair and had neither electricity nor running water, the outbuildings were falling down,
and the yard was full of car parts, tin cans, and bottles dating from
the Civil War. A local farmer told them the soil was rocky and couldn't
support a family of four with a horse and cow, and it was too small for
machines, but they refused to be discouraged. Through donations they
had enough to buy it outright, but there was much to be done, and
they had little money for tools or equipment. It was only after buying
the farm that Dorothy asked John Filigar if he knew anything about
farming.

"I *am* a farmer," he replied.

They cleaned up the junk and turned the yard into a flower garden,
and within a month of moving in, they started planting. Neighbors
plowed the land for ten dollars a day, and John planted potatoes, sweet
corn, watermelon, alfalfa, and cantaloupe.

The striking seamen loaded up the Worker's newly purchased farm
truck with mason jars, blankets, and cots from the city and headed
out to help fix things up. Within a few months there were more than
twenty people living at the farm—Jewish, Catholic, Greek Orthodox,

Protestant, atheist, African American, and white—and in July they opened a summer camp for fifty kids from Harlem. By August they had three ducks named Hope, Faith, and Charity, four pigs, and four hundred tomato plants, and they began trading surplus tomatoes and corn with a local grocery in exchange for food they could not grow themselves. By November Rosie the cow had given birth to Bessie, the first creature to be born on the farm, and by December only two people remained. The rest had fled back to the city, preferring its rats, noise, and days without coal to the isolation and lack of heat, electricity, and water at the farm.

That first winter was harsh. It was so cold, hot coffee went cold in minutes, and people ate while wearing their overcoats and slept with hot bricks. All was not bad, though. Rosie, the cow, was giving five gallons of milk a day, and they had butter and buttermilk, and her calf was the most beautiful thing on the farm. They bought four black pigs, one of which Mr. Breen bought with a check he received for a book review in *Commonweal* and then gave to Tamar.

The spring of 1937, they expanded by first renting and then buying another farm with a small house and two barns at the foot of the hill, connected by a quarter-mile-long steep, rocky road. They were able to purchase the lower farm for four thousand dollars, Dorothy claimed, by praying what was often called the "gimme" novena, better known as the rosary novena. For three novenas (nine days each) you asked for what you needed, and then whether or not you received your request, you started three more novenas in gratitude. If that didn't work, you repeated the entire cycle, and before you were finished you'd have what you prayed for. "This is the kind of a story," Dorothy wrote, "that infuriates those who term us superstitious."

The Worker now had a total of seventy acres and would be able to think about making the farm self-supporting. A group of women, including Kate Smith, was living at the lower farm, or, as some called it, the Downstairs Farm. They cleaned and whitewashed the rooms and painted the woodwork. They had big plans to house fifty women and children and to convert the two barns into chapels, dormitories, libraries, classrooms, and even a dance hall.

They now had two sheep and a lamb, the bills continued to be paid, and that summer the farm was a happy place, with, as Dorothy wrote, "bright sunny days, the heavy odor of milkweed blossoms coming in the window and the daisies studding the fields. Every night we have black raspberry shortcake, and there is all the cherry jam you can eat." Rosie wasn't giving as much milk but they got a new cow, Mollie, three goats, a horse named Jim along with a horse-drawn mower and wagon, bee equipment, and, most happily, a newly dug well. They had their first Easton wedding when Jim Montague married Helen Brennan at St. Bernard's Church, where Tamar herself would get married seven years later. They began hosting retreats, and visiting priests took the children swimming or worked in the fields and went deer hunting. At harvest time, while the women's dorm leaked, and they had to shift the beds back and forth to avoid the drips, the farm was able to supply Mott Street with potatoes, beets, carrots, and cabbage.

Dorothy felt there was progress, but one of the men said to her, "We've been there a year, and all we have is a home for celibate seamen."

Those seamen that the Worker had helped during the strike of 1936 sent money in addition to helping spread the *Catholic Worker* paper all over the world. A grateful Portuguese seaman brought two bags of dirt from Mount Carmel in the Holy Land, which they sprinkled on the garden. As he left for India, Dorothy asked him to bring back a spindle, and five months later he returned with three.

Taxicab drivers, miners, and fishermen all were curious as to how the farm was going, and many asked after the animals by name, and so Dorothy wrote of them in her column, to the amusement of others. In the spring of 1938, they bought another horse, Prince, and John began plowing the fields. Jim was the hardest working and fastest horse John ever knew, but Prince was elderly. In addition to the two horses, they had the usual poor man's livestock—a milk goat, thirteen rabbits, two hundred chickens, and Tug Boat Annie, the sow, with her litter of ten pigs, and ten other pigs besides. John estimated that by the following year they would have one hundred fifty pigs.

During the spring school holiday, Tamar moved into a little house Mr. O'Connell, a skilled carpenter, had built for her on the lower farm next to a narrow, sloping field of alfalfa and oats and amid cherry and pear trees and a hedge of raspberries. Tamar had saved her Christmas and birthday money from Forster until she had fifty-eight dollars to buy the materials for her house. It was a tiny place, nine feet by twelve feet, with room for two bunks, a table, and a chair. Mr. O'Connell also built shelves for the specimens Tamar collected from the fields and woods, including a rattlesnake rattle Dorothy found one day while sweeping. The house also would come to store Dorothy's coffin, which Mr. O'Connell made for her, an idea she may have gotten from Ade Bethune, who had built her own coffin, or Ade may have gotten it from her. In any event, Ade managed to keep hers long enough to be buried it in, whereas Dorothy's coffin was appropriated by Tamar to store blankets.

Dorothy wished the cottage was larger—it was so small that even a tiny potbellied stove made it unbearably hot—but Mr. O'Connell had been adamant on keeping it small.

"So no one but you and Tamar can sleep there," he said to Dorothy.

Mr. O'Connell was an Irishman in his seventies who had traveled the world. He had been a policeman and a fireman and had fought in the Boer War and in India, where, after going bootless for seven months, he took the boots off the feet of an Irishman who had been fighting in the English army. He was from a family of twenty-one, his father a carpenter and his mother a saint who never failed in anything, he said, unlike the women around the Worker. No woman could measure up to Mr. O'Connell's mother. He shared his goat's milk with those he liked, and he had a great love for animals and the children, who clustered around him outside his house while he told stories and twilight deepened over the patchwork fields sloping down into the valley.

"All the animals," he would say to the children, "kneel down before they rest. Far more faithful than men, who forget their prayers, who forget to kneel morning and night. You can see the animals around here doing it, even that bit of a goat out there—down on her knees she goes before she lies down. The gentle creatures."

But Mr. O'Connell had no time for the others at the farm, and as an ex-soldier, he had no truck with pacifists. He couldn't work with anyone, and no one could work with him, and he went on his drinking binges alone. But he was a man with practical skills, and he built his own tool shed and house and renovated the chicken coop into a two-room shack. He finished the Montagues' cottage, a long, rectangular, utilitarian building with three small, narrow rooms, in time for Helen to come home from the hospital with their first child. There was nothing beautiful or imaginative about Mr. O'Connell's buildings, but he refused to use secondhand materials, and Dorothy had to buy new pine boards, barrels of nails, and tar paper for the roof and sides.

Dorothy asked, "How do we be charitable but write as things really are?" She could only write honestly about Mr. O'Connell after he died in 1952. "The truth was that like many old men, Mr. O'Connell was a terror." Hateful, venomous, suspicious to men and women alike, Mr. O'Connell often spurred Dorothy to ponder on the folly of the Cross. Was it right to let him get away with stealing the tools and locking them up so no one else could use them, and then selling them for drink? But the Worker was Mr. O'Connell's home, and he would come to die at the Easton farm after almost everyone else had gone.

Mr. O'Connell made the altar, the sacristy closet, and the benches for the chapel, which was in the cement barn on the lower farm and had hay bales stacked to one side and the sound of the pigs coming from underneath. Ade Bethune carved the cross and her mother sewed the vestments, and on Friday, July 22, 1938, on the Feast of St. Mary Magdalene, they celebrated Mass for the first time on the farm. The first confession heard was that of Tamar, who sat on a rock on the hill with her confessor, Father Joseph Woods, a young Benedictine priest with a glass eye.

By the end of summer, the barns were full, and there were stoves in all of the bedrooms heated by wood gathered from the eight acres of forest. The trees began to turn to gold and red, the sunlight shone like liquid honey, and the September mists filled the valleys hiding the towns of Easton and Philipsburg from view. The farm hadn't become self-sufficient, but the Workers had put up twenty quarts each of beets and blackberries and were sending pears, apples, potatoes, turnips, and tomatoes to Mott Street.

It was at Easton that Tamar found for herself the heart of the Catholic Worker. She learned all she could from John Filigar about planting and animal husbandry while befriending some of the Worker's most difficult people. On her school holidays she planted roses and radishes and helped care for Helen Montague's growing number of babies. She walked with her mother along the upper pasture, where John was plowing with the horses, and searched for four-leaf clovers with Stanley.

"Life at the farm was beautiful," Stanley said decades later. "We never wanted to go away."

"That whole foolish trip," Tamar called it. "Back to the land while living in chicken coops and tar-paper shacks." But then she added, "I was happy at Easton." It was her dream too and would always be.

CHAPTER SEVEN

Dorothy wrote in the paper of contentment and warm autumn days at Easton and how the "sweet smell of the good earth enwraps one like a garment"; she wrote of the smell of apples and alfalfa in the barn and wood fires in the house, and of canning pickled green tomatoes. But her diary reveals something different. She was often laid low for days by migraine headaches, and she endured bouts of depression, which she tried to fight through with writing and praying.

Of all the bohemians and radicals who had been in her circle in the twenties, Dorothy had embarked on the strangest life of them all. Those Depression-racked thirties had started her on a path that no one, least of all herself, could have anticipated. She had found her own answer to the world's ills through starting the paper, the house of hospitality, and the farm, but it was not easy. People came to the Worker and could not endure it—the lack of room, lack of peace and quiet, lack of beauty, lack of money—and they left.

Both her mother, Grace, and Peggy Baird were shocked when they visited. "It was horribly dingy," Peggy said. "I tried to say something nice about it, but you couldn't really." Maybe that's when Grace said, "Dorothy bites off more than she can chew."

Dorothy asked, how are we going to do the work without our poverty? How are we going to reach people with the teachings of the Gospel? How are we going to pay for printing the paper and buying food for a thousand hungry people daily, unless we do without? They lived and slept crowded together, much coming and going of visitors and of those in need, people sleeping on the floor, with no baths and only cold

water. There was a chronic lack of paint and soap, and an abundance of
bedbugs, cockroaches, rats, and body lice.

"Is this what you mean by houses of hospitality?" she had asked Peter.

"At least it will arouse the conscience," he replied.

Many at the Worker saw no use for voluntary poverty. God never
meant anyone to be poor, Dorothy responded. Voluntary poverty was a
means to an end, not only as a way to reassure those they were helping
that the Worker shared in their poverty and was not simply giving away
what they didn't need, but also as a way of helping to address societal
imbalances. "Take less so others have more," Peter often said. But it was
important to distinguish between poverty and destitution. Large families in the slums of New York lived in two to four dark and badly venti-
lated rooms. They threw their garbage out the windows, and the streets
and alleys smelled of sewage and rotten refuse. The tenement next door
to the Worker, abandoned because of fire violations, collected trash so
deep it blocked light and air. Then because this poverty wasn't all there
was, and this description was unfair to the neighborhood, Dorothy
wrote of all she loved about it, of the colorful pushcarts heaped with
food, the baby carriages lining the curb, the music, and the friendship.

"Where there is no love, put love—and you will find love," says St.
John of the Cross.

As people arrived, Dorothy realized the Workers were accepting the
responsibility of caring for many of them for good. Some came for a
few days or a few months, until they were able to find jobs and homes,
but most were unemployable and would always be. Some found a niche
of duties they would take on at the Worker such as mopping floors or
folding papers, something that gave them a bit of dignity, but Dorothy
did not push this. "We are doing this with no picked group but with the
human material, which has come to hand," she said. Editors, writers,
the young, the old, the unemployed, the lame, the halt, and the blind, all
of whom did not choose one another but somehow had come together.

Some had been at the Worker since its first months and would
come to die there, such as Joe Bennett, who helped distribute the paper
on May Day 1933 and who died of heart failure in 1935 at the age of
twenty-four. They began to lose those they loved and those who weren't

so lovable, like Mr. Breen, but had become part of the family. By 1939 five people had died at the Worker, young and old, of tuberculosis, heart attacks, or just being worn down by long-term, untreated diseases.

As in all families, there was discord. "Trials and trouble-ations," as Farmer John liked to say. There were those in which nothing about the Worker stuck, one of whom was Tom Coddington, who had married Dorothy Weston. In 1937 he tried to take over the Worker while Dorothy Weston sued for part ownership of the paper. (The two Dorothys did reconcile years later.) In the paper, one of the editors wrote about "our dear Miss Day who seems to be better able to guide us from afar than when she is here."

Jim Montague, the farm manager, was discouraged—there was not enough money and too many visitors, sometimes eighty to a hundred on any given summer weekend. There was too much work to be done, and food was rotting on the vine. Tension was growing between the farm and Mott Street over resources, over authority, over the vision.

"All looking," Dorothy wrote in her diary, "for organization instead of self-organization, all of them weary of the idea of freedom and personal responsibility—I feel bitterly oppressed, yet confirmed in my conviction that we have to emphasize personal responsibility at all costs. It is most certainly at the price of bitter suffering for myself. For I am just in the position of a dictator trying to legislate himself out of existence. . . . Freedom—how men hate it and chafe under it; how unhappy they are with it."

At Mott Street, some wanted the resources to go into the paper, which sometimes missed an issue for lack of funds, and not to the men on the line or those staying in the dormitory. People asked why they were feeding those derelicts and freeloaders who would do anything for a drink but not lift a finger to help another. In other words, the Worker was feeding and housing the unworthy poor.

Dorothy's response was to say that the works of mercy are difficult, and no one can attend to them all, but we have the obligation to try. She also said, "Be generous—and lavish. Christ is lavish with His gift to us—why should we fear to be extravagant in return?"

Dorothy could drive the others mad with her extravagance. "Send a cablegram—no, two cablegrams to Spain," she cried, remaining, as a more levelheaded soul described it, "magnificently unconcerned about costs," and who was he "to argue with Miss Day when it was a question of Saint Joseph?" When the bills piled up, everyone took turns heading to the Church of the Most Precious Blood to "picket" St. Joseph for funds. (When Dorothy asked one of the young girls to take her turn at the picketing, the girl asked, "Do I need to carry a sign?")

When the utility company, the phone company, the grocer, or the printer (who once sent his bill with the words "Pray and pay!") called up looking for payment, they were told that St. Joseph would take care of it immediately. The head of the utility company, having received this message from his secretary, wanted to know, "Who is this man Joseph who's paying the bills?"

In 1938 the printing of the paper had reached 160,000, a peak (other than for its fifth anniversary issue in May of 190,000) it would never again achieve as cancellations poured in, in the aftermath of many of Dorothy's controversial talks or when Dorothy's refusal to side with the nationalists in Spain became known or after a picketing or demonstration. (The Worker had led the first mass demonstrations of Catholics, confusing the police, who felt they were arresting the pope himself when they confiscated signs of his quotes.)

They joined anti-Hitler protests and had already been writing articles against Hitler's policies. In 1935, when all Jews were stripped of their rights in Germany, the Catholic Worker, alongside the communists, picketed the German consul and the SS *Bremen*, protesting the persecution of the Jews and the opening of the first concentration camp in 1933, which they had learned about from a priest who had fled Germany. Ade Bethune made the picket signs. Peter's, quoting Pope Pius XI, said, "Spiritually, We're All Semites."

"That was a very good action," Dorothy would say forty years later. In response to Elie Wiesel saying in the 1970s that no one cried out about the Holocaust while it was happening Dorothy said, "But the *Catholic Worker* and *Commonweal* did," though she felt the Worker had not done enough.

Some Catholics either didn't believe the stories coming out of Germany or were attending anti-Semitic meetings in the basement of a Catholic church. At a talk Dorothy gave in which she spoke of the conditions of the Jews in Germany, a woman got up and said, "I don't believe you," and the rest of the audience applauded. When Workers protested anti-Semitic tirades by a priest at the St. Francis of Assisi Church, they were thrown out, and Monsignor Edward Lodge Curran, admirer and, to some, successor of Father Charles Coughlin, the anti-Semitic radio priest, wanted to buy the *Catholic Worker* paper for two thousand dollars, promising increased circulation and large expense accounts.

Then came the investigations and building inspections. Within a year after moving into Mott Street, they were threatened with eviction because of fire code violations and underwent a massive renovation. They knocked out walls, put up partitions, and ripped out the old wooden banisters to make way for steel railings. They enlarged the dining room and kitchen, and the upper floors were made into dormitories, giving people even less privacy than before.

"It is either one kind of poverty or another," Dorothy wrote.

At Easton, Prince the horse died of old age less than a year after they had bought him, and they needed another horse for the spring plowing. They also owed the printers twelve hundred dollars, and a thousand more in bread and grocery bills, and there wasn't a cent in the bank. They shortened the breadline by an hour, and Dorothy bought groceries using her royalty check from *From Union Square to Rome*, which she had been saving to pay the farm mortgage. Joe and Gerry tried to protect Dorothy from the worst of the Worker's woes while she was away giving talks. Joe sometimes had to borrow money from George Shuster, managing editor of *Commonweal* and the man responsible for sending Peter Maurin down to Dorothy that December of 1932.

Dorothy's discouragement, sadness, and sense of failure didn't lift, and she wrote, "Went to confession last night and communion this a.m. but feel a great sense of conflict, almost a beginning of the struggle all over again." To fight this, Dorothy took Tamar and the other children up the hill at the farm to hunt for salamanders.

But these were pinpricks compared to the two big blows of 1939. The first was when Peter left the Worker for a year, and most of the time

Dorothy didn't know where he was. She heard he was in Arkansas and then in Minneapolis traveling from university to university, talking to whoever would listen. Peter had almost walked away from the Worker twice before. When some of the young men wanted to stop wasting money on the house of hospitality and focus on the paper, Peter said to Dorothy, "Let us go. Let us leave this to them." But Dorothy wasn't about to give in. This was her paper, and it was the young men who left. The second time, two men in charge of the house struck others, and Peter said that if he ever again saw such violence, he would leave.

There were many at the Worker who didn't understand Peter, and Dorothy felt that some didn't respect him, though Peter didn't seem to be affected by this. Dorothy herself had some ambivalence about him and his ways. His catchy phrases embarrassed her, and she didn't understand why, when given an opportunity to speak to striking workers, he would go into a scholarly discussion of a French philosopher. Even his clothes bewildered her. But he had taught her many things, including how to have hope that others would listen, and she loved him. Dorothy continued for the rest of her life to refer to Peter as the founder of the Catholic Worker, though at times it seemed out of a need to blame him for having started it all. But it wasn't until the deterioration of Peter's health, and she could no longer talk to him about her problems, that I can see and hear how much she relied on him for support—and it was after his death that I could see how much she missed him.

When Peter left that year of 1939, he had been hurt when people said, "Peter Maurin is the philosopher, and Dorothy interprets him."

He responded, "No one needs to interpret me. I speak plainly."

He felt that the Worker was not reflecting his philosophy and that sometimes Dorothy was too involved in other things to listen to him. She was away traveling a great deal, leaving the dissension behind. People were at odds within the Worker—they hadn't gotten the point. Peter spent two years digging ditches at Easton, patiently placing a few extra tools nearby for others to pick up and help, but no one ever did. Even John Filigar didn't agree with Peter. Scholars weren't becoming workers; workers weren't becoming scholars.

"They don't want me," Peter said sadly.

It wasn't that Peter believed people should agree with everything he said. He understood that people had different concerns and came to different conclusions. But still, he believed we all have something in common, and he wanted everyone from all backgrounds and religions to work together in the search for truth. First, he said, we have to love each other, see each other as people, and see each other's dignity. He loved Dorothy dearly, but he was hurt that even she didn't seem to understand him, and so he left to travel around the country.

It was a difficult year. Dorothy was feeling the weight of trying to help the pale, dirty, and distraught women who showed up at the Worker and of the failure of trying to help the severely alcoholic or the mentally ill who could be better cared for by the hospital psych wards. There was also the day-to-day work at Mott Street and the farm, getting the paper out, and her second book since beginning the Worker, *House of Hospitality*, which she was writing in addition to the column and hundreds of responses to letters to the paper. There were also the speaking engagements on both coasts, which made her psychically ill, as she described it. She doubted herself often. One night in Arkansas she woke up with "a terrible sense of futility and helplessness." Why was she doing this—this speaking and traveling? She asked, "Who am I anyway to be so presumptuous?" And then "a most wonderful sense of the glory of being a child of God swept over me, so joyous a sense of my own importance," which would stay with her for years.

There was also mothering a thirteen-year-old child. The criticism of Dorothy's parenting came fast and hard, but Tamar was not the only one to say that Dorothy did the best she could. Ade Bethune saw this, and she knew more of Dorothy and Tamar's relationship than anyone else.

"Dorothy had collected all these dregs of humanity," Ade said. "This was not an ideal place for a child. People complained—'Dorothy made a terrible mistake. She should never have founded the Catholic Worker, started this nonsense. She owes it to her child to make a home for her.' But then I try to envision that, seeing Dorothy being a very Greenwich Village–type bohemian. Dorothy was not a good housekeeper. She had no sense of stability. If she had not started the Worker, this poor child without the benefit of religion would not have had a happy child-hood anyway. Dorothy had morals, but [they weren't] what the critics thought [they] should be."

Dorothy was sensitive to these criticisms, and ten years later at one particularly low point between mother and daughter, she accused Tamar of propagating stories of neglect. "Remember all those trips we took," she said to her. "To Mexico, Florida, Nova Scotia? You've had a wonderful childhood." But Tamar had not accused her of neglect and never would.

"It was hard for the both of us," Tamar said. "She had her work and yet at the same time she had me, but I wasn't the only child of a single parent sent away to boarding school. She was torn, and she always felt guilty. All her life she felt guilt about everything."

Dorothy was tired and discouraged, and then when Peter left, she withdrew into herself. She missed him, but the only way she knew how to reach him was through an open letter in her column. In the letter, she goes on awhile before getting to what is in her heart and on her mind—the second, much harder blow of that year. "This is truly a woman's let-ter, rambling, not telling the important things first. But one does not like to tell sad news. My father died last week. He was seventy years old, and worked right up to the day before he died."

In her diaries she wrote even less about her father's death: "May 16, Pop ill." He had been sick for three days, but Dorothy did not hear of it until a late-night phone call from Della, and she wasn't able to see her father before he died of heart trouble. After writing "May 17, Pop died this morning 7:30," she wrote nothing more for a month.

Grace and Pop hadn't been living together, and Grace flew up from Florida to attend the funeral with Della, Sam, John, and Dorothy. Only Donald, who was living in Finland, was absent. Pop was well-known and well-respected in the newspaper and turf worlds, and his passing was marked in sports pages around the country, and his ashes were spread on the Belmont racetrack on Long Island. For months after her father's death, Dorothy was in deep shock and felt weak and drained.

That autumn Dorothy sat on a bench drinking hot coffee with the Italian mothers while the babies toddled up and down, enjoying the last days of summer. The air was clear and chilly, the stars shone brightly with a half-moon above Canal Street, brilliant even against the street-lights. Mott Street had become home, drab and densely crowded slum that it was. The neighborhood churches had become involved in the Catholic Worker family, with its growing number of marriages, baptisms, and funerals, and the neighbors celebrated with them.

Dorothy felt weighed down not only by Peter's departure and the death of her father but by the years of unemployment and unrest, and the brewing war, which was beginning to be felt even at the Mott Street house. Two girls who were in trouble, as the saying went, were staying on the fifth floor. One was Jewish and the other a Southerner in love with a blond German waiter and a Nazi sympathizer, and she hung a swastika on the wall of the women's dorm. But somehow the peace was kept between them, and the swastika disappeared.

Germany had just invaded Poland, and within a week ten countries would be at war. And the decade of the thirties, that exuberant beginning of the Catholic Worker, which would remain in many minds its golden age, came to an end with a moment of peace on Mott Street before the firestorm of war.

Part Two

THE
MYSTERY
OF LOVE

CHAPTER EIGHT

Coming out of those first heady years of the Worker, when it mushroomed under the conditions of the Depression, when people thirsted for what Dorothy wrote and what the Worker offered, there occurred a series of missteps between Dorothy and Tamar that, to make things more complex, coincided with a series of what many would call missteps within the Worker. Again, it seemed, Dorothy was beset with restlessness. No matter how extraordinary the Worker's growth had been from the first issue of the paper written in her Fifteenth Street apartment to its explosion of a printing of 160,000 copies to Mott Street to the purchase of the Easton farm followed by houses and farms cropping up all over the country, she still struggled with an interior conflict. Just as family and motherhood, joining the Catholic Church, and doing what was expected of her had not satisfied, there remained something else, something just beyond, that whispered to her, drew her in, and kept her restless.

By the beginning of 1940 many of the quotes Dorothy loved and lived by were in place, and she solidified the framework of beliefs for the Worker. The need to perform the works of mercy, the need to give reason for the faith that is in us, the need to remember we are all members of the Body of Christ, and the need to keep hold of the vision of working for justice. Unions, cooperatives, credit unions, houses of hospitality, and farming communes would minister to the needs of the body, and for the soul, daily Mass to pray and be reminded of the Christ in each other. It was then that she wrote a powerful statement that still echoes down the decades.

"What we do is very little. But it is like the little boy with a few loaves and fishes. Christ took that little and increased it. He will do the rest. What we do is so little we may seem to be constantly failing. But so did He fail. He met with apparent failure on the Cross. But unless the seed fall into the earth and die, there is no harvest. And why must we see results? Our work is to sow."

What was lacking, then? What was it that Dorothy continued to search for, and that led her into what Tamar would come to call her severe-and-pious decade?

Piety. Tamar used to spit the word out, for she was angry, and it took many years for Dorothy to understand Tamar's aversion to it. By the 1940s, faith began to drift into piety, and Tamar felt that this diminished Dorothy's natural vibrancy. That it led her to become judgmental and narrow-minded. Most people when faced with Dorothy's complex and often contradictory character can choose what is most important to them and ignore the rest. But of all the people who knew Dorothy, Tamar was the one who had to live with all of who she was, all her contradictions and paradoxes. She could never throw up her hands and walk away, and she never wanted to, but she had to learn to navigate through much of what she didn't understand and some of what she couldn't abide.

How did this battle between the two of them begin?

The winter of 1939 was the coldest in seventeen years, the war in Europe was worsening, and tensions were yet again rising within the Worker, and Dorothy was under attack. Several grievances grew, one of which would set Tamar on a path that was to be endured, and yet, as is common, had started out benignly enough. There were grievances over leadership and finances. Days went by with no money coming in at all while there were seventy people at Mott Street, and eight hundred to feed on the line. The soup often ran out, and they relied on coffee and cake donated by Macy's department store. The phone was disconnected, and people had to leave messages at the candy store next door. The gas and electricity were about to be turned off, and they owed the printer a thousand dollars. Things were so dire Dorothy thought that maybe Mott Street should be shut down and everyone moved to Easton, though she was able to budget twenty-five cents to Tamar so she could feed her mice.

Easton too was suffering. That winter when Dorothy left on a West Coast speaking tour, which was fueled, rumor had it, by Peter's opposition to Dorothy and her "way of working" (Dorothy missed Tamar's fourteenth birthday along with their tradition of planting radishes, and instead sent Tamar flower seeds), the farm was showing signs of deterioration, demoralization, and apathy. The lower farm was filthy, someone had left seventy-five pillows outside to rot in the snow and rain, along with the tools, and the bees were left to freeze to death.

The farm still retained some glimpses of happiness, hope, and idealism. Dorothy returned home from yet another speaking tour in time for Tamar's graduation from St. Dorothy's. As a graduation present, she gave Tamar her first goat, which Tamar milked throughout the summer while attending, as the youngest student, Peter's classes on farming communes at what they were now calling the CW School. Dorothy visited as much as she could, staying with Tamar in the little cabin, and they took the occasional trip into town to see a Shirley Temple movie. They helped plant two hundred apple trees and took great delight in canning asparagus, beans, tomatoes, berries, and applesauce, and harvesting potatoes, carrots, beets, and corn. And then there was the hay to mow, the cows and goats to milk, bread to bake, and firewood to collect from the woods. Readers of the papers were still interested and still desiring their own return to the land.

Then on a rainy August afternoon at Mott Street, while people sat upstairs in the dining room, Father Pacifique Roy arrived. "Love is the measure by which we shall be judged," he boomed out, catching Dorothy's attention.

Father Roy was a Canadian who lived in Baltimore, Maryland, where he liked to organize interracial basketball games. He was a tall man, well over six feet, lean and handsome, slow and sure in his movements, with warm eyes in a rugged face and the rough hands of a worker. "The only thing necessary is love," he said, and all who walked in the door that day, according to Dorothy, set aside their work and sat down to listen. For her, hearing these words was like falling in love again, but innocent as he was of any such intention and as much as Tamar came to love Father Roy, for he was a simple and good man without guile, he set in motion a rift between Tamar and Dorothy, leaving wounds that would take almost fifty years to heal.

Dorothy invited Father Roy to the Easton farm, and he fell in love with it. He would hitchhike regularly between Baltimore and Easton, sometimes catching lifts from bishops and priests who felt embarrassed to see one of their own out on the road, robes flapping in the wind and thumb out for a ride. Father Roy was a practical man, and he arrived with carpenter and plumbing tools. He had a passion for work and over the years had built schools and churches, sawmills and feed mills, in the Gaspé Peninsula in Quebec and in the Louisiana swamps. The Easton farm was still in such a state of poverty and hardship that the austerities he preached were more comfortable than the reality, and so he got to work wiring the farm for electricity and installing a stove in the kitchen to keep people warm as they ate. He piped water from a spring on the hillside to the house and barn, and built a dormitory for the young women with an indoor staircase so they didn't have to walk outside to get to the dining room. He built a chapel in the barn at the lower farm and cemented over the floor and the cow stalls to create a dining room, living room, and kitchen all in one. He built a fireplace and chimney that warmed not only the sitting room but the chapel and dormitories. And he placed a six-foot cross on the highest point of the farm, where it could be seen by all the neighboring farms. Father Roy also loved to sing French folk songs while he worked. "One must reach people in many ways, you know," he said. He threw parties and celebrated many feast days.

Both Stanley and Tamar loved him and appreciated all he brought to the Worker. "He did everything to make life more comfortable for us," Stanley said. Tamar agreed. "We had nothing at Easton until Father Roy came," she said.

During the summer of 1939 Easton had held a retreat, a period of six days of silence and conferences. By then Dorothy had become so enamored of the retreats that she strongly encouraged, or insisted on, or demanded the presence of all Workers who could make it. Seventy people showed up, some traveling from the West Coast, taking the bus or hitchhiking.

After Father Roy's arrival, Dorothy insisted that he begin leading retreats in which he preached a life of asceticism and detachment from worldly pleasures, and the need for penance, without which you could not see God. He believed in bread-and-water fasts during his retreats, but Dorothy drew the line when he tried to eliminate coffee. Black coffee kept them awake for conferences, she said, but didn't mention that not only she but the entire Worker ran on coffee, despite Peter's exhortation to eat locally. "No matter how broke we were," Stanley said, "we always had coffee."

Father Roy also disapproved of having a radio (coffee and a radio—it is hard to imagine Dorothy without either one of them). It let in too much of the world and that made for tepidity, and God vomits the lukewarm out of his mouth. But Father Roy also believed that the fast should be followed by a feast, and at the conclusion of the retreats, he'd walk the four miles into town with empty burlap bags to beg for meat, fish, and leftover vegetables at the markets.

Father Roy wasn't happy with his ability to lead retreats. He loved people, and he loved to be building and tinkering, hammering and sawing, sometimes until midnight. But he felt he was not a speaker or a teacher, and he was not an intellectual like most of the young priests showing up at the Worker. He told Dorothy that if she wanted a truly good retreat, she must invite Father John Hugo. Dorothy had already heard of Father Hugo through Sister Peter Claver Fahy, the nun who had given Dorothy one of the very first donations and who spoke about something called "the Doctrine." She gave Dorothy her notes of retreat talks given by Father Hugo, a man of thirty and a college chaplain in Pittsburgh, Pennsylvania, and by Father Onesimus Lacouture, a Jesuit from New England who had spent years in the Yukon, and when he emerged from the wilderness began retreats for priests. Within ten years, more than five thousand priests had made the retreat. Father Roy, then on the verge of leaving the priesthood, was one of those priests, and, as he said to Dorothy, meeting Father Lacouture turned his life around.

Sister Peter Claver's retreat notes didn't impress Dorothy at that time as she preferred to go for her spiritual instruction to the New Testament and to the saints. But she took Father Roy's advice, and the summer of 1941 she traveled to Pittsburgh to attend Father Hugo's retreat, and as a result was led in a direction that, according to Tamar, brought about the ruination and rejection of all that was good and beautiful.

"The retreat was cruel," Tamar said, "and the only good to come out of it was that Dorothy quit smoking."

Dorothy had been smoking two packs a day for years when Father Roy announced, "Stop smoking for the love of God," while, Stanley claimed, a pair of twin Irish priests from Texas handed out cigarettes saying, "Have a cigarette for the love of God." Dorothy prayed for six months to lose the desire to smoke, and her prayers were answered. She not only never had a cigarette again but, she claimed, no longer had the desire for one, though for several years she took up knitting to keep her hands busy.

It was an odd meeting between Father Hugo and Dorothy Day, one a young priest for whom love seemed an intellectual exercise and the other a middle-aged woman whose capacity to love seemed bound-less. The basic teaching of the retreat was to develop purity of inten-tion and to do everything for the love of God. This required giving up anything done for your own reward, the natural motive, and doing it only for a reward from God, the supernatural motive. "The best thing to do with the best things in life is to give them up," Father Hugo said. And the spiritual life required a deliberate break with every last attach-ment, for even one attachment was one too many. This meant absolute distrust of self and absolute trust in God, and the tools required were prayer, spiritual reading, and spiritual direction. Father Hugo rewrote the beatitudes, Dorothy's beloved beatitudes, and instead of blessings they became condemnations. Blessed are the poor in spirit became a condemnation of those who put their hearts in earthly wealth. Blessed are the meek became a condemnation of those who put their hearts in bodily comforts. Blessed are they that mourn was a condemnation of those who put their hearts in natural joys. You were to have contempt for the world, and all that was natural was to be condemned.

Father Lacouture, for his part, was a warm and likable fellow who loved his family. As a young seminarian in the wilds of the Yukon, he had been surrounded by simple people and by beauty and solitude. He then brought this simplicity of beauty and spirit back to a world in which priests were living luxurious lives, and he was shocked by it.

The retreat did not go down well with either Hugo's or Lacouture's superiors. They were accused, among other things, of "inexactitude of expression" that caused people to go to extremes in mortification, which Dorothy admitted happened. One young man at Easton practiced penances by rolling in the brambles at night. Because of the controversy, invitations for Dorothy to speak at seminaries began to dry up. Even Sister Peter Claver was forbidden by her superiors to see Dorothy, but neither she nor Dorothy made much of it, and over the years the ban wasn't so much lifted as it just faded away.

Father Hugo quoted Dorothy as saying that the retreat was a fore-taste of heaven, that it gave her courage to persevere, and it was like hearing the Gospel for the first time. "Dorothy," he said at a memorial Mass given for her, "now had almost all that she desired—a program of action that would merge her concern for the neediest with her hunger for God. . . . Even after her newly founded movement was already flour-ishing, she yearned for the fullness of love, an all-encompassing love, still to be brought to her by the Church she had chosen and entered." Then he quoted Sister Peter Claver: "The retreat is what made the wheels go round in the Worker movement. It is what led Dorothy to holiness."

Tamar could never understand Sister Peter Claver's enthusiasm for a doctrine that focused on all that was negative. "She didn't get the harsh-ness of the retreat. At the end of your life you realize that you do have to give everything up, but in the meantime, you have to live."

Sixty-five people from houses around the country attended Father Hugo's first retreat at Easton in the summer of 1941. The day began with a sung Mass followed by a series of five conferences of one hour each and fifteen minutes of silent prayer. If you needed to read, the only book was the New Testament, though this later was loosened to include a handful of other books. Between conferences, retreatants worked on the farm, as Dorothy preferred retreats where there was physical work to be done. The retreats did bring in better food. Most meals at Easton were bread and black coffee for breakfast and lunch, and roast groundhog or pigs' feet in a thin soup with bread and applesauce for dinner. Or on the lean days, they ate oatmeal twice a day, and the oats were so rough, John Filigar had to cook them for twenty-four hours in a double boiler. But during the retreats, they had milk, meat, bread, and rice.

The retreat, which lasted for seven days, required absolute silence. This was meant for people to be alone with the word of God, without argument and only to listen. Without silence, the retreat was a waste of time. This wasn't a problem for either Tamar or Stanley. Dorothy claimed that mothers loved the silence while the men were oppressed by it. Aldous Huxley sent the Worker a contribution of five dollars, saying, "Anybody who does something for silence, as you are doing, is performing a real act of charity." It was through silence that the Holy Spirit spoke, but it being the Worker, silence was hard to come by. Father Hugo claimed that the Catholic Worker's greatest attachment was not to smoking or even to coffee but to talking. "It was pretty hard to get silence at the CW, so you didn't fuss too much," he said, whereas Father Lacouture would kick even a bishop out of his retreats if he wasn't silent.

"To us," Dorothy wrote, "the retreat was good news."

She knew, though, what others felt about it. All those who were closest to Dorothy made the retreat, but they all came to reject it. Peter was silent on the subject, but then, he avoided controversy and conflict and seems to have attended only one retreat. (Father Hugo couldn't understand Peter and went no further than to read Peter's Easy Essays.) Stanley drew the line at being told that he who loves the world is an enemy of God. "What kind of a religion is this where God creates beauty, and then tells us you can't have it?"

To Ade the retreat was too intellectual and did not lead her to love God more. "How do you tie your shoe for love of God?" she asked. She preferred St. Benedict, who didn't believe people needed to go through "tricks of difficulty." Dorothy told Ade that in life you had to work against yourself, but Ade disagreed. Look for good things to do, she said. Those are guaranteed to be difficult, and you do them despite their difficulty not because of it. But Ade didn't argue with Dorothy, for she recognized that Dorothy needed the retreats. They allowed her to get away from "her hell-bent situation," one of Ade's pithy descriptions of the Worker. She knew Dorothy didn't bother with the theological nuts and bolts. "She just loved a peaceful time to think about divine mysteries." But the retreats, Ade felt, emphasized what Dorothy already had more than enough of at the Worker—austerity and penance. Ade did argue with Father Hugo. "No amount of hatred can ever produce the love of God," she wrote to him. She didn't like the language of the retreat, and she didn't believe taking it could lead to conversion, while Father Hugo believed that Dorothy had undergone a deep conversion because of it.

Father Joseph Woods, who since 1938 had been spending his summers at Easton and had celebrated the first Mass there, and who heard Tamar's confession on a rock on the hillside, also rejected the retreat. He was a Benedictine at a priory in Rhode Island, young and fresh out of the seminary, who had once told Dorothy, "The moral theology we are taught is to get us to heaven with scorched behinds." Father Woods liked to sell the *Catholic Worker* on the streets without wearing his Roman collar, and when he visited Mott Street, he stayed at a Bowery flophouse. He was keenly aware of the problems at Easton, especially when the men drank and how it affected the women. As a Benedictine, he became unhappy with Dorothy's swallowing the retreat, hook, line, and sinker, as Ade put it. He participated in Father Hugo's first retreat after lodging his objections, saying the proper time for such things was Lent. Beauty, friendship, all these things are good, he said, while Dorothy felt he was attacking all she was working for in the movement.

The retreat was meant to be shock treatment, and for Tamar it was. At Dorothy's insistence, Tamar made the retreat every year starting when she was fourteen and just beginning to be introduced by her mother to art, music, and books. For a teenager filled with love and wonder for the natural world and for the liveliness contained within the Worker and within her mother, being told to give up everything that was good was devastating. The nuns at St. Dorothy's had impressed upon Tamar the need to find a vocation based on what she liked to do. No, Father Hugo said. Do what you *don't* like doing. Ade Bethune was the only one to say to Tamar during this time, "You need to first find out who you are."

The retreat was about afflicting the comfortable, but it could also, in its rigor, which included all-night vigils and fasting, afflict the afflicted. It could lead people to despair for fear that they wouldn't get into heaven, and it created a rift in the Worker between those who had made the retreat and those who hadn't, and between those who had given up smoking and those who hadn't.

By the mid-forties, Hugo and Lacouture were forbidden to give their retreats. Father Hugo's papers were locked up, and he was sent away from areas of influence and controversy, as his bishop explained to him. He remained at his parish in Pittsburgh for the rest of his life, while Father Lacouture was sent to an Indian reservation in northern New York. There he could administer the sacraments but wasn't allowed to teach. This didn't worry Dorothy much as she knew that archbishops had put a stop to quite a few "good and wise" men over the centuries. The ban was eventually lifted, and Father Hugo would once again lead retreats from the sixties until his death in 1985.

At the time Dorothy became enamored of the retreats, she was under criticism from within the Worker and from without. She was repeatedly called to the chancery office beginning with the Spanish Civil War, when Franco was seen by many Catholics as the rescuer of the Church. Her pacifist position on this war lost them subscriptions to the paper. She was also assailed for it from the other direction by her leftist friends, and a rift formed between Dorothy and her brother John that took years to heal. Then there was the gradual loss of Peter's support after his return from his mysterious year away when his health began to decline. With the increasing likelihood of the United States entering World War II, her pacifist stance was creating deep dissension within the Worker, leaving her feeling alone and opposed. Maybe she needed a solid spiritual base on which to stand and ponder all the complex questions she was expected to have answers for, and the retreat gave her that ground. She was able to take what she needed from Father Hugo and leave the rest.

The process of conversion is a strange path, and perhaps Dorothy could not at that time have had the strength to continue without the retreats. In photos of the early years, Dorothy often seems to have this deep sadness about her. Maybe because of her lonely wandering as a young woman and her awful mistakes, she was trying to find a way of making sense of and enduring the choice she made leaving Forster, who was still on her mind.

But the retreat conferences were grounded in theological discussions given by highly educated intellectuals (and sometimes these conferences seemed to Dorothy to be priests preaching to priests), and she did not operate that way. As with all creative people, many of Dorothy's ideas were genius and many disastrous, but it was when she tried to follow her intellect by overthinking and overanalyzing, and not following her instinct, that she most often failed. While Father Hugo spoke of austerity, she was more often guided by the soul's profound need for beauty, and her desire for an austere spiritual life contrasted with the needs and desires of those who came for help, both workers and guests. Ultimately the severity of the retreat would not be of help for those coming to the soup line, which she slowly came to recognize, and the delight and enthusiasm of St. Teresa of Avila would prevail over Father Hugo.

At Dorothy's death, it was suggested that Father Hugo conduct her funeral Mass, as Dorothy had asked him in 1976, the last time she made the retreat. Tamar, still reeling from her mother's death and before she could soften all the years of anger toward Father Hugo, found herself blurting out, "If he comes, I won't." She later regretted her vehemence, but she and Father Hugo never reconciled.

After Tamar's death I found in her bureau clothes that looked to be from the thirties and forties, flowery and bright dresses that I could only guess were Dorothy's, as Tamar would have been too young. They gave me a glimpse of Dorothy before she began to dress more somberly, more religiously. Couldn't she have seen what this doctrine would do to her child? A child who had already had to give up her father and had to learn to share her mother with thousands of others?

What, I want to ask my mother, was the best thing you felt you were being asked to give up?

Father Hugo liked to quote Luke 14:26, often within Tamar's hearing, "If anyone comes to me and does not hate his father and mother, his wife and children, his brothers and sisters—yes, even his own life—he cannot be my disciple." And I know the answer to my question. Tamar was asked to give up Dorothy—to give up Dorothy the mother for Dorothy the saint.

CHAPTER NINE

In Tamar's mind, first the retreats and then the war brought an end to those idyllic years of the Catholic Worker. During the summer of 1940, while Tamar was happily milking her goat and attending Peter's school, it became obvious that the war in Europe was not going to bypass the United States, and Dorothy went down to Washington, DC, to testify at a Senate Military Affairs hearing in support of Catholic conscientious objector status. But this was not a united Catholic Worker position. Dissent was so profound with what many viewed as Dorothy's uncompromising stance that tales of the *Catholic Worker* being destroyed at some of the other CW houses trickled in. Hurt and angry, Dorothy wrote a letter to all the houses telling them that if they wanted to be a part of the Catholic Worker, they must distribute the paper whether they agreed with her pacifism or not. That it was their duty to do so, and that those who didn't want to do so must disassociate themselves from the Catholic Worker.

Dorothy immediately regretted the letter. She called a meeting at Easton during which she said that as a result of the Catholic Worker's opposition to the war and to conscription, the government would probably crack down on them, and people were liable to go to jail. She added that anyone who didn't want to risk this should disassociate from the Worker. At this point, some people, believing they had the right to voice their say regardless, left.

In September 1940 the conscription bill was passed, in October draft registration began, and most of the Worker's young men left to enter training or to become conscientious objectors. By the end of 1941, while life on Mott Street remained largely unchanged, many of the houses and farms around the country were closing down, and people blamed it on Dorothy. Even the town of Easton turned against them, and the police were on the lookout for any reason to arrest those on the farm. Hurt and defensive, she insisted at one point that the withdrawal of support came more from people's belief that they were helping the undeserving poor rather than as a result of her pacifism. The Baltimore house closed in part because of their interracial work, she said, but also because the two men in charge were drafted and were now working in a mental hospital as conscientious objectors, as had happened in other houses and farms. She rejected the claim that half of the houses closed because of her pacifism, and she said circulation of the paper fell after cutting back on bundles, which had bulked up the numbers. But even she must have been hard put to believe that this was the sole cause. In 1941 printing had plunged to 75,000, and by 1945 it would be at 50,000.

While writing *The Long Loneliness* years later, Dorothy was able to look more honestly at the times, and she wrote that maybe it would have been better to remain silent and pray. "Men are not ready to listen," Peter said to her, and he may have been right. "But I do not know," she wrote. "God gives us our temperaments, and in spite of my pacifism, it is natural for me to stand my ground."

But these were hard years for Dorothy when she felt attacked from all sides. Little to nothing remains of her diaries from 1942 through 1944, perhaps because she destroyed them or perhaps because she was so low she couldn't write.

After Tamar's graduation from St. Dorothy's in June 1940, she attended Immaculata High School on Thirty-Third Street for a year while living at Mott Street and spending every free moment she could at Easton. The young men started to fall in love with Tamar for she was turning into a beautiful girl, and it was with the arrival of one of these young men, Dwight Larrowe, that Dorothy began to notice. Dwight saw a quiet and intelligent young girl whom he would drive out to Easton or to a craft school where she was learning tin work and soldering. They danced together at the folk dances held at Mott Street, and he wooed her delicately and brought her bags of candy. Dwight asked Tamar to marry him, though she was only fifteen, and maybe it was his proposal that prompted Dorothy to take Tamar out of Immaculata and send her to Canada, where she entered her into a convent school an hour outside Montreal. It was hard for Dorothy to leave Tamar in Canada, though she told herself it was not so far away. An overnight bus trip.

"I was never so unhappy," Dorothy wrote, "never felt so great a sense of loneliness. She was growing up. She was growing up to be married. . . . I was always having to be parted from her. No matter how many times I gave up mother, father, husband, brother, daughter, for His sake, I had to do it over again."

It was the influence of a priest that sent Tamar so far away from her mother and the Worker, even though by that time Dorothy knew priests' limitations. She liked to quote a priest, "no one gets up to the pulpit without promulgating heresy," and she had a habit of talking to them in her mind as they gave homilies, correcting and contradicting them. Nevertheless, she began to make decisions about Tamar based on advice from priests, a course that would set the stage for misery, first by compelling Tamar to attend the retreats and then sending her, at the age of fifteen, far away from all that she loved, to attend a French-speaking school with only one week of French classes to prepare her. For Tamar, it was the first exile of many from the Catholic Worker.

Dorothy claimed it was Tamar's initiative to go to Canada because she was in rebellion against the school system and city life. The plan was that when she turned sixteen the following spring she would settle at Easton, help with the cooking and gardening, teach spinning and weaving, and care for the animals as John Filigar was talking of leaving for a job.

Dorothy heard Tamar say: "Why wasn't I a retarded child so that I could go to one of these schools where they teach crafts?" While Tamar tried to say: "You think I'm one of these retarded children to be sent off to a school where they teach crafts." Tamar would always feel she didn't measure up to Dorothy's expectations and that Dorothy underestimated her intelligence because she was not articulate and couldn't make herself understood. And because Dorothy believed Tamar wasn't bright, she took the advice of a priest who told her that French Canadian schools for girls were the best. For a tuition of eighteen dollars a month, the sisters taught spinning, weaving, dyeing, sewing, knitting, and cooking. According to Dorothy's understanding, to graduate the girls had to be able to spin, weave, and sew a suit of clothes. The school also emphasized housework in the expectation that the girls would go on to raise large families.

At the convent Tamar was so shielded from events that she would not find out about the bombing of Pearl Harbor until Dorothy picked her up for the Christmas holidays. There was such strict separation between boys and girls that they weren't allowed to see glimpses of each other, and excursions outside were carefully timed. She had to bathe in a cotton shift as the girls weren't allowed to be naked. The hardest part, though, was the language barrier, and Tamar hardly spoke a word the entire time she was there. The other girls laughed at her, and the fainting spells she had experienced at the Oak Knoll school began again. Still, she learned how to cook, spin flax, knit, and weave, and she knitted a pair of knee warmers and wove a scarf for Dorothy. Dorothy told Tamar to read history during her free time, but Tamar was unhappy, so she read novels that Dwight sent to her, holding them on her lap under the desk to read during classes. *Sense and Sensibility*, *Villette*, *Kristin Lavransdatter*, and *The Scandal of Father Brown* got her through the worst of the winter. She read *Pride and Prejudice* in three days followed by *A Tale of Two Cities*, *Wuthering Heights*, and *The Swiss Family Robinson*—and during her last month there, *Martin Chuzzlewit*.

At the end of March Dorothy went to Montreal in the midst of a blizzard to retrieve Tamar along with her new spinning wheel and loom. On the way home they visited Dwight, who was at a camp for conscientious objectors in New Hampshire where he had become a leader in the task of obtaining conscientious objector status for Catholics. Dwight had written Tamar almost every week while she was in Canada and sent her books at a time he and others at the camp were on the verge of a starvation so severe their camp was forced to close. For much of her life she kept one book on gardening that he had given her for her sixteenth birthday.

Tamar returned to Easton and her small cottage and took up her role caring for the animals. She planted herbs, flowers ("flower colors cannot clash," she told Dorothy), and vegetables around her place, while Dorothy took off on a speaking tour, leaving one of the more stable couples, Eva and Victor Smith, to keep a watch on her. "Tamar is lonely," Eva wrote Dorothy, while Victor wrote, "Tamar is well, and a great help and getting to be quite a talker. That seems to be news."

Tamar had returned home to find five families living on the upper farm and half a dozen single men on the lower farm, which Dorothy now called the retreat center in the face of the farming commune's failure. All the young men and many of the homeless men had been called up and were gone.

"All the strong men were sent off to war," Tamar said, "while all the damaged ones remained."

Joe Zarrella, house manager at Mott Street, married a girl he had met at the Worker (there would be seven marriages that year) and was accepted by the American Field Service ambulance corps. Gerry Griffin, the other manager at Mott Street, also became a driver in the ambulance corps. Joe wrote to Dorothy from a Red Cross hospital ship, and Gerry thought of Tamar whenever he saw goats eating debris. Other Catholic Worker men were in training in the signal corps, a machine-gun division, and in a commando division in Texas, or sent off to Australia, the Solomon Islands, or England. Even though Dorothy was heartbroken over the young men heading to war, she published their letters in the paper, and they all would return to the Worker on their furloughs.

Then, inexplicably to Dorothy, Dwight gave up his CO status and while waiting to be called up, he lived at Mott Street. He also decided that he had a vocation for the Trappists and hoped to get into the monastery before being grabbed by the army, but he was drafted as an infantry private. "Dirty fighting with bayonets," as he described it. He was wounded by shrapnel and received the Purple Heart. Many years later, he said, "I realized I wasn't a pacifist because I had a lot of anger." He was angry at Dorothy for reasons he didn't articulate at the time, but abruptly changed his position about the war two months before Tamar, just turned eighteen, married another man.

On her return from Montreal, Tamar met a twenty-eight-year-old man, David Hennessy, living at the lower farm who had been lured to Easton by Eva Smith's farm column in the *Catholic Worker*. Eva was a physically strong woman in her late twenties, with dark hair and round glasses. She was the daughter of a German military officer who, after he divorced Eva's Jewish mother, became the head of Lufthansa. Labeled a "non-Aryan Christian" by the Nazis, Eva and her mother fled Germany in 1939. Eva's husband, Vic, a lantern-jawed man with a shock of hair, was, as Tamar said, the kind of person who would move in with someone else and call it community. He came from an upper-class Rhode Island family and was a well-educated journalist who, for a brief time, became a Trappist novice until he had a nervous breakdown and disappeared from the monastery. He came to the Worker in 1939, and Eva arrived soon after. They were married within a year and moved to Easton. The following winter the first of their ten children was born at the hospital in Easton, and all the remaining children would be born at the farm.

Eva wrote in loving detail of the farm, and that got the attention of David, a city fellow from Washington, DC, who was drawn to the agrarian life and the philosophy of distributism, an English land movement propounded by G. K. Chesterton, Hilaire Belloc, Eric Gill, and other writers popular at the Worker since 1936. With David's arrival, those in Easton added "our fathers"—Gill, Belloc, and Chesterton—to what they'd previously taken to calling "the M's": Mauriac, Mounier, and Maritain. David was so full of enthusiasm for distributism that there would be a dialogue at the Worker, for and against, that would last fifteen years. It meant a great deal to him that "the great Belloc," as he referred to him, was interested in the Worker and had lunched with Dorothy, which Dorothy would remind David of at fractious moments.

David was the only son, along with seven younger sisters, of working-class parents. He was a devout and traditional Catholic and, though he never finished high school, he was a reader and a thinker with a phenomenal memory who liked to quote in Latin and German. He also seemed driven to get in trouble by saying what he felt was the truth. He loved to write and as a teenager had organized his friends into a club of letter and diary writers, though he would never come to touch a typewriter. By 1936 he was in correspondence with a good number of contemporary writers including Ezra Pound and Eric Gill, and he had subscribed to the *Catholic Worker* almost from its inception. He was also a follower of Father Coughlin's radio shows, although, to his credit, he stopped listening when the priest began his deeply racist rants. After David had dropped out of high school at age seventeen, his father found him a job in the government printing office, one of those "good" jobs that would have taken care of him for life. (His sisters also would all find good government jobs, including at the Pentagon.) But after nine years he either quit or lost his job, and in November 1941 he headed to the Easton farm, called by the Worker's agrarian idealism and back-to-the-land movement. But, as Tamar described it, his attraction came more from the desire to be a laird of the land rather than from any real interest or ability in farming. He wasn't a worker with farming skills but a scholar with a library on English agrarians, decentralists, and distributists. "A very good library," Tamar said. "One of the best in the country," Dorothy said.

David impressed Eva with his help on the farm, but after several months, David found the Worker too radical ("I'm not one of that unholy trinity—anarchist, pacifist, and distributist," he would come to say to Dorothy). He left to attend a family wedding and while away decided to return only to pick up his books. It was one of those odd, throwaway strokes of fate that David arrived back at Easton just as Dorothy sent Tamar to the farm with Peter, who was recovering from a stroke. David fell in love with Tamar and stayed.

"Dorothy returned from a speaking tour to find me thick with Dave Hennessy," Tamar said. (In her later years, Tamar always referred to her husband as "Dave Hennessy.")

David was different from all the young men Tamar knew and who had surrounded Dorothy from the beginning of the Worker. Here was someone who wasn't in awe of her mother, and his biting comments made Tamar laugh. David was sarcastic and contrary and liked to stir things up, and he was not called up to fight in the war. Not a pacifist, he had enlisted but was rejected. And maybe Tamar was still hurting from her exile to Canada and angry at her mother. She was still angry about the retreats, and David agreed—he referred to them as that "damnable Doctrine."

"By the end of the summer," Tamar said, "I had decided I wanted to get married, and I roped him in. He had cold feet, but his confessor insisted he had to get married. What a bunch of loonies!"

Dorothy, frightened and unsure, said that Tamar could marry only when she turned eighteen in two years' time. David was willing to wait, and so he remained at Easton. Dorothy asked Forster to help stop the marriage, but he was concerned with only the war, and he didn't understand what she was getting so upset about.

"Let her do what she wants," he said. "It's not a matter of life or death."

"He didn't think as a Catholic would about these things," Tamar said. "And I thought I wanted to get married, have lots of babies, live on the farm. We both were in love with the idea of Catholic families on the land, and the distributist model of local, non-mechanized farming and community. We also thought we had to save our souls by getting married. But I knew David didn't like the Worker."

Dorothy was uneasy about David. Not only was he thirteen years older than Tamar, but he drank, and she was already witnessing several Catholic Worker marriages sinking under the weight of alcohol. She wrote to Tamar, "I strongly disapprove of the way you are sitting around all summer doing nothing, not even weeding your garden. . . . This protest on my part has nothing to do with Dave. As far as I know him, he is perfectly all right, but my protest is the way you are wasting your time and devoting yourself exclusively to him." She then added, "You know yourself you should have regard for my wishes, even my orders, on this subject."

Dorothy wrote to Ade in Rhode Island suggesting that she take on David as a printer, but it was Tamar who, at Ade's mother's suggestion, headed up to Newport. Ade had been thinking of providing a home for Tamar since 1935 when Tamar had spent part of the summer with her, but Dorothy had told Ade then that while she did not want Tamar to become a victim of Dorothy's strange career, Tamar was too young to be sent away.

Compelling Tamar to attend the retreats and then sending her away to Canada had been poor decisions, but in Dorothy's desire to remove Tamar from David's influence and give her a chance to grow up, sending her to Ade's was the best thing Dorothy could have done. It would turn out to be, according to Tamar, the happiest year of her life, but ultimately the plan failed.

Ade created and led an art apprenticeship program in 1939 she called the Preparatory School for Women Returning to the Land, which Peter Maurin affectionately called the Regressive School for Backward Studies. Half a dozen girls from the Worker attended, and Dorothy felt all the Catholic Worker girls should spend a winter studying with Ade, where there was never an idle moment, and Ade expected the girls to lead as disciplined a life as she did.

"Scrubbed and industrious," Dorothy enviously described Ade's studio, where the girls slept on cots and cooked on a coal stove. It was one of the more interesting outcroppings of the Worker, although unlike the other houses it had no breadline or house of hospitality, and its emphasis was on art, crafts, and skills for simple living.

Working under the gaze of the saints Ade had painted on the walls and with her stained-glass art flooding the studio with color in the morning sun, the apprentices were taught how to draw simple items, such as a hammer, a lamp, or a stairway. They learned calligraphy and how to make their own pens with reeds and quills. They cut up rags for hooked rugs while discussing war, conscription, and labor unions. They made book covers, woodcuts, bookplates, engravings, and wood carvings and built their own beds. They learned how to split wood, garden, and raise chickens and rabbits, and they had weekly classes on metaphysics taught by one of the monks from a nearby priory.

The girls took turns shopping, cooking, and cleaning for a week at a time so that the others were free to concentrate on art. There were two rules to shopping—don't buy any canned goods except tomatoes and tomato paste, and don't spend more than $1.50 per person per week. "A practical way of learning to live in the spirit of poverty," Ade said. But as spartan as the life was, there was plenty of food, and mealtimes were happy affairs. They ate potatoes, tomatoes, soup, and brown bread, and meat once a week. They grew garlic, marjoram, and thyme, and Ade's mother provided apple, grape, and quince jam and taught them how to sew, bake bread, and make Belgian lace.

When the weather was good, they went for walks along the cliffs, had picnics, and explored the coastline. In the evenings they listened to Bach, Beethoven, Gregorian chants, and sea shanties. They held parties and square dances for the sailors on leave, and they visited wounded soldiers at the naval hospital and were visited by refugees fleeing the Nazis.

The girls all loved Ade. She was warm, funny, loving, well educated, and an accomplished and successful artist. She was full of enthusiasm for everything she did—her art, her animals, her garden, her girls. She believed in doing work for others out of love and with skill and creativity, and she believed that everyone was an artist.

Within a month Tamar was cooking, shopping, and running errands to the library and post office, tasks that had been impossible before because of her shyness. She was spinning, printing, chopping wood, caring for the chickens and rabbits, and making a small loom. She even made Christmas cards for Father Hugo. She cared for Michael, the pet rat who ran loose on the studio workbench while Tamar worked on reducing Ade's Stations of the Cross with a pantograph. She baked potatoes while on kitchen duty and left them in the oven until they turned to burned shells. She danced with the sailors and collected mussels on the beach. Within two months Ade was leaving Tamar in charge of the studio when she had to travel to work on commissions. Tamar, though, was still shy and quiet, and the other apprentices didn't come to know her very well. "A very, very pretty girl," one would describe her, but that was all she could say.

Tamar and Dorothy continued the postcard exchange they had begun in Montreal (daily for Dorothy, twice a week for Tamar). Tamar was learning calligraphy and used it to write a few of her postcards but soon gave up and reverted to her terse notes and terrible handwriting, which Dorothy chastised her unfairly for, considering the state of Dorothy's own handwriting. "Why should I write longer postals?" Tamar asked. "I have nothing to say and my writing gets worse."

She was always working on gifts for her mother—a knitted sweater and dress, a hand-lettered copy of the words of Christ at the Last Supper bound in sailcloth, a chapter from the English artist Eric Gill's essay "What Is Christianity?" which Dorothy viewed as the result of too much of David's influence.

Dorothy came up to visit as often as she could and, as Tamar put it, offer unhelpful advice. "She was certain that when she was a child they used channel coal in the grates, but she mistakenly sent Ade off to buy soft coal, which was an entirely different thing. And we're trying to cook with this and keep warm in winter. It was a disaster. Coal dust everywhere in an art studio!"

Tamar loved Ade, who was a breath of sensible air after the rarefied atmosphere of the retreats, and she in turn provided Tamar with a contrasting philosophy and a life more in line with the Benedictines. Ade understood everything, Tamar said—her shyness, her complex love for her mother, her need for stability. She also understood Tamar's desire to study biology, as many in the Bethune family were scientists. "The artist and the scientist," Tamar said, "what a marvelous combination." Ade had wanted Tamar to return to high school and acquire the necessary education, but Dorothy would have none of it.

Dorothy later claimed that Ade's suggestion that Tamar return to high school "was the thunderbolt that started the whole thing off." To Tamar she said it had been quite a wrench to take her out of high school in the first place, and now she was talking about returning. In June 1943, when Tamar had been at Ade's for seven months, Dorothy began to put her mind to Tamar's next step, and she wrote to Ade saying that she knew how happy Tamar was, but added, "she's apt to get in a rut and get a bit spoiled for the rigorous life."

"I was happy there," Tamar later agreed, "but Dorothy came and decided that she wanted me back. She was always wanting me back." Dorothy's letters reveal some of what Tamar had to live with—jealousy, high-handedness, and contradiction, along with love and concern.

Tamar, though, was not the same girl who in Canada had lived for her mother's daily correspondence.

"The general consensus of opinion," Dorothy wrote, "is that you are a docile creature and easily led, but I do know also that you know what you want very decidedly." She then followed this with a statement that took the possibility of self-determination away from Tamar, who was considering becoming a nurse, though she actually wanted to be a doctor: "And I think what you want is farming and a country life more than nursing and a city life."

For two months they corresponded, but only Dorothy's half remains. By July, Dorothy talked about the possibilities of high school or taking science and math at the Farmingdale agricultural college on Long Island. "What do you want to do? Would you like to stay at Newport another year? You love it there, I know. Ade would love to have you, she says, and you could earn your way." But then Dorothy adds something Tamar would have had a hard time rejecting, "My selfish reason for wanting you at Farmingdale this winter is so as to have you near me." And she keeps at it. "I'm all in favor of the idea if [Farmingdale] will take you with what credits you have. . . . I know you are happy at Ade's but you cannot be a child all your life, and I disagree with her idea that high school will help you. I do not think it will. I also think you are more mature than she and her mother think. I have seen you for seventeen years to their one, and I do think that no matter how mistaken mothers may be, they do know their daughters a little better than others."

Dorothy saw no reason for Tamar to return to high school. "My two brothers went one year to high school," she wrote, "and were practically illiterate when they launched themselves into the world. Now one is the editor of the *Journal American* here and the other speaks four languages and has been a foreign correspondent for twenty years. This high school business is the bunk."

A week later, maybe in response to Tamar continuing to fight her, Dorothy turned against Ade. "Your writing continues atrocious in spite of a year's association with Ade. Has she given you up as a pupil and that is why she wishes you to go to high school? . . . I feel rather hurt about it. Ade fails to teach you and then calls you illiterate and begins talking about high school."

Tamar could make up her own mind, Dorothy said, but only after a visit to Farmingdale. Dorothy allowed that Ade might be right about Tamar needing to return to high school, but since Tamar was not making a stand either way, she would decide for her. And then with the usual confusion, two weeks after Dorothy decided to let Tamar remain another year at Ade's, Tamar was back in New York and applying to Farmingdale. What neither Tamar nor Ade had known was that spring while Tamar was in Newport, Dorothy had plunged into illness, loneliness, and depression, and her nights were full of "sadness and desolation." Each night was "a rack of bitterness and pain," and each day an act of faith to go on. Then Ade also became ill, and her apprenticeship program would soon come to an end.

"Why didn't you insist on staying at Ade's?" I asked my mother.

"I don't know," she said sadly. "I had a hard time standing up to Dorothy, though as a young child I used to scold her all the time." She paused for a moment. "For some reason she didn't want me at Ade's. Sometimes I wonder if Dorothy wasn't jealous of how close I had become to Ade and Ade's mother. She *did* have a jealous streak in her. A lot like Aunt Della. But of course I came right back to Easton that summer and immediately took up with Dave Hennessy again."

In order to prove her competency and be accepted into Farmingdale that fall, Tamar had to pass the New York Regents Exams. "This was unthinkable for Catholics because it included biology," Tamar said. "They didn't want to teach biology. At Immaculata High School, it was taught by the same nun who taught catechism."

Farmingdale accepted Tamar based on the results of their entrance exam, which she passed handily though she had completed only the ninth grade, but because she lacked a high school diploma she would not receive a degree. This did not concern Dorothy at all.

The month before classes began, on the advice of Father Hugo, who was concerned that Tamar had missed the retreat that summer, Dorothy took Tamar to visit the Grail, a Catholic laywomen's movement, in Illinois, where they attended a course to help prepare young women for marriage and life on the land. Dorothy hoped that Tamar would be attracted to the deeply religious rural life the Grail girls led, but it seemed to be a contradictory plan to convince Tamar not to marry while also preparing her for it.

On their return, Tamar began her agricultural studies. Tuition was free, but fees were $135 a term. Tamar contributed forty-five dollars she had saved by helping Della that summer, and the balance was divided between Forster and Dorothy. Tamar was up every morning at five o'clock to care for the animals, followed by classes in bacteriology, chemistry, and English with students who were mostly Jewish girls preparing for life on a kibbutz. To graduate, according to Dorothy's understanding, you had to milk six cows in an hour and plow five acres. Tamar never mentioned having to milk six cows in an hour, but it was at Farmingdale that she began her lifelong advocacy of organic farming, provoked by the school's method of using tear gas as a pesticide in the greenhouse.

When Tamar entered college, Dorothy temporarily quit the Worker. In the October issue of the paper she announced in what came to be known as the "Farewell Column" that she was going on a year of retreat. "Mary," she wrote to a priest, "lived a hidden life. That's what women ought to do. . . . We must ever put family first. . . . I had long since given up my family and my father used to reproach me, saying that charity began at the home. Now I see my mother, my sister and my two brothers more often, remembering that the family is the unit of society."

Dorothy's decision to leave the Worker was more complex than that. Perhaps she was reluctant to list the many problems at the Worker that were wearing her down. It may have been the discouragement at the deterioration of the Easton farm, the schism within the Worker over pacifism, the paper's plunging circulation, or the realization that, contrary to the ideals of the early years, Dorothy couldn't invite in all who knocked at the door. Also, Peter was not well—he was losing weight and tired easily—and everyone else had scattered. Gerry Griffin was in Palestine training for ambulance driving in Tunisia, Joe Zarrella would be off to Africa soon, and most of the conscientious objectors were working in psychiatric hospitals.

Rumors came to her that many people believed the movement would come to an end without her. "Nonsense," she said.

It may also have been that after ten years at it, Dorothy simply was exhausted. But part of the reason she, as some people described it, tried to quit the Catholic Worker was her fear that all that time she spent away from her daughter was now coming back to bite her, in Tamar's desire and insistence on marrying a man everyone knew was trouble. Dorothy was haunted by the Worker's inability to deal with the needs and disasters of family life. While Tamar was at Ade's, Dorothy wrote Tamar an uncharacteristically frank letter about the goings-on at the farm, perhaps in an attempt to impress on her the reality of some Worker marriages. Jim Montague, a severe alcoholic, physically abused Helen, whom Tamar loved, while Helen was eight months pregnant. Dorothy was distraught and did not know what to do. Helen had the protection of neither the law nor the Catholic Church, and unless she asked Dorothy for help, there was little, if anything, Dorothy could do. If she kicked Jim off the farm without Helen's consent, Helen would have left with him, probably putting Helen and the children into further danger through destitution and isolation. In her letter to Tamar, Dorothy then added what I imagine she hoped would bring Tamar to her senses, "David has been drinking with [Jim], I am afraid."

While Tamar attended classes, Dorothy lived half a mile away in an old convent school surrounded by empty chicken hatcheries and potato fields. Tamar visited each afternoon after classes and before evening chores, and they shared hot cocoa and bread with honey. Once a week they visited Grace, who had moved up from Florida after Pop's death to live with Dorothy's brother Sam, his wife, and their toddler son. Uneasy about Grace's health—they suspected cancer at the time—Dorothy thought that maybe she should live with her, but Father Hugo said she had an obligation to Tamar but not to her mother. Dorothy felt she had to explain to people why she had left the Worker and her desire to be with Grace. "I'm the only link the family has with the Church," she said, but Grace was not interested in Dorothy's religion. *Repelled* was the word Dorothy used.

On this personal retreat, this year of "sacrifice and prayer," Dorothy set a hard schedule for herself. She planned to keep completely separate from the Worker, not even exchanging letters. She wrote, baked bread, carded wool, made soap, and prayed for three hours a day in the chapel. The three hours turned out to be fifteen minutes of actual prayer as her mind wandered, full of internal conversations and debates. Dorothy thought she should give up music, plays, and art, but after being called to the chancery for some unstated reason, she headed to the Metropolitan Museum of Art. She started to write more of the natural world, finding it helped relieve the "dryness and pain of prayer." She was also worried sick over at least five Catholic Worker men who were overseas, including Jack English, who was a prisoner of war in Romania, and she worried over her brother Donald, who was in Finland working as a foreign correspondent for the *Chicago Tribune*. She prayed for them all while listening to Sibelius's Second Symphony in D Major.

She had hoped to repair the damage between her and Tamar, but her loneliness made her bitterly unhappy even with Tamar visiting every moment she could. Tamar turned eighteen that March, and calmly, competently, and without fuss, she passed her term exams. The two of them then returned to the Worker, where, to the others, Dorothy seemed tired, subdued, and heavyhearted, not the vibrant woman they knew. Dorothy's conclusion at why she ended her year away from the Worker after six months? Women are not meant to live the hermit's life.

Tamar, though, had succeeded in her however brief and incomplete college experience in proving she was capable of higher education, and she was now eighteen and free to marry. She fought as best she could for the right to decide her own path, and Dorothy tried to make the best of it. Tamar was marrying, she wrote, "someone who accepts poverty, manual labor, loves country life and literature, and of course first of all, loves her." Dorothy read to comfort herself while Tamar worried about the cold and squalor of poverty.

The misunderstandings between Dorothy and Tamar during those years from 1940 to 1944 festered with both of them for decades to come. Dorothy was not wise in the ways of teenagers, maybe because she was never allowed to be one herself given her own insular and proscribed

Dorothy's mother, Grace Satterlee, holding Dorothy, Anna Satterlee (*seated, right*), and Charity Washburn (*seated, left*), Dorothy's grandmother and great-grandmother, respectively, c. 1898

Dorothy, c. early 1920s

Dorothy on Staten Island, c. 1925
(*photograph by Forster Batterham*)

Forster in his dinghy on
Staten Island, c. 1925

Forster and Dorothy on the beach at Huguenot, Staten Island, 1926

LEFT: Dorothy holding Tamar, 1926 (*photograph by Forster Batterham*)

RIGHT: Batterham family photograph, New Jersey, c. 1926: (*back row*) Virginia Batterham (Forster's sister), Eleanor Forster Batterham (Forster's mother), future renowned literary critic Kenneth Burke (Lily's husband), William Forster Batterham; (*center row*) Rose Batterham Houskeeper (Forster's sister), Lily Batterham Burke (Forster's sister) holding her daughter France, Dorothy holding Tamar; (*front row*) Eleanor Burke

Dorothy and Tamar in Florida, c. 1930

Tamar around the time of the first issue of the
Catholic Worker, c. 1933

Dorothy and Tamar with a group of Catholic Workers, including
Stanley Vishnewski (*standing, third from left*), Ade Bethune (*seated,
second from left*), Peter Maurin (*seated, fourth from left*), outside the
Fifteenth Street building in New York City where the Catholic Worker
began, c. 1935

Dorothy and Peter Maurin at the
Catholic Worker's first farming commune
in Easton, Pennsylvania, c. 1939

Tamar in front of her cottage in Easton, c. 1941

Tamar and David Hennessy on their wedding day in Easton, 1944

Tamar with Dorothy holding Tamar's first child, Becky, after Becky's baptism, the Easton farm, 1945

Dorothy (*back*) holding Eric, Tamar (*center*) holding Becky, with Susie sitting to their left, West Virginia, 1949

Dorothy and Stanley Vishnewski with Tamar's children in front of Tamar's farm in Vermont: (*standing, left to right*) Becky, Nicky, Eric, Susie; (*seated, left to right*) Hilaire, Martha, Mary, Maggie, c. 1960

Tamar (*left*) and Dorothy (*right*) on the lawn of the farm at Tivoli, New York, c. 1969

Dorothy (*left*) and Tamar (*right*) in Tivoli's dining room, c. 1970 (*photograph by Stanley Vishnewski*)

Dorothy (*left*) with Susie (*center*), Tamar (*right*), and Susie's daughter, Tanya (*front*), in front of Tamar's home in Vermont, c. 1971 (*photograph by Stanley Vishnewski*)

Dorothy during her final summer at the cottage in Spanish Camp, Staten Island, 1978 (*photograph by Stanley Vishnewski*)

Dorothy in her room at Maryhouse, reading *The New York Times Book Review*, c. 1979 (*photograph by Stanley Vishnewski*)

childhood and the responsibility she had over her baby brother when she was fourteen. Then at sixteen supporting herself at university with harsh and wearying jobs, followed by those life-and-death experiences at the ages of twenty and twenty-one—witnessing the death of Louis Holladay and working as a nurse during the Spanish flu epidemic. Dorothy had grown up quickly, and she did not recognize that her daughter's needs were different.

I tried to talk of these things with my mother in greater depth, but as usual she was elusive. I followed her around her apartment and garden, when she could still garden, trying to collect the snippets of information or insight she would let drop only when she didn't feel she was being pinned down by my questions. I could feel her trying to be scrupulously fair and honest. "I don't intend to blame Dorothy," Tamar said, "but you know how you do [with parents]. She could have said, 'You can just wait a little while more before you get married.'"

Dorothy fluctuated during those four tense years from being dictatorial to stepping back to do nothing. Her natural warmth and loving nature would eventually lead to reconciliation, but damage had been done to a young, impressionable girl. And Tamar, after being uprooted one too many times, made a decision to begin her own life and her own family, though her decision was based in part on the feeling she had no choice but to marry, given Catholic teachings on sexuality and marriage. But maybe she saw it, in her hurt, anger, and confusion, as an attempt to wrestle her fate out of her mother's formidable grip and do what she had always wanted—live at Easton without having to worry whether her mother would send her off yet again.

On a warm, sunny April day, in preparation for Tamar's married life, she and Dorothy scrubbed one of Mr. O'Connell's larger cottages that he had built on the farm with carbolic and kerosene to rid it of bedbugs. While Tamar whitewashed the cottage, Dorothy left to care for the children of the upper farm. She walked along the steep and rocky road between the two farms, passing the Stations of the Cross and an outdoor shrine to Our Lady where she often said the rosary. The hill was steeper than she remembered, and she stopped along the way to sit on a hay rake and read matins and lauds. At the upper farm, after the children were all fed and asleep in their carriages in the sun, and Eva and Vic's oldest daughter was running around with the chickens, Dorothy settled in to write.

Later that afternoon, Tamar walked up the hill to meet Dorothy, and they visited Helen and her children, sitting on the hillside, looking out over the dusty fields of New Jersey and the Delaware River sparkling in the sun. In this peaceful moment, Vic came running up. Wild dogs had attacked the goats, killing one and injuring three others so badly they had to be killed. The only survivors were three newborn kids. Practical person she was, Tamar fried up the dead goats' livers for dinner that night. "Sometimes," Dorothy wrote, "it seems to us that the Easton farm is productive only in misfortunes and sufferings, but we love it all."

As always Dorothy wrote beautifully about what was wrapped in tragedy. Part of her genius was this ability to see beauty in what didn't seem to possess it. To repurpose the words of St. John of the Cross, "Where you find no beauty, put beauty—and you will find beauty." But Dorothy wrote about Tamar's wedding in the paper with the tone of a social columnist, and nothing of her own thoughts survives from her diaries.

On April 19, 1944, six weeks after Tamar turned eighteen, on a cold, sunny morning, Tamar and David were married at St. Bernard's, the Irish church in Easton where the Catholic Worker weddings took place. In preparation, Tamar had planted a rosebush the evening before ("I don't care if we have no food—I'm going to have flowers around my house," she said to Dorothy). Uncle John's mother-in-law, Mrs. de Aragon, hand-stitched and embroidered her bridal gown and a starched white lace Dutch cap. Tamar wore white sandals and carried a bouquet of red roses. She had no mirror and therefore "never did see how lovely she looked," Dorothy wrote.

One of the men provided everyone with neatly repaired shoes, and a neighbor loaned them his car for the three-mile drive to eight o'clock Mass. On the way, Dorothy snapped at Peter for the first and only time. He calmly accepted her outburst.

"I know a fellow who slapped his daughter on her wedding day," he replied to comfort her.

Before the ceremony, the priest, Father Halahan, turned to Dorothy and, within Tamar's hearing, asked sternly and referring to David, "Do you know this fellow?"

The wedding party was small. Stanley was in Minnesota, and many of the others were overseas. "They wouldn't have wanted to come anyway," Tamar said sadly, though Dwight sent her twenty-five dollars from France as a wedding present.

Peter walked Tamar down the aisle, and Dave Mason, just out of jail for refusing induction and ultimately rejected for the war because of ill health ("a very, very fine person who helped me enormously," Tamar said of him) brought by train from the Mott Street bakery a traditional Italian wedding cake made from cookies, which they dipped in wine before eating. John cooked the wedding breakfast and Eva baked the bread.

Catholic Worker legend, fed by Dorothy, has it that during my mother's wedding breakfast, Peter gave a sermon against raising pigs for profit, though Tamar had begged Dorothy not to let Peter talk. Dorothy claimed it was the last speech he ever made. Tamar's version was different. "I never asked Dorothy to not let Peter talk, and I don't remember him talking," she said. "By that time, he wasn't able to. It was very sad." But the story of preaching against raising pigs for profit is a good one. Possibly Dorothy wanted to squash a scheme cooked up by John Filigar, and here was a way to lay this decision on Peter, whom she still referred to as the founder and leader of the Catholic Worker.

"I don't remember much of the wedding," Tamar said, "except that everybody kept giving me animals as presents." She received a Jersey cow from a priest, John Filigar gave her two pigs, and Vic a hen with eleven chicks to add to her four ducks and three goats, one an Angora whose wool Tamar spun and wove a blanket from (the blanket survived for decades though her children often left it out in the sun and rain). After Mass, her first words were "I must get home to feed the baby goats!"

David, "bibliophile, roofer, and farmer," as Dorothy described him, had waited two years at a community he had rejected until he could marry Tamar.

"He married me because he thought I could save him," Tamar said.

In a photo taken on the day of their wedding David looks away from the camera, maybe to hide the damaged side of his face, the result of a gunshot wound. They sit outside their cottage, and he is turned to look at her while she frowns into the camera, looking young and beautiful, fragile and irked, or maybe it's just the sun in her eyes.

CHAPTER TEN

The demise of the dream that was Easton, for Dorothy, for Tamar, and for many others, paralleled the demise of the dream that was Tamar's marriage. I don't know how much Dorothy knew of what would become of the upper farm, but it was not all, not the worst of events. Tamar wouldn't hear a fuller story until she was in her seventies, and when she did she grieved over the fate of Vic and Eva Smith's children.

The year following Tamar's wedding, hope still lingered at the farm; there was pleasure to be found in the long summer evenings and in Tamar's growing orchard. The cottage too held promise even though it was a tar-paper shack, twelve feet by thirty, cold in winter, hot in summer, with no electricity or running water, and they had to use an outhouse next to the chicken coop. Dorothy and Tamar could watch the sun set as they sat on the front steps, a forsythia bush on one side and a mulberry tree on the other. And Tamar and David would hoe between long rows of beans, Tamar, a teenage girl, her hair in long braids, wearing a peasant blouse and skirt, and barefoot, which is how I remember her as I grew up, barefoot well into her fifties, her toes always in the soil. And there would be my father beside her, and for a moment, for a brief moment, he seemed to be a hopeful young man, undefeated and full of dreams, not yet revealing the signs of a body and mind under siege.

There was still vision, hope, and energy for the farm. Just the year before, they talked of buying an adjoining one hundred acres to grow grain. Dorothy was optimistic, rested, and full of plans. But underneath? I can only piece together through letters, diary entries, and photos what lay beneath, hobbled as I am by my mother's silence.

Tamar spoke little of what happened at Easton, and that only because I kept at her. Dorothy, of course, had much to say, but her story was not complete.

Dorothy's time away the previous year, taken at a time when she felt everyone, even Peter, thought she was a hindrance to the work, turned out to bring validation. While the work could go on without her, it was stagnant. Nearly dead, some said. Mott Street was half-full, and only ten houses remained around the country. No new young people had shown up, and nothing was gained except a three-thousand-dollar printing bill. Nevertheless, Dorothy was delighted to be back at Mott Street and happy to attend the seven o'clock Mass at the Church of the Transfiguration, where the same women knelt at the same pew. And happy but worried about Tamar's pregnancy. A girl of eighteen, she consoled herself, is ideal for having children—she has no nerves. She believed Tamar had entered into marriage and motherhood without any illusions. Tamar had seen the catastrophes, but all wasn't dire—there were a few Catholic Worker families doing well.

Tamar and David spent their two-week honeymoon using sulfur candles, kerosene, and carbolic acid in another attempt to clear the bedbugs from their cottage, which David had named Cobbett Cottage after William Cobbett, a forerunner of the distributists.

David, who turned thirty-one within weeks of the wedding, had been working a few days a week as a slate roofer earning eighty cents an hour.

"I had two requirements of him for our marriage," Tamar said. "He had to buy a stove and get a job. When he came home with his first paycheck, I asked him how much he had earned. He screamed at me, 'You just married me for my money!' He accused me of everything in the book, and I never spoke to him about work again." David lost the job before the month was out, though through no fault of his own. The Professor got into the dandelion wine and then fell into a ditch. David found him on his way to work, picked him up, and brought him home. Because of that David was late to work and got fired. "He didn't get a job [other than occasionally as a day laborer] for another six years," Tamar added.

David started up his mail-order company, Hennessy's Bookstall, through which he sold books, pamphlets, and cards of Gill and Chesterton, never making much more than twenty dollars a week. Dorothy and David were getting along. Tamar was lucky, Dorothy wrote a friend, for David loved poverty and books, animals and the farm. Cobbett Cottage was improving. They put in wallboard and storm windows and painted the door and trim red. They built a cistern to catch water off the roof and put a pump in the kitchen. Tamar baked bread and churned butter from their Jersey cow. She was spinning, making baby clothes, and looking lovely while calmly awaiting the birth of her first child. David had been thinking of baby names, mostly after popes, months before their wedding. For girls it would be either Tamar or Rebecca. Tamar claimed to want a son, but that was David speaking, Dorothy said, optimistically considering that Forster had six sisters and David seven, and between two such families, the genetic odds didn't seem favorable.

That January it was six below outside and eighteen degrees inside Cobbett Cottage. David often headed into town to drink at the Black Horse Inn. Book orders were trickling in but not enough to support the family. Dorothy suggested he start a monthly paper hand-printed at the farm. David liked the idea as he had already been thinking about writing a book on the back-to-the-land movement titled either *Signs of Sanctity* or, even better, *Mud in Your Eye*. It suited his sense of humor. But nothing came of the book or the monthly paper, though David filled his diaries with brief notes—orders received, work hours, births and deaths of both animals and people, and Dorothy's comings and goings, as she divided her time between Mott Street and Tamar's old cabin at Easton.

Tamar, eight months pregnant and weighing 133 pounds, planted radishes on her nineteenth birthday. The farmwork continued with new fruit and nut trees, fields planted with clover, and gardens of herbs and salad greens. "Remind people in the column," Tamar said to Dorothy, "that they once sent rosebushes and irises for the farm. Maybe they will send some more." Dorothy and Tamar picked watercress from the brook for salad and a bouquet of forsythia for the table. They sat on the front steps of the cottage while David pitched manure with John Filigar and helped to plow the fields. John, back from his wartime job of cleaning cesspools, took over the care of their one remaining horse (Jim, their best horse, had died), half-blind Dolly, and with the loan of another horse, he began the plowing once again.

On April 3, Tamar, without fuss, gave birth to her first child, Rebecca, or Becky, as she would come to be called. Stanley, who had returned from attending university in Minnesota, was godfather, and one of David's sisters godmother. Less than three weeks later, on their first wedding anniversary, Dorothy handed them the deed for Cobbett Cottage and three acres of land. The first thing they did was put up a new slate roof, and Della sent Tamar money for a chimney.

John planted fields of potatoes with the help of a new team of horses, though they kept Dolly, unable to bear the thought of selling her to the knackers, the men who slaughter animals unfit for human consumption, as they had done to Rosie the cow. Dorothy and Tamar would go out walking with Becky in the long evenings and then sit on the front steps of the cottage as the sun set and the kitten played and the mother cat chased crickets. They washed a fleece from the sheep Father Magee of the Syrian church had given to Tamar as a wedding gift, and then teased, carded, and spun it on Tamar's new spinning wheel from Montreal to make blankets and clothing for the baby and a blanket for Peter. Tamar let the ewe and her lamb run free, and as they said vespers, the ewe stood at the door with her long solemn face looking in.

After returning from her year away, Dorothy had had great plans for Easton. She envisioned a community of silence and prayer, the girls from the Grail coming to help, and Peter, priests, and others giving instructions on books and ideas, crafts and carpentry. Emphasis needed to be on work, work as if it were any wage earner's day. Let's build shrines and beautify the place, she had said. Let's have more room for guests and visit the prisons and hospitals, and go on picnics on feast days. The lower farm, she announced, would become a retreat house, and it would be for not only those doing the work but also the men coming to the soup line on Mott Street, having forgotten her determination in the early years not to ask anything of those who came for help. "They need more, far more than food, clothing, and shelter. They need retreats too—they need the word of God preached to them."

But the euphoria of the early days at Easton was long gone. The farming commune failed, Dorothy said in her column, because people did not have enough voluntary poverty. They lacked interior discipline and a philosophy of work, along with the willingness to make a gift of their labor. The land hadn't been cultivated in several years, and the orchards and animals were neglected. Even John Filigar, on whom they depended, couldn't maintain his energy and enthusiasm, and he refused to plan for the planting seasons because he had seen too many plans fall by the wayside. People had no sense of obedience but plenty of individualism, Dorothy said. After also chastising the women for not cooking enough, she then turned on Peter in this same column. "He was always willing, for the sake of making his point, to sacrifice order and success. He was always afraid of the argument of the pragmatist. 'Be what you want the other fellow to be,' he kept on saying. 'Don't criticize what is not being done.'"

Peter suffered because of what was happening. The farming commune was his dream, but the dream had turned into a battle of demands. "I have never asked anything for myself," he said sadly to Dorothy.

Dorothy framed the problem as the battle between workers and scholars, but things weren't so simple. Sometimes both the workers and scholars went on drinking binges. Sometimes the scholars were only scholars in that they liked Peter's acute sense of personal responsibility since it meant no one ever obliged them to work. Sometimes the workers were so bitter and unkind that no one could work with them.

Explorations into cottage industries failed. They had tried running a bakery, and they made wooden crib sets designed by Ade, a successful venture until someone walked off with the earnings. An accomplished silversmith living at the farm made chalices for the priests, and encouraged by his success, some of the other men set up a still and tried to sell liquor. A social worker urged Dorothy to discover what the men who were doing nothing at the farm were good at and to encourage it. "Oh no," Dorothy said, remembering these earlier efforts. "If the men feel like doing something, let them do it, but I'm not going to urge them."

The farm teetered from one near disaster to another. One summer people spent days canning hundreds of jars of fruit and vegetables only to have one of the women drive away with them all—she had used cigarettes to bribe some of the men to load them in the back of a truck for her. Then there was the troubled young woman who tried to heat water in a wooden bucket on the woodstove.

"God takes care of fools, children, and Catholic Workers," some unnamed wit said to Dorothy, possibly Stanley as it was indicative of his brand of humor.

There was still the conflict among the needs of the farm itself, the needs of the families living on it, and the needs of the poor. Tamar felt that Dorothy had a romantic notion of what it was like living on the farm. "To her it was just living off the fat of the land, and how happy it all was. All you had to do is reach out and pick your lunch off the trees. Remember that *Wizard of Oz* book, the one with the lunch box tree? Dorothy got hell for not understanding the agricultural needs of a farm, as she got hell for a lot of things. People weren't thinking of her as a saint back then. Sometimes people put too much on the opposition she had from the archbishop, or from her family, or from Forster, but really the worst came from within the Worker."

The majority of Catholic Workers were against the idea of the retreat house, but Dorothy didn't let this dismay her. She planned to travel around the country to enlist supporters and priests. She envisioned retreat houses springing up across the country just as the houses of hospitality and farming communes had. They began to convert the lower farm's barn into a retreat house. They still had only outhouses and bucket bathing, but this lack of running water did not deter her either, and in September 1944, they began holding retreats again.

Fourteen people attended the first one, a far cry from the old retreats where they had up to one hundred twenty-five. From that fall through the end of 1946, the farm was filled with retreats, though they rarely drew more than a dozen people at a time and most were women even when the war ended and the men returned. Stanley called it the Year of the Retreats. During the summer they held one every two weeks, and as one ended, they would prepare for the next. Each was led by a different priest, but none by Father Woods, with whom Dorothy had not spoken in the two years since he had told her that by focusing on the retreats she had taken a great movement and perverted it. When one priest arrived with alcohol on his breath, Dorothy later commented, "The ways of the Lord are unscrupulous." She looked for a priest who would give retreats that followed Father Hugo's, but she failed, so she begged his bishop to allow Father Hugo to once again lead retreats. She failed in that also.

With the end of the war, the Catholic Worker men were returning from overseas or from the CO camps or from jail. Some got married or went back to college. Some started their own farms, and some returned to the Worker. Gerry Griffin was home after three years in Syria, North Africa, Italy, and Holland as a lieutenant in charge of thirty ambulances. Dwight was not yet out but visited on furlough. On the line, there was a change with the men who arrived. Before the war, the greatest problem had been alcoholism, but as the soldiers returned, the Workers began to see more men who were suffering from mental illness or shell shock.

Dorothy was under attack both at Mott Street and at the farm and was feeling surrounded by a hatred so strong that she sometimes felt in physical danger, and she would flee to Della's. "[It is m]ost uncomfortable to be hunted," she said. "And very humiliating to be afraid." One of the men attacking her had been in a mental hospital for seven years for trying to kill his brother. This kind of attack she could survive, but it was the hostile opposition she suffered from the families on the farm that lingered.

Dwight had visited Easton, where he found Tamar and David to be an almost reclusive couple, and the families were aligned against Dorothy in what he called a "discipline and organizational struggle." (After the war Dwight returned briefly to Mott Street. Dorothy hadn't been in contact with him since she left for her year off. She was happy to see him, as they had parted badly. At the time he had been so angry with her, he could barely speak. She still didn't seem to understand how angry he had been over Tamar's marriage and how he blamed Dorothy for it. He then left to join the Trappists for twenty-five years before leaving both the order and the Catholic Church—he was "spiritual but questioning organized religion," as he described it. He married happily, remained active in issues of social justice, and continued to receive the *Catholic Worker* until his death at age ninety-seven.)

From the first moment Dorothy announced her intention of turning the lower farm into a retreat center, she was met with resistance from the Smiths and the other families of the upper farm, and eventually from David and Tamar. They had been attending Father Roy's retreats, but David was fed up. "Nix on that damnable Doctrine," he said, and wondered whether he should attend Mass in town rather than on the farm.

"He went to war with Dorothy," Tamar said. "Everyone went to war with her over the retreats."

Some people fought her, some left in anger, and others just waited it out, trusting that it was a phase she would come out of and that the Worker would survive. Dorothy tried to find solace and support from Father Hugo, but he could respond with only his own troubles. "We are all so alone," she wrote, in this "cold and desolate fear."

In an effort to compromise and bring peace, Dorothy, after deeding Cobbett Cottage and three acres of the lower farm to Tamar and David, deeded three and a half acres to Vic and Eva, but they weren't interested in three acres and a cow. Each family wanted twenty acres, and the rest of the land, they said, could go toward the retreat. Vic also believed that the money coming in should go to the families to establish them on the land and not to the soup line. In Dorothy's mind the farming commune could work only if it were self-sustaining. She felt a responsibility to those giving money to the Worker—donations were for the poor. The farm was not to support families who could support themselves. In protest, Vic and Eva retreated to the upper farm, and the steep climb between the two farms helped widen the schism. To make matters worse, both Peter and Father Roy were not well. Tamar's orchard was the only thing that seemed to be thriving.

"Everything changes and everything remains the same," David said to Dorothy. "So don't worry."

Then in the midst of the conflicts at the farm came another personal blow. Seven months after the birth of Dorothy's first grandchild, her mother, Grace, died at the age of seventy-seven. For months Grace had suffered from not only a heart condition but also worry over her oldest son, Donald, who had been missing in Europe since the end of the war. In the weeks as her mother lay dying, Dorothy was also ill. "Heartburn from fatigue," she said, but she wrote nothing of Grace's death in her diary, only in her column, yet again holding in silence that which hurt her the most, though she would return to it again and again in later years, delicately, as if she didn't want to probe too much.

The November after Grace's death, the Catholic Worker Penny Press—that is, Stanley—printed an Eric Gill book list for David, while John plowed the lower field for winter wheat, and farther up the sheep and Angora goat grazed, their wool long and heavy. Dorothy restated in the paper the Catholic Worker program of action, but this time at the top, before the works of mercy, she put the retreats. In response, some people claimed she was turning the Catholic Worker into a religious community.

Always the first to recognize her failures but rarely able to admit her mistakes, Dorothy believed that people didn't hate the retreat—they hated her. It was all due to a lack of understanding, she said. One of the reasons for the Worker's existence was to bridge that "terrible gap between clergy and laity," and she believed the retreats were a way to do this. Also the Worker was laying too heavy a burden on people, and the retreat would give them strength. She insisted the retreat house *was* a part of Peter's program of agronomic universities. They were not houses of penance but the basis of the work—learning to know, to love, and to serve God.

It was, during these years, an unfortunate part of Dorothy's character that she believed that what was good for her was good for others. Because Dorothy chose not to finish university, degrees, such as from Farmingdale, were "the bunk" for Tamar. Because she couldn't remain at the convent on Long Island for what was meant to be her year away from the Worker, women were not meant to be hermits. And because the retreats gave her strength, they were just what everyone else needed. As Dorothy said, she always did learn the hard way. What other way was there?

When asked his views on the retreat, Peter couldn't respond.

"He still spoke a bit about land and community," Tamar said. "David and I lapped it up. We were the only ones he spoke to at that time, the only ones who still listened. But he'd often say, 'My mind is tired. I can't think.'"

Peter and Mr. O'Connell sat in the barn next to the stove for hours in silence, Mr. O'Connell with his pipe and a book, and Peter, as Dorothy described it, "motionless, his chin sunk in a great sweater that had all but engulfed him." They realized he was losing his mind when he began to set up the altar for Mass at random times throughout the day.

Dorothy was at the farm for Becky's first birthday, and they had tea at Tamar's old place with applesauce and soft-boiled eggs. Tamar, pregnant with her second child, planted black walnut trees next to her peach and apple trees, while David took care of the sheep and cows. Dorothy planted a small garden of medicinal herbs, collected wild herbs, and meditated on a future filled with years of tending to grandchildren and not much time to write. She realized that she'd better write now while she could. To comfort herself, she went to see the opera *Tristan und Isolde* in the city. There will always be music no matter what, she thought. She tried to see good in Tamar's marriage and believed she saw happiness. "She had just been married a week and she looked so proud and happy. She said with a warm note of joy—'He does just what I ask him to do,'—so happy in her power over him, the power of love. . . . Just last week Tamar said in relation to some zinnia seeds David had bought for her—proudly, confidently—'He always gets just the right things.' She talks so little that these remarks are indicative."

"She talks so little." That Tamar silence. Perhaps because of my persistence that spanned almost thirty years, perhaps because Tamar was finally ready to speak, to me she said, "Within weeks of the wedding, I knew I had made a terrible mistake. I went into solitary confinement. Dave Hennessy made all these rules. I couldn't do this and couldn't do that. At my best friend's wedding I was heavily pregnant, but he wouldn't let me stay the night, so I had to travel a long train journey round-trip in one day. I could never spend one night away from home. I could never have a babysitter."

That August, while waiting for Tamar's second baby to arrive, Tamar,

Dorothy, and Becky picnicked on the hillside or down in the meadow under the pear trees. They sat on the porch of Tamar's old cabin, where they sewed, knitted, or teased wool and watched visitors arrive. Tamar washed the fleece from her sheep and in the evenings teased wool for a mattress for the cradle, while learning from two visiting Hungarian women how to grow and prepare flax. Tamar spun the rest of the fleece and made a coat, hat, dress, afghan, and five pairs of socks. They had sent away the wool from the other sheep to be spun so she could use it to weave on her loom. And then late in the month, Tamar and David's second child arrived—another daughter, Susanna.

By then the only person interested in learning from John Filigar how to plow with the horses was a fourteen-year-old girl who lived nearby, and the farm columns were coming to a stop, though Dorothy clung to her optimism. Down at the farm, she wrote in her column, "we have cult, culture, and cultivation. All summer we have had priests to offer Mass for us and to give us conferences on doctrine. We have the sung Mass; we have our own carved statues, done by our friends; we have folk dances on Saturday nights, and picnics and walks; we write, we print, we carve, we draw; we till the earth and build and cook and bake and wash. We have many children. We eat well and sleep well, and we are trying to pray well. Down at the farm it has been beautiful sultry weather. . . . Long quiet days. . . ."

It would be the last summer Dorothy spent on the farm, and after writing of the plans that didn't work out and those that did—two shrines built, one to St. Joseph and a crucifix on top of the hill, house and barn painted, a stone wall repaired and whitewashed, a new slate roof, and Tamar's new loom arriving from Canada. After writing of the smell of roses and clover, of the birds singing, of the cattle grazing on the hill; after praying for the dead and expressing the hope that all of them would be buried in the cemetery just down the road where Tamar wheeled the babies to get them to fall asleep; and after eleven years of trying to put meat on the bones, as she put it, of Peter's vision of a farming commune, Dorothy came to her final decision regarding Easton. That fall she walked away from the farm. And within a year so did Tamar and David.

At that time Dorothy passed over in silence the dissolution of the farm. Years later she wrote very little, and said, "We did not remain at the Easton Farm. Life there became too difficult."

"One problem," Tamar said, "was Dorothy never really understood Peter's idea of the farming commune, and she didn't understand the needs of a farm. She could never just let it be a farm. First, she said the farm's priority was to care for the poor. And then when it was obvious that that had failed, Dorothy announced that the farm was to be a retreat center." Tamar paused. "For me, it was first the retreat, which changed Dorothy, and then the war, which took away all the young men, that destroyed it. After those first marvelous, so hopeful years, Easton was never the same."

Then she added sadly and with her characteristic way of seeming to change course, echoing her mother's roundabout way of approaching a difficult subject, "The families on the upper farm were so hungry they came down at night to steal food."

The story of the upper farm, that beautiful farm with its skyline fields and view over the Delaware River, where Tamar spent winter holidays sliding down the hill and summers gathering four-leaf clovers with Stanley, where she learned all she could of animal husbandry and gardening from John, and where she collected her specimens and stored them in her little cabin built by Mr. O'Connell, would become one of the saddest and most tragic stories in Catholic Worker history. Tamar could barely bring herself to talk about it, although she wouldn't learn the worst of what had happened until sixty years later.

When all is said and done about Dorothy's dictatorial ways, about the battle between worker and scholar, about too much drinking and too little work, about the retreat, all of which were real difficulties, it was another, darker battle that dragged down the wonders and joys of Easton, destroying it so thoroughly that all Dorothy could think to do was lift her hands in defeat and walk away.

CHAPTER ELEVEN

When Tamar returned from Canada in 1944, cracks had already been appearing between the upper and lower farms. The families of the upper farm, particularly Vic and Eva Smith, were starting to fall under the influence of a French lawyer in his forties, Guy Tobler, who did pro bono work for Catholic institutions and alcoholic priests. When he first visited Maryfarm, Eva thought he was a fine gentleman, and he gave the upper farm a life-sized statue of the Blessed Mother. In 1945 Guy moved in, and Vic chose him as his spiritual adviser, vowing obedience and placing himself entirely in Guy's hands, while Eva named their third child after him. Vic and Eva wanted Tamar and David to join them, but whether this was seen as a deliberate strike against Dorothy, Tamar didn't know. Tamar never understood Eva and Vic's manipulations to get her married as quickly as possible. Perhaps the presence of a beautiful, young girl at Easton was too unsettling, or perhaps they wanted more families to align against Dorothy.

Trouble had begun as soon as Guy moved in. He began to demonize Dorothy and the farm manager, Jane O'Donnell, attacking them because he did not believe women should be in charge. Dorothy didn't speak in detail of the personal vitriolic abuse and threat of physical violence she experienced from Guy, so relentless that she feared visiting the upper farm.

Guy began to exploit the tensions between the families and the retreat and was so successful in creating a schism between the two farms that by 1946 he was in complete control of the three families and the handful of single men living on the upper farm. Though he forbade any contact between the two farms, tales of oppressive and cultish behaviors began to trickle out. Guy demanded vows of strict obedience and began to impose penances and rules within a hierarchical system based on class and gender. He wore a skullcap and beard as symbols of authority, which the other men were forbidden to do. Women were ordered to be silent in the presence of men, could speak only when spoken to, and had to knock at the doors to be admitted into the room. If anyone wanted to speak to Guy they had to kneel before him. He took all their money and personal belongings, and they weren't allowed to hold outside jobs. Only Guy, who had inherited wealth, could have money. Through Vic's propensity to submit himself to another's authority—he had tried to do the same with some of the farm managers—and through Eva's desire to live on the land at all costs, the Smiths were constantly on the verge of starvation. When Dorothy saw Vic several years after leaving the farms, at Mr. O'Connell's funeral, she was shocked at how gaunt and hungry he looked. The families at the upper farm never came down to the lower farm except to raid it for food and furnishings, often in the middle of the night, and to tell visitors that they were the true Catholic Workers and that the retreat house was a perversion of the movement. Dorothy felt helpless. Vic, Eva, and the others, whatever their reasons, had chosen to submit themselves to Guy Tobler. She could not change their minds, and she would not force them to leave. These were families she knew and loved, and she had helped care for the children. These were members of the family. Dorothy spoke of the troubles as the struggle for power and authority, which developed into the heresy of the family, of the priesthood, and of the relationship between men and women.

By the end of 1946, in despair, Dorothy severed all ties with the upper farm. She deeded the property over to two families and left them to go their own way, but she had no way of knowing just how far Guy Tobler would go. By feeding Eva's dream of community on the land that Guy, through his inheritance, was able to pay for, by using vulnerable children and families, and by controlling food and money, he was able to groom and manipulate the families of the upper farm into a cult of isolation, violence, and sexual abuse. For punishment, the children were locked in the chicken coop or placed in a hole in the ground for hours. When one of the boys broke a cup, he was forced to kneel with it in his outstretched hands for a long period of time. Physical violence was endemic—the men beat each other, Vic beat Eva, and the children could be beaten by any of the adults. The women were subjected to sexual humiliation while having the model of the Blessed Mother held up to illustrate their submissive role.

Undeterred, the Smiths put a call out to the monasteries for single men to come and work at what Eva called their "contemplative lay community on the land." In response a young man by the name of Arthur Lacey arrived in 1948 unaware that the Worker had disassociated itself from the farm. Dorothy Day, he was told when he arrived, was the devil, and no one was allowed to read or even mention the *Catholic Worker*. They had nothing to feed him but a plate of beans, but he remained for a year until something snapped in him—he did not say what—and Arthur, a tiny, mild man, went after Guy with an ax. Guy ordered the oldest Smith child, who was seven years old, to take the ax away. Arthur left the farm and headed to the Worker in the city, where he lived for the rest of his life.

"There was something evil lurking there," Arthur said. "You didn't know what it was; you couldn't put your finger on it. Guy was diabolical, with a wild temper and easily upset."

While Vic was dangerously foolish about whom he submitted himself to, it was Eva who kept them tied to Guy. Vic was honest, hardworking, generous, and conscientious, and he was unsettled by Guy's treatment of the children. But Eva approved of the strictness, and she was living her dream, and so Vic, wanting to keep the family together, did nothing. The other families soon left—one couple later apologized to Dorothy saying Guy, through cleverly manipulating existing tensions and promising many things, had led them to act foolishly—the single men stopped coming, people no longer came up that steep and rocky road to visit, and the Smiths became lonely and isolated.

After one of the families broke away, the wife, Ann Thornton, wrote a letter to Dorothy asking forgiveness for "the cruel part I have played against you." Through exploiting the quarrel over whether the farm was for families or for the retreat, this "fake prophet," Ann said, who referred to himself as a great mystic, "cunningly led us to finally be worlds apart and it was the distance between Heaven and Hell."

Tamar, who at the time was facing the anger, explosions, and provocations of her own husband, and who was settling into the endurance test of a bad Catholic marriage with many children to come, never spoke of this time in any detail. But David may also have helped give the final blow to the lower farm at Easton. He also seemed seduced by this idea of man as lord and husband as dictator. In response to talk of selling the upper farm as a way to solve the problem, David wrote a letter to Gerry Griffin, who was managing the finances, and within it lay the seeds of some of what Tamar came to despise in David. Earlier that month David had asked Dorothy that he be given a voice in management and made one of the trustees to reform the farm, because, as he put it, "drunk Filigar" couldn't run it. He claimed Dorothy refused because he was a married man and didn't go to Mass daily.

David questioned Dorothy's right to change the farm into a retreat house. "It is the Catholic Worker land movement I'm interested in being a part of—I need none of that hellish born 'Doctrine.'" He questioned her right to sell the farm in part or in whole. He attacked Gerry, who had been made a trustee, and called him woman-ridden because Dorothy kept him under her thumb. The farm trust was a legal fiction, he said, and Dorothy was an absentee landlord. He accused Dorothy of covering up the "moral issues" of who should own and manage the farm with "pious talk and clever writing." He finished by telling Gerry to show the letter to Dorothy.

Four days later, Dorothy asked Peter, who was visiting a friend in upstate New York, if she could spend Christmas with him. She had had a run-in with David over the letter, and she feared she would never see Tamar and the girls again. The intense, two-year opposition over the retreat house from the Smiths and Hennessys, along with the attacks from Guy Tobler, had worn her down. She was ready to give the place up, but dissolution would not be easy. In order to sell the upper farm, Dorothy would have to evict the families, which she was not willing to do. Years earlier in the paper she had suggested that families squat on empty monastic lands, and now the families had taken over Easton. "Poetic justice," one of the men said.

The decision would be hard for all those who had worked to improve the place, eleven years of people coming to help, even the men off the road who stayed long enough to contribute some skill. Little of the work at the upper farm had been done by the families now living on it, Dorothy added. But worst of all she believed she had to give up Tamar and the grandchildren.

Just before Christmas 1946, Dorothy left the farm permanently, and in February 1947 she officially severed all ties to the upper farm, informing the archbishop that the Easton farm was no longer part of the Catholic Worker. It would take her another two years to be legally free of it.

"It may all seem a failure, but at least we made the attempt," Dorothy told Gerry. "Few there are who will accept authority and exercise it. And plenty to taunt and criticize, to tear down and discourage."

John and a handful of others, with the two new horses (Dolly had died) then left for a new farm in Newburgh in upstate New York, which Dorothy insisted was to be a retreat house and not a farming commune. But the retreats, while continuing on occasion for another five years, would never again have the importance they had from 1940 to 1946. "It's strange about the retreat," Stanley said years later, "how at one time it was the dominating influence in the Worker, and now it's not there anymore." Just like so many other ideas, but, Stanley added, the Worker was not wedded to any particular cause. It needed to be flexible. In Stanley's view there was only one thing essential to the Catholic Worker, and that was hospitality.

As for Tamar and David, on the night of October 19, 1947, while Tamar and the girls were in the city visiting Forster, after the garden was harvested and the orchards had borne their fruit, David sat alone drinking beer in an empty cottage. The lower farm, including Cobbett Cottage, had been sold to a local family, and the price included a squatter, Mr. O'Connell, who remained in his cottage until 1951, when Vic and Eva took him in and cared for him the last year of his life. By May 1949, a new deed to the upper farm was written in the names of Victor Smith and another family man, and Guy Tobler bought one of the houses on the lower farm.

The upper farm at Easton, the place of so much hope and beauty, delight and promise, staggered on under Guy's control until 1956, when he died suddenly of a heart condition, and for the first time in nine years Dorothy heard from Eva. After Vic's death in the 1960s, the Smith children scattered, and in the early 1970s the house burned down, and Eva moved into town. Maybe as an apology, she wrote to Dorothy about wanting Maryfarm, as she still called it, to be a retreat center once again, but the buildings were in such bad repair, nothing came of it, and Eva, choosing not to leave it to any of her children, sold the place, and over the following years, the farm became subsumed into the suburbs of Easton.

It was during those harsh years of the 1940s that Dorothy in a moment of despair asked Peter, "Do you ever become discouraged when you see our failures?"

"No," he replied, "because I know how deep-rooted the evil is."

CHAPTER TWELVE

For years Tamar claimed she never read anything her mother wrote because she found it too painful. But this wasn't true. Tamar read *On Pilgrimage*, in which Dorothy wrote of the two months she spent with Tamar for the Hennessys' first winter near the town of Berkeley Springs, tucked in the northeast corner of West Virginia. Dorothy wrote of bitter, bitter things in a way that gave them beauty and grace. Life in their new place glowed.

Dorothy's ability to make anything sound beautiful sometimes irked Tamar because Dorothy either took license with the details or had what seemed to be a loose grasp of some of the facts. Sometimes she would give several versions or change names and facts in a belated sense of privacy. She was always careful about issues of privacy and had a delicate touch for what was unspeakable. And who is to say that she was wrong not to dwell on the worst? When she did describe things as they were, she soon discovered that people preferred to hear the good. But she also saw beauty where many couldn't. She saw things in all of us that lay beyond the ragged threads of our miseries.

The previous summer Dorothy and Tamar had gone down to visit Berkeley Springs, and even they were dismayed by the isolation and poverty of the area. But after three years at Easton as a married couple, it was a move David wanted to make as a way to establish their life apart from the Worker. They had been invited down with two other young families and a promise from a priest to help them establish a small farm-based community, their toehold on the land, as David called it. For Tamar the move to West Virginia was just another exile from all that she loved, and a loaded gesture in the battle between her mother and her husband.

Dorothy wrote *The Long Loneliness* at that time, and the title partly came out of compassion for that lonely, young mother on a derelict farm in West Virginia. And yet she wrote a harsh letter to Tamar in 1949 that said, in essence, you've made your bed, now lie it in—and stop being so ungrateful. Tamar kept that letter throughout the years, the moves, and the burning down of her house in Vermont. The letter is crumpled, and the edges have been chewed by Tamar's pet budgie, the one who chewed *The Eleventh Virgin*.

That first winter, Dorothy spent two months with them waiting for the birth of Tamar's third baby. Dorothy was herself recovering from an operation, Tamar was ill with stress, and the temperature plunged to fourteen below zero. They had one woodstove in an uninsulated house, and they couldn't mop the floors for fear the water would freeze. Becky and Susie woke up crying in the night from the cold while Dorothy wrote in bed covered by her coat and with a whiskey bottle filled with hot water at her feet. A blizzard raged as they waited for the baby.

"It'll be a girl," Tamar said hopelessly.

David shouted, "Don't you dare come home with a girl! We just bought a farm. We need a boy to farm it."

They sat in the kitchen huddled around the woodstove while, by the light of Aladdin lamps, Tamar read *Kristin Lavransdatter* and David read *Blackfriars*, the Dominican publication from England. Dorothy and the girls had a tea party with bread Dorothy baked and homemade blackberry jam from the neighbors, and Susie flung her cocoa about while Becky imitated her grandmother and wrote in an old notebook and then too flung the pages about.

Every morning Dorothy sat in the wicker chair and sang to Becky and Susie as she had done for her brother John and then for Tamar when she was a baby, "All ye works of the Lord, bless ye the Lord; oh ye ice and snow, oh ye cold and wind, oh ye winter and summer, oh ye trees in the woods, oh ye fire in the stove, oh ye Becky and Susie, bless ye the Lord, praise Him and magnify Him forever."

On a warm break in the wintry weather, at a quarter to one in the morning, Eric Dominic was born, and they added another verse. David was ecstatic for he now had a son. After Eric's arrival, Dorothy stopped writing about Tamar's family, and readers who had been following the story in her column sent letters saying, "What about the baby?"

In March, one month after Eric's birth, the Hennessys moved across Sleepy Creek to a farm they had bought for $1,200 in Stotlers Crossroads, a tiny hamlet of abandoned tomato-canning factories. They had $1,000 from the sale of their cottage at Easton, plus $750 from the sale of two Staten Island plots on Prince's Bay that Forster had given Tamar in 1939 and that Dorothy had turned into an interracial summer camp that burned down in 1943. Forster gave them an additional $250, and Tamar was grateful for his help and tried to get him to come down. The creeks are stocked by the state fish hatcheries, she wrote, and there are wild turkeys to hunt. He didn't come, though he did send Tamar a quilt, a baby mattress, scissors, and a radio.

The property had seventy acres of land that hadn't been farmed in years in an area that still had no electricity. The windows were broken and the doors rotted. The yard was full of broken glass, weeds, scraps of wallpaper, and tin cans. The cellar was flooded but there was no running water; the only source was a spring five hundred feet from the house. The roads were so bad, people used horses rather than cars, and Sleepy Creek, which they had to cross to leave the place, was often flooded and impassable, cutting them off from town and church.

David put crucifixes up in every room and on the porch, and called the farm the Flying Inn after an anti-Prohibition novel by G. K. Chesterton. He began to advertise his book business again in the *Catholic Worker*. He suggested Dorothy print the pope's 1939 encyclical, which listed the flight from the land as one of the evils in America, and he wrote a letter against industrialism to *Commonweal*.

Soon the kitchen was full of babies—humans, kid goats, and kittens—while Tamar baked, knitted, crocheted, wove, and in the evenings read seed catalogs. In the spring she planted tomatoes and cucumbers to can and pickle in the fall. She planted peach trees and grapevines and dreamed of planting weeping willows by the creek.

That first summer there was a severe drought that burned up the garden and killed their best milk goat. David worked as a day laborer at a tomato cannery, a ramshackle barn a mile down the road, where for sixty cents an hour he stacked cans to be boiled. He cut corn and helped with the neighbor's haying while Tamar wove rugs to sell. She went berry picking and got chiggers, which left welts on her legs and arms and an itch worse than poison ivy. She began to sponge herself with kerosene before and after picking. There were flies everywhere and, worse, black snakes and copperheads, and she lived in fear that Susie, who ran off to the creek whenever she got a chance, would get bit. Their first harvest was persimmons, walnuts, potatoes, cabbage, turnips, tomatoes, and apples. That winter they lived on beans, boiled barley, and canned applesauce, peaches, and tomatoes. David made elderberry wine and trips to the tavern when he had the cash, while Tamar and Dorothy had food on their minds. Dorothy remembered the abundant food of the summer while Tamar remembered the hunger of the winter.

By spring 1948 they had paid off the house. They now had fifty chickens and were selling eggs to the local store, and a cow who was giving six quarts of milk a day. David's book business brought in some cash, but they were so poor Tamar made dresses for the girls from feed sacks, and they all went barefoot in the warm weather. The day began and ended with carrying buckets of water from the spring. Tamar did the washing, including diapers for three children, in the creek, laying them out on the grass to dry in the sun. They had no light but kerosene lamps and no heat but a defective kerosene heater, and the winter wind blew in through the walls of the house.

Dorothy visited every six weeks, often with Stanley. Mama Hennessy and her daughters also came up regularly from Washington, DC. Even so, "swimming and loneliness" was Tamar's succinct comment on their toehold on the land. She was again pregnant, ill, and exhausted. Worried, Dorothy sent her *Gone with the Wind* along with D. H. Lawrence's *The Rainbow* and *Women in Love*. She said there was nothing like having a good book to look forward to at night.

It seems sex and babies were on Dorothy's mind, what with Helen Montague pregnant with her seventh child, and Tamar, only twenty-three, with a fourth child on the way and a husband she no longer cared for.

"By then he was just something to put up with," Tamar said. "But that was the dream—having a bunch of children, living on the land, and in poverty."

"One of the troubles with love," Dorothy wrote, "is that it gets buried in the debris of life, the hardships of child-bearing, the drain and drag of children on the mother is such that she is apt to neglect her husband and lose that love of body and soul so that she has to explore and search in her depths and seek it and pray for it, wooing it and caressing it again into life."

Along with the novels, Dorothy sent shoes for the girls that didn't fit or weren't matching pairs. In winter the kids again suffered from the cold, were unable to sleep at night, and got sick often. In spring, her plan to plant willow trees long past, Tamar went ahead with the garden but doubted whether they could take care of it. Both she and Dorothy continued to worry about food. Tamar often had to buy groceries on credit.

Every time Tamar wrote Dorothy, at least one of the kids was at her, either Susie hollering for the pencil or Eric fussing. The letters were short and jagged, a combination of Tamar's dislike of writing and the short bits of time she could grab between the demands of her children. And then when it seemed she was sunk by it all, she would write a simple sentence that revealed her love for the land and her love of Dorothy's visits. "I'm sorry you couldn't get here in time to see the redbud and dogwood in bloom together. The radishes and lettuce were even ready for you but they'll still be here. You can go swimming when you do come."

While Tamar slipped into depression, Dorothy continued to write in glowing terms about life on the land. "You make it sound too nice," Tamar commented with her usual understatement. She tried to tell Dorothy the state of her mind, but Dorothy gave her little comfort. Compared to the mad and the homeless in the municipal shelter, Tamar was well-off.

Dorothy visited Tamar in the summer of 1949, and they canned tomatoes while watching the stove because it was liable to go up in smoke. They canned until their hands ached, and Dorothy could barely write afterward. David had gone to Washington, DC, to look for work and a new place to live. Dorothy wished he could find work at Stotlers Crossroads, but she could see how lonely Tamar was. Even the cow didn't want to live at the farm and ran away any chance she got, breaking her chain and deserting her calf.

"She is looking for a herd to join," Tamar said to Dorothy. "Not a community," she added pointedly, "but a herd."

Even though she had just that spring planted twenty peach trees, Tamar was pushing for selling out and leaving. Dorothy suggested that they be joined by another Catholic Worker family to help keep them company, but Tamar discouraged it. Food was scarce, of poor quality, and high-priced, and there were no jobs. "This is no place fit for living even if rents are cheap," Tamar said, and reminded Dorothy of the priest and two couples who had moved down with them. One couple had abandoned the venture within the first month, the other couple a year later after both the deterioration of the wife's mental health and their relations with David, and the priest washed his hands of the whole thing.

David was unconcerned. "We seem to thrive on conflicts," he said to Dorothy.

Tamar and David did not fit in at Stotlers Crossroads, no matter how poor they were. They had paid for their farm in cash, and they were literate. David wrote letters for the neighbors, while Tamar with her new driver's license drove them to their dentist and doctor appointments in the 1932 Chevy Dorothy loaned her. There was Old Man Diddiwick, a farm laborer who raised his eight children on wages of fifty cents a day, and Mr. Unger, from whom they had bought their farm and who lived with his daughter-in-law Freda, even though she had left Mr. Unger's abusive son and was living with another man. Freda had a skunk and three groundhogs she loved like children. She had completed only first grade and worked like a man in the fields, though she was small and had polio as a child. Another neighbor, whose uninsured house burned down that year, destroying the family's life savings, had had five miscarriages, three stillborns, and seven surviving children.

Dorothy reassured Tamar that she understood how lonely she was, but she tried to discourage them from moving to Staten Island, where the Worker had bought a new farm. The rents were too high, Dorothy said to her. Then, maddeningly, a week later she asked David if they had thought of Staten Island. "How I would love to have you near us," she told him.

Tamar snapped. "Why should we hold out here I don't know. There will never be a living for us. Charity doesn't apply to families, and God helps those who help themselves. You don't seem to know what it's like to be expecting lots of babies and no sign of help anywhere. The only thing this place provides is space but nothing else. People don't live on air. I've just been begging at the neighbors for tomatoes to can."

In reply, Dorothy snapped back and wrote the letter that Tamar kept for decades, crumpled and bird chewed, the one in which she blamed Tamar for letting herself and the West Virginia farm go, for being the one who wanted to move, for always complaining and criticizing. For being ungrateful and needy, and taking and taking from the Worker without a thank-you. For not loving her husband enough and not supporting his good qualities. And most unfairly, for accusing Dorothy of neglecting her as a child. Grit your teeth and bear it, she told Tamar, and she wasn't going to write anymore until Tamar made the best of things, did her share in the marriage, and quit complaining.

Three days later Dorothy wrote a more relaxed if not loving letter, an apology that wasn't quite an apology. "Don't talk about your poverty because besides others you are rich. I've been reading *The Imitation of Christ* for comfort every day. Wish you would. After all, all we really have is our faith. Nothing else satisfies—husband, children, friends, comfort. Please pray more. And forgive me if I am harsh. You get little comfort from me, but I can send girls [from the Worker] down to help."

Dorothy said she would look for a place for them on Staten Island if that was what David wanted, as she at that time seemed to fully embrace the idea that the man, as the Christ figure in the family, was head of the household. "His is the decision after all. I know he does not want to live off the CW and that is the temptation if you are too close . . . I want to help where I can. . . . But you may be in such a state of resentment over my letter that you don't want to write. So if you don't answer, I'll not write again."

Relations were the lowest they had been since David's demands to have a leading role in the Easton farm three years earlier. Tamar left it to David to communicate with Dorothy, and David wrote her thanking her for the money she had sent, saying, "After Tamar received your tirade about a month ago, I asked her not to get all worked up—so that's why she hasn't written." A month after that he wrote again to ask Dorothy not to visit for a while either alone or with a girl to help. "We do not need your opposition. . . . We have withdrawn from the CW and now is the job to find out where the family line is to be found between us."

But Dorothy was back in West Virginia several weeks later for the birth of the fourth baby. She waited fretfully with Tamar at home while the children slept and David was out helping free the midwife's car, which had gotten bogged down in the mud and snow. A second son, Nicholas Joseph, Nicky, was born on a cold winter's morning before dawn. For months on end in the following year, all Tamar had to feed Nicky was oatmeal and applesauce.

In the spring of 1950 Dorothy headed down to West Virginia. She was thinking of asking for help from Forster to get the house wired, as Stotlers Crossroads finally had electricity. She arrived to find the family living on turnips and fried pumpkin but refused to be dismayed. "It is so beautiful that I cannot think, only breathe and bask in the sun." Tamar was still slender and lovely, while Dorothy weighed 180 pounds, a "disgrace," she said. Dorothy was now fifty-three and her hair, which had turned gray in her thirties, was completely white. David seemed to have had something drained out of him, and by that last year in Stotlers Crossroads, he had aged fifteen years.

That July, without Dorothy's help, they found what seemed to be the best solution. David got a job in Maryland with a Catholic publisher, the Newman Press, and with the job came a house with electricity and running water. They sold the livestock—three milking goats and five kids, a cow, a sheep, two pigs, and seventy-five chickens—and put the house up for sale, and with that toehold on the land slipping out of their grip, the three years in West Virginia came to an end.

Tamar and David weren't the only ones to fail in their return to the land at that time. Dorothy received many letters from people who said it just couldn't be done. The greatest problem, she believed, was that each family wanted its own farm. No one wanted to join with others, and being short of cash, they bought the cheapest land, which meant isolation from neighbors and from friends and family. The flight was meant to be from the city, not from one another, she said, and the call wasn't for everyone to become a self-sufficient farmer. "There is an infinite variety of ways to get out of the cities."

However, David and Tamar hadn't yet seen their last days on a farm. They still believed in the land movement or, as Tamar would eventually come to call it, that whole foolish trip.

It was during these years that Dorothy received yet another blow—Peter died on May 15, 1949, after being ill for more than five years, both in body and in mind. He had to be told when to go to bed, where to go to bed, when to arise, what to eat, and what to wear. His face was distorted and had settled into an expression of endurance, and he dragged one leg when he walked. Dorothy wrote less and less about Peter as his illness worsened, but the slow, steady loss of his faculties started Dorothy on a lifelong meditation on how we are pared down to the bone by life. Those who had known the caliber of Peter's mind found it painful to watch, but what Dorothy found the hardest to bear was how people treated him as simpleminded and shouted at him as though he were deaf. He seemed destined for oblivion after all his years of being misunderstood. In an effort to preserve something of him, and after much struggle on Peter's part, Dorothy recorded fifteen minutes of Peter reciting his Easy Essays, only to have them immediately erased by someone who didn't know how to work the machine.

In his last year Peter had to be watched over, as he liked to wander, and in March 1949, he disappeared from Mott Street. The Workers thought he was out visiting, so they did not begin to look until late that night. They scoured the Bowery and the lodging houses, and Dorothy sat up all night praying and worrying. They called the police to look for him and the cloistered nuns to pray for him. It was cold, and Dorothy worried that he would be mugged for his coat. Would people be able to understand his accent? Would he ask for directions? She lay awake listening for his footsteps on the stair, waiting for him to call out, "Dorrity."

"Have you found Peter?" Tamar wrote.

Four days later, he reappeared, thinner and happy to be back. He had gotten lost and rode the buses up to the Bronx and down to South Ferry. He ate and slept in coffeehouses. He was sitting in a cafeteria on Forty-Second Street when he saw a bus he knew, and it brought him back to the neighborhood.

It was a long dying for Peter. For a time, his mind functioned only with great effort. More and more he lay in bed unaware of what day it was. He would rally for visitors, but the visits left him exhausted. He lived his last year between Mott Street in winter and the Newburgh farm in summer, where he sat under the crab apple tree in the sun. On the day he died, he went to Mass in the morning and had a glass of wine in the evening, and then that night the men sat at his bedside as he lay dying. Dorothy, on the road, heard the news by phone.

Tamar headed up to New York City for the funeral, leaving the children with David, for even though David had known Peter well and had accompanied him on one of his last speaking tours, Tamar had known Peter the longest of anyone but Dorothy. After the funeral, she sent David a letter, the only one I have found from her to him. She was her perfunctory self, uncomfortable as usual with writing, but sad and quiet. It had been a joyful funeral, the Church of the Transfiguration was packed, and they had sung the Requiem Mass.

Peter remained on Tamar's mind for the rest of her life, as did many people at the Worker—the children she cared for, the women she loved, along with the funerals she attended, the graves she visited, and the quiet thought she gave them all. "He was just Peter," she would say. He lived on another plane. He didn't hold conversations, he indoctrinated, and she loved to listen. He was unfailingly kind to everyone, including that little girl, Tamar, who also didn't chatter idly. "Peter," Tamar said, "opened the door for Dorothy."

*   *   *

And so closed the decade of the forties—the decade of the famous retreat and when all the young men were sent to war, and of the shrinking of the Catholic Worker, during which Dorothy was no longer quite as respectable among the clergy and seminarians. It was the demise of Easton and with it the vision of a life beyond the endless soup lines. It was the call to return to the land and the men who listened but couldn't free themselves from their own inner demons, and all Dorothy could do was watch and pray through the devastation wrought through alcohol, breakdowns, abuse, and mental illness. It was a decade that led Dorothy and others at the Worker to take a hard, hard look at questions of authority and obedience, conscience and freedom.

Peter believed in something that few others could conceive, including the Church itself. He believed in absolute respect for the other and that you can never command or coerce another person. You can only put ideas before them and try to lead them to think for themselves. Recognizing the Christ in others means recognizing their right to act according to their conclusions and their conscience. That was the folly of the Cross.

What did Dorothy believe she could achieve by requiring everyone, workers and guests, to attend the retreats? She was certain that only through this could people be strong enough to do the work. But her mistake was to insist, against Peter's most cherished principle, that people do what she believed was best for them. And the most unfortunate part for Tamar was that Dorothy did this just at the time Tamar was trying to find out who she was and what she wanted to be.

That was the forties, and I hear Dorothy saying, "I always learn the hard way. It's the only way I know how to learn." And I hear Tamar saying, "Everyone must live their own disasters."

CHAPTER THIRTEEN

In the fifties the Worker endured, as did Dorothy, Tamar, and David. It wasn't that life was easier after the forties, when Dorothy had been in danger of losing everything, including her daughter. But there were three returns in Dorothy's life in the beginning of the fifties—the return to Staten Island; the return of some of the old crowd whom she had, in the aftermath of the war, been reluctant to contact for fear they would be angry with her; and the return of Tamar to the Catholic Worker fold.

The decade began with a blow. Within weeks of Peter's death, the owners of the Mott Street building put it on the market and told the Worker it had to move out, and the Mott Street era came to an end. The building may have been a wreck—they kept saltshakers filled with DDT powder to keep the lice, cockroaches, and bedbugs at bay, and rats walked across Dorothy's desk or ran over the cook's hand as she sliced bread—but it had been their home for fourteen years.

Dorothy rarely wrote of the Mott Street building—it was the neighborhood she loved. Before the war it was much the same as when the Worker first moved in, but above Canal Street, the tenements were now almost half-Chinese, as were the businesses. Chinese music wafted through the streets from the growing number of clubs, replacing the sound of the Italian neighbors singing the songs of Mario Lanza.

By the end of the forties, the old men still played cards, and the babies still learned to walk on the street, and the children said "Cross me" to any nearby adult to get to the playground, which was still noisy until ten at night. The Third Avenue El, the only elevated rail left in Manhattan, still passed over Chatham Square, sending the house trembling. But the young men now watched ball games on televisions in store windows, the restaurant where the Gypsies came to eat roasted sheep's head and listen to the violins was gone, and the building next door was abandoned and full of rubble except for the shoemaker's shop.

The eviction and search for a new place strained everyone's nerves, and people were afraid they would be turned out into the street. They found a place six blocks north on Chrystie Street for thirty thousand dollars. It was a double redbrick building set back from the street with iron lacework on the front stoop and a paved courtyard in the back.

"I hear you have a fine place now," the traffic cop called out to Dorothy. "You deserve it after all these years."

But the new neighborhood was not as accepting and welcoming as Little Italy had been, and life was no easier for Dorothy. "Will we ever get peacefully settled so I can write?" she wrote in her diary. She turned away a drunken woman and was chastised for doing so. She had to fight her impulse to say no to people wanting to stay. She was sick, exhausted, and depressed, and it brought back memories of the spring of 1943, when Tamar was at Ade's. Dorothy was diagnosed with uterine fibroids, and she had an infection of the tear gland that left her eyes red and watery as if she were constantly crying. And bad news came from Easton and from some of the other Catholic Worker farms.

"We are beginning our nineteenth year," she commented, "and it seems we have just begun."

The new Catholic Worker farm on Staten Island was on Bloomingdale Road in the town of Pleasant Plains, which Dorothy named the Peter Maurin Farm. It had twenty-two acres, including three acres of asparagus, a ten-room farmhouse, a woodlot, and a barn. Dorothy blamed Peter for her decision to spend sixteen thousand dollars for the farm on the heels of purchasing the Chrystie Street house. She felt his absence keenly, still finding herself wanting to turn to him for advice. Peter would have approved, she felt, because he was never one to limit you in your desires. There's enough money in the world, he would say. And also, with the new Staten Island place she could once again ride the ferry and taste the salt spray while watching the gulls overhead and the sun set over the warehouses and piers of Brooklyn. Once again she had that half-hour interlude, that time when she so treasured being neither here nor there and filled with peace, silence, and the healing power of the sea.

The Worker was, as usual, struggling, and Dorothy was feeling its many failures. She was not much admired, and the Catholic Worker was called a band of nuts, Catholic puritans, or marginal radicals. That steady flow of priests, who since 1934 had stopped on their way home from Rome, had long slowed, and seminarians had their vocation questioned if they expressed interest in the Worker. Dorothy found herself relegated to the fringes of the Catholic Church, much like a poor and batty aunt who can't be gotten rid of and is embarrassing in what she could come out with at indelicate moments. Even Father Hugo seemed to be affected and failed to visit while he was in town. Dorothy felt stung and abandoned.

It was a time of growing laws and growing suspicion, of loyalty oaths and conformity. The McCarran Act was passed in 1950, and there were plenty who believed Dorothy was a communist. "Trying to talk about these things is not so simple," she said, but no one wanted nuanced answers.

A passerby said to one of the men selling the *Catholic Worker* on the street, "I want you to know that I took your picture, because I want to remember your face. Pretty soon this cold war is going to turn into a shooting war, and you're going to be one of the first ones I kill."

A lieutenant colonel told Dorothy that the Worker's position on war was right while Dominican theologians told her it was wrong. Dorothy was either a saint or she was the devil. "As the philosopher said when he received a great deal of applause, 'What have I done wrong now?'" she wrote in response to good publicity, though she couldn't help herself from being defensive about criticisms. Nevertheless the circulation of the paper stabilized, and the Worker began to grow again.

In the fifties, attitudes toward the poor were not the same as they had been in the thirties, when many were poor. Even within the Worker there were those who believed their job was to help people help themselves, but Dorothy, in a tone much different than in 1944, when she believed she could lead people from the soup line to the retreat, felt that people who came to their door needed kindness, courtesy, and acceptance, and most often just to be left alone to rest and recover mentally, spiritually, and physically. "Who knows what is in their hearts and minds? Who knows their pain?" she said. It is hard to do nothing, and yet often that is all you can do—do nothing but listen and give the person a cup of coffee and a bowl of soup.

Have we failed? Dorothy asked. Yes, and on every front—failed to clarify thought, failed in running houses of hospitality, for though they flourished, they weren't, as Peter wanted, places to teach "cult, culture, and cultivation," as he called it in his play on words, *cult* meaning liturgy, *culture* meaning literature, and *cultivation* meaning agriculture. It was all they could do to practice the works of mercy. They failed in even establishing farms, never mind beginning to build a new social order.

"I must say that I am not much concerned," she concluded. "Failures are inseparable to a work of this kind, and necessary for our growth in holiness."

Dorothy's aestheticism of the forties lingered. She spoke of a fear of the senses, of constant sinning, and love was measured by the cost of giving it up. She fasted on bread and water for twenty-four hours on the first Friday of each month, and she thought, briefly, about attending two Masses a day. At the Peter Maurin Farm they held regular Sunday retreats, though no one at Chrystie Street supported Dorothy in the retreats. She felt she needed to continue even if they sometimes were a strain even for her, for she had heard it all before.

After twenty years of living in community, Dorothy still felt tormented by people's moods and unhappiness. She still grieved when her most beloved books were stolen or left out in the rain or used as doorstops. "Community is sword grass in the hand," she would quote, and then leave, as usual, to go traveling.

"Dorothy," Stanley said, "lives on buses. She created the Worker for the rest of us."

Tamar agreed. "Whenever things got to be too much at the Worker, Dorothy got on a bus. No matter where she was, she had an anxious

family waiting to unload all their grievances, but on a bus she was neither here nor there."

She began to hear from the old Greenwich Villagers, including Mike
Gold, whom she hadn't seen since the East Fifteenth Street apartment.
Maybe it was an outcome of the marginalization of the Worker, the soft-
ening of some of Dorothy's ideological stances, and the politically hardening times that led those from that radical past to seek one another
out. And perhaps it was because Dorothy kept moving in the face of
the hostility of the McCarthy era, unperturbed, unshaken, and unafraid.
Along with Mike Gold, she was a radical who endured, who never got
tired.

The times must have brought back memories to them all. The execution in 1953 of Ethel and Julius Rosenberg as Dorothy, her heart heavy,
bathed her grandchildren and put them to bed, echoed the executions
of Sacco and Vanzetti when she cared for Tamar. McCarthyism now
and the Palmer Red Raids then. So much must have seemed familiar.

The fifties also brought several deaths, including that of her old companion Lionel Moise, who died on August 8, 1952. He had continued his
peripatetic journalist's life, traveling and working in all the major cities
of the United States, leaving behind stories of his irrepressible nature.
Lionel worked as an editor for the Hearst Predate Service in New York
City the last decade of his life and died of a heart condition at the age of
sixty-three. His death provoked a flurry of stories, mostly from his early
days, about "that ol' devil Moise" and the fights he gravitated toward—
the articles he wrote with his hand in a cast, the flights out of town without notice. How once when the weather turned cold, he flipped a coin
to decide whether to buy a winter coat or to head to Los Angeles, and
Los Angeles won. How he knew more tricks of the trade than any other
newsman—how to get information out of reluctant informants, how to
spot lies, and how to give the editor the impression he had worked hard
at a story when it had fallen into his lap. He was openhearted and open-
handed, people remarked. He was tough but didn't push it in people's
faces and was "nearly always pleasant," and he had been a top-notch
hooch maker during Prohibition.

About himself Lionel seems to have said very little. "I know nothing," he was claimed to have said, "except what I have read in the papers. I attribute my success to clean living and the use of Lucky Strikes. I pronounce my name Mo-eez, but don't ask anyone else to unless he wants something."

A year after Lionel's death, in December 1953, Dorothy wrote in her diary, "Gene O'Neill died," as brief as always when she was grieving. Before she had heard of his final illness, Dorothy had had a curious experience. She was at Chrystie Street praying the rosary when the candle fluttered, and the phrase "tear drippings" suddenly came to her, and she knew Gene was ill. She immediately sent word to Cardinal Cushing in Boston asking him to send a priest to Gene. Gene's wife, Carlotta, refused to let the priest in, and he later told Dorothy he believed that Gene had wanted to see him. Gene had told Eddie Dowling, an actor, a playwright, and the director of *The Iceman Cometh*, that he thought about returning to the Church but couldn't bring himself to. He would have if the Holy Father had told off Hitler, he said.

Two months after Gene's death, in February 1954, Max Bodenheim and his third wife, Ruth, were murdered. Dorothy wrote an obituary because he and Ruth had lived at the Worker for three months the previous year, arriving the same time that two other poets, W. H. Auden and Allen Ginsberg, had come to visit. Over the years, Max had kept turning up in Dorothy's life—Greenwich Village in 1917 and 1918; Chicago in the early twenties, where he read his poetry in the Bughouse; and then later on Staten Island when Max's son was one of the children Dorothy cared for. When Max was sixty, he arrived at the Worker with Ruth, his beautiful, much younger wife, and a broken leg.

Ruth headed into the city once a week to try to sell Max's poetry, while Max remained at the Peter Maurin Farm and quietly lay on a bed in the hall, full of gratitude, and waiting for his leg to heal. He never drank, just smoked his pipe and wrote, producing a poem every few days. Dorothy wrote, "Every day that he was with us he worked on a series of sonnets, dedicated to each one of us, polished, stately, courteous, often obscure, and he came to meals happily to read them aloud." Max wrote an ode to Agnes Lawrence, who kept the house clean: "You must have been a miracle of fire when you were still a girl."

When spring came and his leg healed, Max and Ruth left, and Dorothy never saw them again. They had found a place sharing an apartment with an unhinged young man who murdered them and then told the police, "I'm a hero—I've killed two communists." And so in the space of two months, Max and Gene, two of the three who sat at a café table the winter of 1918 writing a poem, were gone.

As people aged, they began to reminisce about those early years, though it seemed everyone had a story to tell about the drunken antics of others while remaining forgetful of their own. Even Peggy, who wrote an article on her brief affair with the poet Hart Crane and who had returned to Staten Island and lived near the Peter Maurin Farm, threatened to write one on Dorothy. "Ah, me," Dorothy sighed. There was also Agnes Boulton's memoir, *Part of a Long Story*, of her marriage to Gene O'Neill, and Agnes visited Dorothy to give her the manuscript to read and stayed for supper. Agnes's visit, along with a visit the year before by Louis Sheaffer, Gene's biographer, provoked Dorothy into thinking about writing on her months with Gene, but other than a short unpublished essay she did no writing about those years.

Tamar spent her decade of the fifties either pregnant or nursing. The same year Dorothy bought the Staten Island farm and Chrystie Street house, David and Tamar moved to Maryland. Tensions eased between Dorothy and the Hennessys, and David again put an ad in the *Catholic Worker* for his book business. But the house and job in Maryland didn't last more than eight months. Dorothy was visiting when David's employer arrived at their home with oranges for the children and an eviction notice for the parents. They had to move out at once, and then less than two weeks later David, who had been working long and late hours, was fired. The following month they sold the West Virginia farm for three hundred dollars more than what they had paid for it. David shouted what sounded like an old West Virginian saying—"Hill folks are always free!"—and they packed up and moved into the barn at the Staten Island farm. Tamar was heavily pregnant.

David had found work in the mail room at Sheed & Ward publishers at forty-five dollars a week and a house a mile from the Worker for six thousand dollars. After paying their debts, they had enough for a down payment, but until they could take possession of the house they lived at the Peter Maurin Farm.

Tamar's fifth child, Mary Elizabeth, was born at the farm on Sunday, July 22, 1951, at dawn. It had been a long wait in the summer heat for the baby's arrival.

"Don't have the baby until I return," Dorothy said to Tamar, and she drove into the city to deliver bread. She rushed back, forced to listen to her passenger speak of "scriptural, speculative, moral, pastoral and ascetical theology," and all the while she could think only of Tamar. "Tamar is such a wonder. No false alarms, taking everything calmly," Dorothy wrote after the birth while listening to the rampaging and shouting children. "The first five are the hardest," she said, quoting a Catholic Worker mother.

After seven months at the Peter Maurin Farm, David, Tamar, and the five children moved into their new home, a small cottage with four acres at 201 Winant Avenue, four and a half miles from the beach at Huguenot where Tamar learned to walk. It was a four-room house, tiny but warm, with an attic they planned to turn into another bedroom and a study for David. He reopened the David Hennessy Distributist Bookshop, and the Worker paper began advertising a list of twenty titles.

The house was surrounded by peach, cherry, plum, and pear trees, and four mulberry trees in back that Dorothy sat under while watching over the children and writing—the same trees David would sit under with his buddies drinking Pabst Blue Ribbon beer. The place felt rural as there were few houses on the road, and they were surrounded by acres of scrubby fields and woods with sandy soil. And yet just to the north a mile away was the largest Standard Oil storage plant in the world, and across Kill Van Kull they could see the factories of New Jersey.

Tamar had great plans for the garden. She and Dorothy went to a flower show and returned with dozens of bulbs and seedlings. They spread manure, compost, and mulch to build up the poor soil. Tamar and

David started to share keeping a diary, and while Tamar wrote about the garden, the animals, the children, and the weather, David wrote about attending Mass, his book business, and letters he had received. It was a fresh start for the both of them.

Once again, mention of Tamar appeared in the *Catholic Worker* paper, and one of the writers of the farm column wrote, "It may be because she was born in the Catholic Worker, it may be her ancestors, it may be because she has Dave and five children, but Tamar has always seemed to me to be possessed of a remarkable maturity, a satiric and gentle objectivity."

But life hadn't become any easier with the move. One winter Eric came down with pneumonia, Susie possibly with jaundice, and Becky with a cough, so Dorothy, also sick and voiceless, canceled a trip to the Midwest, and drove Eric to the hospital in the old 1932 Chevrolet that had no windows. Two weeks later Becky was running a fever of 106. She too had pneumonia and went to the hospital, where she broke out in measles and was put in quarantine. Then Susie and Eric came down with measles. Then Susie got the mumps. And then there was the trip to the Newburgh farm when the kids all came back with chicken pox.

Dorothy's columns those years were full of descriptions of the children. Mary was "big as a minute, but full of a tremendous energy and joy of life" and "Eric is quiet, helpful, forever busy taking things apart with wrenches, helping carry lumber, carting out the trash, bringing in the mail" while

Nicky, the terror, is the most talkative member of the family. He is a great conversationalist and his tones contain all intonations, moods, emotions. He boasts, he thrusts out his chest, he is deep-voiced and aggressive, he struts; or he is tender, embracing his little sister, having just knocked her down; or "I'll kiss Granny," implying that none else will, and he will come to the rescue; or he is full of fierce excitement over a dog, a bird, a truck, a bus, which he calls upon everyone to share; or resignation, "Okay, all right, I won't," whereupon he goes and does. He is rollicking, big-

mouthed, shining-eyed. And the place is never still for a minute while he is around.

Nicky would shout, "God was not ever a little baby! I wasn't ever a little baby!" He was "pugnacious, aggressive and then suddenly falls asleep like as not with a toad under his pillow."

Dorothy, Tamar, and the children lunched under the mulberry trees and had birch beer and pretzels at Wolfe's Pond Park. They ran about in the woods, Nicky with a foot-long carving knife, and looked for frogs at the pond. They got infected feet from glass, splinters, and thorns, and fell out of trees while Dorothy prayed to their guardian angels.

They revived the Hot Chocolate and Walking Club from when Tamar was a child. Dorothy, Peggy Baird, Tamar, and Rita Ham, a young artist newly arrived at the Worker, roamed the countryside with the children in search of places to fish or have sketching parties. They went for evening picnics on Mount Loretto beach, where they fished and collected mussel shells and horseshoe crabs. They used a raft as a playpen for the baby and as a backrest for Dorothy as she wrote, or she wandered the beach carrying under her arm letters to be answered or with a manuscript or the notes for columns she should be writing. Dorothy and Tamar headed to the beach every chance they got, even in midwinter, and Mary, along with the next two babies, learned how to walk on the beach, just as Tamar had. The boys collected snails, and Susie, always brave, floated on a raft, while Tamar, heavily pregnant and looking startlingly young in her pale yellow seersucker apron, loaded up the car with driftwood to heat the house in the winter.

While Tamar nursed the baby and David read, Dorothy took on the children's religious instruction and tried saying the rosary with them. Becky and Susie knelt for a while and then sat for a while, and Susie said her beads while winding them in and out between the toes of her dusty feet, and Eric wove his rosary in and out the back of the chair. Nicky would for years claim defiantly that God was not a little baby, or if he was then Nicky was bigger than God, and then he'd puff out his chest. Dorothy wrote, "He is taking much interest in theology so his father calls him his little theologian." Their religious instruction, though, had its up and downs. While Stanley read out loud pious tracts, Nicky and Eric listened with huge tomato worms on their noses, but Dorothy remained optimistic. She snatched moments to read the Psalms to the children out under the mulberry trees, and for a moment or two they would all be quiet. "We don't give our children half credit enough for intelligence even," she wrote in her column, "let alone recognizing what miracles grace works in their souls."

While Dorothy taught the children their prayers, Tamar was preparing them to be gardeners. Susie planted carrots, hollyhocks, and pansies, while Eric planted marigolds and lettuce, which Nicky pulled up. Tamar would send the older kids, all still under the age of seven, to pick vegetables for dinner.

The move to the second Cobbett Cottage had been a fresh start, but a year and a half later Tamar developed stomach problems. Dorothy worried that Tamar would get stomach ulcers and told her not to keep unpleasant thoughts. "Mother used to go in for reading Christian Science & Unity," Dorothy said. "Just as she said she went downtown and bought a new hat when she got melancholy. Sometimes there is nothing on this earth we want, and I've been through those times. Neither food nor drink, not a movie or downtown or a new hat, not a book or anything else. Father Farina calls them tunnels and temptation to discouragement. I always get through them by manual work. Or take a walk. Forster used to insist on a walk, a regular Britisher, and it did me good though I never wanted it." She suggested Tamar read—Dickens, Sigrid Undset, Jane Austin, the Brontës, something to pick up at night and look forward to during the day. And she was careful to tell Tamar how wonderful and strong she was.

Tamar was pregnant with her sixth child, and things weren't going well for David at Sheed & Ward, and after working there for two years, he resigned. Dorothy prayed to Chesterton and Gill to find David better and more satisfying work, and he soon had a summer job for the city of New York working in the woods and on the beach of Wolfe's Pond Park. When that job came to an end he became a gravedigger for seven dollars a day at Saint Joseph's Cemetery a mile away.

The children continued to thrive. "Mary is at the giddy age of two," Dorothy wrote, "dancing and singing and shouting all the day long. 'Rowdy Irish,' David calls her. She is beautiful and good, and it is most edifying to see her fold her little hands in prayer at each meal. Nicky thinks the act of folding the hands, the gesture, is enough and dives right into the meal. He is the shoutingest member of the family." Eric was turning into a carpenter, and built a table. ("The table is very weak," he said, "but I think it is strong enough to eat ice cream on!")

The doctor convinced Tamar to have her next baby in the hospital, and at dawn early in August 1953, Dorothy drove Tamar to the hospital while David, always wanting more sons, recited in enthusiastic optimism Chesterton's poem "Lepanto": "It is Richard, it is Raymond, it is Godfrey at the gate!"

"But it was not—it was little Margaret," wrote Dorothy. A week later the Peter Maurin Farm had a day of dedication to Christian marriage, but neither Tamar nor David came.

Dorothy babysat to help Tamar and David get away. "You must be a 'lawyer, doctor, nurse, philosopher, historian, theologian, story teller, poet, musician,' as Chesterton says, when you take care of children. But don't let me frighten you. Love takes care of it all."

Dorothy was learning much about childhood education from Tamar, for Tamar was not about to raise her kids using the Day family method. She didn't believe in Pop's principle of absolute control and that children must not be heard, nor did she believe in striking them. Dorothy liked to quote Grace, "Never a lick amiss," whereas Tamar did not, and not hitting her children, however lightly and sparingly, was a form of pacifism Tamar taught her mother. There were times when they were overwhelmingly noisy and chaotic, frustrating and destructive, for Tamar believed in expression rather than repression. "Children have their own order," she told her mother. "Don't look," she then suggested.

The kids went almost daily to the Peter Maurin Farm to play and sometimes spent the night there to give Tamar a break. Stanley told them his stories "The Girl and the Miser," "The King and the Nightingale," and "Oswald the Hungry Lion," while Rita taught them how to draw. Just as he had done when Tamar was a child, John Filigar took them for rides in the hay wagon, and in the spring they followed him on the plow. Things were going well at the farm. "You can't work for twenty-two years without improving conditions somewhat," Dorothy said, while Tamar, who had seen farms go up and down since 1936, said they were just going through a clean and efficient period.

When they had first moved onto the Peter Maurin Farm the soil was utterly depleted and the smog was killing the fruit trees. Help came in the person of Father Duffy, an Irish priest from a farming family. He had been associated with the Worker for years and was, in Dorothy's word, "incorrigible." He was a man of strong opinions and a strong drinking habit. In the forties both Mott Street and the Easton farm had become known as places for alcoholic priests to stay until they got back on their feet. "Dorothy," Tamar said, "was the first person to recognize the problem with alcohol and priests. She would take them in, and some of them were in terrible straits. She realized the Church wasn't doing it, so she did it." By the early fifties, there were five priests at the Peter Maurin Farm and three at Newburgh, priests on drunken binges, mad priests, renegade priests, disturbed priests who had had nervous breakdowns or violent episodes or who drank and fought at the local tavern, and priests desperate for any sign of affection.

The Chancery of the Archdiocese of New York told Dorothy to encourage Father Duffy to return to Ireland, but under his direction the Workers cleared the brush, sumac, and witch grass and planted six acres of corn and a hayfield of clover, rye, timothy, and other nitrogenous legumes to help improve the soil. They dug ditches to control rain runoff and catch topsoil, and then planted the raised banks with pine trees and multiflora to provide a windbreak and cover for wildlife. They mulched the three acres of asparagus with seaweed they collected from the beach, pruned the grapevines and fruit trees, limed the blackberries, and spread manure they had traded for grass and hay from the neighboring goat and horse farmers. They had ducks, geese, chickens, rabbits, cows, laying hens, and pigs. Three years later, the pear, cherry, and apple trees and grapevines began to bear fruit. Father Duffy thought it would take another three years to bring back the soil. "If this can be done here," he said, "it can be done anywhere in the US because the farm was as poor and low as any can get."

After the relative calm of the early fifties, in 1955 things began to shift both at the Worker and for the Hennessy family. Since the bombing of Hiroshima and Nagasaki in 1945, nuclear war and nuclear weapons were on everyone's minds, and the thorny topic of pacifism returned to the forefront at the Worker. In June 1955 Dorothy was arrested for the first time since Chicago in the early twenties, this time for refusing to take part in the "duck and cover" air-raid drills in New York City. She would continue protesting them for the next six years.

Those years from 1955 on were also a period of tightening housing regulations and harassment, and Dorothy was accused by a judge of being a slum landlord running the house for profit, and she was told to vacate Chrystie Street. The case generated a huge amount of publicity, and help came from all over, including from Lucy Burns, the suffragist Dorothy had been jailed with in 1917. Their certificate of occupancy at Chrystie Street was withheld because their night watchman wasn't making his rounds every hour on the hour, and they received summonses for leaving garbage can lids off, even though the garbage truck was approaching, and for dripping paint on the sidewalk while painting the fire escape.

At the Peter Maurin Farm the fire department said they couldn't have a chapel in the barn, and the building department said they couldn't have a fire escape on a wooden dwelling. They also could have only one family and four people living there, and if there was no biological link, a family was defined as one person. Dave Dellinger's wife, Betty, gave birth in a room off the kitchen, the second child after Mary Elizabeth to be born at the farm. Dorothy was there to give moral support, and then was later visited by health officials who threatened to arrest her for delivering a child without a midwife's license.

Meanwhile, David had a new job as a night watchman at the Nassau Smelting and Refining Company, where salvaged metals were smelted into ingots of copper, brass, lead, and zinc. The hours were irregular and alternated between the swing shift and the graveyard shift.

Perhaps in an effort to find concordances with David, as she would say, Dorothy reintroduced the English distributists in the paper. David was always worth listening to on these subjects, Dorothy said, because he was a worker and a scholar. He worked for a huge monopoly, belonged to a union, and yet also owned a four-acre homestead in New York City with goats, chickens, ducks and geese, turtles and chipmunks, rabbits and parakeets, in addition to his bookselling business.

"Industrialism can't give man the three basic necessities—food, clothing, and shelter," Dorothy quoted David as saying. "Mass production can make fridges, but not the food to go in them. Of course people can argue that we do have factories in the fields and we do have mass production of food. But all rural-lifers who are working for the family farm can tell you that such mass production does not produce as much per acre as smaller units, and the soil is depleted and poisoned, and the health of the whole population lowered. Under industrialism the world is starving and the vitamin factories are flourishing."

Within the Worker the exchange on distributism had become heated, but David's voice in it had disappeared. His book list was shrinking, and his last ad in the paper was in the summer of 1955. He was failing to fill orders, and Dorothy feared accusations of mail fraud. And by the time she wrote her last article on the subject, "Distributism Is Not Dead," there was no one left to support her.

Back home after her first air-raid drill arrest, Dorothy went over to Tamar's house. David was working the graveyard shift, and Tamar asked Dorothy to stay. Just past midnight, they were off to the hospital just in time for another daughter, Martha, Tamar's seventh child, to be born. The following day after visiting Tamar and the baby in the hospital, David went to the tavern and got into a fight.

Dorothy began to notice that he seemed tormented and that led him to torment others with his rage, his rants, his sheer destructiveness, as Tamar called it, and his determination to alienate every friend he had. He alternated between telling Tamar to ask her mother for money and descending into abusive rages against Dorothy.

"Dorothy tried to keep her distance," Tamar said. "She tried to be so wise about it all. Not bringing things up that she felt were hurtful. But I think she suffered awful when she saw how things were. Dave Hennessy's hostility to Dorothy shocked everyone. He called her a communist. He hated the paper, and called it her red rag. He hated women. He would descend into tirades against Dorothy until all our friends just fell away, didn't visit any more. Dorothy was very kind to not make it worse in any way."

David also tormented Tamar. "I never grew up to the extent that I could get away from my mother and the Worker," she said. "And boy, did he let me know!"

So there was Tamar having her babies neatly and efficiently while David unraveled. West Virginia was poverty and isolation, while Staten Island was drunken parties under the mulberry trees with his sisters or trips to the White Horse Tavern, where he could get muscatel for thirty-five cents a pint and to where Tamar would send Becky and Eric, both still under the age of twelve, running through the woods to the tavern to tell Daddy to come home.

"It is only when I am drinking," he said, "that I feel like a man."

He had a mean mouth when he drank, and he began to turn it on his children. Sometimes he provoked his friends into physically attacking him (it had been his best friend who shot him in the head in 1940), and he provoked Tamar until she threw a tin cup at him and hit him in the head. "That was during those last months in West Virginia," she said, "when Dorothy was coming down on mercy errands. He bled so much it frightened me to death."

Tamar and Dorothy could see underneath David's hostility that something was terribly wrong. Responding in the only way she knew how, Tamar, who had turned thirty, filled her garden with jonquils and tulips and wove every free moment she had—coverlets, diapers, tablecloths, and curtains on the Leclerc loom, which would take days to set up, what with children underfoot and their heads too near the beater. She spun wool on a spindle and flax on a Hutterite spinning wheel. She set aside the softest wool for clothing for the babies and used the coarser wool for afghans, scarves, hats, and socks. She taught Becky and Susie how to knit, and headed over to the Peter Maurin Farm to teach people there how to weave.

The house was a mess as Tamar hated housework. The woodwork and walls needed paint, and the furniture was broken. But the place was full of plants, shells and specimens, books, desks, hooked rugs, and the piano on which visitors would give Schubert recitals on keys sticky from the kids' fingers. Tamar preferred to fill the days with trips with her children, the neighborhood kids, and the Peter Maurin Farm children as well, to the fields, woods, and beach to bird-watch and gather specimens, to swim and fish, and to dig for clams. These things, Dorothy said, make for much happiness and joy and gratitude to God for His creation, while Tamar added there was no point in relying on the school or the parish to provide this connection to the natural world—it was up to families to do it themselves.

Dorothy, Stanley, and Peggy tried to help Tamar as much as they could. Stanley took them on trips into the city or to visit Aunt Della, while Dorothy took them to the Central Park and Bronx Zoos, or Peggy babysat while David and Tamar headed into the city to explore bookstores. Dorothy longed to spend more time with Tamar and the children, and she dreamed of writing books and with the proceeds buying a beach house where they all could stay in the summer while she worked from there. Instead, the summer of 1956 she was arrested again at the air-raid drill and spent five days in jail. She would come to know the city jails well, including the Women's House of Detention on Sixth Avenue in Greenwich Village, where Forster and Della stood outside protesting the arrests and sentencing.

In the photos of Dorothy at this time, she seems so conventional even as she is being arrested, and looked like anyone's grandmother as she was led to a police van. In photos of Tamar, she is pregnant and surrounded by children. ("Over sixteen years," she said, "of either being pregnant or nursing.")

On August 17, 1957, after Nicky's First Communion at Our Lady Help of Christians Church, where Dorothy and Tamar had both been baptized, and after the third air-raid drill protest, for which Dorothy was sentenced to thirty days, Tamar's eighth child was born. The baby was a boy they named Hilaire Peter, after Hilaire Belloc and Peter Maurin. "How David crowed," Tamar said, "to have another son."

Three weeks later the family left Staten Island to move to Vermont in yet another attempt to solve the difficulties of Tamar and David's marriage. "A lot of what makes me feel like a destroyed person," Tamar said in the last months of her life, "was living with a husband who so hated the Worker while I loved it."

CHAPTER FOURTEEN

Tamar could barely tear herself away from her garden—the marigolds, zinnias, and cosmos were in bloom—when she, Dorothy, and the eight children headed up to Vermont on a clear and cool, early-September morning. Dorothy drove a 1949 jeep station wagon, full of rattles and with no hand brake, while Becky, Tamar, and the new baby sat in the front, and the others filled up the back. They arrived at the farm late in the afternoon on the second day, and soon after David and two companions arrived in a rental truck. Tamar was devastated to discover that the truck was too small, and many things had to be left behind, including the mulberry seedlings and house plants.

The new house was a large, traditional, continuous New England farmhouse. Grapevines grew on the front of the house, and in the yard there were two butternuts and two maples, the sizes of which dwarfed the Staten Island trees. In back there were eighteen acres of hillside fields with an apple orchard full of ripe apples nestled in a serene, south-facing valley among gentle hills surrounded by nothing but hundreds of acres of woods. Dorothy felt suffocated by the trees and hills of Vermont. She preferred having a long view, growing up as she did in Chicago, surrounded by the prairie and Lake Michigan, and then living on Staten Island, where she could gaze out to Raritan Bay. Tamar, on the other hand, left behind trees wherever she lived—at Easton, Stotlers Crossroads, Staten Island, and her two homes in Vermont. There were never enough trees for her, not even in Vermont, where if you turn your back for a moment you will find oak, hickory, and maple seedlings uprooting your foundations.

The house on Cady Hill Road delighted them all. "The geographical cure," Tamar later came to call it. She and David made plans while the older kids wandered about, dumb with amazement at the size of the house—it had nine bedrooms—and the younger ones raced from room to room. David unpacked his books in one room, while in another Tamar set up the loom, always the first thing she packed and unpacked in their moves. Her spinning wheel had been stolen from the Peter Maurin Farm, but she found a spindle and a box of raw washed wool in the house. Eric eyed the surrounding woods nervously for several days before he and Nicky finally headed out with two fishing rods they found in the barn.

Dorothy wasn't aware that it was Tamar who made the decision to move, exhausted as she was by David's hostility toward Dorothy and no longer able to shield Dorothy from it. Tamar rarely spoke of what happened to drive her away from all she loved—the Worker, her mother, the beach, and her small homestead filled with fruit trees, flowers, goats, and chickens—but once again she was in exile; once again, as she gave up her connection to the Worker, giving up her mother. And this time there was no name for the house, no Cobbett Cottage, no Flying Inn; there were no more romantic names to be had.

David put ads in the *Catholic Worker* to get the bookshop business going again. Tamar made grape juice, applesauce, and cider with an old cider press she found in the barn. Eric chopped wood they gathered, and Susie milked the new cow, Chrissie. And in the evenings before supper they walked up the hill behind the house to watch the sunset.

Winter came, and David wrote to Dorothy, "Our first Christmas in Vermont! All seem happy, holy, and healthy." But when Dorothy drove up with Stanley, they found Tamar and David in a state of raw nerves. The temperature had plunged to thirty-five degrees below zero, and the snow kept falling. The winters in West Virginia had been nothing like this. To keep the animals alive, Tamar kept eighty-five baby chicks near the woodstove in the living room along with a lamb who liked to curl up against Dorothy's feet as she washed dishes.

The long Vermont winter ended the tradition of planting radishes on Tamar's birthday. Instead, that March Tamar tapped the sugar maples and boiled four gallons of maple syrup. In May she planted strawberries and asparagus while Dorothy watched from the summer kitchen, where she could see lady slippers, dogtooth violets, and trillium blooming in the shadow of the old stone wall running along the back of the house.

David began work as a day laborer for a neighboring farmer, Dave Green, in exchange for plowing and harrowing, and he became tanned and strong from being out in the fields spreading manure and putting up fences. "Dave Green was a kind and generous farmer, an old-timer of the very best," Tamar said. "He took all of our animals when we couldn't care for them." They bought apple cider jelly and hay from Gus Aldrich up the road, and Slim Jacobs down the road would show up half-drunk wanting coffee and sociability and with a gift of sugar cubes meant for his horses.

Other neighbors took advantage of them. The man who sold them the house was open about his grasping nature. "I'm not interested unless it's a steal," he'd say, and he sold them green wood that first winter, and they almost froze to death. Another neighbor sold them what they thought was a useless cow, though, under Tamar's care, the cow ended up living a long and productive life, and they didn't even have to breed her to keep her producing milk.

Becky, now thirteen, did the washing and ironing, while Susie cooked, milked the cow, and cleaned out the barn. Maggie, four years old, was already helping Tamar thread and wind the warp by sitting inside the loom frame, while Eric and Nicky set out early in the mornings to go fishing and sometimes stayed out until dark and brought home trout for Tamar to cook. The boys were soon mad for fishing and hunting just like their grandfather, Forster, who sent up a hunting rifle.

While Tamar was learning how to boil maple syrup, Forster had closed the store on Broadway that he had owned since the Depression and from which he had been sending gifts to Tamar and Dorothy throughout the years. He gave away the remaining stock of knives, lamps, and other housewares to the Catholic Worker, and put his Staten Island cottage up for sale. That summer, after Dorothy had received an unhappy letter from Tamar and an eviction notice for the Chrystie

Street house ("You take care of it," she said to the statue of St. Joseph, and stuffed the notice around it) and before Forster and his partner, Nanette, left for Florida to retire, she and Forster sat one evening, the moon full, on a boat on the beach like old times. Though they had rarely seen each other over the past fifteen years, they had remained in touch, mostly as it concerned Tamar. As Dorothy and Forster watched a flock of great north loons overhead, she spilled out all her worries about Tamar.

Even the beauty of Vermont could not heal David's demons or ease the financial worry. June 11, 1958, David wrote, was the day the money stopped. His unemployment benefits came to an end, the worker's compensation money he received for breaking his arm at the smelting factory was gone, and neither were they receiving rent from the Staten Island house, which they hadn't yet been able to sell. Tamar couldn't speak to her mother without being on the verge of tears. To help, Dorothy took the five oldest children to the two newly purchased Staten Island beach cottages. The cottages were a short walk along the water from Huguenot Avenue, close to where Dorothy's old cottage had been, though her plot of land had long been washed away and the beach changed beyond recognition from tides and storms.

By July Tamar wanted to give up the Vermont house. She was again lonely and feeling isolated, and she missed the beach, but most of all she worried about feeding the children. One week she had peanut butter but no honey, and the following week she had honey but no peanut butter. Sometimes she was tempted to just forget the next meal, take a walk with a wildflower book, and enjoy the beauty.

"The worrying about money and having not a soul to talk to is ruining," she wrote to her mother. "David needs a job. Manna and dandelions help not at all. If you have any money it would string us along, but I'd just as soon sell out and rent a cottage on the beach."

Unable to keep the house warm or the car running, Tamar wanted to spend the winter on Staten Island, but she didn't know how they could go or how they could stay. The phone and electricity were about to be shut off. They had no hot water and the septic system was failing.

Work on the farm had become more than David could handle, and most of it fell to Tamar and the children. Once again unopened book orders and uncashed checks piled up, and Tamar had to tell Dorothy to stop running the ads.

"I'm losing my mind," David said to the priest whom he went to see at Tamar's urging.

"No, you're not," the priest replied. He told him to see a psychiatrist who, in turn, prescribed David sleeping pills.

"He's changed so and lifeless," Tamar told her mother, and so helpless he couldn't even make a decision about selling a chicken.

During their second winter in Vermont, after giving birth eight times without fuss or mishap, Tamar had a miscarriage. Her health continued to be poor, and she, along with Chrissie the cow, got pneumonia. That April they had their fifteenth wedding anniversary, and David got drunk and attacked Chrissie so severely, she ran off. On their sixteenth anniversary, he wrote in a large drunken sprawl on a page splotched with what looked like tears: "And tell me how love comes? / Love comes unsought and unsent. / And tell me how love goes? / That was not love that went."

Readers still asked about Tamar and the family, and so Dorothy wrote as cheerfully as she could, and her columns resulted in requests for Tamar to write about living on the land. This exasperated Tamar. "They want encouragement and enthusiasm when we're the ones who need encouragement. Our attempts wouldn't be fit to print."

Dorothy tried to visit every several months, and Mama Hennessy came up for a summer, but Dorothy had difficulty speaking with her. "They are all inarticulate, Irish and English, Hennessy and Batterham as they are. One does not know what they are thinking and feeling."

"Love and hatred so close together," Dorothy also commented on the Hennessy family, while Tamar said, "His family nearly drives me out of my mind with their constant sheer destructiveness, no wonder he is off-balance."

Tamar and David finally got an offer for the Staten Island place for more than double what they had paid for it eight years before. But even that was too little and too late. David's liver was damaged, and his blood pressure was out of control. Eric and Nicky brought in the wood and milked the cow while David flew into rages, threw stones at the children, and locked them out of the house. He would then fall into a deep, dark silence. He had no intention to stop drinking even though the kids were becoming angry and bitter. Dorothy thought that maybe he was jealous of Tamar's delight in the children and that Tamar needed to give him more attention. "Poor David," she thought, "he is a city man and lives in the country for love of Tamar. My heart aches for him and for her." To relieve the tension they went for rural rides along the back roads, but David remained restless, unhappy, and drunk. Tamar had heavy pains in her chest, but she persevered and brought in the harvest before the killing frost.

In October 1959, Forster called Dorothy—Nanette was ill with cancer. They flew up from Florida and stayed in Dorothy's cottage until they found one to rent several doors down. Dorothy canceled her speaking engagements, postponed a cross-country trip, and settled into her cottage to help care for Nanette. The story of Nanette's death is sad, pain-ridden, and brief, and would send both Dorothy and Forster reeling. This was how the fifties would come to an end for Dorothy. This was how the past rose up to bite her, and perhaps the shock softened her and finally brought to an end the severe-and-pious phase that so pained Tamar.

Dorothy began spending weekdays at the cottage while Forster's sister Lily (who kept calling Nanette "Tamar") came on weekends, and Dorothy could then head to Chrystie Street to catch up on work. At the cottage, Dorothy ran errands, swam in the sea while the weather remained warm, and ate meals with Forster and Nanette. She listened to the sound of crickets and the steady rhythm of the waves, surrounded by the scent of the blooming privet hedge that sheltered the cottage, the sweet clover drying on the windowsill, the seaweed, and the salt air. Her bedroom faced the bay, and it was only a few yards to the wooden steps that led down to the beach, where she waded barefoot in the water and poked through the seaweed and horseshoe crabs with a stick and collected driftwood for her woodstove. She tried to keep to her rules and keep up with writing. She answered mail and read proofs while ruminating about voluntary poverty. It had come to mean something much different for her than simply doing without. Now it meant to be generous—of oneself and of one's time, talents, books, understanding, patience, and love. She continued to speak on occasion in the area, but mostly hers were quiet autumn days of waiting, writing letters, watching the sea, saying the rosary, and listening to the waves crashing against the shore in the middle of the night when she could not sleep, wondering if she was doing any good trying to care for Nanette.

Dorothy kept to her early-morning prayers and reading—praying during the day seemed to invite everyone to interrupt. Then she made the short walk down the lane to Forster and Nanette's cottage, where they ate breakfast together. Like the old days, Forster read aloud from the *New York Times*, and they sat and talked throughout the morning.

Dorothy kept in close contact with Tamar as David wasn't doing well. "Sorry David worried you so on the phone," Tamar said to her. "His impatience and suspicious nature has caught up with him." At every meal, every time the children were in his sight, and whenever there was work to be done about the farm, he descended into screaming fits. "Ask your mother if she knows of a place I could go and rest," he said to Tamar. He also asked if Dorothy could find him a job in a bookstore.

Nanette's condition was deteriorating, and Forster woke Dorothy early, weeping and saying that Nanette couldn't get up.

"Why did it have to be her?" Forster asked as he wept.

Dorothy wondered if she should stay or go to Vermont. Or should she give up this presumptuous idea that she could help either Tamar and David or Forster and Nanette, and leave for a speaking tour instead? Unable to sleep, she said the rosary while looking out her bedroom window at the heavy swells crashing against the shore. Could she bear Forster's deep need for her?

"One would think he is taking up where he left off with me, or that I have always been with him, as Lily has. I am part of him," she wrote in her diary.

Then David called up frantic. Tamar was in the hospital with either gallbladder troubles or appendicitis. Flu had weakened her during the summer, and now she had severe stomach pains. The doctor arrived in the middle of the night to take her to the hospital as David still didn't drive, and two days later he brought Tamar home, her illness undiagnosed. Dorothy rushed up with Stanley for a grueling weekend visit, the only time she spent away from the beach that month. They arrived to find a demoralized household—no beds made, no meal, the house a mess. Dorothy lent them money and paid for a neighbor to clean and cook. Becky and Susie took care of the laundry while Stanley got the wood in for the winter.

Dorothy had little strength to sympathize with either Tamar or David. David refused to do any work and was jealous of the attention Tamar paid to the children. He was bitter at the Catholic Worker yet expected help. When he wasn't raging and belittling the older children, he sank into silence, which Tamar found almost worse than his rages. He should eat his meals separately, as Pop did, Dorothy thought, and Tamar needed to be "more considerate of his comfort, more appreciative of him" and stop her nagging and criticizing in front of the children. Even the children didn't escape Dorothy's censure. She called them greedy, rushing at meals like a pack of wolves.

"Two very good things," Dorothy concluded in her diary. "One, at least D. and T. are suffering, not complacent and content. They see each other's faults and are solidly Catholic so they'll stick together and work it out. And two, the children being so many take care of each other, and of themselves. They are never at a loss for something to do."

Dorothy returned to Staten Island with a growing sense of pressure, unnamed, undefined, and wrote that men want maidservants, though it's unclear whether she was speaking of David or Forster or both, and that they want to settle with another in isolation. "What to do, be submissive? Give in to selfishness?"

Tamar said to Dorothy, "Can a person be told morning, noon, and night that everything they do is wrong, and survive? Damned if I'll stand it as long as Della." Della and Tamar were eyeing each other's marriage closely, for they had similar difficulties. Dorothy tried to speak to Della of Tamar's troubles. "Too many children," Della responded, and Dorothy walked out on her.

Tamar sent Dorothy a card for her birthday. "I wish I could send something but am in prison," she said in bitter commentary on her marriage. She added, "You write a sad letter."

Dorothy turned sixty-two that November. She was still strong and beautiful, and I find it hard to reconcile the doubts and fears she lived with at that time with the power of her sheer physical presence. The topics of life and death were on her mind, and the poetry of Francis Thompson, which she could still recite from memory: "Life is a coquetry of death . . . a mean and single scene." She read parts of Dostoyevsky's *The Idiot* and was struck by what she described as Ippolit's "fierce rebellion against death." She and Lily talked late into the night about death and religion. They also talked about Forster's rebellion against responsibility, family, religion, and tradition. He was selfish and a coward, Lily agreed with Dorothy, but she loved him dearly and never left him without feeling guilty.

The daily routine continued—the early-morning prayers and reading followed by breakfast and talking with Forster and Nanette through the morning. In the afternoon Dorothy wrote or collected driftwood on the beach, followed by supper with Forster and Nanette and evenings of Scrabble with Forster and Lily.

Dorothy bought a record player to learn French, and brought from the city her typewriter and an electric heater, while Stanley arrived with a radio and a battered album of Beethoven's Ninth Symphony. She had a few visitors, including a young man with whom she discussed the philosophy of work. "He kept holding to the primacy of the spiritual, and necessity of someone's praying, and I tried to emphasize man's duty to earn his living." David must have been on her mind. She gave occasional talks in the city but to indifferent or hostile audiences. She planted chrysanthemums and gathered wood while Stanley and Forster competed in who could make the best fire for her. As winter approached, the wind blew up through the cracks in the floor, and sitting down at the typewriter became a cold job.

Dorothy felt pulled by the constant needs of the Catholic Worker, of Vermont, and of Forster and Nanette, and it wore her down. Sleepless from nerves and fatigue, she felt like an empty cistern, and sometimes while on the ferry she said she didn't know if she was coming or going. One day she ranted against Forster to Johannah Hughes, Marge Hughes's oldest daughter (the Hugheses were another long-term Catholic Worker family). Johannah, wanting to be supportive, said a few words in agreement, and Dorothy suddenly turned on her and defended Forster. But one of the most extraordinary clues of the state of Dorothy's heart was the morning she came into the Hugheses' cottage carrying freshly made cinnamon buns and announced she had had a dream of being in bed with Forster. "You can't be held responsible for what you dream!" she said delightedly to Marge.

By Thanksgiving, Nanette was in great pain. Dorothy felt helpless, and only the rosary and the Jesus Prayer kept her going. She wished she could attend daily Mass, but instead she walked on the beach under a new moon. There was an offshore wind and the tide was out, revealing mudflats and seaweed, and grebes swam in the water, diving under for food, while the gulls flew over to the Fresh Kills garbage dump. She didn't know what to say to Nanette, and yet Nanette didn't like to see her go. Her pain was so great, Nanette lay there crying, and Dorothy told stories to distract her.

"How hard it is to comfort you," Dorothy said. "One can only keep silent in the face of suffering."

"Yes," Nanette said bitterly. "The silence of death."

Disturbed by the news from Vermont, Dorothy visited in mid-December. David was doing nothing but sitting, uninterested in even his books. They had received payment for the Staten Island house, half of which immediately went to paying debts, and they now had money to live on until David could find a job.

"He has everything to be happy about," Tamar said to Dorothy, "but just sits around feeling sorry for himself—except when he gets mad. I don't know what to do."

While at Tamar's, Dorothy spoke at a neighboring town, where she was heckled by a man who flung abuse at her so cruel she never spoke publicly in Vermont again. She got ill and stayed in bed reading Jane Austin. When Dorothy returned to Staten Island, it was clear that Nanette was in her last days. Dorothy clung to her routine of cooking and cleaning, writing and praying before light broke, and she and Forster stood by helplessly watching Nanette die. By Christmas, Nanette wished she could commit suicide. The decay, the colostomy, the pain, the pressure, the swollen face and legs, and the weakness were all too great.

Nanette now needed full-time nursing, and Dorothy asked for help from a young nurse, Jean Walsh, who on her days off volunteered at the Catholic Worker and often drove Dorothy out to Staten Island. Jean would come to be one of the few people who remembered Nanette enough to describe her. Even Lily's daughters could not remember much other than that she was sweet and ordinary (though compared to the Batterham women, any woman would be ordinary). Nanette had no family and few friends, and no one knew her last name as she had changed it to Batterham.

"Nanette was a precious, precious woman," Jean said. "Joyful, pretty, outgoing, childlike. She was simplicity. She said with great enthusiasm, 'When I get better, I'm going to be just like Dorothy.' She wanted to live like her. I remember vividly the three of them—Dorothy, Forster, and Nanette. They were so very beautiful."

Forster was terrified that he would be alone with Nanette when she died and clung even more fiercely to Lily and Dorothy. To keep busy, he hung pictures and fixed a table at Dorothy's cottage. When Forster wept, Dorothy found herself barely able to withstand it. "I get so impatient at him and his constant fleeing from her, his self-pity, his weeping that I feel hard and must fight to overcome it. Such fear of sickness and death." But then she remembered the priest who said not to add one straw to the burden another is carrying.

"I feel as though I were bolstering him up, urging him on to courage and perseverance. When he reads aloud to us from the *Times* he is calm. She will no longer let him turn on the radio to listen to the news. She is in a way hostile to everything he loves—flowers, plants, birds, the sea, and now she can no longer share his interest in the news. She is concentrated on a fight with death, a struggle, day to day, for life. She longs for it to end, but she says, 'I am strong-willed and stubborn. No one can help me . . . I am alone. No one knows.' We are all Job's comforter—no one knows another's pain. Forster feels this, too."

Nanette cried out that she was losing her mind and that everyone was lying to her, including the doctors. Lily and Jean tried to calm her.

"It is inexpressibly painful to hear her despairing. And Forster keeps running away."

Jean began staying overnight and gave Nanette morphine for her pain.

"This Cross was not as hard as this," Nanette said to Dorothy. "People in concentration camps suffered like this," she added, showing Dorothy her damaged and emaciated arms.

Nanette asked to be baptized, and Dorothy and Lucille, another nurse Dorothy had asked to help with Nanette's care, baptized her. And then she died the next morning, January 8, 1960. She died so quickly that Jean, who was the only one with her, didn't have time to fetch Dorothy and Forster. As soon as she could, Jean ran up the lane to Dorothy's cottage, where they had just finished eating breakfast. They looked at her when she told them the news, and neither one said a word. When they went to see her, Nanette had a slight smile and looked calm and peaceful.

When Lily arrived, she exclaimed, "She is smiling!"

Jean said, "I wondered how Dorothy must have felt."

"I was numb and dumb," Dorothy said to Jean later, apologizing for her silence. "I had to flee, and when you can't handle a situation, it's best to flee."

CHAPTER FIFTEEN

Dorothy found herself being unkind to Forster, who was hanging around "like a lost soul," so she fled, first to visit Della and then to Vermont. Tamar, Becky, and Susie met her at the bus station on a cold and icy night, happy to see her. Her bedroom was neat and tidy, and the house warm. David seemed calm, but he did nothing but stay up late reading paperbacks and sleep late in the morning. Tamar too had little energy. Her back was giving her problems, and she was pregnant again. The burden of Hilaire's care at night fell on Eric, who was just about to turn twelve, while Susie, thirteen, took care of Martha.

Even with David's inability to cope, the family had taken to the Vermont life. Tamar was in her element in the garden, always planting more than enough, believing in abundance, and the rich Vermont soil didn't disappoint. They had cows, sheep, pigs, and laying hens. The steer had been slaughtered and packed away in the freezer with the vegetables, and there were apples, carrots, and squash stored in the cellar. They had learned how to split wood and make maple syrup. They'd adjusted to the harsh winters—the car that wouldn't start, the boiling water that had to be poured down the drains to thaw the pipes, the ice covering the animals' water troughs that had to be smashed every morning, and the furnace that needed to be fed three times during the night.

Tamar showed Dorothy her new spinning wheel, an antique walking wheel. During her insomnia-ridden nights when she was wakened by Hilaire or by nightmares about Maggie getting injured, she set up her loom and wove curtains for the living room and bedroom windows, blankets from wool she had dyed, and linen towels and tablecloths. The harder things became, the more Tamar spun and wove.

Dorothy, in trying to break through David's sense of futility, spoke with him on his old favorite topics and about recent attacks on agrarians. "It is always Eric Gill and Chesterton they are attacking, and they also disregard the pronouncements of Pope Pius XII," he said.

Dorothy then headed out west on a four-month speaking tour. She talked in Fargo until midnight about the old crowd—Hart Crane, Malcolm Cowley, Kenneth Burke, Mike Gold, and Gene O'Neill. With whom, she didn't say. She read Henry Miller and D. H. Lawrence on the long train ride from Chicago to Seattle. She wrote to Tamar from Minnesota, South Dakota, Montana, Seattle, San Francisco, Los Angeles, Albuquerque, New Orleans, St. Louis, and Detroit. She visited Native Americans, Hutterites, and Doukhobors. She spoke to young seminarians and college students about farming communes, though, she added, the Worker had yet to create one. She spoke of nonviolence, of the bishops' silence on nuclear war, and of honorable occupations, while in her diary she wrote about love.

Forster was still on her mind, but when she returned, having arrived too late to take part in that year's air-raid drill protest, she refused to see him and instead turned to Dostoyevsky. "The world will be saved by beauty, and what is more beautiful than love?" she wrote. "Those who do not believe in God—they believe in love."

Carrying Nanette's ashes and his clothes, fishing rod, and binoculars from the beach cottage, Forster moved in with Lily. He was drinking heavily, but began to drink less after he got a job in a neighborhood electrical shop. While Dorothy was traveling, he asked Della when Dorothy was returning. In his grief, he wrote Dorothy the one letter that remains of his correspondence with her:

Dear Dorothy, I am sorry you so misunderstood me but over the years there have been many times that you have done so that I am not perturbed that you do so now. My association with you has been so purely human that neither of us has the privilege at this time to lean on any position but the most apparent one. I am sorry to write so but you forced me to take this attitude by your last note to me. All I want, Dorothy dear, is just the addresses of the two nurses that you, from the bottom of your heart (the one that you withheld from me) supplied for my dearest Nanette's last hours of breath and heartbeat, so that I can make a gesture of very lowly basic human feeling. As always, Forster.

Then less than three months after Nanette's death, Forster was dealt another harsh blow. Lily was diagnosed with a brain tumor, and Forster stayed with her until she died the following year.

Tamar, now thirty-four, pregnant, and possibly with a kidney infection, was in despair over David. Both Della's and Tamar's marriages, along with problems at the Worker, were keeping Dorothy awake at night. She tried to write her column, but it was full of troubles, so she threw it away and instead wrote of all the good she could see, knowing that that too would get her in trouble. She wrote about Eric and Nicky fishing—Eric caught thirty-one trout and Nicky thirty-three. And of Hilaire, red curly hair, blue eyes, broad red face, who did not talk much, and of Martha, who did.

"When Mommy says prayers with us at night, the kids laugh. I don't like the way Daddy says prayers. He prays too loud and long," Martha said.

"Probably," Dorothy commented, "she does not like them because Daddy's prayers usually end in a roar for quiet. Tamar goes downstairs, leaving them to their usual riotous play before the great silence drops all at once over the house. Suddenly you realize there is quiet, blessed quiet."

That July, Tamar and David's last child was born, a girl, Catherine Ann, me. Tamar gave birth with her usual matter-of-factness—the doctor chastised her for not waiting for him. When she brought me home, she introduced me to each of my siblings and had them hold me, as she had done with all the babies as they each arrived. Until then Dorothy hadn't missed a single birth of her grandchildren. Easton, West Virginia, and Staten Island—she had been with the family for all of them. She wasn't present for my birth through no one's fault but mine—I wasn't due for another two weeks.

Now there were nine children and still no job yet for David, but Dorothy was determined not to worry. "As the Spanish saying is, a baby is always born with a loaf of bread under its arm." Then, within weeks after my birth, and after three years of seasonal day laboring for the neighbors, receiving workman's compensation and unemployment checks, the rent and then sale of the Staten Island place, and sporadic income from his book business, David finally found a job as a night desk clerk at a hotel half an hour's drive away. He worked twelve-hour shifts for forty dollars a week plus room and board. "I begin to feel better," he told Dorothy.

Although it meant more work for Tamar, and he came home on his days off demanding her full attention, everybody was relieved. Dorothy came up for a visit, sick, tired, and suffering from arthritis, though she was finally free of the migraine headaches that had plagued her all her life. At first it was a disastrous visit, and she couldn't wait to get away. Becky and Susie were moping, sullen teenagers who did nothing and were interested only in clothes and movies. "Is adolescence such a disturbance of the body that it affects the mind?" Dorothy wondered.

She also fought with Tamar because the roof and chimney needed fixing, which was paid for by the Worker. Dorothy, painfully aware of possible accusations of misuse of funds, paid the money back almost immediately, and yet Tamar wanted to buy another loom. Greedy, Dorothy called her, and chastised her for being indulgent toward the children, provoking Tamar to lose her temper. "I will be glad to be gone," Dorothy wrote, feeling scorn and contempt from Becky and Susie and feeling used by Tamar. But all blew over within a day or two, and Dorothy was sad to leave.

At first David's job seemed to go well. Tamar wrote Dorothy, "David had a good day this week finally. How much better it makes me feel! Work is so essential and healing." But he was still sinking into his moods, and in another letter she wrote, "David came out of a lurid mood. I hope it lasts. When he feels good, I feel we can do anything." To Dorothy, though, David looked sad on her visits.

"Hold the baby," Tamar would say to him when he couldn't do much else, and then it was time to hold me, and he had a breakdown.

"I was the straw that broke the camel's back," I went around saying when I was old enough to know the story—or part of the story.

My mother responded, "You were a joy from the moment you were born."

By spring 1961, Tamar was sick with colitis from worrying, and she struggled with weariness and needed to take a daily two-hour nap. Mary and Maggie were looking so poor and ragged, it depressed her. Becky was now sixteen, and Hilaire, Martha, and I were the only ones not at school. Martha was bossy, busy, and helped with the dishes. Hilaire, who at the age of four could manage the cows, cut his foot in the barn and had to have stitches, and I was an angel with a bad cold. Mama Hennessy wanted to spend the summer, as she had the previous one, but Tamar told her not to and felt badly for doing so. She had no visitors for months save for the nuns and Father Sevigny, the twenty-six-year-old priest from St. Mary's, our parish church, though she did hear from Dorothy every day either by letter or phone.

At work David began to raid the liquor cabinet and shoplift from the pharmacy next door. Stealing was something he had never done before, Tamar said, as he had the morality of a good Catholic child—you don't lie and you don't steal. At home he wandered around the house in the middle of the night crying out for help while Tamar sat on the couch in the dark, and the children listened from their bedrooms. After a year of working at the hotel, he resigned, writing in his diary only one word of explanation—"sick." Four days later he asked to be admitted to a psychiatric hospital. "Going to the State Mental Hospital at Waterbury for observation—nuts."

"I'm relieved," Tamar said when she told Dorothy the news. "And he is really trying."

Dorothy arrived immediately to find Tamar calm and with no self-pity. They visited David at the hospital, and he said the ward he was in reminded him of the Catholic Worker.

"The doctors had no idea what was wrong," Tamar said, "so after a month they gave him a job as a dishwasher. It was the best thing they could have done. The doctors and priests tried to help, but everyone seemed helpless in the face of it all. Father Sevigny caught himself saying that a separation would be a solution for birth control."

To Dorothy, David wrote that the doctor told him he "must give up for good drinking and laziness." He lost weight and looked much better for it. He asked for books as he wasn't interested in television, and the other men in the ward weren't talkers. Stanley and others from the Worker came up to visit him, and Tamar wrote frequently. "Said she was enjoying the vacation," he told Dorothy.

Dorothy had wept all the day long when she heard David was hospitalized, and Tamar wept all the night long when she decided not to have him back home.

Dorothy was with Tamar when Tamar made her decision to end the marriage. "I don't know how you stood it for so long," she said.

"With that," Tamar said years later, "I forgave Dorothy everything."

She didn't speak about the days and nights of crying that followed, though on that visit in October, the house was filled with the warm, early-autumn sun, and the boys were chopping and splitting wood while Tamar put food up. They had evening picnics with hot dogs, marshmallows, and squirrel meat. Everyone, including Dorothy, seemed relaxed, cheerful, and helpful.

Tamar forgave her husband for his inability to care for his family, for she recognized he had been given a burden he could not bear, but there were some things she could not forgive. She could not forgive David for the war he waged against all that was meaningful to her, and she did not want her children to grow up learning that kind of destructiveness and bitterness.

"I am very sorry for him," she told her mother, "but don't intend to be a victim and have the children be also. Hate, fear and antagonism are so catching."

Tamar felt she had not handled things well with the children, particularly the boys. She never explained the separation to them. They had gone away to camp, and when they got back, he was gone.

After three months at the Waterbury hospital, David headed down to Washington, DC, the bus fare paid for by one of his sisters. "Left Vermont. Seventeen-hour bus trip," he wrote in his diary. "Got a haircut for a dollar fifty. Ninety-eight cents for this notebook. Stayed with Momma." He went to confession, and the priest told him to go to Alcoholics Anonymous. He wrote Dorothy inviting her to visit and asking for help in finding a job, but soon moved to Atlantic City, where he found work as a dishwasher in an old hotel. He signed the farm over to Tamar while she began the process for a legal separation. She needed forms filled out by David, his priest, and four witnesses, and even then the bishop could refuse permission. She also for the first time applied for state assistance as neither the Hennessys nor the Days were willing or able to help. Dorothy felt they were all looking to her to take care of Tamar's family, but she wasn't earning enough money through her writing, and Forster, now retired and on social security, could help out in only small ways.

David and Tamar wrote each other, but he more often than she. Two years later, he was still in contact, but the calls and letters were fewer and further apart. Then in January 1965 he wrote a letter to Dorothy. "Dear Granny Day, I dislike to worry you and Tamar with my troubles but thanks to Tamar [for] telling me to go see a priest and I did—I talked to two—they both saw I was near the end of my rope and said to leave town and be near my mother and sisters. . . . I need to get back home again with Tamar and the children—but everything looks black and helpless to me. I am going bad to worse. Anyway, thanks for the help and please do help Tamar and the children all you can. I'll write you again when I get to Mama's. God bless you. Love from David H."

He came up to Vermont for a brief visit, the first time since leaving four years previously. I was five and remember nothing. Tamar said I ran around saying, "Daddy's coming, Daddy's coming." She added, "It broke my heart to see your excitement."

That September, Eric, then sixteen, went down to visit, and he found his father sitting on a park bench so drunk he didn't recognize his own son. David was living with a woman, Madge Johnson, above a tavern with a steep, narrow flight of stairs that he kept falling down. Eric came home and said little about the visit to either Tamar or Dorothy. Dorothy wrote, "Eric came to New York from Atlantic City where he was visiting his father, a sad experience. I am glad they love him, the children, and want to keep close to him, and that Tamar never utters a bitter word about him." While Tamar said, "Eric seemed crushed by it, shocked by what he had found. I didn't know what to do or say."

"I thought I would never see him again. That he would be dead before the year was out," Eric recalled years later.

Soon after, David wrote to Dorothy one line on the back of an AA announcement, "My dear mother-in-law, Come see and talk to me and save your Tamar's David." Then there was nothing.

My mother and I sat together at her kitchen table soon after David had passed away at the age of ninety-two while living in West Virginia near my sister Maggie, who had helped care for him the last years of his life.

"Was it alcoholism?" I asked.

"No," she said.

"Mental illness?"

She gave me a brief, sharp glance I couldn't read. "No," she said.

"What was it then? What was he battling with?" I asked, and I knew as soon as the words were out of my mouth that I was pushing too hard. Her jaw was firm, her lips closed in that straight, thin line that I could never cross. What could have been so unspeakable? I wondered, frightening myself so much that I dropped it. I couldn't bear the thought that maybe there were things that *were* unspeakable. We moved on to something else, and I had to wait two years for her to return to the topic on her terms, again while we were sitting in her kitchen.

"If you want to understand my marriage," she said, "there are three books you should read."

Her list was brief and harsh, and as I reveal this, I feel I'm revealing some of my mother's deepest secrets, but not my father's. I would need to read something quite different to discover those. She began with *After the Fall*, Arthur Miller's play based on his marriage to Marilyn Monroe. "Read that if you want to know something about the kind of neediness that destroys a relationship." Followed by Pat Conroy's *The Great Santini*. "That one will show you the sheer destructiveness of families, particularly of what a father can do to a son."

"And the last, Mom?"

"Lolita."

I was so shocked I didn't know what to say.

"It's a classic," she said. "Goes beyond being a dirty book." Then she fell silent, and I was relieved. If she had had anything more to say, I didn't want to hear it.

Tamar didn't like labeling people either with problems or beliefs, much like Peter Maurin didn't like to be labeled as an anarchist or pacifist. Dorothy didn't understand that. She loved words and terms, and believed it was good to state things as clearly as possible. But these labels held no interest for Peter, and neither did words like *alcoholism* or *mental illness* interest Tamar. She rejected the idea that the human condition could or should be so categorized. I should have known better when I asked Tamar for something as definitive as a diagnosis, but she didn't hold it against me. She knew that I just wanted to understand my own father, and she tried to help as best as she could by pointing me to literature, to stories, just like her mother would so often do.

In the winter of 2005 Martha and I went down to West Virginia, where David and Madge had moved in the mid-1990s to be near Maggie, who had a farm there. He was ninety-two and in a nursing home dying of congestive heart failure. His laughter was a shadow of what it had been but still there, mirthless, a tool I never understood. A weapon, I thought, but maybe I am wrong. Maybe he just never really knew how to laugh.

I shouted in his good ear, the one that wasn't shot away, "Hi, Daddy, it's your youngest daughter, Katy," but I didn't know if he heard me. An elderly woman across the hall cried out, "Mommy, Mommy," again and again. Maggie, Martha, and I sat with him, and we waited, and I didn't know what I was waiting for until he said, "Where are the boys?" and "You girls can go now." And I realized that I had been waiting for him to say something hurtful, which he did, and I survived.

Each day he slipped further away.

"Why can't I fall asleep and be done with it?" he asked, and then a few hours later, "Am I going to heaven or hell?"

He called out Tamar's name, but I couldn't understand what followed, just as Tamar would speak of him when she lay dying three years later. Soon he was speaking in an unintelligible stream as he slipped in and out of consciousness.

In the evenings, after sitting with him, we crossed a bridge of iron poles, the river flowing muddy underneath, and walked the mile up Buckeye Holler to Maggie's house. We sat around the kitchen table reading his diaries by the light of solar-powered lamps. Like my grandmother and like me, my father wrote his way through life, though his diary entries were short and sharp, as sharp as his handwriting, which I knew well as a child for he liked to fill the margins of his books with comments.

After several days, David had largely fallen silent, mostly asleep or in a coma, I didn't know. Martha and I left then. Perhaps we did the wrong thing, leaving him when he had so little time left, but we made him anxious and agitated. Only Maggie could calm him, and she was the only one of his children to be with him when he died within the week on February 28. The funeral was on Tamar's seventy-ninth birthday. It didn't feel real to her that he was gone and that she was now a widow.

Since 1942, Dorothy and Tamar had been witnessing and discussing the plight of Catholic Worker families. "Dorothy saw it all," Tamar used to say. Tamar liked to quote *Zorba the Greek* and call it "the whole catastrophe." Regardless, Dorothy continued to try to help as best she could, though she often didn't understand how relations within families could become so dire, while Tamar would shrug her shoulders and say, "Families." Tamar also said to me, "You can't use marriage as a garbage can for men's weaknesses."

When I looked for clues in his diaries as to how my father became the man he was, I found bleak sentences describing the condition of his mind and his life. When he was twenty-two, he was mixing Hennessy cognac with Bénédictine and, as the years passed, he moved on to whiskey, red wine, and sherry. By the time he was twenty-six, he knew something was wrong. "Mass by Father Spense," he wrote, "who preached on Sin and Death—must go see him about my mental and spiritual decay." A year later, in 1940, after a night of drinking, he was shot in the head by one of his closest friends with a 30-30 Springfield rifle, his right ear and skull partially blasted away. No one claimed to remember anything, and no one was arrested. One and a half years later he arrived at the Catholic Worker full of ideas about distributism.

The diary entries during his marriage are terse and sporadic, mostly birth announcements, birthdays, and mentions of babies in the hospital with pneumonia or measles. But there were also quotes from Chesterton: "Marriage is a duel to the death, which no man of honor should decline." And Samuel Johnson: "Marriage has many pains but celibacy has no pleasures."

After he moved to Atlantic City, David met Madge Johnson, a coal miner's daughter from West Virginia and an incest survivor. He left brief clues of their relationship: "Miss Johnson left me again" and "Miss Johnson left with the sherry." Madge went to jail for ten days for what he doesn't say but it may have been prostitution. He couldn't pay the fifty-dollar fine, but he visited her every day. Eventually, after too many fights between them, Madge gave up drinking. She couldn't have children, and she and David never married since my parents never divorced. By the 1970s David's entries became a litany of drunken brawls, getting arrested, getting tossed out of taverns, and breaking his arm or bashing his head open on the sidewalk. They also contained comments on missed Masses and missed kids' birthdays.

He and Madge moved to Philadelphia after all the old Atlantic City hotels were torn down and the cost of living rose. In 1988 Martha and I visited him there, and he greeted us loudly but sober, while I pretended he wasn't my father but a distantly related uncle of sorts. It seemed easier that way as I was more likely to enjoy the visit and less likely to have any expectations destroyed by brief but poisonous comments. Our visit was short and uneventful. They lived in an Italian neighborhood in a tiny brick house with a grapevine and fig tree in the garden. He seemed glad to see us, grateful even. He asked about the old Vermont neighbors and touched briefly on Tamar, asking us in an odd, childlike way, "Did your mother divorce me?" He teased me, but not unkindly, about my unmarried state. He would later write in his diary of Martha and me, sadly, succinctly, "I don't know them." Madge and I would exchange Christmas cards until she died eight years later.

"I'm really sorry," he wrote to Tamar in 1994, when she was sixty-eight, and he was eighty-one and had had heart surgery. "I'm really sorry for leaving you and our children. Something gave in and lost responsibility." His words dip and scrawl at the last, as if he could barely contain the pain. When he turned ninety, David called Tamar to again say he was sorry he didn't stay to take care of his family. He was afraid of dying because he believed he was going to hell.

"Being raised a Catholic," Tamar said, "you're liable to believe that mortal sins are around every corner, and you don't lose that fear."

I had thought that having nine children destroyed my father and then leaving them destroyed him all over again, much like those Irish myths where people die first by drowning followed by hanging, burning, and dismemberment. But as I came to discover, the seeds of his destruction began long before his marriage, and the clues were to be found in his early diaries.

There was a time in my father's life in which he surrounded himself with all he loved—his books, his family, his friends. When he worked hard at a job he did well at, when he educated himself by reading all he could lay his hands on. When he was a devoted grandson to his paternal grandmother and a normally tormenting and loving older brother to his seven sisters. When he was in correspondence with many of the thinkers of the time and delighted in collecting autographs. When he discovered the three great minds he would admire all his life—Chesterton, Belloc, and Cobbett. When he went to Mass daily, prayed the rosary, and venerated the Blessed Mother. There was a time before he started drinking. There was a time when he was content.

David dropped out of high school at the height of the Depression when he was seventeen. He got a job with the Department of the Interior and spent his free time in the Library of Congress, the Senate, and the Supreme Court. He collected autographs from the poet Robert Bridges and the essayist Agnes Repplier, as well as from Ezra Pound and Eric Gill. He wrote to Eugene O'Neill, W. B. Yeats, and George Bernard Shaw and received signatures from the latter two. T. S. Eliot sent him an autographed volume of his poems. He refused to attend dances with his friends and instead stayed home nights to read Thomas Aquinas, Byron, Tennyson, Chesterton, and Belloc. He often stopped in churches to pray, and he gave money to beggars. He wanted to travel to two places only—Rome and Ireland. He refused to smoke or chew tobacco, and he drank little.

Then he began to write about someone he referred to as "M" who worked with him in the press room of the Department of the Interior, where they made maps for the Geographical Survey. M and he took their meals together and talked and talked, and there began more and more references to M—a chance to talk with M, the days M wasn't at work, the times they went to Mass together. But it wasn't until after months of entries that David revealed that M was a man, a lithographer, two years older than David.

They began exchanging letters via special delivery even though they saw each other daily, and his coworkers began remarking on how much time David and M were spending together. Then M would pull away, and David would agonize. He couldn't read and sat and daydreamed "thinking foolish things that could happen but impossible." He couldn't help himself from buying gifts for M, while claiming he just had them hanging about. Every conversation and meeting was treasured and examined. "Air between us together was very close . . . I do think we would make a great pair." "Now I breathe a prayer for our mutual love and devotion." He was overjoyed when they took a trip together to see the painting *Whistler's Mother* in Baltimore. He wrote in detail about how M looked, what clothes he wore, and where the two of them sat when they visited. "My M," he would often write.

This went on for a year until tensions began to arise between the two men. M told David that he had a girl whom he wanted to marry. The three went to church together, and David remarked about the "woman between us." He wanted to live with them when they got married but he was devastated. "I'm awful lonesome—tired of it all—miserable. Pray that soon I shall find the true course and live to be a good Catholic." Surely, he wrote, this is not what God intended. "Virgin most fine, console my mind—control my soul."

After the wedding, David sat alone on the front porch until late into the night, feeling empty and lonely. Teddy, M's wife, got pregnant almost immediately, and David sunk into further depression. He thought of joining the Dominicans and becoming a priest. He and M still talked and argued about everything, including "woman and her causes and effects."

Then it begins—the trips to Baltimore to drink twenty-five-cent shots of Golden Wedding whiskey followed by beer and a swill of bootleg. Or muscatel and Bénédictine, that "elixir of heavenly odor and divine taste." He was starting to lose his temper at work and got into fights with his coworkers.

M tried to convince David it was time for him to get married, while David still thought he should become a priest. He read Latin, Cobbett, Maritain, Aristotle, Gerard Manley Hopkins, and Aldous Huxley while drinking Hennessy and Bénédictine. His entries became shorter and bleaker. Sometimes his handwriting took on a huge sprawl, and I know he was drinking while he wrote. "Longing for my M." M gave David a shave, and a few weeks later David wrote, "May the Archangel help me through Grace to forget and erase something of [the] day's later part." He moved in with the couple, and the entries disappear.

For three months he lived with M and Teddy helping to care for their daughter—his goddaughter—and drinking port. They were evicted for failure to pay rent, and the two men moved to another apartment, while Teddy and the baby moved in with her family. Within days, David wrote, "My Dearest Mother, cleanse me with thy prayers of petition at the throne for the hateful sin I have committed this day." Then two days later, "The bachelor and the married bachelor are just living together in one big dream. God Bless them." This dream world lasted two months until M returned to Teddy. David went to confession for the first time in months and then retreated even further into his books.

While my mother never spoke of this element of her husband, something in her insistence that his troubles went much deeper than alcoholism and her reluctance or inability to speak further makes me think that she knew, and that within this knowledge lies a large part of her own struggles with the Catholic Church.

A photo has survived of my father and M. M is a slender, handsome man with a pleasant face not so rugged as David's nor with the same intensity. I look at this photo of the two of them, and I know I am witness to the shredding of a man's soul because of his love for another man, and his Church and his faith could not abide this. "God cannot rest in an unquiet heart," St. Teresa of Avila said, and what is more unquiet than a heart filled with self-hatred?

Part Three

THE
MYSTERY
OF FREEDOM

CHAPTER SIXTEEN

I grew up in two houses of hospitality, two expressions of Dorothy and Tamar's lives—the farm at Tivoli, New York, on the banks of the Hudson River, and the house on Cady Hill Road amid the trees of Vermont. Tivoli was large, boisterous, uncontrollable in a derelict mansion and a former hotel—that was my grandmother's house of hospitality on the land bought after the Staten Island farm was sold. Cady Hill Road was a small Vermont farm with a derelict house on the south side of a hill surrounded by stone walls and cows—that was my mother's house of hospitality on the land, created in the aftermath of her marriage. It was within the embrace of both of these beloved and battered farms that I was dropped into that immense pot of Catholic Worker soup, one small additional ingredient.

In December 1963, when I was three and all my siblings were in school (Becky was in her first year of university), just weeks after Dorothy had listened to the news of President John F. Kennedy's assassination on the radio and wept, she found the Tivoli farm listed in the *New York Times*. "Suitable for a religious group," the ad said. It was an eighty-seven-acre gentleman's estate on a bluff overlooking the Hudson River, one hundred miles north of New York City. It had two large buildings, one a hotel with thirty-two bedrooms and a swimming pool, and the other a mansion with fourteen unheated rooms and a large veranda near a seventy-foot embankment overlooking the river. Part of a string of nineteenth-century mansions built along the eastern shore of the Hudson River, in 1905 it was sold for a dollar and became the Leake and Watts Farm School for boys. During the Second World War, the Land

Army took it over and filled it with young people working crops along the Hudson Valley. The Jehovah Witnesses then ran it as a camp until they sold it to a building contractor, who renamed it Tivoli Manor and transformed it into a summer resort for families where for sixty dollars a week, patrons could golf, fish, go horseback riding and dancing, swim in the new swimming pool, or lounge in the casino and bar. Tivoli Manor didn't last long before the owner put it on the market for seventy-eight thousand dollars. Dorothy fell in love with the place and made an offer for three reasons—the Hudson River, the driftwood that could be collected along its banks just like on Staten Island, and the words "Beata Maria" chiseled on the side of the mansion.

She had dreams for Tivoli, and it was a place made for dreaming. She wanted a folk school and farming commune, a place for study and discussion, a house of hospitality, and a retreat house. They would fish for shad in the river, grow vegetables, keep goats and chickens, and plant trees. Students from the nearby college could come and have work camps, and the scholars would become workers and the workers scholars, just as Peter had always wanted. Once again the hope was to create a place of study and prayer combined with manual labor and hospitality. She wanted the place to be staffed by the artist Rita Ham, who was now married to Martin Corbin and mother to three children. Marty would become editor of the paper, and Rita would run the house, Marge Hughes would become the bread baker, John Filigar would teach the young ones how to farm, and Hans Tunnesen, another seaman who had arrived at the Worker in the 1940s, would cook. And she and Hans, Dorothy claimed, were going to sit on the mansion's front porch overlooking the Hudson, which the Lenape Indians called Muhheakunnuk, the river that flows two ways, and watch the oil tankers and freighters pass by in the deep channel that ran near to shore.

Even knowing they were moving to a place of such beauty, leaving Staten Island, especially the beach where Dorothy had spent so much time writing and praying, was hard. By then the island was changing irrevocably. The few remaining farms were making way for roads and housing developments while the small beach cottages were torn down to be replaced by large houses. The landscape was filling up with sewage treatment plants and oil storage tanks, the air with pollution from New Jersey, and the skyline with, beginning in 1959, the building of the Verrazano-Narrows Bridge, so massive it could be seen from all five boroughs.

With the sale of the two beach houses, they were able to make a down payment of twenty-five thousand dollars on the Tivoli farm, and on April 25, Dorothy drove up from the city with five others, including Stanley, who recalled the very first night at Easton, when he was one of three men who slept on the floor. It took two months to collect thirty people with all their belongings, along with the contents of the library, chapel, and loom room where Tamar had given weaving classes—fourteen years of life at the Peter Maurin Farm and six years at the beach houses all packed and shipped up to Tivoli. Dorothy hoped it would be the last move the Worker farm would make. Stanley, "the melancholy Slav," as she liked to call him, said that doubtless the state would want to build a highway along the river, and they would have to move again.

Tivoli was a three-and-a-half-hour drive from Cady Hill Road, and within two weeks of the move Tamar showed up for a quick visit with all her children and some of the neighbors' children as well. Stanley, who had set up his printing press in the mansion, greeted us. He stood in the lobby of the main house, his arms stretched wide, and called out, "Pick a room, any room!"

That first summer was a summer of "beauty and happiness," with Hans in the kitchen, Rita and Marge doing the baking, John in the garden, and Stanley at his printing press.

"The best place we've ever had," Dorothy said.

"We've moved into the mansion class," Stanley said.

When summer ended, Dorothy headed up to Vermont to spend four months with us. She had been staying close those years after the end of Tamar's marriage. Every three months or so, and always for Tamar's birthday, Dorothy was up. Sometimes she'd arrive on the bus, and we'd pile into the car to meet her at the station. Other times she'd arrive in a car driving up the steep, narrow driveway that was often washed out in spring or iced over in winter. The dogs, at times half a dozen of them, including her favorite, Rex, with his red hair and large silky bat ears, surrounded the car and barked excitedly, and she'd ride the clutch in fear of hitting them.

"Don't ride the clutch!" Tamar would call out to her.

Both Dorothy and Tamar were early risers, and as soon as Tamar saw light coming through the cracks of Dorothy's door, she brought her coffee and breakfast in bed—a soft-boiled egg in an eggcup and toast sliced in fingers for dipping, just as Eleanor had done for her children and Dorothy had done for Tamar. Just as Tamar did for me, and then I did for her.

Dorothy spent most Christmases with us, making the long winter drive up with Stanley or Hans. The visits were as peaceful as a house filled with nine kids could be, the peace that came with David's departure. Riotous, Dorothy described it. It always seemed to be fifteen degrees below zero, with frozen pipes, buckets of water to be hauled, a car that wouldn't start, and the house full of kids, not all of whom were Tamar's. Sledding, skiing, skating, rushing in and out of the house, the floors awash in discarded boots and coats, the heat registers from the forced hot-air furnace covered in socks, hats, and mittens. A fire in the kitchen woodstove, and another in the living room, a mother hen and her chicks in a box in the kitchen chirping, the radio blaring, and Maggie and Nicky arguing over a game of Monopoly.

"The louder the noise, the louder the canary sings," Dorothy commented. "One can only try to keep the kitchen orderly, and find a quiet corner to read, write, tease or card some wool for a comforter."

She tried to shut out the noise by placing a pillow over one ear and into the other plugging an earpiece connected to a small transistor radio that she never traveled without. As she became deaf, she would lie on the bed with her good ear to the pillow and her deaf ear to the noise. While Tamar cooked for thirteen people and wove silk scarves, Dorothy tried to write. She took refuge in Tamar's small bedroom off the living room, but Tamar would come in for a talk, soon followed by me, and then one by one all the others would pile in.

Still, Dorothy treasured her visits to Vermont. "I get to feeling torn in so many directions sometimes," she wrote Tamar. "You alone do not make demands on me but welcome me when I come and do not reproach me. You do not know how grateful I am for that. You are a real comfort to me always."

Dorothy was in Vermont to see the oldest of her grandchildren get their first jobs, Becky at a summer resort, Susie babysitting, and Eric on a neighboring farm. She was there to see Becky turn eighteen and receive a full scholarship to the University of Vermont, but she wasn't there when Eric shot his first deer. She watched Eric work hard at school and around the house, chopping wood and still caring for Hilaire (Susie still cared for Martha, and Maggie, at thirteen, began caring for me). Nicky was as wild as he had always been, and with his keen eyesight he became a skilled fisherman and hunter. Mary tended the babies, Maggie read, Martha washed the dishes, and Hilaire, at five, caught fish about the same height he was.

We seemed to be doing well, but in those first years following the disintegration of Tamar's marriage, we were more ragged than usual— with holes in our pants and ripped shirts—and it broke Tamar's heart to see what each of us needed and what she couldn't provide. She had to appeal to the overseer of the poor, which in those pre-welfare days every town had, and she and Becky drove to the overseer's farm to beg for surplus commodities of milk powder, peanut butter, cheese, and butter. It was also customary in Vermont for poor families to farm out their daughters, and one of the neighbors suggested Tamar do this. "We'll take the two older girls," they said, but Tamar politely declined. Poor as she was, she wasn't about to break up the family or send her daughters off to be unpaid menial workers. She was planning to send them to college. Dorothy contributed what money she earned through her writing, fifty dollars here, a hundred there. She still hoped that Tamar and David's separation was temporary, but David was not improving, and the letters between him and Tamar dwindled until Tamar often didn't know where he was.

Then, twenty-three years after dropping out of Immaculata High School in Manhattan, Tamar took the high school equivalency test, not sure of what she wanted to do, knowing only she was interested in science and that she needed to find work. She settled on nursing.

"Why nursing?" I asked her.

"I thought I needed to do something useful," she replied.

It seemed an obvious choice. No one doubted her abilities, and those who knew her well said to Dorothy that of course Tamar needed to return to school. Even Uncle Donald in Finland thought it a great idea. He had always admired Tamar for her strength and intelligence, if not for her wisdom in her marriage or her religion. Tamar herself was excited and looked forward to being in school again.

That September of 1964, after the first glorious and happy summer at Tivoli, Dorothy headed up to Vermont full of fears and memories of Susie breaking her arm the previous year. And so began four months of praying and caring for the Hennessy brood, minus the three most mature members of the family, Becky, Susie, and Tamar, who were all away at college.

Tamar loved and excelled at her classes, but she came home on weekends to dream at night of unfinished homework.

Dorothy tried to be encouraging but ended up sounding dismissive to Tamar's ears. "Oh, you don't need this training," she said. "You know it all already."

"Nursing," Tamar replied, "is not the same as it was in 1918 when you were in training."

To me Tamar said, "How in the world Dorothy expected me to know everything without training or an education was beyond me."

Dorothy had great hopes of writing while the six kids were in school and only I, four years old, was at home. She got up at five thirty each morning for an hour of silence and to gaze out the kitchen window watching the stars before they faded in the morning light. Then it was all she could do to get everyone dressed, fed, and off to school with their lunches by seven fifteen. Before they left, she would give each child, even Eric and Nicky—both dressed in tight pants and button-down shirts and with slicked-back hair—a quick sign of the cross on the forehead trustingly raised to her. Then Granny and I would write letters before the mailman came and take a nap in the afternoon before the kids returned. September was full of letters, diary entries, her column, an appeal for funds, an obituary, and an article, but by the end of October the writing had slowed to a trickle. It was hard to think or write while the older kids repeatedly played the song "Devil Woman" at full volume on the turntable.

Dorothy tried to get the older kids to pick up after themselves and do the dishes, which outraged them and bemused Tamar. "I don't remember Dorothy trying to put structure in my life," Tamar said, although she allowed that the household needed it badly. The place was filled with not only seven children but also the neighborhood kids, all teenagers and all showing up to let off the steam they weren't allowed to in their own homes. Dorothy's solution, after shouting, "Stop your roughhousing!" and not being listened to or, worse, being laughed at, was to retreat to her room, hold the transistor radio to her good ear, and read.

She tried to get Eric, Nicky, and Mary to pray, even if it was on their way down the driveway to meet the school bus. Only Maggie, Martha, Hilaire (a "good and serious boy"), and I ("a quiet, biddable child") still took our prayers seriously, and we liked to be specific in our requests.

"How good Nicky has been to fetch water from the brook," Dorothy included in their prayers. (The well had gone dry, as it did every August.)

"Tell Him something about Hilaire," I'd say. I adored Hilaire.

"And so we ask protection for Hilaire, who is seven, so that he won't chop off a foot with the ax which he insists on using or get shot by a hunter when he is out with the other boys." (Hilaire had been using a hatchet since he was three, Dorothy claimed, and it was probably true. Even at seven he went out in the woods with Nicky and Eric when they hunted rabbit, squirrel, and partridge until dark.) Dorothy wasn't keen on hunting. She found it painful, and she found the boys hard-hearted. But she also saw how they loved the woods, and she hoped that their awareness of the beauty around them would stay with them always.

Washing and cooking was hard on Dorothy's arthritic hands, her feet ached with the labor, but most of all she worried. She worried about the car, about Nicky injuring himself while playing football, about Martha learning to ride a bicycle, and about the boys hunting rabbits. Dorothy wasn't following her daughter's advice not to look. She worried as we filled our days with skating, skiing, climbing trees, and falling out of trees and into icy brooks, but trips to the emergency room were rare.

After Christmas, when it was time for Dorothy to leave, things seemed to be going well at the Worker, and Dorothy wondered if she should remain in Vermont until the end of the school year. Tamar would have to leave early each morning to her job at the local hospital, and the kids would have to get themselves to school, leaving no one to take care of me. But, as it turned out, things weren't going as well as she hoped at the Worker, and she didn't stay. To help Tamar, she made arrangements to send me to live with one of Della's sons and his young family. Tamar did not like the idea, but Dorothy was insistent. She had left Tamar when she was a child with Della for two months, and she believed it had done Tamar good, widening her perspective and giving her a sense of family. I was several years younger than Tamar had been, a fact that Dorothy with her loose sense of childhood development did not take note of.

Dorothy spent a month at Tivoli watching the ice form and break on the river and the tide carry the ice floes toward Albany. The fog was sometimes so thick it seemed as if they were living on the edge of an abyss, and she felt melancholy for she missed the kids and was unable to write. She had been happy at Tamar's. She missed the simple life of preparing food, washing clothes, and keeping everyone fed, warm, and healthy. Those daily tasks had been a break from all her other obligations, including her writing, and now she felt pulled in every direction. Forster was ill and begged her to visit often, and Della was also frantic to see her. She left for a three-month cross-country speaking tour. The times were tumultuous—Malcolm X was assassinated, Lyndon Johnson announced air strikes in North Vietnam, and Martin Luther King Jr. led the march in Selma, Alabama.

Tamar began her nursing job at the local hospital, and I left Vermont to live with the cousins, a stable and kind family with a mother and father, an orderly and clean house, and clothes that were beautiful and neat. I was not happy. "Where are my kids?" I asked again and again, speaking of my brothers and sisters. Dorothy always had ideas to help lighten Tamar's load—sending Eric away to a Catholic boarding school in Massachusetts, Martha to Dr. William Miller's family in Florida, and me to my mother's cousin—but none of them worked out for she never understood just how attached we were to one another and to our home.

In the spring, Dorothy finished her speaking tour and came up to Vermont for Hilaire's First Communion. There she found Tamar frantic over her homework, her stomach in knots, and dreaming at night of everything being half-done and going to the hospital half-combed and half-dressed. "Live your own life," Dorothy woke up hearing one morning while feeling bound up in Tamar's.

That fall, back with the cousins after some time home, I entered kindergarten. "Eve of Destruction" played on the radio while we practiced duck-and-cover drills at school. Eric entered technical college, and Tamar had to get up even earlier to drive an hour to get him to classes before she went to work. He was also working in a soapstone factory on weekends and would come home covered head to foot in white soapstone. Becky had fallen in love with a young man from New Hampshire while working at a summer resort, and Susie, in her last year of nursing school, was reading Aldous Huxley and mysticism.

The following spring, while Hilaire tapped sugar maples and Tamar turned forty, Becky and Eric both dropped out of college. Becky, now twenty-one, told Dorothy, to her shock, that she was getting married. That October, within hours of the death of Uncle Donald in Finland, the first of the Day siblings to die, Becky got married.

"A first grandchild's wedding is a wonderful thing," Dorothy wrote to her readers.

The following summer of 1967, the summer of love, was when I fell in love with the Catholic Worker.

Things weren't going well with Tamar's work. She was getting sick often, and when she was sick she didn't get paid. Tamar had chosen nursing because she believed that you do the things that are needed, but it was not a good choice for her. She still battled her extreme shyness and sensitivity, even though her patients and coworkers came to love her for her good sense and calm and caring disposition, and forty years later patients and nurses still remembered her. She begged to be able to work in the pediatric ward with the newborns as she didn't know how to deal with the neediness of people. "People want more than you have to give," she said. But her request was denied. She couldn't sleep at night and took Valium to get herself to work. Much of the time she was terrified. Her days became filled with dry mouth, chills, and uncontrollable crying, and when things went wrong with the patients, she was devastated.

To help relieve the pressures on her, at every opportunity Tamar stuffed us six younger kids into the car and headed to Tivoli. We left the house unlocked and gave animal-care instructions to our neighbor, who occasionally fronted the gas money to get us there.

Tivoli was the Worker I grew up with, with its guitar liturgies and outdoor Masses underneath the hemlock trees. It was the only aspect I knew of my grandmother's life and work at that time, and I loved it. I still sometimes dream of the road that leads down from the village of Tivoli toward the railroad tracks and the Hudson River. The road then turns north and runs along the train tracks up through the woods, along the foot of a cliff, and past the Peter Maurin House, which was full of books, drawing me like a kid to a candy shop. But there was too much religion and too little storytelling, and I'd be out of there in a flash. Then through the arch under the tower of the decaying mansion, where I explored feeling on edge because of the ghost stories. Then up to the main house, where I'd jump out of the car into the wonder that was the Tivoli farm, hotbed of idealism for some, the last bastion of hope for others. I was interested only in looking for Maggie Corbin, Rita Corbin's daughter, whom I'd be dying to see, but we both were so shy, it could take a day before we talked to each other.

Dorothy liked to book the place with conferences organized haphazardly in Catholic Worker fashion. Sometimes there would be more than two hundred people camped out in every available space. Life was lived on the front lawn and celebrated with plays and puppet shows, volleyball and dancing in front of the mansion. And in the evening everyone watched the sun set across the river and over the Catskill Mountains, beyond the cypress tree that grew at the edge of the lawn just before the wrought iron fence that kept us all from plunging down the cliff onto the railroad tracks below. At the previous summer's Pax Conference (the US Pax Conferences were established as a way for Catholics to explore

Catholic teachings on nonviolence and address the issues of conscientious objector status), Mary Lou Williams, the jazz pianist, composer, and arranger of sacred music, performed on the Steinway piano Dorothy had received from a local chapter of the American Legion in exchange for the bar at the end of the casino. (She then turned the bar into the chapel and placed a statue of Our Lady, carved by John Day's sister-in-law Tina de Aragon and given to the Worker for the Easton farm, to the right of the altar.) Karl Stern, a psychiatrist who spoke on ambivalence, violence, and the acceptance of mystery, played Mozart on the violin while Dorothy wondered how they were going to feed them all (including a yogi from Ananda Ashram, an Indian poet, and a communist seaman full of questions about God), when all they had were toasted cheese sandwiches.

That August 1967, Tamar, who had taken leave without pay from the hospital, piled Eric, Mary, Maggie, Martha, Hilaire, Rhonda, who lived down the road, and me in the 1961 red Corvair, another one of our far-too-small, short-lived, and overused cars, and headed down to Tivoli. Nicky stayed home because he was in love with Rhonda's sister and was planning to marry her as soon as they graduated from high school. Susie was living and working in Canada, and Becky was living in New Hampshire with her husband. We arrived in time for a Peacemaker Conference (the Peacemakers were a pacifist network founded in 1948 who held yearly conferences on nonviolence) where they talked under the trees of community, noncooperation, tax refusal, small industries, and cooperatives, and often were interrupted by the sound of the passing trains so loud no one could hear themselves think, and we kids would rush to the fence to count the cars. People gathered around the handful of hemlock trees, which had swings for the children and a small round table in the center where Mass was celebrated, to listen to Dorothy talk. In bad weather she spoke in the dining room, and people would sit among the long tables beneath Rita Corbin's three-paneled mural of an interpretation of Peter Maurin's phrase "Cult, culture, and cultivation." Dorothy was getting thinner, and the fashions of the sixties—a handwoven Guatemalan handbag and a pin with an E. E. Cummings quote, "Damn everything but the circus"—crept into her otherwise conventional wardrobe.

This is when I began to listen to Dorothy's voice. At the time I didn't understand or care what she talked about. I was simply caught up by the sound. One of her topics, which had been handed to her the night before by an organizer of the conference, was "The Urban Poor." She retitled it "The Urban Destitute" and gave one of her usual rambling discourses, telling stories of Agnes sitting up all night in the dining room and how they learned of the plight of migrant workers in upstate New York only when someone dropped off an African American migrant worker at the doorstep of the Newburgh farm.

A man in the audience asked, "What are the statistics on how many men there are who come in on the breadline and become involved in the political aspect of the work?"

Dorothy responded by telling the story of when a man had attacked Arthur Sheehan with a knife.

"What does this have to do with anything?" the questioner asked.

"I don't know," she answered. "Let me be discursive. I've learned to speak in stories." She then spoke of how men became part of the family and found some job such as chopping vegetables. She added, "We don't have records or statistics," for, of course, she was aware—as the questioner, who was not involved in the Catholic Worker, seemed not—that there were men in the audience who would have been part of those "statistics." It was not the intention of the Worker, and never would be, to place any importance on whether or not those who came for help would then be led into political activism, and in her roundabout and gentle way, Dorothy tried to impress this upon the questioner.

That summer, under the auspices of New York State, which provided workers, equipment, food, and transportation, Dorothy opened a daycare center for children of migrants who came north to harvest the fruit crops. Thirty-two kids from ten months to eight years old arrived at the farm, and my sister Mary was hired as one of the staff. Some of the kids were malnourished, and two had pneumonia and had to be taken immediately to the hospital. The Workers filled the old casino at the back of the kitchen with cots and cribs, tables, chairs, and toys for the children, who often would bang away at the piano near the chapel.

The Tivoli farm also held a Pax Conference, a War Resisters League meeting, a Catholic Peace Fellowship meeting, music recitals on the Steinway piano, and the first session of the Tivoli CW School. Nuns played guitars and danced, priests wore shorts and T-shirts while discussing Catholic radical action, and Stanley and I mingled with the crowds on a mission to identify the FBI agent as the FBI could be expected to be at any and all of the events of the Catholic peace movement during the Vietnam War. They had also been keeping an eye on my grandmother. Stanley always claimed to know who the FBI agent was, but they were all just grown-ups to me.

Maggie Corbin and I would race through the dining room, stopping just long enough to grab a piece of toast with butter. We'd run past the outdoor Masses and head out back to leap into the pool. We formed a secret society in the mansion's attic while the grown-ups talked about nonviolence and John harvested the green beans to be taken down to the city for the soup line. And when the summer came to a close, I returned home to Vermont freckled, happy, and with a head full of lice.

CHAPTER SEVENTEEN

Within months after we returned home from Tivoli the summer of 1967, Tamar attended her last Mass with Dorothy and quit the Church without fuss or comment. It is one of the curious ways of this story that the time Tamar was able to rejoin the Catholic Worker, as much as she could, coincided with the time of her leaving the Catholic Church.

In the early sixties my siblings had still been attending catechism on Saturday, and we all went to Mass on Sundays. When Dorothy visited, Tamar and the girls would head to St. Mary's while Dorothy stayed home and read aloud matins and lauds to Hilaire, and I babbled along holding a book to imitate her. By the time I was seven, I knew we were Catholic though not practicing, but I didn't know what this meant beyond the rosary and breviary my grandmother always had with her, the blessing she gave me on my forehead with her thumb, and the three prayers I knew—the Our Father, Hail Mary, and the grace my grandmother said before meals. I have a faint memory of the hard pews in church, the scent of incense, and Hilaire and Nicky carrying on until the snot came shooting out of Hilaire's nose, making them behave even more badly. Or maybe this is a story Hilaire told and not my own memory. Like his grandmother, Hilaire became a storyteller.

I often tried to get my mother to tell her story of how and why she left the Church. Sometimes she would throw me a line or two, which I would repeat back to her much later only to have her look blankly at me as if I was making it all up. She was delighted to tell stories of Easton and of life at Ade Bethune's, but she was silent on many other aspects of her life, and why she left the Church remained one of the subjects she was most silent about—so often my questions were met with that straight, thin line of her lips and vague flick of the fingers as if to toss it aside. The story of Tamar's loss of faith, as she referred to it, took me decades to piece together or, I should say, to piece together into one possible version of the story. My questions started when I was in my twenties, and they continued until she died. And every time we spoke of it, she told a different story, or so I thought until I realized that each of these stories was a small piece of the puzzle.

Over the years people showed up at Tamar's doorstep to ask, "Why did you leave the Church?" To one stranger, she said, "I tried to hold on to those values. I tried to live simply. I tried to follow the Catholic faith. It did not turn out well. Right now I seem to have lapsed." It did not turn out well—such a gracefully muted and polite understatement. Tamar was never one to put flourishes on the facts of her life. She made another understatement to yet another stranger: "I had been trying to be a good Catholic. The kids and I gave up on it and feel much better for it."

To me she said, "I didn't know why I was leaving the Church— I just had to do it." Sometimes, though, her statements were darker, sharper: "The Church's teachings on sex and birth control destroy men. Women are strong enough, but the men aren't." In one of her most bitter moments she said, "One of my greatest accomplishments is that none of my children is a practicing Catholic." She didn't elaborate, so I don't know what was on her mind at that moment, but fifteen or so years later when Martha returned to the Church, Tamar was curious and support-ive of Martha's decision.

The one person, Tamar said to me, who never asked about her loss of faith was her own mother. The joy at the birth of her daughter that had brought Dorothy to faith was never far from Dorothy's mind, and even during the disintegration of Tamar and David's marriage, she believed and hoped faith would see them through. But when her daughter, hav-ing chosen to end her marriage, made another choice, it broke Dorothy's heart.

"Dorothy believed that for someone to lose their faith was the worst thing that could happen," Tamar said.

Shortly before Tamar stopped going to Mass, Dorothy wrote, "I consider the loss of faith the greatest of disasters—the greatest unhappiness." She added, "Of course, it does not necessarily follow that 'one out of the Church' has lost his faith." She wrote much at that time of what held her to the Church—her love for the Psalms, the Sermon on the Mount, the prayers of adoration, contrition, thanksgiving, and supplication. And those she prayed to—the Blessed Mother, St. Joseph, and that whole companionship of saints who were real to her and a daily presence. And daily Mass—the words of the Eucharist, the cup of wine, and the wafer. She received so much from the sacraments, and yet she also wrote of what she battled with—she was bored by theology, disheartened by anti-Semitism in the old writings, driven to distraction by indifferent mumblings of priests during Mass, and suffering over the wealth of the bishops and their refusal to condemn nuclear weapons.

For years Dorothy was sure she could, through her example and force of personality, bring people into the Church, and this often got her into trouble at the Catholic Worker. And perhaps her greatest mistake was with her own daughter, as it so often can be. When Dorothy was fifty and looking back at her conversion, trying to understand it, she said, "I knew that I was going to have my child baptized, cost what it may. I knew that I was not going to have her floundering through many years as I had done, doubting and hesitating, undisciplined and amoral. I felt it was the greatest thing I could do for my child." Dorothy didn't yet know that the cost was not only hers but would become her daughter's. She didn't yet know that not only could she not provide faith for another but she had to guard against the force of her personality, and as the years passed she watched some of those who had come into the Church because of that force begin to leave it.

Tamar left the Church gradually in her quiet way, or maybe she didn't leave it but shed it like the old skin of a snake. Forty-one years old and exhausted, she retreated to a delight in the natural world and a sense of her role in it as a gardener. This is what sustained her, along with the endless spinning and weaving. The Church Tamar experienced wasn't the Church Dorothy loved. "The Catholic Church was something different to Dorothy than it was to me," Tamar said. "She revered priests even though the Worker was often a dumping place for unwanted ones. They could do no wrong in her eyes. She accepted the authority of the Church, but she didn't feel it in her bones like I did. That's the difference between the indoctrination of a child and the conversion of an adult."

The Church Tamar experienced was simplistic, paternalistic, controlling, self-satisfied, and manipulative, and it forced her into contortions of trying to figure out how to make her way through life without committing a mortal sin. Tamar was looking at the Church through a hard-eyed practicality forged, stripped, and scrubbed clean by teachings that dogged her every step as a child, teenager, and childbearing woman, whereas Dorothy experienced the Church as only a mystic can—free of its corruption. The only element of her mother's religion that made any sense to Tamar was the Catholic Worker. All else had been a recipe for disaster.

Early in the 1960s it ate at Dorothy that not one of her siblings had become Catholic, and then she had to watch as her five oldest grandchildren stopped attending Mass. Hilaire and I were too young to care either way, and only Maggie and Martha continued for a time. Dorothy believed Tamar was leading the way by no longer getting to Mass after her separation, which left the kids to feel free of the obligation. But the exodus did not begin with Tamar. It began with my older brothers and sisters, who did not take their religion seriously and never had, unlike their mother. The indoctrination had failed with them, but maybe that was because to have Dorothy as your mother was an entirely different thing than having Tamar as your mother. Mary was the first one to begin the fight openly in 1958 when she spread poison ivy over her face in a failed attempt to get out of making her First Communion.

"What was it you were fighting against?" I asked Mary.

"I don't know. I just knew I wanted no part of it. I didn't believe it, and I never believed it. Then I had to make things up at confession. I'd say I lied or stole, and I hadn't. It was crazy—a seven-year-old lying in confession just to have something to say!"

Sweet, beautiful Mary, the child who was always cheerful and won everyone's heart, and the most serene and constant of my sisters. Was it she and her poison ivy who started the Hennessy exodus from the

Church? So it went, in any case, with all the others, no matter how dar-
ling we were at reciting our prayers. Dorothy, in an effort to influence
matters, brought Tamar a book on whether you should compel your
children to go to church, but each time Dorothy came up to Vermont,
fewer of the kids went to Mass with her. By Christmas 1966 Tamar was
the only one who accompanied her, and by the fall of 1967, we were all
done with it, including Tamar, and it broke Dorothy's heart. But no one
would talk to her about it, and Dorothy did not pry. She comforted herself with the belief that God wills that all be saved. She also said, "How
can I intrude into the personal lives of others, this most interior life of
faith and love, of the heaven and hell that are within us?"

We weren't the only ones losing our faith at this time. Nuns and
priests wrote her letters or showed up at the Worker questioning their
vocation and their faith, and maybe the departure of many of them
allowed my mother to realize that she too could leave. It hurt Dorothy
to see so many people leaving the Church, particularly at the time of
Vatican II, Pope John XXIII's "great and trustful gesture." It got to the
point that if Dorothy saw a priest without his collar, she wondered if he
was on his way out of the Church.

All was not lost though, as the era also seemed to mark the end of a
complacent and compulsory Catholicism and the beginning of a deeper
understanding of the sacraments. Though Dorothy did not trust the
consciences of many of the young people and their "it feels right" sense
of morality, and she called us all, Tamar included, adolescents.

When I was in my twenties, Tamar told me the story of having to
browbeat the kids into getting dressed and into the car both on Saturday and Sunday, and of driving the seven miles to St. Mary's on icy roads
in a bad car that was too small to seat all the kids at once, and Dorothy
claimed that Tamar had to put some of us in the trunk. Tamar also told
me of how one day she sat quietly during Mass, got up when it was
finished, and walked out glaring at the priest—poor Father Sevigny—a
hard, silent glare, her own version of Dorothy's "the Look," as Tamar
called her mother's fierce gaze, and never went back.

"What did Father Sevigny say that finally tipped the scales?" I asked,
but she didn't answer.

As I grew older, Tamar's responses to my questions dug deeper.

"My doubts started long before my marriage," Tamar said when I was in my thirties. "Dorothy never understood what I was being taught in school, and I spent far too much time believing it. But my first quarrel with the Church was when I was told that unbaptized babies went to limbo and not to heaven. I was outraged. I knew that wasn't right. My second quarrel came out of my love for the natural sciences, which the nuns dismissed completely."

It was only at Ade's that Tamar was again reminded of her love of science, which had been squelched among the careless, if inadvertent, destruction of her specimens, the loss of her microscope and chemistry set in their many moves, and Dorothy's and the nuns' indifference to providing instruction in the sciences. Tamar's stirrings of a vocation were so thoroughly trampled, she never was able to retrieve them, and to her never-ending grief she felt this was inherited by her children. By the early sixties, Tamar wanted science and not religion, and even though there were now nuns and Catholic laywomen in the universities studying the sciences, it was too late for her. The Second Vatican Council had arrived too late.

It wasn't just the lack of the natural sciences that led Tamar to dismiss her Catholic education. She also wasn't impressed by the history the nuns taught—"manipulation of facts," she called it—or the teachings about hell. "I don't know why I grew up believing in hell. No one else did. My classmates all laughed it off, but not me."

The doubts didn't end with her education. In the early years of her marriage Dorothy had given Tamar a book for Catholic wives about obedience and submission. "It showed the extreme paternalism of the church," Tamar said. "It would shock anyone today to read it."

She still had the book, which she found for me. Someone, I don't know if it was Dorothy, had underlined particular passages, and I was so appalled by the thought that it could have been her, I shut the book. The book was not on Tamar's shelves after she died, so I couldn't return to it and find what had upset me.

Tamar also didn't trust much of Catholic language. She did not take to jargon at all, and the way she spoke was much like the way she was—

unadorned, to the point, literal, no jokes, no puns yet full of laughter. Tamar and I spoke often of piety over the years, trying to tease out the elements of piety that made it so volatile for her and to understand my own aversion to it. But understanding piety would be much more complicated when it came to her mother's. To Tamar, one of the more egregious results of it was in the forties when Dorothy turned away from her old friends and began identifying people as Catholic or not. Tamar did not agree with Dorothy's belief at the time that being Catholic was best. She did not admire what she saw as the Church's sense of superiority and triumphalism while it simultaneously held on to grievances and a sense of persecution. "We are all children of God. Peter Maurin knew that. I don't know what got into Dorothy."

Dorothy said, "You must accept all of the Church teachings if you are a Catholic." She said this most often when people questioned her about the Church's stand on sex, as they did in the sixties. In search for her own answers to why she left the Church, Tamar had picked up a copy of the missal she had read as a child and couldn't believe what she was reading. "The Good Friday prayer with its mention of 'perfidious Jews.' It's funny how I never noticed that as a child. But really! It was a relief to let that all go."

Another Tamar understatement. It was a relief to let the Church go, a relief not to be subsumed in the paternalism, a relief not to be required to be against homosexuality, against men that she had known all her life, had cared for deeply and had loved, including her own husband. "Do not add one straw to the burden of others," as Dorothy liked to quote. Unable to untangle the web, Tamar simply dropped the Church and never spoke of it to her mother or to her priest.

Gradually Tamar became a supporter of birth control. As for abortion, she did not speak against it—this was not her way—but she suffered for women who chose it, I could see. She would fall silent, a sense of sadness and helplessness settling into her bones, and this led me to think of all the babies she knew of who had been taken away from their mothers, babies whom others forgot and she did not. Even as a mother of nine, she kept a close and interested eye on many children who were not her own. But Tamar also had a cold, scientific eye that looked at the long view—the truly long view of a paleoclimatologist who once said that we all will probably become, no matter our hubris or our suffering, a thin carbon line between the sediments, marking that great and insignificant passing of human beings.

Beyond my childhood memories, I saw Tamar at Mass only twice—at Dorothy's funeral at the Church of the Nativity on Second Avenue and at the memorial Mass the following month at St. Patrick's Cathedral. She kept no rosaries about her, though she had some in her jewelry box, but she hung on her walls the prayer of St. Francis, the beatitudes, and her collection of Russian icons.

Thirty years after Tamar left the Church, she received an unexpected letter from Sister Henrietta, a nun the same age as Tamar who lived in the small convent attached to our parish church. She had left St. Mary's and transferred to another convent in 1965 and had long been retired, but Tamar was still on her mind. After asking Tamar if she ever thought of writing a book about her mother, she said, "You bravely carried a heavy cross." Tamar and Sister Henrietta kept in contact, and ten years later, when she and Tamar both were in their late seventies, Sister Henrietta wrote a letter that my mother made sure I read. "I regret," she wrote, "that I was unaware of the difficult time you and your children had on the farm. I was also unaware that you separated from your husband during that time. I can understand your deep hurt when the Church was not there for you in your need. Forgive us, please."

Horrified to think that Sister Henrietta had been struggling for years with this, Tamar wrote back reassuring her that Father Sevigny had done all he could. Not too long after Tamar and David's breakup, Father Sevigny left the priesthood, leaving Tamar to fear for years that her situation had led him to lose his vocation. (While Dorothy believed the worst thing that could happen was to lose one's faith, for Tamar, who never had the chance to find her own, it was to lose one's vocation.)

During that last decade of Tamar's life, when I was in my forties, our conversation turned away from those teachings of the Church Tamar had battled and settled onto something much more difficult to define.

"What do you mean when you say you lost your faith?" I asked her.

As usual we were sitting in her kitchen, where all the most important conversations took place.

She shrugged. "I just sort of dropped it," she said, making it sound as if it were a book she had started to read and never bothered to finish.

I wanted to ask much more, but she changed the subject in her aversion to others prying into her heart and mind, even her own daughter. I know she received solace from the soil and seeds, from the growth and bearing of fruits, vegetables, and flowers, and from the creatures, human and animal, that came to her also looking for solace. Tamar's faith, if I need to call it that, was a private affair that was hard to recognize in the shadow of her mother's religion.

I have come to believe Dorothy needed to join the Church for the same reason Tamar needed to leave it: in an effort to find out who they each were meant to be. Tamar needed the freedom to choose just as her mother had, but both had so entwined faith with the Church that Tamar's rejection of the Church could be seen only as a loss of faith. I will never know entirely why Tamar left the Church, shrugged it off like an old coat, simply and without argument. Perhaps the difference between Dorothy and Tamar over the question of faith was that for Tamar life was truer without the Church, while for Dorothy life was truer with it.

CHAPTER EIGHTEEN

The year Tamar left the Church was also the year that her oldest son, Eric, was drafted into the army. These years of 1967, '68, and '69 were full of terrible battles and fear faced with courage, and the effects were felt on Cady Hill Road. Dorothy thought and spoke much on the topic of fear during that time of both the civil rights movement and the Vietnam War, and it was the brutality against the civil rights movement that frightened her the most. Not many of us will experience, she said, what blacks were experiencing in the South in terms of hatred, torture, and murder, most of which was never reported in the press.

"I know what human fear is and how often it keeps us from following our conscience," she said. There are many kinds of fear: "fear of losing our bodily goods, fear of poverty, fear of losing our job, our reputation, and least of all there is the strange business of bodily fear." She recalled the fear she felt in the face of the hate, contempt, and venom that greeted her in the South and when she was shot at while sitting in a car at the integrated community Koinonia in Georgia. There was always a sense of terror in the South, she said.

Her awareness of the discrimination against African Americans had begun in the 1930s, when she and Tamar traveled down to Florida to visit Grace. Her protest against the Jim Crow laws began in the late thirties, when she and Tamar would travel third class on the train. At that time third class was meant for only African American passengers, and Dorothy and Tamar's presence sent fear throughout the carriage. "Dorothy was oblivious," Tamar said. "Everyone else was frightened to death." The Worker began to make its stand against segregation in Baltimore, also in the late thirties. The CW house there was integrated at a time when it was illegal to have both blacks and whites in a hostel, and the young man in charge was arrested and jailed for running a "disorderly house." At the same time, one of the young women at the Worker ran an integrated children's camp on the Prince's Bay lot Forster had given Tamar. Soon after the Second World War, another brave young Catholic Worker woman was arrested at an interracial demonstration against a segregated pool in New Jersey, and in Chicago, black and white Catholic Workers went to a beach and were beaten up, victims of sudden mob violence. Workers from around the country had headed down south to help the civil rights movement, and some served jail time, one man for three months. In the early sixties Dorothy was invited to speak in Virginia to African Americans who were trying to register to vote. She prayed to be delivered from fear of the whites' fear. "I haven't the slightest idea now what I said. You do an awful lot of praying on those occasions."

In the thirties she had been labeled a "northern communist whore" when newspapers in Memphis, Tennessee, attacked her for supporting unions for the sharecroppers and again in the fifties when she tried to buy seed peanuts for the Koinonia community. "Racial slurs and the word 'commie,'" Dorothy said, "are swear words that come out of the mouths of frightened, confused, enraged, and vulnerable people."

She was often called a communist or at the least accused of being soft on communism. Her ongoing friendship with Mike Gold, her oldest friend, who had become a communist in 1917 and who died a communist fifty years later, didn't help. He had been a loyal friend to Dorothy, barring the years of the Spanish Civil War and World War II, even though they had taken such different paths. She felt he understood all that she went through and that there was a price to be paid for following one's conscience. He had been best man at Della's wedding, and he was indirectly part of the beginnings of the Worker, as it was his brother George who organized and led the hunger march on Washington in 1932 that helped change Dorothy's life. To some this enduring friendship was proof that she was a communist, always had been and always would be. But there was a special bond between her and Mike that she would not deny, begun when they were engaged to be married in 1917. And of all Dorothy's friends, it was Mike Gold, she felt, who understood the misery she was going through during her conversion to Catholicism.

In the winter of 1965 Dorothy left on a train trip through North Carolina, Alabama, Mississippi, and Louisiana, fortified with sandwiches Della provided and, in her handbag, her missal, the New Testament, and C. S. Lewis. She wrote little in her diary about her time there except for a terse "Had a grim time . . . harrowing." Every conversation she had with people put them in danger, but people were grateful for her presence. In a black drugstore, a young man rushed up to give her a kiss just for coming in.

Dorothy was criticized as an outsider for these trips, but it was an argument she did not agree with. Because of fear you often don't speak when you ought to, and she said, "This is my country, all of it, not just North or South."

Then, just as the South was beginning to integrate, the focus shifted to the Vietnam War. In March 1968 Hilaire collected sap for sugaring while Dorothy and Tamar were beside themselves with worry, for as far as they knew Eric was in the highlands of Vietnam, where the heavy fighting was, and they hadn't heard from him. Tamar was still taking Valium to get herself to her job at the hospital, and Dorothy spent the two years from Eric's draft and induction in 1967 to his return at Christmas 1969 praying and fasting from meat. Even if Eric were to survive, they didn't know what damage he would return with.

"The taking of a life does something to a man," Dorothy said. "It does something to a man whether in war or in peace."

Eric had dropped out of college when he turned eighteen, and he waited to be drafted. In April a demonstration of four hundred thousand people gathered in Central Park in New York City led by Dr. Martin Luther King Jr. to march to the United Nations. Dorothy stood on the steps of the Church of the Holy Family, across the street from Dag Hammarskjold Plaza, listening to the speeches. Three days later she was in Vermont. Eric was in court for totaling Tamar's car while Tamar tried to appeal to the draft board for an exemption based on her dependence on him as her oldest son. The wait was an ordeal, and Eric and Nicky, who was not yet old enough to register, stayed out late at night drinking, but there was no talk of refusing the draft.

Dorothy had first started writing about Vietnam in 1954, and by 1967 she had been invited to go there three times. She refused each time. There was no use it in, she said, unless she were younger and able to go as a nurse. There were many antiwar demonstrations that fall and winter. Dorothy didn't participate, though others at the Worker did. By December we knew Eric was going to be called up in January. Dorothy came up to Vermont for Christmas and to see him off, but he spent his last few weeks of freedom out drinking with his buddies, all of whom were being sent over. No one went to Mass with Dorothy on Christmas Day, and Eric left his gifts unopened under the Christmas tree—they would continue to sit unopened on his bureau for months as a kind of reproach.

The day after New Year's, Tamar drove Eric to the induction center in Woodstock, Vermont, while Dorothy, Mary, Maggie, and Martha watched them leave. Martha wondered if she would ever see Eric again, while Dorothy thought of Forster. Eric was so like him, she felt, similar in looks and disposition and with a similar sensitivity to the world and an inability to go out into it. She feared Eric would break down as his grandfather had done during the First World War. He seemed attached to home and Tamar, and Tamar to him. Four weeks later, the Tet Offensive was launched, eroding any belief that the Vietnam War could be won by the United States. Tamar joined Dorothy at Tivoli to attend a peace conference.

In May, before being transferred from Fort Jackson, South Carolina, to Fort Benning, Georgia, Eric was given a twelve-day leave. He left a message for Dorothy at Tivoli, and she sat up waiting until three o'clock in the morning hoping he would show, but he had gone on to Vermont. Dorothy came up within a day or two, and we listened to Eric and his friends tell tales of basic training and of forced marches, running, push-ups; scrubbing, waxing and polishing the barracks; and not being allowed to lie down but having to sleep standing up or leaning against each other in groups of three.

"One fellow," Dorothy wrote, was "forced, for untidiness, to get on his knees and crawl around proclaiming he was a pig. . . . Fellow beaten to death, his head banged around washroom wall until he died. Men, boys, standing around had to take it. No protest made." This instinct for cruelty plunged her into despair. "'The world will be saved by beauty,' said Prince Myshkin. But we do not want the world saved."

That was what she wrote in her diary. In her column she called it "a delightful visit," during which she and Tamar picked rhubarb and dandelion greens and walked in the garden. The house was so full of young people, they were sleeping on the living room floor, much like they were doing at Tivoli.

That summer, unable to sleep, nervous, and depressed, Tamar took several months off from nursing. She, Mary, Maggie, Martha, Hilaire, and I headed down to Tivoli to spend the summer at the farm. The first of Tamar's grandchildren was on her way—Nicky's girlfriend, Brenda, was pregnant. Dorothy informed Forster, with whom she kept in greater contact as the two of them aged, that they were now going to become great-grandparents, and Forster sent Nicky a double-barreled shotgun for bird hunting.

It was a hot summer, and we all lived in the swimming pool, while Dorothy visited Eric at Fort Benning.

"I don't know how Granny did it," Eric said. "Families weren't allowed to visit during training."

He had finished his course as a Ranger, in which he underwent training so severe half of the class dropped out. He was on his way to several weeks of training in the Florida swamps and the hills of Georgia before getting a month of leave, after which he would be shipped out to Vietnam.

In September, Tamar, her nerves shot, quit nursing and gave Forster the news in her usual unadorned and succinct way: "I was depressed so have given up nursing for now. Will try weaving for sale." She went on welfare while dreaming of starting a small greenhouse. Dorothy longed to help even though she had her doubts that Tamar could run a business. Dorothy went up to Vermont, where she read Eric's latest letter and despaired. To raise their spirits, she and Tamar visited the local historical society two miles up the road, where Dorothy found a copy of

John Ruskin's *True and Beautiful*, which contained one of her favorite quotations on the duty of delight.

While Dorothy was in Vermont, Father Dan Berrigan called to tell her about the Milwaukee 14 draft-board action, in which five priests had taken part destroying draft files. She stood by them regardless of her personal doubts about the actions of these priests and laymen who offered themselves as "a living sacrifice" to somehow offset the obliteration bombing in North Vietnam. People accused her of inconsistency as she had been against the actions of the Catonsville Nine that May, but she saw no inconsistency, for she always respected people's willingness to go to jail. "You cannot go to jail as a gesture," she said. "It is a real suffering."

The draft-board actions were provoking a great deal of self-reflection and soul-searching, and she was full of doubt. "I understand the grief, the horror," she said, "but I do not think them right." She recalled the time when she was working on the *Call*, and its offices were ransacked by the police. In the fifties, Dave Dellinger, publisher of *Liberation*, had his printing press destroyed and the type scattered about in the forest. "Although it was only property which suffered destruction, we ourselves have suffered violence, vandalism by hostile right-wing groups, the beating of individuals, the destruction of mailing lists and records, the burning of houses and barns. So we repeat the golden rule, 'Do unto others what you would have them do unto you,' and its contrary, 'Do not do unto others what you would not have them do unto you.'" If government and industry, she went on, "will not hear the screams of children burned by napalm, do you think they will hear the breaking up of files and office furniture?"

In November, there were false rumors of a cease-fire in Vietnam. That Thanksgiving, we all sat at the big oak dining table, which was loaded with food, and my mother, the only adult, stood to serve it. Turkey, mashed potatoes, cranberry sauce, dressing, and dilly green beans she had canned. Eric called, and Maggie answered the phone. He had finished his Ranger course. The draftee had graduated as a staff sergeant in a class of West Point officers and Navy SEALS, and the hope was that he would teach and not be sent overseas. In the meantime he was coming home for Christmas.

Dorothy drove up to Vermont for Christmas and was promptly snowed in. The temperature plunged to fifteen degrees below zero, and as we waited for Eric, she was forced to go to bed early because of the bitter cold. She and Tamar sewed and knitted surrounded by kids and creatures, three tanks of tropical fish, a squirrel, a mouse, two canaries, three dogs, and eight cats, and Christmas cacti, begonias, and African violets in every corner. Dorothy read Abbie Hoffman's *Revolution for the Hell of It* and was not happy with his bitterness and hatred, but she was fond of Abbie. ("I have known Abbie Hoffman, and have known him for a long time," she said. "He is one of our disorderly children." Abbie, who would attend her funeral, said, "Dorothy was the first hippie.")

Eric finally arrived and now everyone was home, including Susie and her new husband, Jorge. Susie was pregnant, and Nicky's new wife, Brenda, was due in several weeks. Eric, waiting for his orders to go to Vietnam in mid-January, was again out every night with his friends, as he had done the Christmas before.

"But just the same," Dorothy wrote Forster, "this is a better Christmas than last when he was waiting induction. Strangely enough he has enjoyed his training, after he got through basic. It was all survival training in the mountains of north Georgia, in the swamps of north Florida and paratroop training. He loved the South and he loved the rigors of life in the wilds. They walked twenty-six miles a day and starved in the swamps and mountains. He ate rattlesnake meat and one fellow ate a lizard. They didn't give them time to fish or hunt.

"Why is that when forced, men are capable of so much, and do so little when no compulsion is put upon them?" she asked Forster.

On February 9, 1969, in the middle of a blizzard and several weeks after the birth of Nicky's daughter, Tamar's first grandchild and Dorothy's first great-grandchild, Eric called from Fort Lewis in Washington. Mary answered the phone, and he told her he was flying to Vietnam in four days. Eric wasn't old enough to vote, but he was heading to Vietnam as a platoon sergeant. A week after he arrived in Vietnam, Tamar received a letter from the army telling her that her son was now a Sky Soldier in the 173rd Airborne Brigade.

It was a hard, hard winter. War and violence dominated everyone's thoughts, and the peace movement was turning angry. "The battle at home," Dorothy wrote, "is now to conquer the bitterness, the sense of futility and despair that grows among the young and turns them to violence." Again and again she said that we must remember that God loves all men, that God wills all men to be saved, that all men are brothers. "We must do that seemingly utterly impossible thing—love our enemy."

She spent one day listening to the Wagner ring cycle until she felt calm and rested, while Tamar read *Soul on Ice* and *The Autobiography of Malcolm X* and made soap in addition to doing her never-ending spinning and weaving, much like an incarnation of Clotho, one of the three Fates. That winter she was weaving cotton towels.

Young men had asked Dorothy again and again, "Do you think my father is guilty of mortal sin because he was in the army?" Now, during the Vietnam years, they asked, "Do you believe I will be in a state of mortal sin if I join the army?"

If he truly thinks he is striving for the common good, he must follow his conscience, she replied. It is the teaching of the Church. But he has the duty of forming his conscience through study and listening to others' point of view. This is something no one else can tell you the answers for, and if you are not convinced as a pacifist, then it is far better to go ahead and enroll in the army.

Dorothy gave no easy answers for young men faced with the war. The paradox of obedience is that it cannot be asked of someone else; it can only be voluntarily given by oneself, and if your informed and educated conscience puts you in a state of obedience, then good, and if it puts you in a state of disobedience, then also good, but you must be ready to take the consequences. And, she added, you must follow your conscience even if it is a wrong or ill-informed conscience.

Dorothy also said, "It is a hard thing to be a pacifist when men are showing such great courage and have endured so much in the armies." Nonviolence is not as colorful and heroic as the life of a soldier, and the conscientious objector is often despised while the soldier is not. To speak out might mean losing your job or being treated with contempt or being jailed, beaten, or killed. It's a hard thing to set yourself against your church leaders, your political leaders, or your fellow man. Dorothy had now witnessed three wars in which she saw the suffering of men who refused to fight. Again and again she saw young men go to jail for acts of conscience and come out broken, or even die in prison.

"The pacifist has to think in terms of a great sacrifice in order to match the heroism, very often, of soldiers," she wrote. "We're not questioning the motives or bravery of soldiers. We've got to endure as much as they endure. We have to make the sacrifices they make, and as Gandhi said, 'It is far better to fight than do nothing.'"

As the war dragged on, more people in the peace movement turned to violence. In response Dorothy liked to quote Che Guevara: "At the risk of seeming ridiculous, let me say that the true revolutionary is guided by great feelings of love." She also said, "I am convinced that prayer and austerity, prayer and self-sacrifice, prayer and fasting, prayer and vigils, prayer and marches, are the indispensable means. . . . And love."

There probably weren't many people, especially among the young, who wished to hear of prayer as a means of effecting social change, but prayer gave Dorothy strength and helped calm her fears. You can't help but feel fearful, she said, but fear is the greatest danger. It can be handled through prayer and community, to not be alone, for people alone are bound in fear. She was uncomfortable with the anger in many of the antiwar demonstrations and the inflammatory slogans and profanity. And she felt tired after decades of trying to explain her positions and her beliefs on pacifism, even to those closest to her. Once in a while her tiredness and impatience would break through. When she was asked, "Are you opposed to all war including the war on poverty?" she snapped, "Yes," and the next day she woke up feeling she was getting old.

The summer of 1969 was harsh for both Tamar and Dorothy. Martha, Mary, and Maggie attended an antiwar demonstration in New York City, and there was another Pax Conference at Tivoli. While Maggie Corbin and I continued to run around wild, oblivious to all of this, Dorothy discussed Gandhian nonviolence as a response to the Vietnam War. I still didn't understand a word of what she was saying, but these talks I lingered around the fringes of when I was between the ages of nine and fourteen would be all that I would see of Granny in her public persona. By the time I was old enough to begin to truly listen to her, the talks had come to an end.

Dorothy was sick of writing and talking about war—she'd rather have been talking about communities and the work of hope. Look to the civil rights movement, she said. Find out what is happening with the farmworkers and their grape boycott. *They* are the peace movement. But also, let's not judge others so much.

She didn't know what to say to soldiers who believed they were engaged in a holy war against communism. "They try to save their own sanity, you might say. They try to save themselves from bitterness and cynicism by believing they are really doing something worthwhile." She spoke of the stories of torture coming out of Fort Dix and the need for compassion for our young men in the army. She spoke of the growing numbers of hippies whom she saw as young people striving to find their vocation. Look at the hippie communes, she said. What are they but a form of the Little Way? In the news they showed only the marijuana, the group weddings, and "the beautiful nude pictures in *Life* magazine," at which her audience laughed and clapped.

Again and again she repeated, "We are all children of God, part of the mystical body of Christ. God wills that all men be saved. When one suffers, all suffer." To her, as a Christian, all wars were fratricidal. From its beginnings, the Worker had seen nothing but war in some region of the world, and they always had a kind of warfare in their own midst—racial war, class war, and workers versus scholars. Even talking about pacifism aroused antagonism and anger. The roots of violence, she quoted St. James, are fear, lack of forgiveness, and greed.

What can a person do directly? It's hard, she said. It's hard to find the spirit with which things need to be done, but what is worse is a sense of futility. Christ left a new commandment that men should love each other as he had loved them. The Catholic Worker was founded on this concept, and to join this work is a subtle thing. Inform your conscience and shoulder your responsibilities. Remember man's basic dignity. We have no right to coerce or force the conscience of another through the strength of personality, for man's freedom is sacred. The beatitudes are to be accepted or rejected, but never coerced.

Dorothy understood anger, and she understood the desire to fight for others or for an ideal. "I hold in one moment more anger than you will ever hold in your life," she said once after being chided for her temper. But most of us, she said, don't choose to go through life getting what we want through acts of violence. We convince, cajole, try to find accord, to influence, even to find consensus. And so why is what we find unacceptable and illegal in our homes, community, and country, not only acceptable but inevitable when it comes to foreign policy? And those who suffer the most from war do not have the option to "believe" in either its inevitability or its justness—children, the poor who cannot flee, the poor whose boys are culled to fight.

That hot and miserable summer of 1969 ("my sad summer," Dorothy called it) was filled with tension and worries over Eric, and as usual when things were stressful, Dorothy and Tamar fought. Dorothy thought about selling Tivoli because of problems of sex, marijuana, and LSD, but when she tried to kick some of the bigger troublemakers out, someone else would let them back in. The sixties must have in some ways reminded Dorothy of the twenties with the sexual freedom and radicalization of the young. Now her granddaughters were the age she had been then, and they were staying up late at night partying and keeping others awake. Dorothy tried to take the matter in hand but was met with hostility from both Rita and Tamar, "the rebellious middle-age group," as she called them, who believed in permissiveness.

Soon after the Pax Conference in August, my sister Mary, now eighteen, bought five concert tickets with money she earned from working at the migrant workers' day-care center, and she, Maggie, and Martha, along with two friends from Tivoli, headed for Bethel, New York, to attend the Woodstock Music and Art Fair. The *New York Times* called the concertgoers "a well-behaved half million young people," while Dorothy commented that it sounded like a nightmare, but she had been supportive of the girls going, and she jumped to their defense several months later when a priest condemned it as an orgy of sex and drugs. "No compassion for the young," she wrote in her diary, the very accusation Tamar held against her.

At the end of the summer, Tamar, now with only five children at home, returned to Vermont from Tivoli with several "wounded ones," as sometimes Dorothy referred to those who showed up looking for help, plus two abandoned teenagers, leading Dorothy to see how Tamar was creating her own Catholic Worker. Tamar's nonjudgmental nature led Dorothy to regret her outbursts and to once again appreciate Tamar's peaceful and uncritical nature. "I could learn from her," she said.

In November Eric sent word that he was getting out of the army on December 20, and Tamar and Dorothy waited while getting on with the business of living. "What did the women do after the crucifixion?" Dorothy wrote in her column. While the men mourned and prayed, the women had to get on with the business of living. Going about the business of living, we celebrated Nicky's birthday while Dorothy waited by the phone and read a history of the Vietnamese war before US involvement. It started to snow, and Dorothy could not get to Mass.

In her column Dorothy wrote:

> One of his friends who had served in Vietnam came in that afternoon looking for Eric, and he spoke of the Vietcong burying thousands alive in Hue. "I know," he said. "I saw those corpses." He spoke defensively as though I, as a pacifist, was on the side of the Vietcong. . . . Certainly I did not then nor later refer to the terrible stories being printed in the daily papers of massacres, rapes, kidnappings, captives being dropped from helicopters who refused to talk, of the torture of prisoners. But these facts are in the minds of all, and I am sure that young soldiers on leave, or being discharged from service, are going to be on the defensive and will be bending over backwards to defend this country any way. But no soldier I ever met wants to talk about the war itself, about the action, the combat; especially to a woman, to a relative. But I remember an instructor in philosophy drafted into the infantry (he refused officers' training) in the Second World

War, and how he said at war's end that in the midst of the horror of destruction and bombardments, he felt a strange and terrible sense of exultation.

For three days we waited. Eric's friends kept calling, looking for him. It continued to snow, and we would come in from the outside to bury the heat registers with steaming socks, mittens, hats, and scarves. The house was filled with seventeen young people running in and out, eating peanut butter and honey sandwiches; the record player was always on. We headed out to the woods to cut down a Christmas tree, and Maggie wrapped the presents. Christmas Day came and went, and still no Eric. Every time the phone rang, we almost fell down the stairs to get to it. The day after Christmas, the phone rang at nine o'clock in the morning. Hilaire got to it first.

Eric's flight had landed at Kennedy Airport before it was shut down by the storm, and it took him just as long to get from there to Vermont by bus as it had to fly from Vietnam to Seattle. He then spent another two hours traveling the thirteen miles home from the bus stop—by then the storm had dumped almost four feet of snow—and at two o'clock in the morning of December 27, Dorothy wrote, "Eric Dominic Hennessy, Staff Sergeant, Ranger, [arrived] home from the wars." But for a rash from the waist down caused by exposure to dioxin, he was safe and alive.

CHAPTER NINETEEN

Vermont does not hold on to its seasons but tears through them as if there is never enough time. My mother's days, before the arthritis set in, were filled with the rhythm of the seasons: buying seeds in March; planting seedlings in May; hoeing, weeding, and mulching throughout the summer; and the wave of vegetables she harvested, cooked, canned, or froze—asparagus and rhubarb in early spring, then lettuce, peas, beans, zucchini, tomatoes, carrots, beets, winter squash, potatoes, and last, brussels sprouts and kale when the garden was a half-frosted, overgrown jungle of rotting vines. Her gardening philosophy was pretty much the same as her child-rearing philosophy—provide water, good soil, and benign neglect. In winter it was the rhythm of her loom, the treadles and shifting harnesses, the bobbin unwinding as she shot the shuttle through with a quick flick of the wrist, followed by the beater. Treadle, shuttle, beater, treadle, shuttle, beater, weaving herself through her losses and disappointments. Weaving us through our childhood and into adulthood and through the early deaths of two of her children. She had a weaving or spinning project to get her through every crisis. She wove silk scarves as her marriage fell apart and spun wool through Dorothy's last years. During Susie's battle with cancer, she wove a cochineal-red coverlet in a Colonial overshot pattern called Orange Peel.

"The worse the disaster, the more you laugh," she'd also say.

In the spring of 1970, Tamar's oldest son home from the war, her work as a nurse over, Tamar wanted to sell the place on Cady Hill Road and move to Tivoli. Dorothy wouldn't hear of it, and she wrote a diary entry that to me showed how little she understood her daughter. "I'm afraid Tamar gets bitter at the young couples and larger families living off the CW and she is always so concerned for money for food. But I would not have her living off the CW, money sent for the poor. Tamar is rich in that she has a house and twenty-five acres and all the family are in good health." Dorothy still didn't realize that it wasn't to live *off* the Worker that her daughter longed for—it was to live *in* the Worker. While knowing that the Worker was something much more than a soup line, that it was a family, Dorothy didn't recognize that it was her daughter's family and that all Tamar ever wanted was to return to it. Dorothy couldn't recognize this, and Tamar couldn't tell her. It hurt my mother deeply, but Dorothy's decision was wise, though for another reason altogether—we had a stable life in Vermont, far more stable than Tivoli could ever have provided.

"I wanted to live there," Tamar said to me, "because I wanted you kids to have the same experience I had growing up in the Worker. It's complicated, this business of Dorothy not wanting me to return to the Worker. When I got married, she deeded us three acres of the Easton farm. What a ruckus that created! Nepotism, someone said. From that day on, Dorothy bent over backwards to make sure she wouldn't ever be accused of that again."

So we remained in Vermont while continuing to spend as much time as we could at Tivoli. Susie and Maggie lived at the Tivoli farm—Susie for years—and found their husbands there. One of my nieces was born in the mansion, and I got to hear the grown-ups talking just as my mother had.

Tamar never would come to feel Vermont was her home even after living there for what would become more than fifty years. Even so, after ten pregnancies and nine children, after a marriage to a man who fought life and God like a mortally wounded animal, following a faith that did not speak to her condition, and with a mother who could misunderstand her at crucial moments, Tamar carved out a place of her own with what was left to her. (Back in the forties, not long after the bombs fell on Nagasaki and Hiroshima, and stunned philosophers everywhere spoke of the eleventh hour, Tamar responded with her impatience and razor-sharp practicality born from having to hand-wash diapers for four kids without running water. "Well, we still must live.") She was still in her forties, still able to work hard in the garden and go swimming with her children, and late in the summer of 1970, after returning from Tivoli, Tamar and I made an eighteen-foot canvas tepee. She didn't buy the canvas—we never could have afforded it. It had come from Reggie Highhill, one of the Tivoli hermits, who had salvaged it while helping clean up in the muddy aftermath of the Woodstock music festival.

We spread the canvas out in the front yard under the butternut trees, draping the driveway with a swathe of material. While I read out loud instructions from a pamphlet, Tamar measured a large arc using a length of twine and marking it with charcoal. One of Eric's Vietnam buddies wanted to help, but he cut it crookedly, which left the tepee with a permanent draft. Tamar and I erected it on the hill behind our house, and then gathered the blankets from our beds and deposited them in the tepee. I spent two summers sleeping in that tepee. The second summer, Martha glanced out the back of the house and saw smoke and flames. She threw a blanket in the tub to wet it, while Granny got in her way, crying out, "What are you doing?" By the time Martha got up the hill, the tepee was engulfed in flames.

In the early seventies Tamar seemed strong, happy, full of plans and ideas. Her house continued to be full of her children, her children's children as they arrived, and other people's children. It's not that things were easy; marijuana and vegetarianism began to create cracks in family relations. But there remains in my mind's eye a luminosity and magic about my mother. She explored, she read, and she talked about what she read. When she laughed, her eyes lit up. The worries about what she had to feed us were gone. Her gardens were large and abundant, and her animals healthy and content.

"People look to you as a model of survival," Dorothy said to Tamar.

As much as I can hear Tamar sputter at the thought, this seemed to be true. Of all those who had been lured by the return to the land in the forties, she was one of the few still at it, and when the seventies brought a resurgence in the movement, it scooped us Hennessy kids up as well.

She was proud of all that we were doing and learning, and bragged to Forster: "I have had lots of young people dropping by this last year. They are all full of good ideas and are doing so many interesting things. The young people, especially the so-called 'drop-outs' are really a fine bunch. They are all learning cabin-building, tipi-making, gardening, baking, weaving, sewing, painting, leatherwork, jewelry."

After refusing to allow Tamar to move to Tivoli, Dorothy was careful to give her encouragement. She would send a check here and there saying, "Here's a little help for your house of hospitality." She also said, "You have a house of hospitality in the realest sense. We are really all of us foundering towards a better life, a better social order—a real accomplishment in this day and age."

But the disorder that frustrated Dorothy at Cady Hill Road got no better even as we kids grew up. Dorothy told Tamar she longed to clear the junk out of the house, which got Tamar's back up, reminding her of how often Dorothy had carelessly thrown out Tamar's belongings when she was a child. But Dorothy also took delight in what could be found in the chaos. She could always find a good book to read or wool to spin, or she could help Tamar make cucumber pickles, chili sauce, or grape juice. Dorothy visited every three months, and she particularly liked to come when Tamar was either planting her garden or harvesting it. The great-grandchildren continued to arrive, and she came for the baptism of Eric's son. Eric was the first not to marry before becoming a parent, and when five of my siblings started their families without the approval of church or state, Dorothy must have felt she was facing Forster all over again.

Dorothy, the great talker, somehow had difficulty relating to her grandchildren as they grew older. She could see that they were interested, observant, and searching, but once again she found herself faced with the silence of the Hennessys. Even still, she could relax in Vermont. Of all her three sprawling families—the house on Cady Hill Road, Tivoli with its sixty-five members not including the commune hoppers, and St. Joseph's on First Street in the city (successor to the Chrystie Street house, from which they had been evicted to make way for a subway station)—we allowed Dorothy her privacy. She could read without having people around her wanting to talk about whatever book she was reading, and Tamar never made her feel guilty or clung to her. They went for walks in the afternoons with the dogs, and in the evenings Dorothy knitted while Tamar wove, and they read and talked about books.

Our place was like Tivoli, divided by the workers and scholars. While everyone else was out working in the fields or in the garden, I was in hiding and reading yet again *The Lord of the Rings*. Granny and I shared a love for mythology—we both read, at much the same time, as it turns out, Mary Stewart's *The Crystal Cave*, T. H. White's *The Once and Future King*, and *The Hobbit*.

"My visit," Dorothy wrote, "has been like the first chapter of that book when fourteen dwarfs arrived one by one."

It was bound to happen—we still followed Tamar into Dorothy's bedroom to talk. We couldn't help ourselves; she was like a magnet. They both were.

We had prepared Eric and Hilaire's old bedroom for her, which had become the music room and looked out on a greenhouse that Tamar and Hilaire had built. It was, though, still the gun room. "The grandchildren had tried to cover up the rack holding the boys' hunting rifles by hanging over them a beautiful spread Tamar wove, but the butts protruded!" she wrote, not mentioning that she had to demand that the boys cover up the guns.

The youngest of the family, Susie's three-month-old daughter, slept beside Dorothy, the oldest, while the house was quiet and empty, and Hilaire, Maggie, and Martha were out in the garden. Maggie drove the tractor pulling a cart, and we pitchforked the hay from the barn to the cart. We had two Alpine milk goats, ducks, chickens, and two young steers. We ate from the garden from early spring to past the killing frost in September, supplemented by the perch and brook trout Nicky caught. We made butter in an antique glass butter churn from fresh raw milk we bought from a neighboring farmer to put on the whole wheat bread Maggie baked.

Then there were the passels of young people streaming in and out, the overflow from the Catholic Worker, or as one of our neighbors called them, the riffraff from New York. We picked blackberries warmed by the

August sun or wandered in the beech and maple woods listening to the song of the hermit thrush. Martha and Maggie carded wool in a book-filled alcove on the second floor, while Maggie Corbin and I sat on the rooftop reading the sunny afternoon away until we all converged at four o'clock to watch *Kung Fu* on the black-and-white television, which had such poor reception we could barely make out the picture.

Decades later, I still cannot separate my feelings of love from my feelings of shame for that rambling New England farmhouse with its peeling white clapboards, surrounded by burdock, ragweed, and junk cars rusting under the butternut trees. And the inside always verging on squalor, a wreck of battered furniture and indifferent housekeeping, but crammed full of all that delighted Tamar—looms, spinning wheels, wool, and books, thousands of them filling every wall and hall possible.

Tamar always had a book to answer every question and fill every need. Books on Picasso, organic gardening, cooking, art history. Books of poetry by Langston Hughes and Gerard Manley Hopkins, or on psychoanalysis by Jung and Rollo May. Books gathered to her like dust under a sofa, thousands of them, coming in all the time, filling up the house; bookshelves lined the hallways and sagged under the weight. There were books of a questionable nature for a young girl to read, but I read them all, and I read them with Tamar's blessing.

"I had to trust you," she said when I asked her about the time she found me reading an issue of *Playboy* magazine I found in the stacks, left behind by one of the many young men coming through our house. "Dorothy used to take away from me those books she didn't approve of, just like her father did to her. I found it hard to forgive, and I vowed I wouldn't do the same to you kids."

It was the life Tamar wanted to live even if she felt she wasn't able to find and follow her own vocation. She had created her own school, and all of us were involved in what she could teach. She was proud and pleased at how we were growing up believing in what she valued, how we loved the land as much as she did and were looking beyond the desire to make money. The counterculture to her wasn't simply a marijuana culture, although there was plenty of that. It was a continuation of the idealism that she had learned at Peter Maurin's knee and that continued when she got married and was shared by her husband, however unprepared he was. Tamar continued to live inspired by this idealism in her own way, but accusations that her children weren't realistic and didn't understand the need to earn money hurt her. She didn't know how to respond, for she could see how we struggled to find a balance between our connection to the land and what we needed to do to live in the world. Maybe she was utopian, but the Catholic Worker itself, the measure of all for her, continued to thrive in a world that believed in only the realistic and the sensible. She did want us to find out what we were each meant to do, and she never forgot the nuns' advice to find one's vocation even though she felt she had failed to do so herself. It wasn't easy holding on to her vision, and she admitted that she grew up with a peculiar understanding that you achieved your goals through praying to St. Joseph. Going back to the land and providing a house of hospitality wasn't sensible. It wasn't going to get her out of poverty. But then, what she considered a comfortable life, one that she did achieve by her sixties, was, by most people's standards, poor. Tamar had no patience with what people often believed was poverty. "Just because a farmer hasn't mechanized his farm doesn't mean he lives a hardscrabble life," she'd say.

During those years that the house—that beautiful old house with its wide pine floors—rotted into the hillside, Tamar had several offers for it. One man, while standing under the butternut tree, offered her fifty thousand dollars cash, and she stood in front of the woodpile and said no. He was so surprised, he couldn't say a word. For her a good life was a warm house filled with nothing you couldn't make, remake, or get at a yard sale, along with good food on the table and people to share it with. Loneliness was her only poverty. She still craved community, still thirsted for good and kind people, and she waited for Dorothy's visits and for the weekly calls that sustained her when she'd be sitting on the couch, a book in her hands. When the phone rang, she'd leap up and send the cat flying.

There was a dark underside to our bucolic life on the land, and it was welfare. From when Tamar quit her nursing job in 1968 until 1975 when I left home, she received welfare benefits of less than $175 a month. Tamar often piled us kids in the car, the red Corvair or green Volkswagen—there was a long line of great old cars that seemed to be perpetually on their last legs—to head to the local swimming hole. On the way home, Tamar sometimes stopped at the ice-cream stand to buy us each an ice-cream cone. Our neighbor, the one who had on occasion fronted Tamar gas money to get to Tivoli, was furious when she got wind of this. "We don't want our tax money to go for ice cream for those kids," she complained to the welfare office. The harassment became so severe Tamar's caseworker commented, "You don't have nice neighbors, do you?"

With money Forster sent, Tamar was able to buy Christmas presents (sometimes he was the only reason we were able to celebrate Christmas). "I had to hide his gifts from the welfare department, though," Tamar said. "They would cover eighty percent of your needs, and if you tried to make up the remaining, you had to pay them back."

Forster helped pay for oil and wood to heat the house and insulation to keep it warm and a chain saw to cut the wood. He also helped pay the property taxes, make car repairs, and buy food while Dorothy also sent what she could. "Which was quite a lot when you add it all up," Tamar said.

I don't know when I began to see our life on Cady Hill Road through the eyes of others and began to measure us against the neighbors and realized that we were different. We may have been poor but there were families much worse off. Yet we were on welfare, and I was ashamed of it—I think we all were—and I was ashamed of our house. It took me until my thirties to be able to put those feelings of shame behind me, that we all, as a family, had failed our grandmother somehow.

Dorothy again and again tried to explain her position on voluntary poverty. She said she encountered far more trouble over propounding voluntary poverty than pacifism. "The best thing to do with the best things, is to give them up," said Father Hugo. Much of what Tamar owned was given up to anyone who asked or was in need, though her lack of attachment may have been more a result of having learned as a child the futility of fighting to keep things. Back then her toys, books, clothes, pets—every treasured belonging and every gift from Forster—

disappeared into the mists of the Catholic Worker, and so she gave up holding on to the things she loved. As an adult her home was raided repeatedly by family, friends, and strangers, even up to the last years of her life, and it bothered her, even though she also loved to give things away. Dorothy eventually changed Father Hugo's "give it up" to "give it away," which was a different thing altogether, while Dorothy's "do without" was changed by Tamar into the belief that if there is something you truly wish for, then there is always a way to get it.

For Peter Maurin, voluntary poverty could keep man from being fearful. For Dorothy, it was a basic necessity if you wanted to help others without hypocrisy. It was also a form of resistance and a form of generosity. Tamar appreciated how Dorothy helped the involuntary poor without trying to change them. This was sometimes misunderstood, and Dorothy was accused of failing to confront the causes of poverty or being fascinated with some sort of medieval aestheticism.

But in the depths of Tamar's worst times, when she felt lonely and scared, and she wondered how she was going to feed her children, Dorothy sometimes responded in either of two ways, accusing her of lacking faith or of being ungrateful for what she did have. She also said to Tamar, "Do without," but Tamar had never had the chance to do with.

Between the years of the collapse of Tamar's marriage and when she gave the farm on Cady Hill Road to Hilaire and Martha and moved out in 1979, bringing her house of hospitality on the land to an end, that house embodied the one time in her life where, no matter how hard things were—the years of school and working as a nurse, the years of receiving welfare, the years of raising a household of teenagers—she was able to re-create those things she loved most about the Worker—gardening, raising animals and children, spinning and weaving, art and the natural sciences, and hospitality. And for far too brief of a time Tamar had succeeded. She was, in her own way, helping us to find our vocations.

Finding one's vocation was on not only my mother's mind, for her children and for herself, but also Dorothy's mind. Sometimes, particularly during the postwar, affluent fifties, Dorothy claimed that voluntary poverty was the most controversial aspect of the Worker. During World War II and the Vietnam War, she said it was pacifism. After Vietnam, she said, "The whole of the Catholic Worker is this—on finding your vocation, finding the part where you can work best and go there to work at it." It was a question she was asked many times. "You will know your vocation by the joy it brings you," she said.

As a young girl, I wasn't listening to my grandmother speak about vocation—I was watching her write. It had started at the age of seven when I'd peer around my grandmother's door at Tivoli, a timid little thing who just couldn't fight the curiosity, to see her at her typewriter, and then I'd tiptoe away, sneaking glances before I ran off. I never told my grandmother of my own call to a vocation—to write—even though she wouldn't have been surprised. Writing was a family tradition in both the Day and Batterham families.

Given the endless tasks at the Worker, it seems a miracle how Dorothy managed to write as much as she did. She wrote wherever she could find the space and time—in the Tivoli village Laundromat, on the Staten Island Ferry, or waiting for a bus. At the farm, she wrote in her room overlooking the river. She couldn't remember a time when she was not writing a book. She called herself a compulsive writer and had been ever since she was eight years old, when she wrote a story for Della on a little pad of pink paper, and the two of them would go out onto the breakwater on Lake Michigan, where, surrounded by water, they wrote in their diaries. Dorothy was twenty-two when she wrote *The Eleventh Virgin*, which she followed with an unpublished children's book and a published serial novel. She wrote a play and several more novels, including one written right after Tamar's birth, and in Mexico she wrote yet another novel—all unpublished and lost. Then came the autobiographical books of her conversion and the Worker and a biography of St. Thérèse, the "Little Flower." There are also forty-seven years' worth of her column and articles for the *Catholic Worker*, along with articles and book reviews for other publications. She wrote so many letters she was certain that was why she developed arthritis in her fingers, and often her eyes ached. In the last years of her life she was still making resolutions every year to write more, to keep a record of her days so she could see where she was coming from and where she was going, and maybe see the meanings of the storms the Worker was always passing through. And then there were the books that remained unwritten or unfinished—the biography of Peter Maurin, the account of her nights walking the waterfront with Eugene O'Neill, and that last one she called *Notebooks* that she had started too late.

"Dorothy had a terrible time writing," Tamar said. "She used to pace the room, and get into everyone's business, particularly mine, before she could finally settle down to write."

"Writing is prayer," Dorothy would say. Her writing often took form in simple descriptions of nature that to her were expressions of gratitude to our Creator, and often she wrote herself out of her moods and depression. "Writing is work," she said, and made the resolution, year after year, to write more. "Writing is a form of activism," a tool of the spiritual works of mercy for it was always a way for her to instruct, to inform, and to console.

She also said, "We write what we suffer."

In the fall of 1974 Dorothy came up to Vermont to wait for the arrival of Becky's second child and Mary's first. It reminded Dorothy of waiting, five years previously, for Eric to come home from Vietnam. There were now seven great-grandchildren and three more on the way. Eric and Nicky were drinking heavily as always, but the tensions of the previous year seemed to have lessened. We built a goat barn—small, sturdy, and still standing forty years later—and everyone was earning money picking apples. The house was getting shabbier with every year, but we were still afire with those things that Tamar had taught us. The barn was filled with hay, which Martha and Hilaire had scythed by hand, the woodshed was filling up with wood for the two woodstoves, and the root cellar with potatoes, winter squash, onions, cabbages, pumpkins, and brussels sprouts. The pantry shelves were filled with jars of dried mint and sage, dried beans, canned tomatoes, dilly green beans, and pickled cucumbers. All the food for our Thanksgiving meal was homegrown but for the nuts and cranberry sauce.

Maggie, who, closely followed by Martha, was the fiercest in our family for her determination to be self-sufficient on the land, was now living in West Virginia in a cabin she and her partner had built. They made their own furniture, raised their food, and in preparation for the birth of her second child she wove twenty-five yards of material to make diapers. When Dorothy mentioned this in her talks, people gasped. "Everyone is in awe of that," she said.

Then just at the point I was beginning to emerge from being yet another one of that mad tangle of Hennessy children, while also beginning to see my mother and grandmother beyond a child's view, Tamar began to struggle with arthritis and Dorothy with heart disease, and the shape of both the farms on Cady Hill Road and at Tivoli began to change. I left home to attend boarding school, and though I would come home for holidays and one more summer, and though I thought it would be there whenever I needed it, for me life on Cady Hill Road had come to an end.

CHAPTER TWENTY

The last winter visit Dorothy would make to Vermont was New Year's 1975, as the ice and snow now made her fearful of stepping outside. I could see her growing fragility, and she too felt herself slowing down, but not the voice. Some of her talks in the last twenty years of her life were recorded, and what a talker she was. No wonder she found the silence of her daughter and grandchildren incomprehensible. No wonder we were all a mystery to her. Often her voice sounds much younger than the voice I came to know as a teenager, and yet I know it well even though some of these talks were recorded just after my birth. Dorothy told long, seemingly rambling stories she spun out like a thread in her quiet, luminous voice, a voice you couldn't help but listen to. Grace told stories to her children but always with an intention. "Make a point," she'd say to Dorothy. But Dorothy's meandering voice, in both her writing and speaking, lulls you into a sense of listening to a story as comforting as a lazy river running through a hot summer's day—until she wallops you with the realization that you need to change your life and you need to do it now.

In the seventies Dorothy's writings began to have a sense of distillation, and the fire and fury of the earlier years had quieted. The appeals in the paper were gentler and less position-taking and simply explained the reality of the work. It wasn't, however, that the times were easier, as each decade brought its own heartbreak and strife.

In the winter of 1970 Stanley had had his first heart attack, and Dorothy too was diagnosed with heart disease when she ended up in a Detroit hospital with chest pains and shortness of breath. She had an enlarged heart and hardening of the arteries, and the doctor put her on digitalis. (She had been warned back in the fifties that her heart was not good, but as it was a prison doctor who examined her during one of the air-raid drill arrests, she thought the prison authorities, fearing bad publicity, had just wanted an excuse to get her out.) She lost twenty-five pounds and over the next few years she lost twenty more. But there was strength there even as she was changing physically. I hear her voice, strong, relaxed, and able to keep focused on what had been forged from forty years of being at the work. It was a different kind of strength than before. It was as if she had been worn smooth to reveal a great sense of calm, clear-sightedness, and reflection. Maybe this had begun back in 1960 after her time with Nanette and Forster, followed by the breakup of Tamar and David's marriage, and the loss of so many she loved, especially Tamar, from the Church. Maybe it was Eric's time in Vietnam. Maybe it was the sheer number of years of the Worker. Maybe it was the passing of so many of those she had known and loved, those from her past—Gene O'Neill, Mike Gold, Lionel Moise, and Berkeley Tobey— and those who had been at the Worker for years, such as Hans Tunnesen and Peggy Baird (who came to live at the Worker in the early sixties after the death of her fourth husband and who remained until her death).

In 1972 a letter arrived from the IRS stating that the CW owed almost three hundred thousand dollars in back taxes. The IRS didn't believe that no one earned a salary at the Worker. The stress affected Dorothy, and she was having heart problems again, pains in the chest and dizzy spells, and she had to cancel all her speaking engagements. Five months after the arrival of the IRS's letter, she met with the assistant attorney general, and the case was dropped.

Nixon was reelected, and Dorothy turned seventy-five. She wrote to Della, "I'm sleeping and reading, writing a few letters and refusing to see people. They come up anyway, and then I have to make an appearance just to stop rumors I'm on my last legs. Seventy-five seems a terrific age." She wrote to Tamar, "Everybody wants to interview me—*NY Times, NY Post, Washington DC Star*—even *Ms.* I'll have to put up with it—do the best I can." Bill Moyers came to Tivoli, and in response to his show, the farm was flooded with visitors. "Publicity does us no good at all," she said.

Dorothy had an uneasy relationship with the biographies that began to appear during these years, and often with the authors themselves. She wanted William Miller to destroy his interviews with her. Too many mistakes, she said. Later she told him she didn't want him writing her biography—then or after her death. Miller, a kind-hearted man, became caught up in the affairs of the Hennessy family. He sent money to Susie when her second daughter, not even a year old, was in the hospital with a tumor on her spine. He invited Martha to come live with his family in Florida, but within days she returned to Vermont homesick. Because of Dr. Miller's many kindnesses to Tamar and Dorothy, Tamar remained loyal to him, even when he was criticized for publishing his biography after Dorothy had rescinded her permission and because of its many errors, including his colossal mistake of assuming that all of *The Eleventh Virgin* was fact and that all he needed to do was insert the correct names. But Tamar felt badly for the hostility with which his book was greeted, and she made a point of consoling him.

Dorothy continued to feel weak and exhausted and didn't travel for a year other than between New York City, Tivoli, Della's, Tamar's, and once again, Staten Island now that the Worker had gained the use of several cottages there. Dorothy spoke from the pulpit at Saint John the Divine with Coretta Scott King and Cesar Chavez, while feeling an overwhelming need for solitude and to write. With her "fading heart" she felt it may be the last year of her life.

But by April she was traveling a bit more, and breathing and walking more easily. There were worries in Vermont over Eric and Nicky, both of whom continued to drink heavily, and over Tamar, who suffered because of this. On May 1, a time of celebration, Dorothy broke down and cried, shocking those around her, and Stanley tried to comfort her. In June, on the same day the Watergate scandal broke, Joan Baez invited Dorothy to California to attend a peace conference, while Dorothy was looking at a building two blocks from the New York City house, the Third Street Music School, as a possibility for a new women's house. Four days later she headed to California and began picketing with Cesar Chavez and the farmworkers. Bob Fitch's photo of her on the picket line sitting on her cane chair, flanked by large policemen, was to become one of the most iconic photos of her. She was talking at the moment, as only she would be, to a Mexican-American policeman about Tolstoy's story "How Much Land Does a Man Need?" She then told the group of young police officers gathered before her, "Tomorrow, I'll return to read aloud the Sermon on the Mount."

The next day, before she was able to read to them, she was arrested for the eighth and last time for unlawful picketing. She spent "a delightful retreat" in a farm labor camp with a group of Mexican women and thirty nuns who had also been arrested. The Mexican women knelt at the sides of their beds and prayed the rosary with their arms outstretched. People, including prison guards, brought their Bibles and rosaries to Dorothy to be blessed, and the nuns read the office every day. The Sisters of the Holy Child Jesus had been meeting in San Francisco, and some of the nuns spontaneously joined the picket line, where they got arrested. To Dorothy's delight, she found out that they were of the same order that had asked her many years before to take Tamar out of their school.

After Dorothy returned from California, she signed the contract for the Third Street Music School. On the day before her seventy-sixth birthday, she left for England and Ireland on her last trip overseas, and the following spring she went on her last major speaking tour, traveling by bus from Boston to South Dakota. She continued to travel back and forth between the city and the farm managing crises, and there were always crises. She was often awake at four o'clock in the morning, her mind troubled. At hand were her bedside books—a missal, Julian of Norwich—and her radio with Berlioz, Schubert, Chopin, or Brahms's fourth movement of his German Requiem. She liked to quote St. Teresa grabbing her castanets and dancing in the cold convent, saying, "One must do something to make life bearable!"

Around her seventy-seventh birthday, Dorothy again had to cancel all speaking engagements due to ill health, and her diary entries were becoming brief and more repetitive. Her memory was suffering, there was a tiredness in her voice, and she stayed close to home. She began to sort through her papers to send off to the Marquette University archives, afraid that if she were to die suddenly all her papers and belongings would disappear as had happened after Peggy Baird's death. She was still losing weight and was weak and tearful. Some kind of nervous exhaustion, she thought.

Forster, who was now calling once a week, called her on his eightieth birthday. "Quite proud of *his* numerous progeny!" she wrote to Becky.

Dorothy was on Staten Island when he called, where she could watch the sunrise and sunset over the bay and listen to the gulls, terns, and grebes and the waves lapping on the beach. For six months she lived in a small, three-room cottage. She sat outside in the shade of the privet hedge or, on calm days, on a log on the beach where, surrounded by yellow sand and rocks covered in seaweed, under a blue sky or in a heavy mist, she wrote postcards to Della, Tamar, and Forster. She would also in her confusion answer a letter one week and answer it again the next. The wind was strong, and the waves pounded on the beach while she listened to symphonies on the radio. It was a time to think, write, study Scripture, and read her beloved Psalms while keeping warm with a pot-bellied woodstove in which she burned driftwood washed up from the winter storms. She read C. S. Lewis on the Psalms, and the correspondence of Emma Goldman and Alexander Berkman. It seemed she had finally forgiven Emma Goldman for her association with Ben Reitman, the doctor who had performed her abortion fifty-five years ago. On the radio she heard the news of South Vietnam's surrender. She tried to keep a daily schedule, to discipline herself with early-morning meditations on the Memorare and with reading and writing to the sound of the waves and the gulls and the smell of salt air and fish, as the early sun streamed into the kitchen. As the weather warmed, she walked along the beach to collect stones, shells, and driftwood, the beach littered with segments of piers washed ashore from the winter storms. A fisherman came to her door with his first catch of the season, a striped bass, and at low tide she searched for starfish and seahorses instead of writing the articles she had agreed to do.

Then after six months with Jane Austen and Trollope and walking on the beach, Dorothy cleaned up the cottage and headed first up to Tivoli, then to Della's, and on to Vermont before returning to Tivoli for another Peacemaker Conference. There she gave a talk, the first since her rest on Staten Island. She sounded calm yet still tired after her winter of solitude on the beach. She repeated herself, had difficulty hearing the questions, and found it hard to keep her train of thought. Names weren't coming easily to her, but she was still formidable in her command of literature and references to current events.

"There are a lot of personal questions here," she said. "Are there any you insist upon?"

People wanted to know about spiritual discipline and maturity. She sighed and then laughed. "The best way to wake up in the morning is to say, as is in the Psalms, 'Now I have begun.' One of the Desert Fathers said, 'Each morning I wake up with all of these solutions, and joyous I lay waste the day.'"

When asked why the Worker didn't obtain federal nonprofit status, she replied, "We don't believe in signing papers." Another person, referring to Vietnam and the devastation wrought on people there, suggested Americans should be bringing in children from other countries, to which Dorothy replied, "That is a typical American show-off gesture—adopting children from countries we are at war with." Then she asked, "Does anyone have any more ideas for me to squash?"

She also said, "Suppress the paper. I don't care. I've been at it a long time, and anyway, other papers will crop up. If they close one house, open up another. You can't stop this type of work."

She spent most of the summer at Tivoli watching the heavily loaded tankers head up to Albany. She walked along the railroad tracks with Stanley and Rita to collect sweet clover, and she often kept to her room. "How glad I am to do nothing—a little writing—that's all," Dorothy told Maggie, but she was doing much more than that. She was opening another house in the city, and just after New Year's, Dorothy moved into Maryhouse, the new women's house on Third Street.

It had taken two years to obtain the certificate of occupancy from the city and transform it from a music school into a house of hospitality. The city seemed to put up roadblocks every step of the way, and she tried to anticipate each one with a team of architects, contractors, plumbers, and electricians. There were delays in getting approval for the architectural plans, and then bathrooms needed to be added, the roof repaired, and all the old wooden doors to the practice rooms had to be replaced by self-closing steel doors. (Dorothy fretted that they would have to replace the lovely wide staircases and old wooden banisters to meet the fire code.) The renovations cost more than the building had, and Dorothy recalled how in the early years they just moved into a building and did the repairs as they went. Now the city regulated the amount of cubic feet of air per occupant per room.

"Certificate of occupancy!" Dorothy was incensed. "The women living on the street, sleeping in doorways and in abandoned and condemned buildings, had no certificates of occupancy."

Still, the place seemed well suited as a house of hospitality. The practice rooms became bedrooms, and Dorothy, music lover that she was, delighted in the idea of women sleeping in rooms in which the very walls were soaked in music. It had heat and hot water (Mott Street was always in the back of her mind) and an auditorium that could hold 150 people. There were several offices, a library, a laundry room, a clothes room, a small backyard, and a room suitable for a chapel where they could hold vespers. Its only flaw was the tiny kitchen.

There were worries—there were always worries. Taking women in meant taking them in for life, and many of the women who moved in at that time would remain there until death—Helen, Margaret, Annie, Lena. And it wouldn't be long before the house, as big as it was, would fill up. All past difficulties and failures pressed in on her even amid the excitement of the opening.

When the Worker finally moved into Maryhouse with twenty women, they were still preparing the rooms one by one. One Saturday afternoon, Dorothy stomped out of her room and said, while giving those who were noisily sanding and finishing the wood floors her fierce look that could send the bravest person scurrying off, "I am trying to listen to the opera." Dorothy's sunny new room faced the street, had its own bathroom, and had a small hall that served as a kitchenette. "I am being especially cherished," she wrote Della. Her room was so comfortable, she joked, "Even my voluntary poverty has been taken away from me."

Within two weeks of moving to Maryhouse, Dorothy began to talk of selling Tivoli, and Peggy Scherer, the farm manager, visited Dorothy with a list of those who wanted to sell and buy a smaller place. Peggy was a young woman of twenty-four, who, after arriving at Tivoli to oversee a Peacemaker Conference and discovering that someone had absconded with all the grocery money, stayed and became such a voice of authority that Dorothy felt she could leave it all in Peggy's hands. Dorothy had decided to settle in Maryhouse, but she couldn't sleep at night, fretting about the farm just at the time she was beginning to feel able to let go, relax, and hand over control to others.

The Tivoli farm had been fueled by the growing peace movement, by the profound changes in the Church itself, and by the shake-up of society led by the hippies, but as early as 1968 Dorothy realized the place was too big, too expensive to run, too hard to get to by public transportation, and too hard to handle. At one point, she was approached by an interested buyer.

"Okay," she said, "we'll sell for two hundred thousand," confident that the outrageous amount would scare him off, but when he seriously considered it she ended up frightening herself. "Probably a temptation of the devil. Or an opportunity to try for a more village type of community. But I am too old to start again and I decided I would do nothing myself—let the others decide."

They were crowded as usual at Tivoli. Seventy people including sixteen children lived scattered about in three houses, along with the hermitages, cabins, tents, sheds, and barns. But it had become, as Dorothy described it, the poorhouse of Dutchess County and an annex to the Hudson River State Hospital. Highway police picked up old men traveling alone and on foot to bring them to the farm. Many of them were the old generation of hobos still hitchhiking and riding the rails, guys with names like Blackie who worked all over the country and could tell you where there was a good Salvation Army or where you could get a good meal in Montana. Dorothy referred to them as men off the road until some of them complained. There were also girls "in trouble," ex-convicts, and growing numbers of mentally unstable young men—dropped off by the Hudson River State Hospital or by the local police or churches—who could hardly care for themselves and whose families no longer knew what to do. One of these young men was from a major tire-manufacturing family. He was a gentle person who couldn't function on his own, but at Tivoli he had found a home and a role as dishwasher, and his family was so grateful that they sent the Worker new tires for their cars. There were many others like him, and the casino, now the men's dorm, was crowded. Tivoli accepted them all, and the community tried to do the best they could, even during the psychotic episodes and outbursts of violence that no one at the farm was trained to deal with. Often it seemed that the only tool they had was kindness.

By 1973 Tivoli had become so well-known for its acceptance of the mentally unstable that an old Village acquaintance asked Forster if he thought Dorothy would take Shane O'Neill, son of Gene O'Neill and Agnes Boulton, who was addicted to heroin. Other than saying, "How we cannot get away from our past," I don't know how Dorothy answered, but Shane O'Neill never arrived, and four years later he committed suicide. (His half brother Eugene had also committed suicide, three years before their father's death.)

In addition to the troubled young men and old hobos, there were still the new kind of people "off the road"—hippies looking for a commune. Many came with grand ideas; one group arrived in caravans and tried to stage a coup. "Nip things in the bud at once," Stanley said, and gently persuaded the caravans to move on.

"If we did not have so big a place," Dorothy said, "people would not move in on us."

She had not forgotten walking away from the farm at Easton, and she worried that their problems, while not as severe as Easton's had been and of a far different nature, would become just as unsolvable.

"We need to pray more," she said.

"A mistake ever to have gotten this place," Stanley said.

"We are a family," Dorothy replied, and, as she often said, if you begin purging people from the Worker, there will be no end to it until there is no one left. But she felt badly at how often she condemned people or disapproved of them, and she felt helpless in trying to control the pot smoking and the promiscuity. Dorothy prayed continually for the young, for she understood them. "Aside from drug addiction," she wrote, "I committed all the sins young people commit today."

During the worst of these times, Dorothy said to Tamar, "I'll not sell the farm. We'll manage somehow." And so she held on to it, and for a while it was doing well. The farm seemed better with the old stalwarts—Stanley, Deane Mowrer, John Filigar, and two farmer priests—along with a small group of hard workers. The problems weren't only over issues of control or of pot and sex. The plumbing had begun to break down, and by the summer of 1975, the smell of the toilets, which could not be flushed for lack of water, was overpowering. This irked Dorothy. "Never have we had such filthy bathrooms. You used to be able to read in them. They were our reading rooms." Because the drainage from the cesspool was polluting the river, the Department of Health told the farm it needed a new septic system, which would be prohibitively expensive.

Even with the physical deterioration of the place, the decision to sell Tivoli came slow and hard. So much had been put into it, including the sale of the two beloved beach houses. It was too big—this had been obvious within the first few years—but it did give people privacy, which meant a great deal to Dorothy. Privacy was part of the works of mercy.

The farming commune was a program people longed for and continued to long for, so why did it keep failing? Stanley said that all Catholic Worker farms become houses of hospitality on the land. "Sometimes," he said, "they are a retreat house, a place for alcoholics to dry out, a recreation center, a home for the mentally ill. No farm could exist the way the Catholic Worker farms do. No farmer could raise enough food to both feed the tremendous numbers of people and to save food for the winter." The Worker, Stanley said, had its high ideals, but at the same time it never let them interfere with the reality of the present moment.

But the accidental nature of Tivoli, the farm that became a conference center and then a hotel for men off the road and commune hoppers, had become too uncontrollable. There were complaints of loafers living off the hard labor of others and complaints that Dorothy was never there, and they needed her presence to keep people behaving. Every time she arrived, she was met with the pent-up frustrations of those trying to run the place. All things that had been happening since Easton.

Tivoli was also a financial drain. Expenses were averaging thirteen hundred dollars a month to house and feed fifty people, property taxes and fees were close to ten thousand a year, and the plumbing problems persisted. Stanley and Peggy Scherer began looking for another place, but Dorothy kept changing her mind. She recalled what a painful upheaval it had been, especially for the elderly and the ill, when they had to move before.

As I entered into my midteens, Tivoli changed in my eyes. I began to see more of its faults and felt less of my old love for it. It seemed shabby and sad, but I don't know if it was because I was pulling away from the Worker and seeing it with more critical eyes or because Tivoli was beginning its decline. So much had been stolen, including a wall hanging Rita Corbin had woven, that only the most ragged of the furniture remained, and the toilets still weren't flushing properly. Farmer John had closed the swimming pool because he could no longer fix the pump and turned it into a greenhouse.

But even so, under the leadership of the small group of hard workers, Tivoli was running relatively smoothly for the time being, and Dorothy refused to look at it as an utter failure. Each morning as dawn broke and she read the Psalms to give her courage to face the day, Dorothy watched the first rays of the sun touch the mountains across the river. She watched the ships—freighters from Finland, tankers, cement barges, tugboats, and the coast guard—pass by in the channel close to shore, and she counted the cars of the train as it passed, just as she had done as a child in Chicago, "ninety-seven of them, many of them marked Pacific Fruit." On still days the fog lingered on the river, and the foghorn at the Saugerties Lighthouse across the river reminded her of Gene O'Neill's plays and the New York Harbor. And the house, perched at the end of a long spit of land jutting out from the other shore, would vanish and reappear as the fog rolled along the river. In the evenings everyone would gather on the front lawn to watch the sun set over the Catskills. How could they give all of this up?

Back at Maryhouse that summer, Dorothy sat in her room surrounded by her usual piles of letters scattered on the bed and books stacked on every available surface; even the typewriter was buried under the newspapers. Her window on the second floor faced the street, and noise and sun poured in. She sat in her rocking chair or the armchair, both of which are still there, and gazed out at the ailanthus tree across the way. It was too hot to sleep with the windows closed, and the sound coming from the Hells Angels' headquarters several houses down reverberated along the street. They were having a Fourth of July block party—they had barricaded the street and were setting off fireworks. Dorothy had returned to Maryhouse to take a rest from the responsibilities at Tivoli, but she was in inner turmoil for a month over an upcoming speech at the Eucharistic Congress in Philadelphia in August. She did not feel at all prepared. She was distraught and full of fear, but she believed that one must go where one is asked. "A few simple words," she wrote. "'Fear not' is a most important message."

Dorothy's state of nerves before the talk, the talk itself, and her state of exhaustion after had its consequences. After the speech, she went on a weeklong silent retreat in Pittsburgh with Father Hugo. She then returned to Tivoli to find a crowd gathering to greet the Continental Walk for Disarmament and Social Justice as the group made their way from California to the Pentagon. Dorothy wanted to meet the walkers because people were speaking as though the peace movement was dead, and it irked her to hear nostalgia for the sixties. "The sixties," she said, "were a time of anger and turbulence."

Then on September 3, two months short of her seventy-ninth birthday (Tamar was fifty and I sixteen), Dorothy felt a pain in her chest and left arm, she had difficulty breathing, and her pulse raced. As people gathered downstairs for an evening meeting, Dorothy, alone in her room, had suffered a mild heart attack. And so this is when we begin to witness the slowing down of a mighty life.

CHAPTER TWENTY-ONE

In my mind my mother's last years intertwine with my grand-mother's—those years when all is stripped away bit by bit. And out of all the losses of old age, I first think of Dorothy's and Tamar's love of driving and of their cars, a long parade of battered vehicles that shouldn't have been able to run. Somehow they were always able to head down the road when things got too unbearable or too compli-cated or when Dorothy got too ill-tempered and knew she had to seek refuge at the beach or at Tamar's or Della's. Those hours on the road were precious to Dorothy as they were the only time she felt free. She liked to make a pilgrimage, she called it, every year in which she vis-ited Catholic Worker houses and farms around the country, packing lunches for the road of peanut butter and honey on whole wheat bread. "Guarding the peace in one's own heart," she called it. And when she had no car, she sat next to strangers on buses and trains who did not know who she was and did not weigh her down with their expecta-tions, admiration, or criticism. On the road she was anonymous. On the road she was neither here nor there. "If I had a good car," she said, "I'd be on the road always."

Dorothy had a reputation as a terrible driver, but I know of only one accident when Tamar was three years old and Dorothy had just learned how to drive in California. She fell in love with driving begin-ning with her first car in Culver City, California, the secondhand Model T Ford she had bought for eighty-five dollars and, after one driving lesson, practiced alone on the back streets of Los Angeles. On their return from Mexico in 1930, she bought another Model T that she drove around Staten Island researching for her gardening column. The first Worker car was a green Ford truck in which they transported vegetables from Easton to Mott Street and returned with a truckload of people singing in Gregorian chant. It was in this truck that Dwight Larrowe taught Tamar, when she was fifteen, how to drive, in the fields of the lower farm. Next they had a panel truck, which was good for transporting vegetables but not for people, and someone fell out of the back on the steep hill to the upper farm. Then there was the car one of the men drove into a tree when he and two others had been drinking. A year later John Filigar was transporting a goat in an old beat-up sedan when the goat jumped out into Easton's town square, and both John and the goat were arrested. During the war two young thieves kept stealing the Worker's car at Mott Street, and the police returned it each time. They had a 1928 Columbia that broke down in the Delaware Water Gap while moving from Easton to the new farm in Newburgh, a 1936 Buick that had belonged to a television actress, and a 1932 Chevrolet donated by a fellow who had lost his license for drinking. Dorothy drove that Chevy to West Virginia to visit Tamar in the late forties, and when Stanley's brother Walty drove down with Dorothy, as they entered a mile-long tunnel on the Pennsylvania Turnpike, he asked her, "Where are the lights?"

"It doesn't have any," Dorothy replied.

The car had broken headlights and no windows, and the wind blew through the cracks in the floor.

Dorothy's history with cars was a history of gas pedals going through the floor, gear sticks coming off in her hand, the battery falling out onto the ground just as she arrived home, or windshield wipers breaking off in the middle of heavy rainstorms.

"I'll tell you what's miraculous about Dorothy," Tamar said. "She could get any car to run."

"They say always mistrust Greeks bearing gifts," Peggy Baird had said to Tamar. "And the same might apply to cars given to the Worker."

There was that one good car Dorothy drove out to California and back given to her either by a priest or by a member of the Roosevelt family, but most cars would last only a few weeks. At the Peter Maurin

Farm on Staten Island, they rolled them down the hill behind the barn to try to get them started, and when that failed, they left the cars to sit in the middle of the field. Dorothy claimed Father Duffy wore down a car "making trips between farming experiments."

"Oh, he'd been drinking," Tamar said. "Totaled the car. I still would like to tell her off about that! She had promised to give it to me. We lived too far from the beach to walk, with the kids being so young, and I longed to get to the beach." Father Duffy's mishap may have been the reason Dorothy announced sometime in the late fifties that the Worker was going to stop owning cars, but her determination lasted only six months.

Dorothy's last time behind the wheel was early in 1976 when she, Stanley, and Nina Polcyn Moore, both of whom had been with Dorothy in 1935 when she picketed the SS *Bremen*, drove the Datsun twenty-seven miles from Tivoli to Poughkeepsie for lunch. On their return, Dorothy, pale and silent, handed the car keys to Peggy Scherer and never drove again. She gave the car to Tamar, and it was in that car that Tamar headed down to Tivoli after Dorothy's heart attack.

The heart attack was mild, just enough of a warning, Dorothy felt, to stop gadding about and write two pages a day. She was determined not to worry about it—everything is providential. Under the advice of Tamar and Dorothy's two doctors, for four weeks she stayed in bed, where she had breakfasts of homemade bread and poached eggs from Farmer John's "girls," the chickens, and drank tea instead of coffee. "It makes me feel very British. I shall begin reading Dickens again," she said.

Her two doctors—"it's convenient to have two doctors"—disagreed with each other over the question of coffee. One said no coffee at all while the other said one cup a day. After a month of drinking tea, Dorothy began drinking coffee once a day, but after two months she was up to two cups.

As time passed it was clear Dorothy was affected by her heart attack more than she realized. It was an exertion to write, to read, and to think, and her memory suffered. In each letter she wrote to Della she repeated the news of the attack. She couldn't attend any meetings but stayed in her room, sleeping long hours, listening to the radio, or reading paper-back mysteries. As the news spread, people sent her books—Martin Buber, Dorothy Sayers, Agatha Christie. A friend sent her ten dollars and told her to buy a bottle of sherry, pour herself a glass every after-noon at four, and read a chapter in *The Imitation of Christ*. On warm days she sat out in the sun under a maple tree while it dropped its red leaves about her.

Tamar visited once a month, and Forster called daily, but she got overtired when she spoke to visitors.

"I talk too much," she said.

"Yes, you do," one of the folks at Tivoli said to her; Dorothy did not identify who.

With Dorothy ill, everyone was worried and behaving well at the farm. Most days it was quiet. No guitar playing and no frivolity, she said, but it was unclear whether she approved or disapproved. The core group of hard workers was keen on homesteading. They had chickens and goats housed in a barn they had built out of salvaged materials, and they tilled the upper fields with John's two-blade plow. In what may have been the last enthusiastic and hope-filled dream for Tivoli, they had planted two hundred tomato plants, which provided the city houses with fresh and canned tomatoes. The farm was growing more than it ever had before, not only feeding everyone there, but sending vegetables to the city for the soup line. They sat around the dining room tables shelling soybeans, pinto beans, and navy beans, which they had dried by laying them out on the roof of the mansion.

Winter arrived, and the men cleared out the dead trees in the woods and collected driftwood from the river, which they towed past Dorothy's window in John's tractor, a 1953 John Deere always in need of repair that he had bought with a back payment of social security. John gave away a good portion of the money, but he drank the rest until Dorothy sat him down and said, "John, am I going to have to bury you too?"

As she regained her strength from her heart attack, Dorothy again woke early to read and write, and John brought her coffee at five thirty. In the evenings she walked from the main house to the mansion to watch the sunset. She thought she was ready to write another book, "a diary of our times," but it wasn't until December that she felt strong enough to sit at her typewriter to write a few letters. In the meantime, Stanley typed her column, while she made him executor of her papers. "Stanley is the soul of delicacy. An invaluable help," she said.

By March she felt strong enough to travel to Vermont for Tamar's birthday ("March fourth was a happy, happy day in my life," she had said to Tamar on Tamar's fiftieth birthday the year before). As subdued as Tivoli felt compared to the late sixties and early seventies, Vermont was even more so. It seemed the fortunes of the house of hospitality on Cady Hill Road were tied to the fortunes of Tivoli, and as Tivoli faded, so did our place. The previous summer Tamar had turned over the property, eighteen acres and the old ramshackle house, to Martha, Hilaire, and me, and the tumultuous, turbulent Hennessy family broke up, each raising his or her own family elsewhere. Dorothy arrived to find only Tamar, Nicky, Maggie Corbin, and the baby chicks and newborn goats who were staying in the kitchen for warmth (Hilaire and I were away at school). Tamar was teaching herself how to make natural dyes using what she collected from the gardens and around the house—lichens, horsetails, goldenrod, wild grape leaves, dahlias, and marigolds. She had three sheep, which Martha and Hilaire learned how to shear, and Tamar carded and spun the wool, dyed it with the vegetable dyes she had prepared, and then set up the Leclerc loom to weave a plaid blanket.

It was a quiet visit. There was no radio or television, no going out because of the ice, and Dorothy missed Mass because the car wouldn't start. Nicky cooked while Tamar wove, and Dorothy read a biography of Solzhenitsyn and Chekhov's plays, and Becky, Eric, and Mary visited daily. The days passed, and Dorothy was still unable to go out because of the bad weather. Tamar continued to weave, while Nicky unraveled before them. Dorothy and Tamar both feared he would die young; they had seen too many Catholic Worker men die from drink, and Nicky had been drinking heavily for five years. He had been arrested three times one year for drunk driving and had been sent to jail. But it wasn't just drinking—he was also losing his mind, and it was hard coming across these words in Dorothy's diary: "*'NICK IS JESUS! NICK.'* Nick wrote those last few lines—those four words. He had a bad spell—where he got the gallon of wine, we don't know. He all but broke his knuckles banging the dining table. I could only keep repeating the Jesus prayer and washing dishes while Tamar tried to calm him."

"Give me money," he said to Dorothy, "so I can get drunk, go to jail again, and evangelize the men there."

Dorothy said to Tamar, "Thank God you do hang on to him." At the Worker, she added, "we get all the people who are kicked out by their families."

Back at Tivoli, Dorothy's health took a sudden turn. She felt weak and again had pains in her chest and arm, and in mid-April she headed to the city, where she was more comfortable, had more privacy, and was surrounded by loving kindnesses. "Tulips, a rose, a picture, food. Tender loving care! We all need it, sick or well."

Dorothy never returned to Tivoli or to Vermont. Susie and her family also left Tivoli within months, and with both Dorothy and Susie no longer there, the bond between Tivoli and Cady Hill Road, those two houses of hospitality on the land, came to an end. The farms themselves would linger for a while, but, no longer infused by Dorothy's presence and energy, they too would soon come to an end.

There is one more story of a "last" for Dorothy, the story of the summers of 1977 and 1978, when she lived on Staten Island, returning to that battered island that she called sacred, and wrote of it with such loving detail. I find myself drawn again and again to Dorothy's writings on nature. Love for nature—it lies within us all beginning with Forster, who opened the door for Dorothy and taught her to love it through the eyes of a gardener and biologist, and then encouraged it in his daughter by giving her seeds and chemistry sets. His grandchildren too—we were such children of the land with the instinct to escape outside and seek refuge in the garden or in the woods or out in the middle of the water in a rowboat.

While Tamar felt that Dorothy, as a city person, did not understand farming, she did have a powerful sense of the earth's beauty. Her relationship with the land was not as a farmer or gardener, like Tamar; it was more as spiritual sustenance and an instinctive awareness of what John Moriarty, the Irish philosopher and guardian of the Irish landscape and its mythologies, called the integrity of the land no matter what abuse it endures—and Staten Island had endured much. In 1947 the city of New York built the Fresh Kills garbage dump, destroying more than two thousand acres of forests, tidal wetlands, and salt marshes, and at one point it would become the world's largest man-made structure. In 1964 the completion of the Verrazano-Narrows Bridge brought the final destruction of the farms and meadows. Dorothy called environmental degradation a form of poverty, and she felt this keenly on Staten Island. And yet Dorothy and Tamar never stopped loving the island, seeing beyond the mountain of garbage and the factory-polluted waters land that was holy and still retained its integrity. Land that still could help bring a sense of God's beauty through its gardens and woodlands; the dogwood, lily of the valley, and violets of early spring, and the sweet clover growing on the roadsides; the sound of the cicadas on hot summer days and the crickets in the fall.

It was after a long stay at the beach that Dorothy wrote, "We need a reverence for the earth. Everything comes from the earth. Alyosha in *The Brothers Karamazov* kissed the earth. . . . I took my grandchildren one day out at the Peter Maurin Farm and said, 'Come on out and let's kiss the earth.' Such a strange, mysterious, and beautiful concept—man being part of the earth." And it was at the beach that she spoke of her prayers of gratitude feeling like pebbles cast onto the water, sending out ripples in all directions, and who knew what could come of them.

I first set foot on Staten Island in the summer of 1977, when Dorothy was there and Tamar had just arrived a few days before with me not far behind, similar to what I had been doing since I was a toddler following her into my grandmother's room. After getting off the Staten Island Ferry, Stanley and I took the city bus along Hylan Boulevard, a lengthy stretch of dreary houses and strip malls that gave way to a desolate landscape with fewer houses, potholed streets, and abandoned, overgrown lots full of garbage that was neither country nor city. We got off at the Poillon Avenue bus stop, which was nothing but a cracked and weed-riddled sidewalk and a telephone pole covered in bindweed.

The cottage, one of three bought by Frank Donovan, manager of the New York City Worker, was part of Spanish Camp, seventeen acres of land on Raritan Bay held in trust. It was a summer community of seventy-five people of working-class families founded in 1927 by Spanish and Latin American anarchists and an ex-bullfighter from Barcelona. Children played ball on a green from which ran narrow streets lined with small cottages. We turned down one of the side streets and walked to the end until we could see the sea and the last two cottages, those of the Catholic Worker. The cottage closest to the beach was in such poor condition it was almost unlivable even by Catholic Worker standards.

Dorothy's cottage had gray asphalt siding with white and red trim around the doors and windows, and three tiny rooms—a bedroom, kitchen, and sitting room. The kitchen had a small gas stove, a white enamel sink, and three windows looking out onto the bay. The table was untidy and covered with letters, newspapers, books, cups of coffee, a radio, and a fan. There were bits of plain and battered furniture draped with shawls—Dorothy always had a shawl about her, usually one that my mother had knitted or woven.

We sat in the tiny postage stamp of a garden, at a green picnic table surrounded by the thick, head-high privet hedges and hydrangea and sassafras bushes. There was an outhouse under a mimosa tree that overlooked a small inlet full of reeds and garbage. A mulberry tree grew beside the front door, staining the ground with its berries and on hot days smelling like a winery and mingling with the scent from the deep crimson rambling rose.

Dorothy was thin, and her face was soft and gaunt, with the delicate cheeks of the aged. She wore a soft gray cloth hat to protect her from the sun, a long gray skirt, a cotton paisley blouse, and sensible shoes, the only new item of clothing she ever had. Her glasses and cane rested on her lap, and her hand-woven Bolivian bag lay at her side. Her arms draped over the armrests, her wrists facing up, her long, slender fingers, aged and arthritic, flicking restlessly, just as Tamar's did, as she talked about old Catholic Worker people and farms, and especially about Peter Maurin, who was still much on her mind.

Stanley and I headed down the wooden steps from the second cottage to walk along the beach. The sand was littered with detritus and driftwood. Anything could be washed up from the winter storms—great tree trunks ripped out by the roots and sent along by the tides, a section of a large pier, and a light blue VW bug with a rusty red door and smashed roof. The inlet was littered with garbage. All I could see was degradation, while Dorothy on seeing the clover and Queen Anne's lace would exclaim, "Beauty in the city!"

The water was smooth and gray and dotted with passing ships and sailboats. Across the bay the flat outline of the New Jersey shore was as gray as the sea and the sky above. The beach still had swaths of undeveloped land of grass and sand, and there was a red clay bank bordering on a stand of trees near where the old Huguenot cottage had been.

Doris Nielsen, a neighbor who had first met Dorothy at the Peter Maurin Farm in 1960, came by with two fleeces of sheep's wool from some local sheep, holdouts of the last farms, which Tamar dyed with goldenrod and inkberries she collected from around the cottage. Tamar then traced an outline of Dorothy's feet on paper, formed the soles for a pair of bedroom slippers with reeds from the inlet just a few yards from the cottage, and spun the wool for the uppers with a spindle she carved from a piece of driftwood.

Dorothy often had company on the weekends just like the old days at Huguenot. Stanley came down regularly from Tivoli after looking for books in the secondhand bookshops along Fourth Avenue. Rita Corbin visited and worked on a woodcut of Sacco and Vanzetti for the fiftieth anniversary of their execution, reminding Dorothy of the summer Della was protesting in Boston with Katherine Anne Porter while Dorothy took care of Tamar, her heart breaking over the disintegration of her relationship with Forster.

When Dorothy was alone, she listened to opera and reread her old article "Having a Baby" at the news of the arrival of yet another great-grandchild. She slept deep and long at night to wake at five thirty, when she read at sunrise Genesis and Psalms, the Ascension and Acts. She sometimes awoke to feelings of joy and gratitude, and other times in a state of depression or worry. She thought of Forster and of Tamar's conception on a June morning at the beach—the beach where beauty had helped lead her to faith—and the picnic not long after at the Tottenville circus when she knew she was pregnant. Dorothy rarely could write of the beach without thinking of Tamar's conception and birth, and of happy, cold spring days caulking a boat with Forster and collecting driftwood while watching the wind rise. Now, decades later, she watched the huge swells in the bay and looked out to the horizon, where sea and sky met, and prayed to have the strength to write, even if just a little a day.

When she felt strong, and when the sea and wind were calm, Dorothy sat on the beach either on a log or in her lawn chair at the edge of the sea, a silk or cotton scarf on her head (often the only splash of color both she and Tamar wore), with a book in her hands, looking out over the bay at the gulls, watching ripples stirring a patch of water here and there and the reflection of clouds. The water lapped at her bare feet while she searched for shells and stones among the bits of plastic and driftwood. If she felt strong enough to walk, Tamar and she would wander barefoot in the sand while reminiscing about the strange plague of horseshoe crabs on the beach one summer years back and listening to the gentle sound of waves lapping against the sand and retreating through the stones and shells.

The following summer of 1978 was much the same. Dorothy listened to *Tannhäuser* as the bay filled with sailboats, and Tamar found the bag of wool in the closet from the previous summer, which she washed and carded. With her driftwood spindle she then spun the wool into yarn and knitted a sweater for one of her grandchildren.

After graduating from high school, I came to visit, again with Stanley, and in the afternoons we sat in the garden listening to Dorothy tell stories. She was still hoping, believing that she could get her strength back if she walked a little more each day. She tried to answer mail, but she got confused, opened envelopes, and stirred them all around. She knew she was failing, but she wasn't giving up.

"Dorothy fought every inch of the way," Tamar said.

She sat in front of the cottage watching and listening to the gulls and waves while writing postcards until either the hot sun or a cold breeze drove her inside. She read George Orwell while sitting on the red bench in front of the cottage closest to the sea. On some days the bay was filled with sailboats and fishing boats, and on other days there was no one in the water or on the beach, and the neighbors were all silent or gone, and then she was reminded of those words "And God made heaven and earth."

"The problem of evolution has never bothered me," she wrote, "nor the exact time when 'God breathed into man a living soul.' It was the observation of these beauties along the seashore that brought me to a stunned recognition of God as creator of infinite beauty and variety."

Then September arrived bringing yet again that old melancholy. Dorothy awakened early from a restless sleep, a cricket singing on her windowsill, mind in a turmoil, feeling ill, and having, as she called them, nostalgic, early-morning thoughts. By the end of the month she was back in the city and settled into her room on the second floor of Maryhouse. There she made a final retreat, in a way, and so ended that lifetime of traveling, her love of which had begun in 1904 when Grace and her four children, all under the age of eight, went by train from New York to California, stopping at the world's fair in St. Louis on their way to rejoin Pop in San Francisco. No more heading to the beach for sustenance and driven by a restlessness Dorothy had long sensed was spiritual hunger. No more moments on the road where she found her solitude, being neither here nor there, freed from all responsibility. No more fleeing, when she felt she got too high-handed, to cross the bay on the ferry and ride the bus down Hylan Boulevard, anticipating the fresh smell of the sea. No traveling around the country or zipping between the city, Tivoli, Della's, and Vermont. No striding, strong and confident, across the lawn at Tivoli or speaking in front of the crowds at the Pax Conferences. No more would we see her driving up our washed-out driveway, trying not to hit the dogs as they circled excitedly around her, and no more would Tamar, when she saw by the light that Dorothy was awake at dawn, bring her a cup of coffee and one of the girls' old missals.

And no more would mother and daughter sit together on a log on the beach on Staten Island, the place where so much had begun, the two of them momentarily free from their troubles and their families—Dorothy with her coffee, Tamar with her tea—listening to the waves and watching the gulls.

Part Four

THE ART
OF HUMAN
CONTACT

CHAPTER TWENTY-TWO

I was fifteen when I first visited the Catholic Worker in New York City with a group of friends from school. A man began throwing rocks at us a block away from the house, St. Joseph's on East First Street, and we fled. It was 1975, and the city—worn, filthy, and bleak—was near bankruptcy. The following summer, I showed up at Maryhouse six months after it opened, and this time I was met at the bus station by Stanley. Everyone needs a guide when entering the wilderness, and it was Stanley who helped me through those first encounters with the Catholic Worker city houses, with his Brooklyn accent, receding hairline, broad smile, and round stomach that he would pat gently and say, "Too much Catholic Worker soup."

I continued to show up for short visits during school breaks, and Lena Rizzo greeted me, as she greeted everyone who walked into Maryhouse. In the summer she lived in Union Square, on the sidewalks between the trash bins and walk signs, surrounded by her belongings, which were kept in canvas US Postal bags she carried in a supermarket cart. In winter she lived on the bench in the Maryhouse foyer—she refused to stay in a room—where she spent her days sewing clothes with large running stitches. Garrulous and friendly, she had her own style of language. "Is Doris on the microphone?" she'd call out, which I learned to interpret as, "Is Helen on the telephone?"

She asked everyone who passed, "Gotta cigarette?" She even asked Mother Teresa of Calcutta when she came to visit.

"No, I'm sorry, I don't," Mother Teresa replied.

To which Lena said the same thing she said to everyone who didn't have a cigarette: "Well, then what good are you!"

While at Maryhouse, I spent time with my grandmother in her room, knitting or reading.

"Frank keeps me locked in," Dorothy joked, speaking of Frank Donovan.

The door was large and solid, a fire code door that creaked before it slammed shut, but I could still hear the noises of the house, people running up and down the stairs, the phone ringing, and from the street, cars driving by and people calling out. Dorothy sometimes sat in an armchair in the corner, where she read her mail and looked out over the ailanthus tree, but mostly she lay on her bed, and Tamar sat in the rocking chair next to her. Stanley had the winged chair at one window, and I sat at the other, where I looked out onto Third Street, the windowsill black and sticky with soot.

Her room was full of gifts she had received—a terrarium with a red glass roof, icons and a crucifix on the walls, books stacked on the floor and on a battered wooden office desk, a caned rocking chair draped with an afghan Tamar had knitted. Each gift led her to speak of the friend or family member who had given it to her, if she was still able to remember.

Her typewriter sat on the desk, although I hadn't seen her type since our summers at Tivoli. She had three overflowing bookcases. There were at least five New Testaments, *Bread and Wine* by Ignazio Silone, and, of course, Dostoyevsky. In a drawer of one of her two bureaus she kept what she called her escape library—the mysteries of Agatha Christie, Dorothy Sayers, and Josephine Tey, the Bony books, and the Rabbi books.

Dorothy lay on the bed with a kerchief around her braided hair and her reading glasses on a chain around her neck. "It's like a Russian novel," she said, looking at each of us sitting in our corners. She sat propped against several pillows with her rosary in her hand. Her shoulders were stooped and her dress shapeless. She read aloud from her letters while Tamar knitted or spun wool, or Stanley read the *New York Times*, and I read from the secondhand books Stanley bought for me. Stanley also often brought cheesecake or a bottle of wine, which he sneaked into the house, and all four of us sipped from small sherry glasses. Tamar and Dorothy had a similar laugh, a high-pitched, joyous giggle that lit up their eyes, one that seemed incongruous coming from faces of wide cheekbones and firm mouths. They also had the same habit of moving invisible objects around with their feet while they spoke, and strong, elegant, and nervous hands that rarely kept still. They both had that crown of braids around their heads, one white and the other graying.

I am grateful for those years from 1977 to my grandmother's death in 1980, though they were hard for her and for Tamar. After I graduated from high school, eighteen years old and restless, I kept returning to Maryhouse, a week here, a month there, getting to know my grandmother, though it seemed I was too late. I could see only the shadows of a life that whispered of events of long ago. I felt drawn to her and Maryhouse. I wanted to be there with her and piece together her life through the stories she told. But I had the same problems with the city that Tamar did; it provoked in me the same combination of borderline claustrophobia and agoraphobia, and I wandered back and forth between New York and Vermont, unable to settle in either place. When I was nineteen, fresh, confused, and shy, and my grandmother was lying on her bed, weak and tired, and yet looked at me with eyes that had lost none of their piercing power, she said, "Well, Katy, what are *you* going to do?" I don't remember what I answered, but I scuttled back to Vermont, keeping my distance from her, which she had first observed when I was fifteen. "You have never written me a letter," she said, though the first postcard I received from her was in 1967, from Gibraltar, when she was sailing from New York to Rome. I did eventually write her, but it didn't come easily.

Dorothy had a second heart attack in the fall of 1977 after returning to Maryhouse from Staten Island. She was so weak she could scarcely walk, and she was even unable to fold the *Catholic Worker* paper, the one job she felt was left to her. Then on October 11, she woke up feeling as if she were being smothered, and under the instructions of her doctor, Marion Moses, she was rushed to the hospital. No simple bed rest like she had had a year earlier.

Before Marion became her doctor, Dorothy had been seeing a Russian doctor, a quack, Marion called him, at Bellevue. To Dorothy, Bellevue was the only hospital in the world, and she liked Russians. But it delighted her to have a woman doctor, and she and Marion became good friends. Marion was a Lebanese-American Catholic from West Virginia whom Dorothy had first met when Marion was a nurse for the United Farm Workers in Southern California. Marion specialized in occupational medicine with an emphasis on the effects of chemical sprays and pesticides on farmworkers. She also cared for Cesar Chavez during his fasts ("Dorothy and Cesar Chavez," Marion said, "were a lot alike"). She became Dorothy's doctor in 1977 and remained so until Dorothy's death.

People were glad to know Marion was there. "When Marion is around, people don't die," they said.

Tamar said, "If it wasn't for Marion, Dorothy would have died three years earlier."

Dorothy remained in the hospital for eleven days, while Tamar and Forster visited daily. Forster brought her books and ice cream, while Tamar sat and knitted socks.

A month later, Dorothy turned eighty. Cardinal Cooke called her with birthday greetings, the *Daily News* wrote her up, and five days later, her fourteenth great-grandchild was born.

"It does not seem possible I am so old," she wrote to Della. "My eightieth year! In my dotage! But life still has its joys—just looking at the river, the beauty of the bare trees, the beauty of children, the joy of reading."

Word spread of her illness, and Joe Zarrella and Gerry Griffin came by. Others wanted to visit for what was likely to be the last time, but Frank, trying to protect her, turned many away. By the following spring, she was able to get out and about, eating downstairs on occasion and writing more. Spring led her to feel the old restlessness, and she wanted to return to Tivoli to sit in the sun and watch the river, but she didn't have the strength. She was sometimes able to get down to the Mass held in Maryhouse, and on her rare good days, she went to the five o'clock Mass at the Church of the Nativity around the corner on Second Avenue, but most days Frank brought Communion to her room. At night she read, sipped a little bit of brandy and water, and listened to music on the radio. Forster called daily, and Tamar visited monthly. Dorothy's world had become very small—visits to the chapel downstairs, vespers and Communion, music and opera on the radio (including Wagner, whom she refused to let Hitler, or even Wagner himself, ruin for her). On the television there was a revival of Gene O'Neill's plays, and she watched *Mourning Becomes Electra*, *Beyond the Horizon*, and *Ah, Wilderness!*, which Dorothy called "his one happy play." She listened to *Elektra*, *Tosca*, *Parsifal*, and *Eugene Onegin* from the Metropolitan Opera, and the refrains haunted her. Stanley gave her a private showing of his slide show of Catholic Worker history, and Marion regularly had supper with her.

Fritz Eichenberg, one of the three most outstanding Catholic Worker artists (the other two were Ade Bethune and Rita Corbin), brought her a book of icons and a book of animal proverbs. Her brother John brought *The Pilgrim's Progress* and Huysmans's *The Cathedral*. Della was now living in British Columbia near her daughter, and she and Dorothy corresponded regularly. Dorothy never heard from her brother Sam. She hadn't seen him in years, maybe not since Grace's death in 1946.

Frank made her a toasted cheese sandwich every day. Frank, she claimed, oversaw her as she opened her mail and grabbed the loot to keep her from going out and living riotously. What she didn't admit and perhaps wasn't aware of was that her memory was so poor she was liable to mislay the donations, some of which wouldn't be found until thirty years later.

Her diary entries were succinct. "'Hell is not to love anymore.' Woke with this quote in my mind. Where is it from? My memory, my memory!"

Sometimes Dorothy seemed to Marion to be low and depressed, yet she liked to tell, over and over, a joke about a woman with terrible memory. Her daughter tells her to go to the doctor, and the doctor asks, "How long have you had this problem?" The woman replies, "What problem?"

Dorothy still loved to talk. She spoke to Marion of the Russian authors, of Tivoli, of her travels by bus and the people she had met, of Della, and of how the family all listened to opera. She didn't talk about Forster other than that he objected to Catholicism, but she did speak often of Mike Gold. She also talked to Marion about when, as a young woman she had overdosed on laudanum and had the abortion. "When I was young and leading a 'free life,' it never occurred to me to have the baby," she said to Marion. "And then I had trouble getting pregnant again because of the abortion."

Dorothy had several medical crises during those years, but she was hard to treat because she wasn't a willing and compliant patient. "How long do I have to take these pills?" she would ask, irritated at every prescription Marion wrote.

"She was stubborn," Marion said to me. "And like many of her generation, Dorothy believed that you only went to the hospital to die. But she liked her cardiologist at Beth Israel, Dr. Goldberg, who, when he was told of his new patient, asked, 'THE Dorothy Day?' They got along like a house on fire. She never refused to visit him."

When Marion went to visit her at the hospital, she said to the receptionist, "I'm here for Dorothy Day."

"Dorothy Day?" the receptionist replied. "The communist?"

During one of Dorothy's health crises, Marion received a frantic call from Frank and arrived to find Dorothy sitting in her bed, nightgown on, hair braids down, arms folded and her lungs half-full of liquid.

"I'm not going to any hospital," she said, glaring at Marion.

For three hours Marion tried to convince her to go until she said, "Dorothy, out of our friendship you need to go to the hospital. As your doctor, I could strong-arm you into doing it, but I don't want to do that. I want you to pray about this."

She then left the room for ten minutes, and when she returned Dorothy said, "Okay, I'll go."

For the first time since her year off in 1944, Dorothy was no longer on the masthead as editor of the paper. Her diary jottings became her column, and each time they reprinted an old article of hers, she was reminded how she had done the same with Peter Maurin. She excused it by saying, "Teachers have to repeat and repeat." On what may have been Dorothy's last outing, she heard a speech by Elie Wiesel, who said we are obligated to keep the memories alive, and that is the work of a teacher.

One morning while she watched the rays of the sun touch on an ailanthus outside her window, a quote came to her. "I know not ugliness. It is a mood which has forsaken me." She wondered where it came from, and then later remembered. Of course. Max Bodenheim. She also often woke up with two lines that haunted her, "the duty of delight" from Ruskin, and "joyous I lay waste the day" from a prayer by St. Ephrem the Syrian. "At evening I say, tomorrow I will repent, but when morning comes, joyous I waste the day." Writing, even if it was only a few words, was still part of her early-morning prayer life, which began at six o'clock with Psalms. She read and wrote until eight o'clock, making instant coffee on a little hot plate. She read the Psalms with her cup of coffee and ruminated. A bad winter storm bringing in snow through an open window reminded her of when she walked the streets through the drifts with Mike Gold in the winter of 1917. Stanley bringing her a bottle of vermouth reminded her of dinners with Della.

Dorothy's musings on her past moved from the early days of the Worker back through the tumultuous years of her twenties to finally rest on her childhood. Her publisher was still interested in one more book, and Dorothy told Della she was going to write about their childhood. Dorothy wrote about Grace, but she talked about Pop. Tamar said that Pop and Dorothy had been hurt by each other's attitude, but now only the good memories remained, and Dorothy remembered how he always made sure the family lived close to a park or a beach, beginning her love of beauty. She told Marion that she had had a very good relationship with her father.

"You don't grow up until you forgive your parents," my mother said the year before she died.

The following year of 1979 was a cruel year—it began with a death and ended with a death. On January 11, Becky's four-year-old son Justin, blond, blue-eyed, with a strong and accurate throwing arm, was struck and killed by a school bus as he slid down the driveway behind a snow bank at Cady Hill Road. Stanley did not visit Dorothy that day but stayed in his room, while Becky turned to Dorothy for comfort, but Dorothy was too shocked and confused to even speak about it. Tamar returned to New York after the funeral, bringing a tiny terrarium she made in a glass Christmas tree ornament. To distract themselves from sorrow, they watched *The African Queen* on television.

That summer the house on Cady Hill Road burned down. After those of us still living there—Tamar, Martha, Hilaire, and I—had asked Nicky, whom Tamar could no longer hold on to, to leave, he lit a fire in the attic one evening while we were downstairs, and we heard what sounded like rain hitting the roof. We all, including Nicky, watched the house burn while the firefighters siphoned water from four nearby ponds, emptying them until they were spraying mud on the white clapboards. Many of our books had their spines burned off, and the rest were water damaged. When the fire was extinguished, only the ell, the wing built at a right angle off of the main section of house, remained untouched. Dorothy was too upset over the news to get to Mass.

Then, less than three months after the death of our old house, Tivoli finally closed its doors. When the depopulation of the farm began, Dorothy thought of all the Pax and Peacemaker Conferences, the visitors from as far as Japan and Australia, guests like Mary Lou Williams and the psychologist Karl Stern, and all the priests who came through, hippies and conservatives. But also she believed that it was the stress of the Tivoli farm that had brought about her first heart attack. The hard workers were leaving to start their own toeholds on the land in West Virginia, Kentucky, and Missouri, where land was cheap. This left only Peggy Scherer and Stanley to keep the place going, until Stanley moved to Maryhouse, and the balance was tipped from the vision of Peter Maurin's agronomic university to a home for the mentally ill.

Those problems of Tivoli were the same old problems Dorothy had encountered before, "our human condition—our discontent." But it always came back to the needs of flesh-and-blood people, for it was there she felt the love of God and could see the face of God. Also, she said, the poor, like garbage, get kicked around until they get lost. Dorothy didn't want to sell the farm until people had places to go to. She couldn't forget the anxiety and fears when they left the Mott and Chrystie Street houses, and how terrified people had been at possibly finding themselves homeless again.

Those who could began to leave of their own accord, but there was a small group who couldn't, and the Worker needed to find another farm for them. Shortly after May 1979, when they had found a buyer for Tivoli, the Worker found a small farm in Marlboro, a town across the Hudson from Poughkeepsie, not far from where Grace had been born. It had two small houses for the older members, fifty acres of good land, a pond, and several barns. The local priest, to their delight, was an old friend of the Worker. Dorothy named the place, which neither she nor Stanley would come to see, the Peter Maurin Farm. And with this move, the open hospitality of Tivoli, which was less a matter of policy and more the result of not being able to shut the gates, came to an end.

On the day after Dorothy's eighty-second birthday, the Worker closed on the Tivoli sale for $215,000, more than half of which went to pay off the mortgage. In the years to come, the place would become more derelict as it passed through the hands of several owners until 2002 when the minimalist artist Brice Marden bought it for $2.3 million. He renovated the mansion but left on the wall of what had been the clothing room the roughly hand-painted words "Men's pants" with an arrow pointing down. The swimming pool, though long unused, remained. The living room and dining room of the main house, where they had held Mass and meetings, parties and concerts, and sometimes where unhinged young men attacked others with knives or peaceably cleared the dishes from the tables, were gone, and only the two wings remained. The old chapel and the casino, which had first been the migrant workers' child-care center and then became the men's dorm, had been torn down and remade into Marden's art studio, and the walls were covered with canvases twenty feet wide and the rooms full of paints and paintbrushes. The only room that remained as it had been was Dorothy's bedroom on the second floor overlooking the Hudson River, coincidentally, as Marden would have had no way of knowing which had been her room.

The final blow of that sad and difficult year fell less than a week after Dorothy's birthday. After the Cady Hill Road house had burned down, I moved to Maryhouse. My sojourn there lasted less than two months, after which Stanley took me to the Port Authority bus station to head back to Vermont. I was disconsolate and humiliated by my inability to live at Maryhouse, and Stanley tried to cheer me up. That was the last time I would ever see him. Two weeks later, Stanley became ill with what he thought was a stomach flu, and on November 14, within five days of the sale of Tivoli, he died of a heart attack in his tiny room at the end of the hall in Maryhouse.

"It was the soup!" Stanley was said to have cried, true to the last, though this could be another Catholic Worker legend.

Stanley's death left us all bewildered. He was only sixty-three, and none of us imagined that he would die before Dorothy. He was like a son to her, an older brother to Tamar, and an uncle to us, though I wonder if he loved my mother. He was so discreet and old-fashioned he wouldn't come up to Vermont without Dorothy. "It wouldn't look proper," he said to Tamar.

"We were very close," Tamar said.

Through the years, Stanley visited Tamar every chance he got, first at the Fifteenth Street house, then Mott Street, Easton, West Virginia, Staten Island, and Vermont. His last trip to Vermont was in May 1976, when he stayed in his favorite room, the book room, and took photos in the afternoon sun out near the outhouse of the four generations: Dorothy, Tamar, and the children and grandchildren.

Stanley left behind few belongings—a shortwave radio, a bookshelf of books, a tape recorder and tapes of Tchaikovsky, Mozart, and Chopin, a sparse wardrobe, and boxes of his manuscripts and papers. But his greatest possessions were his heart and his open, welcoming arms, maintained for more than forty-five years of living at the Worker.

While Catholic Worker lore has it that Stanley arrived in 1934 when he was seventeen and never left, he worked as a shipping clerk for a time while still living at home with his parents before moving to the Easton farm in 1936. He lived on each of the farms until 1978, when he moved to Maryhouse. But over the years he had left the Worker several times.

"I was always glad to come back," he said. "In one way I never left; I always felt I was part of the family."

Stanley not only was a master at hospitality, greeting each visitor warmly and with a joke, but also had an eye for irony, and he kept a running commentary on the Catholic Worker. When the motto of the Catholic Action program of the 1930s was "the love of Christ drives me on," Stanley quipped, "The fear of Dorothy Day drives us on." He was devout, though unobtrusively so. He attended Mass daily and often led prayers, his Brooklyn accent distinct and strong, and he loved to sing Gregorian chants.

He always said the right thing at moments of tension. Tamar called him the soul of discretion and sensible, which was high praise from her. Dorothy often spoke to Stanley of things she never told others, but sometimes Dorothy couldn't see Stanley's worth. In the fifties, when he had been at the Worker for twenty-five years ("Some people," he'd say, "come to the Worker planning to remain the rest of their lives but leave after a few days—others come for a few days and remain the rest of their lives"), Stanley told Dorothy of his grievance over not being included on the paper's masthead. "How one injures people without knowing it," she wrote. He wasn't a gifted writer, but he was a hardworking one. He wasn't a scholar like the bright young men who came and went—Bob Ludlow, Michael Harrington, or Robert Ellsberg. He wasn't a worker like John Filigar, and he wasn't a farmer, though it was the farm that called to him. Stanley identified with the scholars because he felt clumsy and inept in the face of John's impatience and scorn, but the scholars never embraced him either. And the hostility of that old battle of the workers versus the scholars bothered him. "The workers tend to remain workers and the scholars tend to remain scholars," he said, unable to find his place in either camp. Stanley had his moments of discouragement and depression, his Lithuanian winter mood, Dorothy called it, and he had a store of Lithuanian sayings, one of which was "It is better to quarrel than be lonely."

Earlier that year, before he died, Stanley and I had become writing partners, each banging away at old battered typewriters with ribbons so well-worn you could barely see what you had typed. Stanley gave me assignments on what I had seen on our walks together, and afterward we would go out for pizza. He understood my desire to write—he had arrived at the Worker wanting to write. Dorothy was the first writer he had ever met, and she encouraged him. I didn't realize until long after his death just how much he had written. He had published articles and stories in more than fifty magazines. In the fifties, Stanley earned seven hundred dollars one year through his writing. Influenced by my father, he wrote an essay called "The Right Spirit" advocating distributism. He had written several books that he was unable to get published, and he kept his many rejection letters. He wrote a book on the Staten Island farm and for five years tried to get it published but was only able to get an excerpt placed in the *Christian Science Monitor*. He also wrote an unpublished biography of Dorothy, titled *The Long Endurance*, well before any of the other biographies appeared in the seventies. He never showed it to Dorothy. His last book, which he also failed to get published, was about the early years of the Worker. To lift his spirits, he would grab the manuscript, march out the door, and announce, "My book is coming out today!"

It wasn't his writing but his storytelling and his jokes that I knew best. All of us children, the Hennessys, the Corbins, the Hugheses, listened over and over to his stories, especially "Oswald the HUUUUUUN-gry Lion." The story is about a family who takes in a lion. The lion gets hungry, and as they don't have much to feed him, he eats one of the children. But the family is so nice and hospitable, they can't put him out, so he eats another child, and another, until the whole family has been eaten up. It wasn't until I was older that I realized it was a satire on the Worker.

"Here at the Catholic Worker," Stanley also liked to say, "we feed the naked, clothe the hungry, and know each other in the breaking of heads."

Old friends that they were, sometimes Dorothy accused Stanley of taking a book she had misplaced and chastised him for not helping around enough. Offended, Stanley would disappear for a day or two, leaving Dorothy to feel ashamed of herself. "There are the saints and the martyrs," Stanley would say within her hearing. "The martyrs are the ones who live with the saints."

But it was to Stanley that Dorothy cried out in despair during the worst of the Tivoli troubles, "I am being blamed for everything." And when Dorothy had weeping spells in her room at Maryhouse, Stanley tried to console her. "The same thing happened to me when I had my heart attack," he said.

Dorothy wrote Stanley's obituary, one she did not expect to have to write, and she titled it "A Knight for a Day," Stanley's own description of his relationship with her. It was short and full of pain and old age. "A dear friend of mine who had no particular faith said in his last illness, 'Don't mourn for me. But play . . . Strauss's *Death and Transfiguration*,

and recite as a prayer the twenty-third psalm, The Lord Is My Shep-
herd.' I think of that as I mourn for Stanley. I can't help but mourn. I
miss him." In the corner of Dorothy's room, Stanley's chair sat empty.

Dorothy had one more obituary to write after Stanley's death, another
one she did not expect, and it would be the last one of those tender stories with which she formed a history of people at the Catholic Worker
who otherwise would have been forgotten. Five months after Stanley's
death, Dorothy's sister, Della, died, the second of the Day siblings to pass.
That May, Dorothy didn't write her traditional anniversary column in
the paper. Instead she wrote of Della's death and reprinted the postscript
from *The Long Loneliness* under the title "The Final Word Is Love."

CHAPTER TWENTY-THREE

During that final year in Maryhouse, Dorothy's writings became dreamlike and drifting, full of prayer and memories. Her column still came out regularly, not one missed, but they were brief and made up of whatever notes she was able to collect. Stripped to the bone. She kept writing to the last, saying, "I don't want people to think I'm already dead."

I weep at this winding down of a mind and a life, but, every month, there it was. Her voice was like a long, slowly moving river that runs deceptively deep, with a rhythm and a tone that mirrored and echoed her lifelong conversion. The exuberance of this life, this pulsing, passing history—Stanley, the farm at Tivoli, the house on Cady Hill Road, the beach at Staten Island—fading away.

Dorothy was still intuitive and perceptive, and that elemental shyness never left her, no matter how long she had lived in the public eye. She still told stories of all those she had known in her life—the stories were getting shorter and distilled to sentences, often filled with a pain I didn't understand, but I could hear the depths from which they rose. She was tired, deeply tired, heavyhearted, prayerful, burdened with the weight of the world, and yet still able to laugh like a young woman. Still able to call up the glow of delight in her eyes. Still sighing, her head tilted to one side, and saying, "I don't know," when faced with some insolvable Catholic Worker conundrum. Though she was also known to say, "There are always answers—they're just not calculated to soothe."

She often sat silent after reading a few pieces of mail that she faithfully tried to answer, even though the effort was beyond her, holding her rosary, her shoulders weak and slumped, her face, her fabulous face, soft and bare.

That last year of Dorothy's life, Dorothy, Tamar, and Forster made their peace with each other over what had seemed so insurmountable, Dorothy's Catholicism. It still weighed on Dorothy's mind how in becoming a Catholic she had deprived Forster of a child and Tamar of a father.

"Dorothy and Forster were deeply attached," Tamar said. "But it hurt so badly that he kept himself apart. It was heartbreaking. He felt her loss keenly."

The three of them came together again in quiet company those last years. The passing decades had worn away the most intractable of problems—Forster's rigid stance against religion and belief that it was nothing but hypocrisy, along with what Tamar called Dorothy's "my way or the highway" heavy-handedness. And in their place were revealed companionableness, love, and the ties of family, just as Tamar had always desired.

Each brush with death seemed to help sweep all away and bring them closer. In the early seventies, Forster had been diagnosed with colon cancer, and he called up Dorothy asking her to visit. He told her he was "fighting off death," though his sight and hearing were still excellent. With each birthday and medical crisis on both their parts, they spent more time together, and with each hospital stay he would call her up, frantic for her to visit. By the time he turned eighty in 1974, when Dorothy had to cancel her speaking engagements because of her own ill health, he was calling most days. For years they had had a phone signal—let the phone ring twice, hang up, and then call again.

When Dorothy was diagnosed with heart failure, Forster had been in and out of the hospital. He went in with pneumonia and three months later he was back for more surgery for colon cancer. He had six operations, some of which occurred while Dorothy was arrested in California. He was going through "a long agony," Dorothy said, and it was a miracle he survived. Though weak and weighing 110 pounds, a month later he was doing well enough to return to collecting and framing pictures to send to Maryhouse to help cover its freshly painted blank walls. Forster didn't like blank walls. He liked to fill them from top to bottom with framed prints of the old European masters, such as Rubens's *The Three Graces* or Hugo van der Goes's portrait of Maria Portinari with her daughter and Saints Margaret and Mary Magdalene. He sent the Van der Goes over to Dorothy, along with Pere Serra's painting *Annunciation*, which sits in the Maryhouse chapel alongside Our Lady of Guadalupe. I have two of his prints—Modigliani's *Seated Nude II*, which had been a gift to Tamar, and Fra Angelico's *Jesus Appearing to the Magdalene*, a gift for Dorothy.

Six months after his colon surgery, Forster was again in the hospital. He had fallen and broke two ribs and pierced a lung. Like clockwork, six months after that, he was back in the hospital for a cataract operation, another six months, kidney failure, followed by a kidney removal. During one of his hospital stays, Dorothy arranged a Mass for him at the church in which she and Tamar had been baptized.

Before his kidney operation, Dorothy had complained to Della, "Forster calls up whenever he is going through a crisis," but this wasn't quite true. It was only in the hospital that he felt he *could* ask her to visit. Maybe even then Dorothy couldn't admit how much he had loved her and still did. But all this lingering tension fell by the wayside, and by 1979 they were speaking to each other daily, no matter how briefly, and Forster would light up when Tamar showed up at his doorstep to take him over to Maryhouse. He sometimes liked to walk the mile from his place on West Tenth Street.

Tamar's arthritis was so severe at this time, she couldn't get down to see him during his recovery from the kidney operation. Until then they had rarely spoken to each other but had sent messages through Dorothy. Now Forster was so delighted with the regular contact he had with his daughter that he called Dorothy to say, speaking of the grandchildren and great-grandchildren, "We've done pretty well, haven't we?" which made Dorothy laugh. By the time of Dorothy's death, they had sixteen great-grandchildren, and by the time of Forster's death, there were seventeen with two more to come.

Forster didn't seem to resent all the harsh things said about him by people who didn't know him, and he didn't hold them against Dorothy. I'll never know all of what they had to forgive in each other. All Dorothy wrote about Forster he seems to have borne without complaint, and the only objection he ever raised was when people got his name wrong. Forster felt injustices keenly and felt helpless in the face of them, just like Tamar, and Dorothy, who rarely let helplessness stop her, had criticized him for this, but he was faithful to his own ethical code.

It was not until after a lifetime of looking at her daughter and wondering who she was, while also thinking she knew who she was, that Dorothy could come to say, "Tamar is more like her father, and professes no interest in religion. The natural world is enough for her. She has a deep, almost mystical love of the natural world." And when Tamar could say to her mother, "Don't worry—I believe in God."

Dorothy and Tamar weren't able to untangle one element of that web of mistakes and misunderstandings. After a lifetime of feeling uneducated, in January 1980 Tamar entered the local community college and spent much of the year traveling between Vermont and New York. In between coaxing Dorothy to eat, she studied and wrote a paper on trends of the family farm. I don't know why Tamar decided to enter college when her mother was failing so rapidly. Maybe she felt it was her last chance to prove to her mother that she was a scholar and worthy of higher education.

"On one of Forster's visits," Tamar said to me, "Dorothy had to drag out the history of my education. Dorothy said, 'You had the best education in world.' For the feeble-minded, I said to her. I became the feeble-minded child."

Tamar didn't think Dorothy noticed her irritation at Dorothy's claim that Tamar had the best education in the world, when she felt she had been, through Dorothy's influence and peremptory decision making, shepherded away from pursuing a formal higher education. But Forster said to Tamar, "Spare her," so Tamar dropped the subject. After Forster left, they sat up late drinking wine and watching a war movie, but this wound of Tamar's education remained on both of their minds. "I thought I was more than ready to let it go," Tamar said. "But Dorothy couldn't seem to do so."

Perhaps Dorothy did recognize Tamar's intelligence, but formal education had never interested her. Degrees are the bunk, she had said often enough. Most of Tamar's cousins on both the Day and Batterham sides were highly educated. As for Tamar's children, all of the girls got some level of higher education, but her dream that we all be well educated did not turn out as she had hoped. Tamar felt Dorothy had an outmoded understanding of what made a person qualified for certain professions. Dorothy kept saying to her, "You know all that," as though Tamar didn't need training and qualifications.

"She understood it for everybody else," Tamar said. "She always encouraged people to pursue their training. Something slipped there."

Tamar believed that Dorothy had deliberately steered Tamar away from academics and toward crafts, agriculture, and the household arts as subjects she was more suited for. Tamar felt insulted. "Dorothy raised me dumb," she said to me on one of her bad days. Yet Dorothy insisted she had done the right thing.

This was the time, if there ever could be one, to transcend Grace's lethal saying "least said, soonest mended" that Dorothy so admired. Yet she still couldn't seem to talk to Tamar. She had a sixth sense that helped others discern their gifts and vocation and that Tamar had seen many times. Dorothy was rarely fooled by people, and could spot the egotist, the troublemaker, the needy, the lonely, and the fragile, and yet she couldn't read her own daughter. Tamar could sense the guilt that Dorothy lived with because of this, but she was as inarticulate as ever and Dorothy was too ill to talk, so instead they watched *Crime and Punishment* on television.

The turbulence on Cady Hill Road (the house was being rebuilt) continued. Dorothy was still looking for signs that we were coming back to the Church, and she tried to take encouragement from our reading spiritual books and meditating. She was delighted when I went to Mass, but she said nothing of it to me.

Martha and Nicky were both in jail at the same time, one for civil disobedience, the other for burning down the house. Martha was serving what would be three months of an unusually harsh nine-month sentence for leafleting at the public works office against the Seabrook

Station Nuclear Power Plant. It hadn't been clear at first if Nicky would be sent to jail. He underwent a psychiatric evaluation, and each of us was asked if we thought he should be held responsible for what he had done. I was angry and said yes, he should, but now I feel ashamed at my inability to forgive. Nicky was found guilty and served two years of a two-to-five-year sentence.

On her birthday in March, Tamar visited Becky in the hospital. A year after Justin's death, she had contracted a painful and undiagnosed infection. On the same day she also visited Nicky in prison and was shocked at what she saw. He was emaciated and seemed disturbed. His mind was in a whirl, and he insisted that everyone in the family, including my sisters Susie and Maggie and their families, all come back to Cady Hill Road, help rebuild the house, and farm the land. He was suffering from severe hypoglycemia but wasn't receiving any medical care other than an occasional sedative. The prison was overcrowded—eighty-five people with room for only thirty. "Damn the establishment all to hell," Tamar said. "He'll die of that place. He can't eat or sleep." Soon after her visit, they sent him to the state hospital in Waterbury, where my father had spent three months the summer of 1961.

Things had irrevocably changed in Vermont. Susie and her family, who had been living at the Tivoli farm since 1970, asked if they could move to Cady Hill Road.

"No one sympathetic," Tamar said.

Susie and her family left, and Tamar mourned the passing of the Hennessy house of hospitality.

Dorothy said to Tamar, "Why don't you sell the place, scatter them all. Sounds like hell." This hurt Tamar. She saw it as yet another attack on her children and their way of life. She had already been battling with her therapist, to whom she was trying to explain her beliefs about life on the land. He said it was nothing but a counterculture of marijuana. "Like Dorothy, no sympathy for rural life," Tamar said. But maybe Tivoli was still on Dorothy's mind, and that was what she had done there— sold the place and scattered them all.

Tamar had recurring dreams of being lost or anxiously searching for something through endless rooms and tunnels and along railroad tracks. She struggled to understand herself with the help of her thera-pist, her academic adviser, and her doctors, but what could any of them have said that would have made sense for her situation? She was bitterly lonely. She kept a diary that year, the only time she did so, other than briefly during the fifties. Though she intended to write of the past—the past was on both Tamar's and Dorothy's minds—she would come to write of her mother's death.

"I feel as long as I'm alone, I'll have no faith, hope or love," she wrote. One of her kittens severely injured itself in a fall, and Tamar had to put it down. "I lost it. Feel all a delusion. Three beers. Pits. Day alone in house. NG," which was her shorthand for "not good." Her health was poor—in addition to her arthritis, which had already led her to have a hip replacement, she had uncontrollable high blood pressure. She needed a second hip operation. She was drinking too much—beer one night, vermouth another. She had no desire to live alone, but living with one of her children seemed unlikely, as their lives were too unstable. Peggy Scherer, the only one of all the people at the Worker, including Dorothy, who recognized Tamar's feelings of exile and loneliness, invited her to live at the new farm in Marlboro, and Tamar thought about it through-out the year. She was tempted but wrote, what would turn out to be a few hours before Dorothy's death, "I've had to give up my mother and my husband. Do I now have to give up my children also?"

With each visit to New York, Tamar looked more worried. Dorothy's pulse was irregular, and her aortic valve was very small. She weighed only 120 pounds, and Frank brought her ice cream every night after Marion scolded her over her lack of appetite.

"You're cannibalizing," Marion said. "Eat more peanut butter."

"Anything but that eternal soup," Dorothy replied.

Frank and Tamar hovered over her trying to find something she would eat—yogurt, crackers and cheese, a bit of watermelon. One day she would feel better, the next day ill.

"It was like having to constantly plot and persuade a contrary, sick child—to eat, to take medicine, oxygen," Tamar said, while Dorothy said, "Tamar scolds me just as she used to do as a child."

Dorothy forgot the summers, only two years previously, that she and

Tamar had spent together on Staten Island. "I'm so sorry," she said. "I just don't remember."

She still had moments of her quick wit and sense of the absurd, though. When she answered a phone call in the middle of the night, a strange man's voice said, "I've decided to renew our affair."

"It's too late," Dorothy replied. "I'm eighty-two." And she hung up.

Dorothy had a few visitors, but Frank and Marion tried to shield her from many, which, when Dorothy found out, upset her.

"Is she going to live forever? Is it worth it?" Tamar wondered.

It was hard for people to let Dorothy go, and so many wanted to be able to say good-bye. Those who felt they had been a son or daughter to her wanted to see her once more, but she was easily agitated, and visits could leave her ill and shaking for days.

Her days were a round of Communion and music. Maryhouse's resident priest, Father Geoff Gneuhs, held Mass three times a week, and on rare occasions she walked down the flight of stairs to attend. When there was no priest around, Dorothy received Communion in her room from Frank. "The Lord has sent me a son in my old age," she said of Frank.

She immersed herself in the romantics—*Siegfried* and the novel *The First Violin*. On the radio she always had at her bedside, she heard live Verdi's *Otello*, Richard Strauss's *Elektra*, and Puccini's *La Bohème*, which had haunted her years with Forster. Listening to *Salome* or *Tristan und Isolde*, she was once again at the old Metropolitan Opera House on Broadway and Thirty-Ninth Street, where she and Forster saw all of Wagner's operas, buying cheap standing-room tickets and leaning over the top balcony, five tiers up, to look down into the orchestra pit.

She watched Gene O'Neill's play *The Iceman Cometh* on the color television Frank had bought her for her eighty-second birthday, and was reminded of those nights in the Hell Hole. She watched one of the young men run string from the fence in front of Maryhouse up to the third floor for the morning glories to grow on. "Beauty!" she cried.

Early in July, Tamar was back at Maryhouse. As always, Dorothy perked up when Tamar arrived and began to eat and feel better, but she easily slipped back into feeling ill. Dorothy couldn't bear the smell of food, so Tamar often ate downstairs in the dining room.

Tamar missed Stanley. Maryhouse seemed empty without him, and his death had left both Tamar and Dorothy feeling confused and disoriented for months afterward. New York City had always been difficult for Tamar—even as a child she would get sick at the very thought of it. With Stanley it had been bearable, but now she couldn't bring herself to enter the coffee shops and pizza parlors they had frequented together.

In September, Tamar again headed down to the city to find Dorothy extremely weak and ill. She coaxed her into eating a bit of peanut butter, cheese, and crackers. When Marion visited, Dorothy got out of bed and looked so perky she surprised everyone, but her continuing lack of appetite worried them. Tamar suspected that the water pills were making the food taste bad, so she took Dorothy off them for four days, and for a time Dorothy improved and ate most of dinner, even chicken, the only meat she had had in months.

Dorothy checked over the galleys of the paper while Tamar tatted her a bookmark. They listened to Mozart's *The Marriage of Figaro*. Dorothy preferred *Tosca* or *La Bohème*, while Tamar didn't like opera at all. She preferred Beethoven, Louis Armstrong, and the classical guitar music of John Williams.

"I am dying by inches," Dorothy said to Forster. Her pulse was so irregular, it had to be checked five times a day. She told Tamar to open the window and turn off the air-conditioning, then to close the window and turn on the air-conditioning. She ate some fruit and complained it tasted terrible. Tamar gave her oxygen and a sedative.

Most of us grandkids visited her one last time that year, but it was difficult to see her failing, and our visits seemed hard on her. Hilaire stopped by on his way hitchhiking home to Vermont after shearing sheep in the South. Martha visited with her two-year-old son, and Susie and her family stopped by on their way to Tennessee, where they had moved. Mary would be the last of us to see Granny, a few weeks before her death. The last time I remember seeing her, we listened to *La Bohème* on the radio and watched *War and Peace* and a documentary on Charles Darwin on the television. My mother wasn't with me, as she had classes to attend, and Stanley, of course, was gone, so two corners of Dorothy's room were empty. She was no longer reading aloud her letters or answering correspondence, and she no longer had it in her to scold me for dressing improperly or even to tell me stories.

That last month there was time yet for one wound to be healed when Dorothy held on her lap the manuscript of Father Hugo's latest book, *My Ways Are Not Your Ways*, which Sister Peter Claver brought her. He was still giving his retreats in Pittsburgh, still requiring silence for a week. An impossibility in this modern age, Dorothy thought. She fingered the pages restlessly, put them back on her desk, and said to Tamar, "It no longer seems as appealing as it once did."

On November 8, Dorothy turned eighty-three, and Tamar had planned to be there for her birthday but couldn't make it because of her classes. She called, and Dorothy sounded weak. Three days later, Frank called—Dorothy was in Beth Israel Medical Center, and on the first anniversary of Stanley's death, Tamar headed down to New York. Dorothy was in a sunny, south-facing room on the eighth floor, and she seemed stable and in good spirits. The doctors discussed the possibility of aortic and mitral valve surgery.

When Marion arrived, she found Tamar sitting on the side of the bed braiding Dorothy's hair, the two of them as calm and comfortable with each other as they always seemed.

"Dorothy wants to go home," Tamar said to Marion, and she and Marion looked at each other silently.

Dorothy returned home the next day. Tamar returned to Vermont, but just as she arrived home, Frank called, and she was back in the city immediately.

In Dorothy's last diary entry, November 20, she wrote of Jane Sammon bringing her coffee, of Frank bringing grilled cheese sandwiches for lunch, and of the doings of Rita Corbin and her family. And that was it. Forty-six years of diary writing, that fabulous voice that later helped me navigate my way after my mother's death, had finally come to an end.

CHAPTER TWENTY-FOUR

There was no ground in those years after Dorothy's death. Both Tamar and I were adrift. I, entering my twenties, continued to wander in and out of Maryhouse, while Tamar, in her fifties, lived alone in her little cabin on the edge of the woods where she had moved after the old house had burned down, both of us trying to figure out who we were and what we were meant to do. I never saw Tamar cry over her mother's death. Maybe she kept her tears hidden from us as she hid those deepest things; a mother of nine is hard put to keep her privacy. Tamar wrote, "Frank grieves. I don't. I guess I gave up Dorothy long ago, and now I am relieved she is no longer suffering." But she did grieve—she grieved for years, and all any of us could do was watch.

Tamar struggled to answer the many letters of condolence she received from around the world and to write what was on her mind. Her therapist encouraged her. Write it all down, be done with it, he told her, but Tamar couldn't bring herself to do it. "Dorothy would call it the February doldrums," she said, but of course it was more complex than that.

She knew she had to change her perception of herself, and so she embarked on a quest to find out who she was. She took an IQ test in which she scored 145, and her therapist looked at her dumbfounded. "What a trip!" she said. "I can't even do a crossword puzzle." She took the Myers-Briggs test, she recorded her own voice, and she looked at herself in the mirror, a simple gesture that she had for years found impossible. But she still couldn't untangle the knot. Then that spring Tamar was diagnosed with severe degenerative arthritis, and the specter of living as an invalid for the rest of her life frightened her.

The May Day after Dorothy's death, Tamar, Forster, and I went to Maryhouse for the celebration. The visit cheered up both Tamar and Forster, though it must have been difficult to be at the Worker without Dorothy. Tamar and I stayed for a few days at the cottage on Staten Island, and we visited Forster at his partner Pat Erikson's apartment, where she served us strong vodka and orange juice. Forster was slim and spare, with a broad forehead, a receding hairline, and a nose exactly like Tamar's. He dressed daily in jacket, tie, and vest, as he had always done. Pat talked while Forster, Tamar, and I listened. The three of us were so alike in our silence that Pat must have been mystified, just as Dorothy had been.

I was with Tamar on these visits because I had moved to New York two weeks after my grandmother's death. The city in those years suited my mood. Its near bankruptcy in 1975 left it filthy and bleak with abandoned lots filled with garbage and graffiti. There was just the beginning of a scent of change that Dorothy had caught soon after moving into Maryhouse, which led her to wonder how long it would be before the neighborhood was gentrified. In 1980 the East Village was a cheap punk haven centered around St. Mark's Place, still flavored by the sixties, and vibrant and dangerous enough to leave me repelled, attracted, and half-scared out of my twenty-year-old Vermont girl wits.

I relied on the Worker for friendship, shared meals, and sometimes shelter. People there were good and kind to me and accepted me just as I was, but I could not shake this feeling of being an outsider. I explored the Church cautiously, attending Masses at Maryhouse and St. Joseph's, but I couldn't seem to free myself of the conflict I felt between my grandmother's faith and my mother, who was trying to find her own way. I'd sometimes sit in my granny's room in the armchair near the window where Tamar or Stanley had sat, surrounded by her things, which were left just as they had been when she died. Sometimes I sat there for hours, day after day.

My mother tried to comfort me. "Sometimes there is nothing for it but to leave it in the hands of God," she said.

Living in the city did not come naturally to me, but I felt I had nowhere else to go, and one year gave way to two, until ten years had passed. I felt I was, in a way, circling around the Worker, sniffing the boundaries to see if it was, after all, a place for me. One warm, early-spring day, I sat on a garbage can in front of my building. A Hells Angel drove by on his Harley, rattling the windows and setting off a trail of car alarms in his wake. He turned the corner to head up First Avenue, and in a momentary lull of traffic, I could hear only the breeze in the trees and cats fighting behind the building. The street was empty but for one woman, who walked toward me, stopping at each of the garbage cans along the way and peering inside. She slowly made her way closer until I recognized Sister Jeanette Chin, who regularly ate meals at the Worker. She had a large beauty mark on one cheek and wore a turban around her head and thick black streaks of eyebrow liner that never quite aligned with her eyebrows. Her bosom looked as if she had constructed a bra from cardboard and inserted it under her dark, heavy blouse, creating angles and sharp protrusions in uncomfortable places. Even in the hottest weather, she wore a wool hat and several layers of sweaters.

"Hello, sister!" she called out when she saw me. "Alleluia. Looking good, sister, looking good." She held up an unidentifiable rag and asked, "Need a sweater?"

Sister Jeanette was full of generosity, always giving away broken bits of furniture and clothing she found in garbage cans and Dumpsters.

"No thanks, Sister Jeanette. I'm all set for sweaters."

"Alleluia!" she called out amicably once more before continuing down the street, leaving a small wake of goodwill behind her, wafting along with the smell.

I liked Sister Jeanette, but I was also afraid of her. I had a shaky relationship with many of those I knew through the Worker, like Brother Paul, a fierce Italian with a large untreated hernia who used to work in the flower district and had arrived at the Worker in the late fifties. He liked to call me Princess Diana, spitting it out like a curse. He also liked to cook, but he would on occasion threaten people with a meat cleaver. Every day he collected food scraps to feed the stray cats behind St. Joseph House and the pigeons in the small park at Astor Place. In his early years at the Worker, before I knew him, he would take the subway out to the beach, where he had built a shack, and he fed the seagulls, which would see him coming and fly all about him. He would then strip, take a dip in the sea, even in winter, warm himself by a driftwood fire, get dressed, and return to the Worker.

There was also Eleanor, who lived in Maryhouse. She liked to sit in the sun on a water pipe where it emerged from a used furniture shop on the corner of Second Avenue and observe the passing world while she warmed her arthritic bones. On her good days, with a bit of rouge on her papery cheeks and her eyes clear and full of good humor, she chatted with me about how much she had loved my granny and how lovely my mother was. On her bad days, she screamed obscenities as I passed and shouted, "You're nothing like your grandmother!" She was right, I knew, and I crossed the street, face averted, and walked on as fast as I could, nothing like my grandmother.

I wanted to be part of the Worker, but it was hard—the noise, the dirt, the needs. I was terrified of being asked to be on the house not so much for having to cook the meals or hand out clothing, but for what seemed to me to be people's unvoiced and unanswerable needs. I was even more terrified of being asked to take the door during the soup line and face that long line of men who sometimes showed up drunk and angry. Because I was Dorothy's granddaughter, I thought I was supposed to be strong and to pull it off with the grace I felt so many others who weren't related to Dorothy had. But I backed off, frightened by those whose needs seemed bottomless and who grasped desperately at something, anything.

It had been difficult for both Tamar and Dorothy to be in the line of fire of such need, to not instinctively protect themselves from those who latched onto them in desperation. In the forties, while observing Tamar's marriage, Dorothy had written, and I know she was also speaking for herself, "There is so much talk of community and so many who desire to share your life, who look at you with wistful eyes, who want from you what you cannot give—companionship. . . . They want to move in with you, crawl into your skin. This awful intimacy."

Still, for more than a decade I kept showing up at Maryhouse, yet another one in need, and each time I knocked at the door I felt like a hovering stranger. I lived a block away from both Worker houses, Mary-house on Third Street and St. Joseph House on First. From the kitchen window in my tiny, fifth-floor walk-up apartment, I peered into the windows of St. Joseph's and watched people working in the office or Brother Paul feeding leftovers to the feral cats. One reason, among several, that I lingered at its edges was that I too wanted to experience this desire for what I can only call *darshan*—that need to touch someone to gather a sense of the holy. But after years of circling around like a half-wild dog attracted by human activity but also frightened by it, I left. I turned away from the Worker, and I turned away from the Church, for without the Catholic Worker, the Catholic Church made no sense to me.

Those were hard years for us all, beginning that January 1979 with the death of Becky's son Justin, and then seven months later on a hot August night when Nicky burned down the house on Cady Hill Road, followed by Stanley's death in November, Granny's death a year later, and Forster's in 1984. Then we lost Susie and Nicky. Susie had returned with her family from Tennessee to live near the Peter Maurin Farm in Marlboro, and she died in 1986 after five years of fighting cancer. Nicky died the following year of a tragic combination of mental fragility, alcoholism, and fire—90 percent of his body was covered with third-degree burns. Both Susie and Nicky were not yet forty and parents of young children. Alcoholism, mental illness, old age, disease, and accidents—all part of the human condition.

In his diary David wrote one short line on an otherwise blank page, "My dear boy, Nick, died."

Tamar said, "I've cried enough."

Dorothy, Tamar, Kate—we all suffered from depression at times. "Unhinged" was Dorothy's description of when she wept from weakness, discouragement, and the hopelessness of many situations. Then she would escape to either Della's or Tamar's or clean the house (advice from her mother), or she would go to the theater or listen to music. She said that discouragement and wobbly perseverance do not let up, but you can try to manage them through prayer, solitude, and reading. But she also said that if she ever experienced such despair again, she would have tried shock therapy.

Dorothy still struggled with moments of despair in her last years. In her diaries she wrote, "my heart is as heavy as lead. . . . [M]emory and understanding fail completely and only the will remains, so that I feel hard and rigid, and at the same time ready to sit like a soft fool and weep my eyes out."

Here and there, throughout the years, Dorothy's writings contained descriptions of these moments. "Even as a child of six, I often awakened in the dark and felt the blackness and terror of nonbeing . . . a terror of silence and loneliness and a sense of Presence, awful and mysterious." She wrote in 1968, "There are many glimpses of the quiet terror." She added, "And from quiet terror, I go on to quiet joy at God's goodness and love." In 1972 she wrote, "I wonder if Forster wakes in the night sometimes, appalled by a glimpse of nothingness, of not being, of loss of all the beauty he has known."

I read of the nights of weeping and torment, and I know of what she speaks. Tamar said that she herself did not suffer from depression, and I believed her even when she was taking antidepressants in her later years. I believed her because it was disrespectful not to.

Though the eighties was the decade of Tamar's grief over the loss of her parents and two of her children, they were also a time in which she received two unexpected gifts. Through an inheritance from Forster, Tamar left the cabin at the edge of the meadow and bought a comfortable house in the town of Springfield, the last move she would ever make. But perhaps more important, she also inherited that collection of seventy letters Dorothy wrote to Forster, in which she found something of Dorothy that she believed she had lost to hagiography and to Dorothy's own nature—her mother's love for her father.

I separated myself from my family in the 1990s, and those long conversations between my mother and me stopped for a time, though the separation was an illusion. After years of wandering, I arrived back at my mother's house on a bitterly cold December day. Tamar was now entering the last decade of her life, and we resumed our conversations. This was around the time of Dorothy's centenary birthday, and Tamar began to open up to those who came to her door asking questions, but people seemed to want things from her that they did not get. The two of us kept at it. We sat and talked while music played on the radio, John Williams on guitar or the aria from Villa-Lobos's Bachianas Brasileiras no. 5, our conversations jumping from one thing to another. Tamar had a habit of using pronouns instead of people's names, so I often had to guess of whom she was speaking, and I had to learn how to follow her vague, disconnected sentences.

"I can't stand fixers," she'd say, seemingly apropos of nothing.

"Must be a reaction to growing up with your mother," I said.

"Oh yes, and she could be so righteous about it too."

During those last few years of Tamar's life I would often write in her living room early in the morning, and I would know when she awoke because she would press the button on her Lifeline box, and an electronic female voice would say, "Thank you." Sometimes, though, she slept so deeply and soundlessly that fear would grip me, and I'd watch from her bedroom door to see if she was still breathing.

Her mornings were slow and pain-filled. On one particularly difficult morning, she said, "Every inch of me wants to be elsewhere."

"Like mother, like daughter," I replied.

"Dorothy too," we both said at the same time, and laughed.

We ate many meals together. By that time I had eaten in some of the most beautiful places of the world—couscous around a campfire in the Sahara at sunset, dal and chapatis on a veranda looking out to the Himalayas, breadfruit and freshly caught red snapper on an island off the coast of Honduras—but the ones that mean the most to me now, of course, are the ones I had with my mother in the last years of her life. Here's one—breakfast of blueberry pancakes that I made in her perfectly seasoned heavy black cast-iron frying pan. While I was at the stove, she came into the kitchen in her wheelchair and said to me, "Kate, I've been thinking. Don't waste your time. To be alone is a terrible thing. Get married."

I stood still, pancake flipper in hand, and looked at her speechless. I was forty-five years old, she seventy-nine, and she had never before told me what to do. Never. Once she came close to it by saying, "Well, maybe you should become a teacher."

We sat down at her yellow-and-white enamel-topped kitchen table, me on one side, Tamar on another, and Lucy the conure on her perch on the third, and all three of us ate blueberry pancakes with butter and maple syrup, and I thought, "Yes, I will get married."

The kitchen table was never cleared. We'd have to push things aside to make room for the cups of tea. I never knew anyone who could leave such a trail of clutter, litter, and disorganization as my mother could. And it seemed so effortless, coming naturally out of her movements. Her fingers would flutter, and with a shake she'd flick off some bit of broken something. A snap of the wrist and a pile of local newspapers, *National Geographics*, and *Commonweal* magazines would litter the floor around her bed. A flash of a look, and the sink filled with flotsam and jetsam left by the rising tide of her terrible housekeeping. Most times when I went to throw something away, thinking it was trash, she'd grab it from me. I cleaned only when I was feeling brave, as she was suspicious that I'd throw out all her favorite treasures. I thought I was good at discerning what the treasures might be from the general detritus of her daily life, but all it would take was tossing out one thing I couldn't even give a name to, and I wouldn't hear the end of it for years.

It was at my mother's kitchen table that we began to examine those things that remain in the last years of life. As her arthritis advanced, Tamar, like her aunt Della, moved from using a cane to a walker, until finally she was in a wheelchair, but she kept doing what she could as her life began to strip itself bare. In witnessing this, we both thought of Father Hugo and the retreat. "The best thing to do with the best things of life is to give them up," he had said to her when she was fourteen. Now she had no choice. It had begun with losing her ability to go for walks or tend her garden. Then she had to give up driving and spinning, while her weaving was reduced to using a small table loom, until even that was beyond her, followed by knitting, and finally cooking. Like her mother, she read mysteries, though she could barely hold the books. I brought her audio books from the library, but she couldn't work the player, so then she had nothing left but the radio, light paperbacks, and a bay window of plants where she planted seeds in small pots while sitting in her wheelchair.

In her love and curiosity for so much that seemed improbable, she grew a desert plant called the night-blooming cereus. It is an ungainly plant with long, ropelike stems and thick, elongated leaves. The buds are pale, oblong bulbs several inches long and covered with large pink tendrils. We made bets on which night each blossom would open, and then on a hot July night, as soon as darkness fell, two flowers began to unfold, one tendril at a time. By nine o'clock, they were fully open, revealing a cup-and-saucer-sized creamy white universe of layered petals emitting a fragrance more familiar to a tropical evening than a Vermont summer's night. We felt sorry for the plant as it would sit all that night in rooted loneliness waiting for a moth that would never come, its blossoms open and inviting, sending out their scent. When dawn arrived, the blossoms would begin to wilt and, within a few days, hang shriveled from their stems like wads of used tissue.

"Do you pray?" I asked my mother as we sat watching the blossoms open.

"Rarely," she replied.

"Why not?"

She was silent for a moment, her hands moving restlessly in her lap. Tamar's hands always moved restlessly. They would hop about the kitchen table to pick up the saltshaker, then a fork, to put them down in slightly different positions. When she drove, her hands had jumped around the steering wheel in small, jerky movements, as if they were arguing between themselves which way to go.

"Dorothy's prayers were always answered," she finally said. "Even as a little girl I wondered what chance I had."

I didn't ask what she had prayed for, but I felt I understood. Like Tamar, I felt I couldn't pray. I swerved away from the act no matter how strong the urge, for I believed my prayers were bound to be clumsy, prayers of a stumbling faith, prayers of confusion. And any prayer that accidentally welled up seemed small and self-centered compared to the prayers of my granny. That is the danger of holiness on your own doorstep, in your own family. Either you cannot see it for the view is too close, or if you do, you feel you haven't a chance of being the person she was. You feel it is a sad mistake that you are related.

My great-grandmother Grace felt that prayer was not meant to be public. "Exhibitionist piety," she commented. Dorothy said that writing is prayer, as is reading. She often walked into any church she came upon to sit in meditation and prayer, and sometimes just to read. I envy that. The churches now have locked doors. Writing and prayer were the glue that held Dorothy's days together. Often she found herself praying before she was fully awake and praying as she fell asleep. "My job is prayer," she said. "Sometimes I feel it is like a prayer wheel, mechanical." She drank her coffee and read the Psalms first thing each morning. I can just hear her order at the corner café: "Coffee, please, black, with a few Psalms on the side."

I once found inserted in one of my grandmother's copies of *The Imitation of Christ* a prayer by Teilhard de Chardin, on the back of which was, in Dorothy's handwriting, a list of people, living and dead, she was praying for. Below the list she wrote, "There is no time with God." She often filled her prayer books with the names of those she prayed for. "All those that bothered you," Jane O'Donnell, who had been farm manager at Easton and godparent to one of my siblings, said to her. Over the years Dorothy's formal prayers were often pared down to two, the Memorare and the Jesus Prayer, which would come to mind in moments of travail, such as when taking Eric to the hospital with pneumonia in midwinter in a car without windows, or when Nicky was losing his mind, or when a man on the line attacked another with a knife.

Regrets lingered in Tamar's final years, but she rarely spoke of them. At first she claimed her only regrets were moving away from the sea and then not walking in the Vermont woods more often while she could. But then she began to admit that she lived with much regret about what happened in her teens when she left Ade Bethune's and got married.

"I don't want to feel regret," she said. "I don't want to be smothered by it, but I can't seem to let it go. As a teenager I was so immature. I can't believe how tied I was to Dorothy. I'd walk down the street clinging to her, and she would push me away. 'You must be stronger,' she'd say to me. And I knew she was right. Teenagers want to break away from their parents, but not me. I wanted her so badly. I didn't grow up enough. Daughters are supposed to grow up, and mothers and daughters have to part. And she too had a hard time letting me go."

She sat quietly for a moment, her hands as always restless in her lap.

"I adored Dorothy," she added sadly, defiantly. "And I know how that sounds, but it is the truth. I adored her. And I was always, along with everyone else at the Worker, waiting for her to come home."

It wasn't until Tamar would sit still and fatigued, sometimes resting her forehead on a neatly folded linen dinner napkin on the kitchen table for a few minutes, and her face had begun to reveal more of that extraordinary shape of her mother's, that she started to talk a little about the difficulties of those last years with Dorothy.

"There were still moments of humiliation," she said. "Still her defensiveness over my lack of education, which she sometimes brought up with others in the room."

"You weren't able to speak about it?" I asked.

She said nothing, just waved her hand in that motion of futility she used when she wanted to convey something that she just couldn't tease out into words. But in her short, unanchored sentences, Tamar gave glimpses of what she had come to peace with. "Dorothy was full of contradictions," she said. "You can let it upset you, but you do have to get over it."

During these last months of my mother's life, she had one remaining dark night of the soul that we, her children, were only peripherally able to be present for. Twenty-five years after Dorothy's death, her diaries became open to the public, and Robert Ellsberg, publisher of Orbis Books, was asked to edit them for publication. Robert spent several years painstakingly transcribing Dorothy's cramped and jagged scrawl, which filled numerous small notebooks, and when he was done, he sent a copy to my mother and asked if there was anything that she did not want published.

My mother could have a wicked temper. Her rage would rise into her face, and she would sputter, her lower lip straight and thin, her eyes small and fierce. In the years she raised us, sometimes she threw dishes at the walls, leaving gouges in the hundred-year-old plaster, and the gouges remained until the end. She never hit us, but once she grabbed the broom and started chasing Hilaire and me. I ran up the stairs and crouched behind the banister, looking down at her, for the first time realizing she couldn't catch me or any of us. Tamar had one last rage after she read Dorothy's diary entries written in the years before the breakup of Tamar's marriage. The entries were severe and judgmental and brought up the old accusations of lacking faith and being ungrateful. And even though these accusations were forty years old, they left Tamar so angry that she removed all of her photos of Dorothy.

"The devil take the two of them!" she cried, speaking of both her mother and husband, and placed the photos facedown in her bureau drawer. It was largely an internal rage, one that soon became pain that ran up her arm and shoulder and into her neck, keeping her awake and unable to move until she couldn't bear it and began taking narcotic painkillers. My sisters could only watch and worry.

It was those old accusations of ingratitude that lingered and ate at Tamar's heart. Tamar knew as a child that she had to not only share her mother but give her up. Tamar never spoke of this as a sacrifice; it was simply reality. But the accusation of ingratitude would rankle, as did the accusation that she lacked faith when she spoke to Dorothy of her worries about raising her family. Tamar was never able to step away from her anxieties, and even up until her death she had recurring dreams of trying to save babies.

Robert Ellsberg, hearing of Tamar's distress, called up to reassure her that he wouldn't include any part of the diaries she didn't want published. He thought that maybe it was Dorothy's comments on Tamar's marriage that were at the root of her difficulties, but then in the course of their conversation, he suddenly understood. What remained unresolved between Dorothy and Tamar was simply Tamar's desire that her life and struggles be acknowledged.

"I felt Tamar immediately pick up on my moment of understanding," Robert said to me.

It was as if a switch had been flicked just through Tamar feeling that Robert was a witness, in a sense, and the tone of the conversation changed. She began to talk of how much she had loved her mother and what that meant. She then added, "Use whatever you want."

After speaking with Robert, Tamar threw out the painkillers and said to Mary, "I'm done. I'm over it." A few days later she called up Robert, which was unusual as she rarely called anyone but her family and closest friends, and said, "I want to make sure I was clear—include whatever you want." She then added, "Ask me anything, and I'll try to answer as best I can."

"I felt," Robert said later, "a sense of letting go from her. That she was at peace."

I was away for most of my mother's inner torment and anguish, and when I returned home, after a brief discussion—Tamar didn't go into details—she set it aside, and suddenly I knew that this conversation we had been having on and off since 1980, twenty-eight years of it, had finally come to an end.

CHAPTER TWENTY-FIVE

There is a Catholic Worker story, a parable I call "The Woman Who Never Had Enough." In the late fifties, there was trouble in the house because of Catherine Tarangel and her adult disabled son, John, who later died in a fire. The men called Catherine "the Weasel," while she called them drunken bums and worse. She stole sacks of clothes from the clothing room to sell. She beat John to get him to scream when the Worker had visitors. She made demand after demand until Dorothy moved Catherine and John into a hotel on Delancey Street, paying the eighteen-dollars-a-week rent for them. But they continued to be in and out of the Worker for years. Dorothy's diaries are sprinkled with Catherine's name—Catherine raising hell, Catherine calling the police, Catherine's lawyers sending threatening letters. Faced with these years of Catherine, a woman of "many demands but no satisfaction," as described by one of the Workers, Dorothy responded maybe in the only way she could by giving Catherine a diamond ring that had been donated. It created a stir in the Worker.

"Somebody could pay months of rent with that ring."

"We could keep the soup line going for a long time."

Dorothy's response? "Do you think that beautiful things are only for the wealthy? Let Catherine decide what she wants to do with it."

Catherine died in 1973, shortly after Dorothy had written, "I evade Earl, Larry, C. Tarangel, Joseph—the drunken and the mad who bother me!" I don't know if having a diamond ring was enough for Catherine, but she now lives in the annals of the Catholic Worker in that probably apocryphal story. But there is something of Catherine in all of us. Even given a diamond ring, will we feel it is enough?

Tamar up to the last also drew the needy and the marginal to her. She still bled for them and was easily overcome by their loneliness. Rose, a woman in her early fifties, came knocking at her door one day saying she had heard Tamar was Dorothy Day's daughter and wanted to meet her. I immediately, as did Tamar, recognized a Catholic Worker guest, a person living on the edge—the edge of her mind, of her heart, of her wits. Rose launched into a tale of her time at a Midwest Catholic Worker. She was kicked out (they called the cops on her, she said) for sitting in front of a photo of Dorothy and playing a tin whistle for hours on end. "Well," she added, "for days. And then when I left, I stole the photo." My mother and I both burst out laughing.

We didn't know if Rose's story was true, but Tamar took a liking to her, and they became friends. Rose often came visiting tightly wound, and her dog would rest her head on Tamar's lap. "As if she were sighing in despair," Tamar said.

Within a few years Rose died of breast cancer, and the large and loving gathering at her funeral mystified and touched her family, seeing how their daughter, whose mental illness had driven them apart, had finally found a community. It meant a great deal to Rose's mother to meet Tamar and to know that her daughter had found a good friend in her.

Tamar and I inherited Rose's car, a green Ford Escort, so that, according to Rose's will, I could continue to drive Tamar around. (It had tickled Rose to see how often we would hop into the car and head out to explore yet another back road.) As a surprise recipient of Rose's generosity, I felt bad for the little time I had given her. I had found it hard to be with her; her needs and fragility reminded me of those years in New York City trying to find my place in the Worker. She reminded me of how I had failed to find that boundary between meeting people's needs and not being eaten up by them. I have to stop trying to protect myself, I thought. Look at all my mother was able to do just by visiting and talking and having tea.

After Tamar died, and we were going through her things, choosing which treasures we each wanted to keep, my sister Becky said, "Everything she

had was broken." Every piece of Tamar's belongings had some damage—
furniture, dishes, vases, even the ceramic fish she used as a spoon holder
on the stove. Becky sounded sad as she said this, as if Tamar felt she
didn't deserve to have things that weren't broken, but maybe she was
drawn to all things broken—creatures, teenagers, ceramic fish—wanting to help heal them, help make them whole. Maybe she saw beauty in
the cracked, chipped, and repaired. This is a paradox we all live with—
this flawed vessel called to holiness.

Dorothy said, "What a variety of people called to be saints, crotchety,
giddy, cranky ones, bibulous ones." Stanley said, "People come to the
Worker expecting to find saints, and instead they find human beings."
Tamar said, "Everybody wants the other person to be a saint." She also
once, with a slip of the tongue, referred to Dorothy as "being tried for
sainthood."

"Do you believe your mother is a saint?" I asked Tamar during her
last year.

She surprised me, not that she answered. That would never have
happened. But there was no dismissive flick of the hand, no vague
shrug. Instead her eyes lit up, and she laughed.

In that last decade when Tamar got back in touch with some of the
old crowd going back to the 1930s, one of the men who had lived at
Easton said to her, "Dorothy was no saint." She laughed then too and
didn't disagree, but neither did she agree. Again, she kept her own
counsel.

Tamar, ever practical and sensible, said the miracle of Dorothy's life
is the Catholic Worker, this modern-day parable of the loaves and fishes,
and the Church doesn't need to look any further. What riches she spread
about her like St. Brigit's cloak, the one Brigit would hang on a sun-
beam and which, when she spread it out on the ground, grew and grew
until it covered the countryside, a glint of silver running along its edge
as it brought abundance and beauty everywhere it touched. That's the
miracle—that cloak spread out to give comfort and shelter to our most
wounded in body and soul as she handed out riches recklessly and with
abandon to whomever she met.

Here are just a few ways in which Dorothy spread that cloak about her. She gave a young seminarian money to pay for a year's tuition and expenses. She provided rent for a newly married couple who had met at the Worker, supplied a down payment for a house for another, and paid off the mortgage for yet another. She made it possible for Cesar Chavez's wife, Helen, to accompany him to Italy to attend a personal audience with Pope Paul VI, and she helped put the Farm Workers Credit Union on its feet by purchasing more than a thousand dollars' worth of shares. She gave five hundred dollars to a small struggling farm school in Vermont. She put Ade Bethune on the path of her life's work by paying her tuition to a liturgical art course. She donated thirty thousand dollars to help start a housing cooperative in Washington Heights and gave two hundred dollars to William Miller for the Datsun, a thousand to the civil rights activist Marge Baroni, and another thousand to the Rural Advancement Fund. During one month in the early 1970s, Dorothy sent out more than three thousand dollars to various groups and people, including a home for mothers, the Medgar Evers Fund, and other Catholic Worker houses. She gave money to PBS, Danilo Dolci, and the Committee for Artistic and Intellectual Freedom in Iran. She helped people pay rent; tuition for nursing school, real estate school, and special needs schools; and a graduate program application fee. She gave money to local churches, credit unions, and coops and provided seed money for homesteaders. She paid doctors' bills and car repairs and bought computers for a school for children with developmental disabilities. There's a rumor she helped a young woman attend opera school. ("I'd like to come back as an opera singer," she once said. "Then I could bring beauty into people's lives rather than tell them what's wrong with the world.") Royalties from *Loaves and Fishes* helped Becky with college expenses, and an advance for *On Pilgrimage: The Sixties* helped Maggie and Martha go to Spain for a summer. And who could even begin to have a sense of the sheer numbers of meals eaten, shelter given, clothing handed out, and visits to hospitals, jails, and courts—all part of that practical, visible, miraculous cloak?

There are many eyes on Dorothy—those who knew her, those who didn't but look to her for answers, and those, friendly or hostile, who search her every action and word to support what they already believe.

And those who examine her for possible canonization—sometimes I feel their presence too, searching just as intently. There are many ways to dismiss Dorothy Day, to distort her or call her a dingbat or a communist or to say she was obsessed with medieval notions of sanctity. Or call her a social worker, a social activist, a humble woman, when she was so much more.

But perhaps we all have it wrong—it is not us who should be casting our eyes on Dorothy, but we should be feeling her eyes on us. Both Tamar and Dorothy stare at me from the photos I have of them above my desk, like old Italian portraits in which the eyes of the subject follow you around the room. There is Tamar in her fifties, soon after Dorothy's death, in which she is looking into the camera, and every time I sit down to write, I have to meet her intimate yet cool gaze. Next to that photo is Dorothy in her early forties, her hair already white. She looks off to the side so I cannot meet her gaze. And then there is the photo Richard Avedon took in 1969 in which she stares straight at me. She is older, her hair is a bit untidy, and there is still some indefinable energy beneath the surface of her aged face. Her eyes know what they see, and they look straight into mine.

The photos make other people uncomfortable. "Shaman's eyes," one visitor to my home said. "Unsettling," said another. I feel defensive. Don't they see what I see? Don't they see that this is strength of a kind they may never see again?

Dorothy is in danger of being lost in all her wild and varied ways, her complexities, her contradictions, and this sense of power that defies description. The Look, as Tamar described it, with those beautiful and devastating eyes, darting and intense. Her voice, the one she has left for us, is beautiful, simple, and evocative, but then sometimes there is the lecturing, the defensiveness, and the piety. Often it feels as if she tried hard to efface herself. This was partly for good reasons—she *was* fierce, dictatorial, controlling, judgmental, and often angry, and she knew it. It took the Catholic Worker, her own creation, to teach her her lessons.

In my struggles to know the nature of her gifts, I hold on to my relics of her. I hoard my beliefs, my stories, my memories, and those things I have, like her marked copy of *The Imitation of Christ* and the handwoven Bolivian bag she wore when arrested for the last time at the age of seventy-six. Others too hold on for dear life to their Dorothy stories, their Dorothy connection, their Dorothy relics. Stop it, she says. Look to yourselves. Do the work.

But what is the work? Dorothy never said that everyone should work on the soup line. She loved people's vocations and occupations and found so much beauty in our desire to work and create. I suspect she became exhausted by what people said she did or didn't approve of, and her own attempts to direct and control often backfired. When she was seventy-nine she said, "I feel like an utter failure," and she warned us that we always must expect failure. "The older I get the more I feel that faithfulness and perseverance are the greatest virtues—accepting the sense of failure we all must have in our work, in the work of others around us, since Christ was the world's greatest failure."

Still, she said, we must keep moving. Take as many steps as you can. Bear witness, stand fast, huddle together in faith and community. And dream. We have, she said, a responsibility to hope and to dream of a better world. And being a practical mystic, she said one's spiritual life takes at least three hours a day.

It has been said that three things kept Dorothy going—prayer, the sacraments (in particular, the Eucharist), and the works of mercy. Why isn't the word *love* mentioned here? We don't talk much about how she loved, including Lionel and then Forster, her daughter, and on and on, this ever-widening circle of family sheltered under her cloak of love. Always, always, Dorothy spoke and wrote of love. As she said, there is no end to the folly of love, and there is nothing else to write about. In the end, her enlarged heart gave out from the strain. Maybe it was the outcome of having had so many demands on her, spiritually, physically, and emotionally, but I can't see her having it any other way. The miracle was how long she was able to live with it, the love that kept her alive.

Christ understands us when we fail, she said, and God understands us when we try to love.

CHAPTER TWENTY-SIX

On an October evening in 1945, when Tamar's first child was six months old and Dorothy was forty-eight, Dorothy sat with her dying mother. She had stayed with Grace those last few weeks, daily, then hourly, watching her mother struggle to swallow and to breathe. As she coaxed her to eat a spoonful of custard, she remembered Tamar as a little girl saying, "When I get to be a great big woman and you are a little tiny girl, I'll take care of you."

It was not easy for Dorothy and Grace to talk of dying, but every now and then they did.

"What about a future life?" Grace asked. Even Grace, practical Grace, granddaughter of whalers, who at twelve went to work in a factory to support her mother and three sisters, looked for comfort in her own daughter's extraordinary strength.

Dorothy could only point to the chrysanthemums in bloom and to the maple trees outside, stripped now of the leaves of autumn, and say, "These are promises from God, and God keeps his promises."

"Will I see your father?"

"Yes," Dorothy replied with an assurance and authority that when she looked back years later amazed her.

Grace pondered that for a while.

"I'm not sure I want to see him again," she said.

Dorothy laughed at her honesty. She knew how Pop had wronged Grace and had sometimes been cruel to her, for in that last year of her life Grace had finally abandoned her "least said, soonest mended" maxim and let fly the truth about her marriage.

"You will see him as he was when you first loved him," Dorothy replied.

Years later as she approached the age when her mother died, Dorothy wondered just who her mother had been and whom she had loved. "Were there others . . . during those long years when she was raising us five? . . . Did every now and then that wave of sexuality wash over her that brought with it an exquisite and shattering joy at the beauty of a face, a character, or even at the pure masculinity of a friend or acquaintance, the exchange of a glance, a touch? . . . How little we know of our parents, how little we know of each other and of ourselves."

But Grace, in spite of her hardships, knew how to enjoy life, even during the worst of their poverty on Thirty-Seventh Street in Chicago when, dressed in her best gown, she had read Kipling and Stevenson to her children as they ate supper.

"I can only pray the Our Father and the Creed. Is that enough?" she asked her daughter.

"Enough?" Dorothy said. "Books have been written on the Our Father alone."

As Dorothy prayed by her mother's bed, Grace said to her, "Do not pray that I live longer. I have lived through two world wars, the San Francisco earthquake, and a Florida hurricane, and I have had enough!"

"On the very day she died," Dorothy wrote, "she sat up in bed, and, sipping a cup of tea, remarked on how comforting it was. She had taken up a little bouquet of violets, her favorite flower, and, holding it up to her face, smiled with happiness. Life was sweet, even in her last illness." Grace died "so quietly, so gently, saying but a few moments before to John, 'Kiss me goodnight and run along, because I want to go to sleep.'"

Dorothy had prayed for a long time to be with her mother when she died, and she worried as she traveled around the country that she would not, but God granted her prayer.

"I was there, holding her hand, and she just turned her head and sighed. That was her last breath, that little sigh, and her hand was warm in mine for a long time after."

*   *   *

On a rainy late-November evening, thirty-five years after Dorothy had sat with her dying mother, Tamar sat with Dorothy as she lay dying. Mother and daughter were alone in those rooms on the second floor of Maryhouse, Dorothy in that great physical struggle she had witnessed with Grace.

Tamar had rushed down to the city after a talk with Marion Moses, who told her she didn't think Dorothy would survive the year. Tamar was shocked and confused. This year, she wondered, or the next? She found Dorothy weak and not eating. She coaxed her into taking a few sips of chicken-broth-and-noodle soup. She helped her into her night-gown and washed her gray dress.

Forster came over the next day for Thanksgiving. He sat in Dorothy's chair while he and Tamar talked, and Dorothy lay with her back to them.

"I'm sorry," she said, "but I just can't lie on my left side."

Every time Tamar tried to give her medicine, she said, "I can't swallow."

Why do we do it? Tamar wondered. Why force her? Oxygen was the only nourishment she accepted. Forster suggested using a straw for her to sip a little ginger ale with.

Devastated, unsettled, and in his disquiet, Forster, now eighty-five years old, walked the mile across town to his apartment on West Tenth Street, while Dorothy and Tamar watched *The Sound of Music*.

"It's too tiring, too exciting," she said to Tamar.

Dorothy dozed, and Tamar watched to see if she was still breathing, while beginning to feel a great pressure building up in her own chest. She stayed up as long as she could and then went to bed feeling afraid, sad, and alone. She missed Stanley's support, his good sense, his humor, his discretion.

It rained all day on Friday, and Dorothy ate nothing but cranberry sauce and three bits of turkey left over from the Thanksgiving meal. Forster called, and later they listened to music while Tamar tried to write a college paper. Again she went to bed afraid Dorothy would be gone by morning.

On Saturday they listened to the opera. Tamar felt her courage drop from her, and her anxiety increased throughout the day. Dorothy was so weak she was scarcely able to take a few steps. Forster called twice wanting to come over. The first time Dorothy didn't speak to him, and the second time, at four in the afternoon, they talked briefly.

"Should I come?" he asked.

"I'm so tired," she said. "I don't want to talk."

He then spoke to Tamar. "Should I come over?"

Tamar said, "No, come tomorrow." But she felt bad as she said it.

Dorothy's old friend Eileen Egan called.

"What are you doing about the victims of the Italian earthquake?" she asked Eileen. It had been on her mind for several days, though she kept referring to it as Vesuvius.

The afternoon turned to dusk, the rain continued, and Tamar, unable to bear the tension, misery, and growing anxiety, poured herself a glass of wine.

"Do you feel bad because of me?" Dorothy asked.

"I wish I knew what to do," Tamar replied.

"It takes so long to die," Dorothy said, and staggered badly when she got up. Tamar supported her as she walked into the bathroom, and she stood in the middle of the room wondering if she would ever see her mother alive again. The pressure in her chest became unbearable, her heart aching as if she could feel her mother's struggling heart in her own chest.

Frank tried to get Dorothy to take her medicine.

"You're badgering me," she said to him, and flustered him so thoroughly he left, forgetting to ask her if she wanted Communion brought to her, and because Frank did not bring it, Tamar did not leave the room to give Dorothy privacy to pray. And because Tamar told Forster not to come over—if he had, he would have been there for Dorothy's death— mother and daughter were alone, just as Dorothy had been with Grace. But maybe Tamar had to be the only one there. Of all of them she was the one who could let Dorothy go, who knew how to let her go. And so, one more of Dorothy's prayers was answered—that Tamar would be with her when she died.

Just when she reached for Dorothy's wrist to feel for a pulse, just when she realized that Dorothy was gone, the phone rang, then a knock came at the door, and Tamar had had her last moment alone with her mother.

"Shall I bathe and dress her?" Sister Marie Kimball asked.

Tamar nodded, and Sister Marie dressed Dorothy in the gray dress Tamar had washed just two days previous. They called the parish priest, who came over and anointed her.

Within the hour we all knew—Forster, my siblings and I, and the entire Catholic Worker network. Tamar talked to as many as she could. She called Marion and said to her two words, "Dorothy's dead." She sat quietly while Frank and the others prayed, feeling nothing but a sense of relief. The suffering was over.

At the wake, she sat by the coffin as the women of the house visited. Their fears saddened her.

"They wonder if the house will go on," she said to Frank. "They must be reassured."

After the funeral and after the crowds had gone—the Day, Batterham, and Hennessy families, the old Catholic Workers and the new, the famous and the forgotten (Forster found himself thinking every time he saw someone famous, "I must tell Dorothy")—Tamar slept that night in Dorothy's bed, for every bed in the house was needed. The emptiness of the room startled her. She woke up in the middle of the night in terror and loneliness.

Twenty-eight years after the death of her mother, Tamar had a stroke on Holy Thursday and the spring equinox. In the early-morning hours of Good Friday, before dawn, I sat alone, numb and exhausted, with her in the emergency ward of the hospital. Her eyes were closed, as they had been since the stroke hours before. She was intubated, and yet she lay so still I looked closely to see signs of her breathing.

"Are you ready to have the tube removed?" the doctor asked her, and she fluttered her right hand. It was such a tiny movement, I could easily have missed it, but because of it, I thought I would be able to speak with her.

"We're in the emergency ward," I said to her, but she remained still and silent. I kept talking—saying I don't know what—but there was no response.

At dawn they moved her, and for several hours I didn't know where she was. I was terrified she would die alone. And then with the rising sun, the family began to arrive—Tamar's sons and daughters and their spouses, her grandchildren, and her great-grandchildren—to gather around her. We flooded the hospital and took over the waiting room.

I returned home later that day. Tamar's apartment was in turmoil and her bed a wreck with strewn blankets and torn clothes from the efforts of the paramedics. I talked to my mother's parrot. She was subdued and did not complain even though she had been left alone all day. I sat and listened to the laundry cycle late into the night. All I could see was my mother lying on the floor after she fell from her bed. She had been sitting doing her bedtime rituals, combing her hair, rubbing lotion on her dry skin, radio turned on to the jazz hour, and a cup of herbal tea that I had made for her on the bedside table.

All of that was done now. She slipped further into that otherworld and died three days later, in the wee hours, in those dark hours, with two of her daughters, Maggie and me, at her side.

"I'm afraid," she had said in the first minutes after her stroke. "I'm afraid."

"He was a drinking man," she said to no one in particular in the following days.

To Mary she said, "I've failed the children."

To Maggie the atheist, Martha the Catholic, and Kate the uncommitted, she said, "I lost my faith." And it was Maggie who comforted her saying, "No, no, you didn't."

I can see in my mind's eye my grandmother holding Tamar in her arms. Dorothy is young, and Tamar is old, for there is no time with God. In this vision, Dorothy is the age she was when she gave birth to Tamar, and in her strong arms, which are just about to reach out and take on the weight of life, the weight of the world, she holds her daughter, who is in the last moments of her life, frail, gray, her face revealing that softness in her cheeks and that strength in her jaw, just as was in her mother.

Peace . . . peace . . . our wounded hearts will be soothed. The world will be saved by beauty.

EPILOGUE

It is a warm, early-autumn day, and I am visiting my grandmother's room in Maryhouse. Such a deep sense of familiarity resides here. The hallways of the house are shabbier than when she was alive, the walls cracked and covered in soot, the floor worn, but I know the sound my steps make on the stairs and of Dorothy's door as it opens and closes. The scent that greets me is undefinable, and perhaps it's just stale air, but suddenly I feel I am seventeen years old again. The room hasn't changed much, though it's a bit tidier. The floor is the same black-and-gray checked linoleum squares, and her old bookshelves are where they have always been. Her dresses hang in the closet, and her radio remains on the bedside table with a photo of Stanley on top, and in front a small stack of old missals and several editions of the New Testament. Boxes of blank postcards and unused envelopes left over from her prolific correspondence sit on her large wooden desk. Only the bed, covered by a handmade quilt of a simple block pattern, is new.

I walk around the room restlessly, my mind jumping from one thing to another. I pick up objects and put them back down. I circle around and around, seemingly unable to land on anything with either focus or comfort. Restlessness, my grandmother said, is a sign of spiritual hunger. I run my fingers along the spines of her books—Dostoyevsky and Daniel Berrigan, Gandhi and Agatha Christie, Dickens and Chesterton, Mounier and C. S. Lewis.

I can't seem to sit comfortably on any one of her chairs. They are weak or wobbly or the stuffing is falling out. I settle in the armchair, the one Dorothy sat at near the window while she read the *New York Times* or galleys of the *Catholic Worker* paper. I look out the window to the ailanthus tree across the street. It has grown in the years since her death and now reaches up to the fifth story. The neighborhood too has changed. Dorothy had liked to watch the Ukrainian and Puerto Rican neighbors sit on the stoops of the old and tired tenement buildings while their children played ball in the street. Now the stoops are empty, the families gone, and, in any event, the traffic allows no time for ball games. The tenements have had their scrolled granite architraves sand-blasted clean of the layers of soot, and inside the apartments have been gutted and renovated. What had been an empty, boarded-up building on the corner of Second Avenue, where Eleanor used to sit and curse me out, is now a busy café. The old tenement on Second Avenue and First Street that once had housed the Worker's men's clothing room is now a fifteen-story building with a bank branch. The Catholic Worker has been ignoring offers for their buildings from property developers with large, unimaginable amounts of money. There are always people in need, so the Worker has not yet moved out of the neighborhood. How long will Dorothy's room be with us? I wonder. Is this yet another thing to let go of?

While sitting amid these remnants of her intimate life—the gifts people had given her, the collections of rosaries and relics, shells and stones—I look for signs of my mother. After Dorothy's death, Tamar had taken away most of what she had given Dorothy over the years, but my gaze falls on a small hardcover book that Tamar had turned into a loom by wrapping cotton string around the book as warp and using emery boards for heddles. She must have made it in a moment when she had no other tools and materials at hand—she never could keep her hands still. I see also signs of Forster. Two of his framed prints remain on the wall, including Hugo van der Goes's portrait of Maria Portinari, and taped to Dorothy's desk is a small piece of paper with his phone number in her handwriting.

These are the small items that remain. Of the larger elements, in addition to Maryhouse, there are both St. Joseph's on First Street, which still operates the men's soup line as it has been since the mid-1960s, and the Peter Maurin Farm in upstate New York. The hillside property on Cady Hill Road that my parents bought in 1957 is still raising Dorothy and Forster's progeny—Tamar's grandchildren are now rearing their children, and many of them love to have their hands and feet in the soil just as she did.

As for Staten Island, Dorothy's remains are buried at Resurrection Cemetery, two miles from the site of her Huguenot cottage where she underwent her conversion. The gravestone is simple, flat, and small, and decorated with flowers, stones, and odd items left by visitors, much like the sites of holy wells in Ireland. Spanish Camp, where Dorothy spent much of her time in the last five years of her life, no longer exists. In 2001, while preservationists were in the process of obtaining landmark status in recognition of her occupancy, the cottage was razed to the ground by a developer who had intended to build luxury homes but instead subsequently went bankrupt. Only a handful of the other cottages remain, most derelict and boarded up, while the lot where Dorothy's cottage stood is a mound of rubble.

In the decades since Dorothy's death, there has been a slow and steady increase of Catholic Worker houses of hospitality and farms. There are now almost 250 communities in the United States and internationally. Each is autonomous, and each decides what is needed in the area and what it can provide. Dorothy's reputation has also been growing, and it is now common to find people all over the world who know of her. In 2000, Cardinal O'Connor of New York City initiated her cause for sainthood, and Pope Francis, while speaking to the US Congress in September 2015, held her up along with Abraham Lincoln, Martin Luther King Jr., and Thomas Merton as a remarkable American, an "individual with a dream."

I sit for some time in my grandmother's room surrounded by her shabby furniture and simple artifacts. The incessant noise of the street contrasts with the stillness within her room. I find it extraordinary how deeply Dorothy has influenced people, but then here I am still probing and examining all that she has meant to me, and all that her daughter—my mother—has meant to me, and I imagine I always will be. I hear from the street below the sound of women arriving at the door. Many of them are greeted by name as they are welcomed in. It must be lunch-time. I glance at a book I had picked from the bookshelves—Caussade's *Abandonment to Divine Providence*. Great title, I think, but I've never been able to read the book. I set it aside, rise from the armchair, and walk downstairs to join everyone for a meal.

ACKNOWLEDGMENTS

Many thanks to my siblings—Becky, Eric, Mary, Maggie, Martha, and Hilaire—for their unconditional support, for sharing their stories, and for delving into memories that are bittersweet for all of us. I also add my brother Nicky and sister Susie, even though they both died years ago, for any list of Tamar's children, particularly in this context, is incomplete without them.

I am deeply grateful for that great, wonderful Catholic Worker family. The folks at Maryhouse in New York City, including Joanne Kennedy, Jane Sammon, and Frank Donovan (who died before this book was finished), always welcomed me and gave me a bed. Jim Allaire's website, www.catholicworker.org, saved me an incalculable amount of time as he and a crew of typists, including Johannah Hughes Turner, transcribed Dorothy's writings from the *Catholic Worker*. Pat and Kathleen Jordan provided not only their stories but vital support at crucial moments, Rosalie Riegle generously shared her oral history transcriptions, and Michael Harank gave me permission to use his story of Lena Rizzo and Mother Teresa. Robert Ellsberg, publisher of Orbis Books, spent years transcribing and editing Dorothy's diaries and letters. He also shared with me his conversations with Tamar in the last months of her life and gave me invaluable editorial advice.

I am also grateful for my two local libraries—Brooks Memorial Library in Brattleboro, Vermont, and Moore Free Library in Newfane, Vermont—and the librarians who through interlibrary loan provided dozens of out-of-print books, and who never said a word those times I couldn't help pay for the postage costs. Also, Louise Sirois, librarian at

Moore Free Library, trustingly provided me with a key to the library and a desk tucked away in a corner so I could work undisturbed after hours. Speaking of writing spaces, deep thanks to Alex and Jerelyn Wilson, owners of Deer Run Farm, where most of this book was written.

Then there are the archivists and their archives—Benjamin Panciera of the Louis Sheaffer–Eugene O'Neill Collection at Connecticut College, Deborah Kloiber of the Ade Bethune Collection at St. Catherine University, St. Paul, Minnesota, and Phil Runkel of the Dorothy Day–Catholic Worker Collection at Marquette University. Phil is a treasure who never failed to answer my many questions, and I am deeply grateful for the care he takes of a collection that includes so much family history and many items of family memorabilia.

Many thanks to Roger Freet of Foundry Literary + Media and to Kathy Belden and her team at Scribner. In addition to being thankful for their brilliant professional skills, I am grateful for the personal interest both Roger and Kathy have taken in my grandmother and for the opportunity to first meet them on a visit to Dorothy's room at Maryhouse.

Finally, I come to Garry Jones, my husband. He cooked for me, listened to me, and helped me through my most difficult moments even though for the five years I spent writing this book he had no way of knowing if I was actually writing anything. Garry never once wavered in his faith and patience, and for this I am truly grateful.

INDEX